BILL HICKS was born on 16 Dece... ... ... Georgia. Hicks began his stand-up career while still at high school and went on to become one of the most influential stand-up comedians of his generation. He died on 26 February 1994 at the family home in Little Rock, Arkansas. He was thirty-two years old.

'All he did, really, was to tell the truth about himself, and about the way he saw the world – and this is the hardest thing to do on stage and still be funny with it. Hicks' life was spent in this quest and he succeeded brilliantly, and to me and to countless others he remains nothing short of inspiration.'   **Bill Bailey, *Independent***

'Bill Hicks – blowtorch, excavator, truthsayer, and brain specialist, like a reverend waving a gun around. He will correct your vision. Others will drive on the road he built.'   **Tom Waits**

One of the best comedians in the world: a discernible point of view, great mind, attitude – the whole bag. He works completely for me.'   **Dennis Miller**

'Bill was right up there with Lenny Bruce and Richard Pryor. He was easily the best comic of my generation.'   **Brett Butler**

'With his clarity of vision and gift of words, if Bill Hicks had had any more time he might have started a revolution.'   **Keith Olberman**

'Hicks's stand-up act is about taking a stand – and occasionally dodging a chair.'   ***Rolling Stone***

'Ten years after his death, his words still burn with righteous truth. This book could change your life.' **Paul Brannigan, *Kerrang***

'That this house notes with sadness the 10th anniversary of the death of Bill Hicks, on February 26th 1994, at the age of 32; recalls his assertion that his words would be a bullet in the heart of consumerism, capitalism and the American Dream; and mourns the passing of one of the few people who may be mentioned as being worthy of inclusion with Lenny Bruce in any list of unflinching and painfully honest political philosophers.'

Stephen Pound MP, Early Day Motion, House of Commons, February 2004

LOVE ALL
THE PEOPLE
Letters, Lyrics, Routines
BILL HICKS

CONSTABLE • LONDON

The publishers would like to thank Matt Harlock
for his generous assistance in compiling this collection.

Constable & Robinson Ltd
3 The Lanchesters
162 Fulham Palace Road
London W6 9ER
www.constablerobinson.com

First published in the UK by Constable,
an imprint of Constable & Robinson Ltd 2004

This revised edition published by Constable, an imprint of
Constable & Robinson Ltd, 2005

A copy of the British Library Cataloguing in
Publication Data is available from the British Library

ISBN 978-184529-111-2

Printed and bound in the EU

Contents

FOREWORD
The Goat Boy Rises

I

On October 1, 1993 the comedian Bill Hicks, after doing his twelfth gig on the David Letterman show, became the first comedy act to be censored at CBS's Ed Sullivan Theatre, where Letterman is now in residence, and where Elvis Presley was famously censored in 1956. Presley was not allowed to be shown from the waist down. Hicks was not allowed to be shown at all. It's not what's in Hicks' pants but what's in his head that scared the CBS panjandrums. Hicks, a tall, thirty-one-year-old Texan with a pudgy face aged beyond its years from hard living on the road, is no motormouth vulgarian but an exhilarating comic thinker in a renegade class all his own. Until the ban, which, according to Hicks, earned him 'more attention than my other eleven appearances on Letterman times one hundred,' Hicks' caustic observations and mischievous cultural connections had found a wide audience in England, where he is something of a cult figure. I caught up with Hicks backstage on a rainy Sunday last November at the Dominion Theatre, in London, where a record-breaking crowd of two thousand Brits was packed so tightly that they were standing three deep at the back of the dress circle to hear Hicks deliver some acid home truths about the USA, which to him stands for United States of Advertising. Hicks thinks against society and insists on the importance of this intellectual freedom as a way to inspire others to think for themselves. 'To me, the comic is the guy who says "Wait a minute" as the consensus forms,' Hicks told me as we climbed the stairs to his dressing room. 'He's the antithesis of the mob mentality. The comic is a flame – like Shiva the

Destroyer, toppling idols no matter what they are. He keeps cutting everything back to the moment.'

Even then, the talk about courting comic danger had Hicks worrying about his prospects in America. 'Comedy in the States has been totally gutted,' he told me when we'd settled into the dressing room. 'It's commercialized. They don't have people on TV who have points of view, because that defies the status quo, and we can't have that in the totalitarian mind-control government that runs the fuckin' airwaves. I can't get a shot there. I get David Letterman a lot. I love Letterman, but every time I go on, we have tiffs over material. They love me, but his people have this fictitious mainstream audience they think they play to. It's untrue. It doesn't exist. I like doing the show, but it's almost like working a puzzle: How can I be me in the context of doing this material? The best thing I do is make connections. I connect *everything*. It's hard to do it in six minutes.'

Hicks certainly went for broke and pronounced his real comic self in the banned Letterman performance, which he wrote out for me in a thirty-nine-page letter that also recounts his version of events. Hicks had to write out his set because the tape of it, which the Letterman people said they'd send three weeks ago, had not yet reached him. He doubts it ever will. But the routine, which he had prepared for a Letterman appearance a week earlier (he was bumped because the show ran long), had been, he wrote, 'approved and reapproved' by a segment producer of the show. Indicating stage directions and his recollection of significant audience response, Hicks set out some of the 'hot points' to which the network took exception.

> You know who's really bugging me these days? These pro-lifers . . . (*Smattering of applause.*)
> You ever look at their faces? . . . 'I'm pro-life!' (*Here Bill makes a pinched face of hate and fear; his lips are pursed as though he's just sucked on a lemon.*) 'I'm pro-life!' Boy, they look it, don't they? They just exude *joie de vivre*. You just want to hang with them and play Trivial Pursuit all night long. (*Audience chuckles.*)

You know what bugs me about them? If you're so pro-life, do me a favor – don't lock arms and block medical clinics. If you're so pro-life, lock arms and block cemeteries. (*Audience laughs.*) . . . I want to see pro-lifers at funerals opening caskets – 'Get out!' Then I'd really be impressed by their mission. (*Audience laughs and applauds.*)

I've been travelling a lot lately. I was over in Australia during Easter. It was interesting to note they celebrate Easter the same way we do – commemorating the death and resurrection of Jesus by telling our children a giant bunny rabbit . . . left chocolate eggs in the night. (*Audience laughs.*)

Gee, I wonder why we're so messed up as a race. You know, I've read the Bible. Can't find the words 'bunny' or 'chocolate' in the whole book. (*Audience laughs.*)

I think it's interesting how people act on their beliefs. A lot of Christians, for instance, wear crosses around their necks. Nice sentiment, but do you think when Jesus comes back, he's really going to want to look at a cross? (*Audience laughs. Bill makes a face of pain and horror.*)

Ow! *Maybe* that's why he hasn't shown up yet. (*As Jesus looking down from Heaven*) 'I'm not going, Dad. No, they're still wearing crosses – they totally missed the point. When they start wearing fishes, I might go back again . . . No, I'm not going . . . O.K., I'll tell you what – I'll go back as a bunny.'

Hicks, who delivered his monologue dressed not in his usual gunslinger black but in 'bright fall colors – an outfit bought just for the show and reflective of my bright and cheerful mood,' seemed to have a lot to smile about. Letterman – who Hicks says greeted him as he sat down to talk with 'Good set, Bill! Always nice to have you drop by with an uplifting message!' and signed off saying, 'Bill, enjoy answering your mail for the next few weeks' – had been seen to laugh. The word in the Green Room was also good. A couple of hours later, Hicks was back in his hotel, wearing nothing but a towel, when the call came from Robert Morton, the executive producer of the Letterman show, telling him he'd been deep-sixed. Hicks sat down on the bed. 'I don't understand, Robert. What's the problem? I thought the show went great.' The following is a condensed version of what Hicks remembers from the long conversation.

'You killed out there,' Morton said, and went on to say, according to Hicks, that the CBS office of standards and practices felt that some of the material was unsuitable for broadcast.

'Ah, which material exactly did they find . . .'

'Well, almost all of it.'

'Bob, they're so obviously jokes.'

Hicks protested that he had run his routine by his sixty-three-year-old mother in Little Rock, Arkansas, and it passed the test. Morton insisted that the situation was out of his hands. He offered to set up another appearance and, according to Hicks, shouldered the blame for not having spent more time beforehand editing out the 'hot points.'

'Bob, they're just jokes. I don't want to be edited by you or anyone else. Why are people so afraid of jokes?'

'Bill, you've got to understand our audience.'

'Your audience! Your audience is comprised of people, right? Well, I understand people, being one myself. People are who I play to every night, Bob. We get along just fine. We taped the show at five-thirty in the afternoon, and your audience had no problem with the material then. Does your audience become overly sensitive between the hours of 11.30 p.m. and 12.30 a.m.? And by the way, Bob, when I'm not performing on your show, *I'm* a member of the audience of your show. Are you saying my material is not suitable for me? This doesn't make any sense. Why do you understimate the intelligence of your audience?'

'Bill, it's not our decision.'

Morton apologized to Hicks, explaining that the show had to answer to the network, and said that he'd reschedule him soon. The conversation ended soon after that exchange, and in the intervening weeks Hicks had had no further word, he says, from Morton or Letterman. He has, however, heard indirectly from the CBS standards-and-practices office. A man who heard an interview with

Hicks on the radio and was outraged over the censorship wrote to CBS to upbraid the network for not airing Hicks' set. He faxed the reply from CBS standards-and-practices to the radio station, which faxed it to Hicks' office. 'It is true that Bill Hicks was taped that evening and that his performance did not air,' the letter said. 'What is inaccurate is that the deletion of his routine was required by CBS. In fact, although a CBS Program Practices editor works on that show, the decision was solely that of the producers of the program who decided to substitute his performance with that of another comedian. Therefore, your criticism that CBS censored the program is totally without foundation. Creative judgments must be made in the course of producing and airing any program and, while we regret that you disagreed with this one, the producers felt it necessary and that is not a decision we would override.'

Hicks, who refers to the television set as Lucifer's Dream Box, is now in Lucifer's Limbo. He can't get the Letterman show to send him a tape of his performance. He can't get to the bottom of who censored him. And, as yet, he has no return date on Letterman. I called Robert Morton two weeks ago, and, when pressed, he finally grasped the nettle. He had begun by saying that the decision not to show Hicks' routine was made jointly by the Letterman show and CBS and ended up telling me that the producers of the show were solely responsible. 'Ultimately, it was our decision,' he said. 'We're the packagers and owners of the program. It's our job to deliver a finished product to the network.'

'It's been a strange little adventure for Willy,' Hicks told me at the Dominion last year, referring to his American comedy career. And so it has proved – stranger, in fact, than Hicks' most maverick imaginings. The farce came full circle in the week following the Letterman debacle. A friend called Hicks to tell him about a commercial she'd seen during the Letterman show – a pro-life commercial. 'The networks are delivering an audience to the advertisers,' Hicks said later. 'They showed their hand. They'll continue to pretend they're a hip talk show. And I'll continue to be me. As Bob Dylan said, the only way to live outside the law is to be totally honest. So I will remain lawless.'

* * *

Outlaw is how Hicks was styling himself last year for the Dominion performance as he put on his black rifleman's coat and Stetson in the dressing room. When the curtain came up on his performance, Hicks was revealed in his hat, long coat, and cowboy boots, while behind him huge orange flames licked the air. Images of heat and hunting are the perfect backdrop to Hicks' kind of comic attack. He was a hostile sharpshooter taking aim at the culture's received opinions and trying to shoot them down. The British, who have an appetite for this kind of intellectual anarchy, embraced Hicks with a rare and real enthusiasm from the moment he stumbled onto the vivacious English comedy scene in November 1990, as one of eighteen comedians in 'Stand Up America!,' a six-week limited engagement in the West End. The next year, Hicks was at the Edinburgh Festival, where he outclassed the native talent and won the Critics' Award. This led to his 1992 'Dangerous Tour' of Britain and Ireland, which culminated in appearances in the West End, at the Queen's Theatre, that May. The response was overwhelming, and now Hicks was doing one of the final performances of the 'Relentless Tour,' his second lap of honor around the British Isles in one year. Hicks was at home with the English, whose sense of irony made them more receptive to his combative humor than the credulous American public had been. 'There's a greater respect for the performer,' he said. 'If you're onstage, people think you've earned it. In America – I'm not kidding – people bark their approval.' I looked at him dubiously. 'Ask around,' Hicks said, and he simulated the sound. 'They bark like animals. It's frightening. It's what American society has reduced people to. Ironically, in this show I call myself Goat Boy. They shouldn't be barking, they should be *baaing*.'

My first encounter with Hicks was his Gulf War routine, which had been broadcast during the postwar euphoria at the beginning of 1992 on England's Channel 4. My sixteen-year-old son, Chris, was bellowing from the living room for me to come quickly. It was midnight, and he was sprawled, laughing, on the sofa, watching Hicks at the Montreal Comedy Festival calling a massacre a massacre. 'So scary, watching the news. How they built it all out of proportion. Like Iraq was ever, or could ever, under any stretch of the imagination, be any threat to us *whatsoever*. But, watching the news, you never would have got that idea. Remember how it started? They kept talking about "the elite Republican Guard" in these hushed tones, like these guys were the bogeyman or something. "Yeah, we're doing well now, but we have yet to face . . . the elite Republican Guard." Like these guys were twelve-feet-tall desert warriors – "NEVER LOST A BATTLE. WE SHIT BULLETS." Well, after two months of continuous carpet bombing and not *one* reaction at all from them, they became simply "the Republican Guard" – not nearly as elite as we may have led you to believe. And after another month of bombing they went from "the elite Republican Guard" to "the Republican Guard" to "the Republicans made this shit up about there being guards out there."

'People said, "Uh-uh, Bill, Iraq had the fourth-largest army in the world." Yeah, maybe, but you know what? After the first three largest armies, there's a *real* big fuckin' drop-off. The Hare Krishnas are the fifth-largest army in the world. And they've already got our airports.'

Most TV comics trade in brand-name jokes or jokes that play off physical stereotypes. They don't question their culture so much as pander to its insatiable hunger for distraction. But Hicks' mischievous flights of fantasy bring the audience back to reality with a thump. Hicks is a kind of ventriloquist of his contradictory nature, letting voices and sound effects act out both his angst and his appetites. Occasionally, the instinct for Goat Boy comes over him, and Hicks, a man of instincts, goes with it. Goat Boy is Pan, or Hicks' version of him – a randy goat 'with a placid look in his eyes, completely at peace with nature' – through which he celebrates his own rampaging libido.

'I am Goat Boy,' he would say in the act that night, in a grave baritone. 'Come here, my little fruit basket.'

'What do you want, Goat Boy?' he answered, in a coy Southern falsetto. 'You big old shaggy thing.'

'Ha, ha, ha, ha,' Hicks growled into the microphone. 'I am here to please you.'

'How?'

'Tie me to your headboard. Throw your legs over my shoulders, let me roll you like a feed bag.' Hicks brought the microphone close to his mouth. He snorted, slurped, and finally screamed, 'Hold on to my horns!' Then, as suddenly as the impulse had come upon him, Hicks broke off the fantasy, saying, 'I need professional help at this point.'

The secret of Hicks' psychic survival has always been comedy. He started writing and performing his jokes as an alienated thirteen-year-old in Houston in 1975, and, by his own count, for the last five years he has been performing about two hundred and sixty-five days a year, sometimes doing as many as three two-hour gigs a night. Few contemporary comics or actors have such an opportunity to get their education in public. Hicks uses the stage time to write his material in front of an audience. 'I do it all onstage, *all* of it,' he said, and then began to relate how he'd started on his eccentric journey. 'When I was about eleven, it dawned on me that I didn't like where I was,' he said, speaking of the subdivision where he lived, which was called Nottingham Forest; of Stratford High School, which looked like a prison and where he was bored out of his skull for four years; and of his father, who was a midrange executive with General Motors. The Hicks family lived in 'strict Southern Baptist ozone.' The memory still rankled. 'One time a friend of mine – we were nine – runs over and goes, "Bill, I just saw some hippies down at the store." I go, "No way." He goes, "I swear." My dad goes, "Get off this property! We don't swear on this property!"

'We were living the American dream. This was the best life had to offer. But there was no life, and no creativity. My dad, for instance, plays the piano. The same song for thirty years – I think it's "Kitten on the Keys." I don't play the piano, but all my friends are musicians. My dad goes, "Do they read music?" I go, "No." "Well, how do they play it?" I go to the piano and I write a song. What's the difference? He can't improvise. That, to me, is the suburbs. You get to a point, and that's it – it's over.'

Once he'd seized on the idea of writing jokes, Hicks closeted himself in his bedroom and went to school on comedians. He started watching Johnny Carson. 'I thought he was the only comic in the world, because I never stayed up later,' he said. Soon Hicks began burning the midnight oil, taping other comic acts on television. 'I'd take their jokes and also write my own. I performed them around school, and what I loved was when both got equal laughs. I knew which one was me and which one I'd seen on TV the night before. I learned how to mesh these things. How to get into character. I was very, very popular and known as a comedian at school. I'd always have to have material, constantly, all day. It got to the point where my English teacher gave me five minutes to do before class. My older brother Steve encouraged me. I typed up about two pages of jokes – whimsical stuff in the Woody Allen vein, which really appealed to me – and slipped them under his door. He came in later that night and said, "What's this?" I said, "I dunno. I'm writing these things. They're jokes." He couldn't believe it. "These are funny, man. Keep doing this."'

Hicks' first partner in comedy was Dwight Slade, with whom he formed the act Bill and Dwight in the eighth grade. A tape exists of Hicks and Slade giggling through some of their early routines, which involved pretending to be brothers with 'many, many problems.' 'Ladies and gentlemen, the comedy sensation Dwight Slade and Bill Hicks. And here they are!' it begins, and then the two of them collapse into roars of amusement at their own vain attempts to strike adult postures while reading gags about God, sex, abortion, and parents.

The jokes illustrated Hicks's precocity, and suggested how comedy both masked and admitted the hostility that kept him sullen and virtually silent around his family. 'I can remember being at dinner when Bill would come down to eat,' Steve Hicks told me. 'He'd sit there with his face buried in a book. Absolutely no conversation from him or to him. Nothing. Then he would go up to his room and close and lock the door. We had no idea what he was doing.' Hicks' room, which had nothing on the walls but a guitar, was a cell of rebellious solitude. He kept a typewriter under his bed and hid his pages of jokes inside its case.

In 1976, there were no comedy clubs in Houston. Except for school, the only outlets for Bill and Dwight's routines were talent shows and nightclubs. They scoured the paper for auditions, and often rode their bikes the seventeen miles into town and back for a tryout. That summer, when they were both fourteen, a talent agent to whom they'd sent a tape liked it enough to get them airtime on Jerry Lewis' Telethon from 2 to 2:45 A.M. Their big break posed three immediate problems: (1) they didn't have forty-five minutes of material, (2) they'd never performed as Bill and Dwight in front of a live audience, and (3) they had to tell their parents. The first two problems were surmountable, but the third proved the sticking point. Hicks' parents said no. Hicks and Slade had to cancel, explaining that they were too young to drive themselves to the job. But in 1978, when the Comedy Workshop opened on San Felipe, in Houston, they talked their way into the lineup. This time, they made the gig. To get to it, Hicks had to climb out his window, shin down the drainpipe to the garage roof, jump from the roof to the ground, and hightail it to the Catholic church behind his house, where Kevin Booth, a friend who had a car, picked him up and then drove both performers to the club. Bill and Dwight did fifteen minutes – a kind of double solo performance, each doing Woody Allen shtick without the actual give-and-take of a comedy team. 'What was really funny was when my friends would come and I'd go, "I . . . uh . . . I have trouble . . . trouble with women,"' Hicks said. 'And my friends would go, "No, you don't!" I'd go, "My parents are very poor." "No, they're not!" They were amazed we were in this adult world. They were seventeen and could drive us there, but when they got us there we were in the adult world.'

The comedy team performed five times before Slade moved to Portland, Oregon, where he still lives, working as a standup comic. Hicks put his anarchic energy into a hapless punk-rock group called Stress, in which he sang a song called 'I'm Glad I'm Not a Hubcap (Hubcaps Don't Get Laid).' At some point in his seventeenth year, Hicks' parents took him to a psychotherapist. 'There was no connection between me and my parents – none,' he said. 'They had no idea of who I was. They still don't get what I do. How could they have understood it fifteen years ago?' The therapist met with the family, then with Hicks. At the end of the session, the therapist took Hicks aside. '"Listen, you can continue to come if you feel like it,"' Hicks recalled him saying. '"But it's them, not you."' Soon afterward, at the beginning of Hicks' senior year, his father was transferred to Little Rock, Arkansas. He and his wife left Hicks behind in the house and gave him the keys to the car. Hicks began doing comedy every night. His parents thought he was studying. The comedy club put him on first, because he had to get home early. Sometimes the phone would be ringing just as he walked in the door. 'The conversations were like this,' Hicks said. He fell easily into his father's Southern accent: '"Where were you?" "Library." "Again?"' Even after his parents left, his material was almost entirely about them.

To this day, Hicks continues to mythologize his parents and his relationship with them, in comic routines that spoof their Southern propriety. But this is only professional acrimony, and doesn't stop Hicks from thanking his parents on his record albums or turning up regularly for ritual family occasions. Hicks, like all comedians, picks at ancient wounds to keep open the soreness that feeds his laughter and to demonstrate his mastery over the past.

In 1982, Hicks' parents finally saw him perform. They had been visiting Steve in Dallas, where the family had assembled for Thanksgiving, and his parents decided to surprise him. The plan was to drive the three hours to Austin, see the show, and drive back to Dallas the same night before setting out the next day for the six-hour ride to Little Rock. Steve and his wife waited up for them but finally fell asleep around 3 a.m. At nine, their phone rang. The Hickses had been so appalled by their son's act that they'd got in their car and driven nonstop to Little Rock. 'They were in a state of shock,' Steve says. 'They didn't say a word to each other for nine hours. They didn't even realize they'd driven through Dallas!'

At one end of Hicks' long, corridorlike dressing room at the Dominion was a window overlooking the stage. Hicks walked over and looked out at the paying customers. 'It's about that time,' he said. Isolation suddenly fell over him like some fog blown in by his unconscious. Showtime was approaching, and he wanted to be alone. Fifteen minutes later, he brought his aggression roaring onstage. The narrative swung into attack as Hicks, like a man driven to distraction by the media, fought his way free of its overload by momentarily becoming its exaggerated voice: 'Go back to bed! America is in control again . . . Here . . . here is "American Gladiators." Watch this! Shut up. Go back to bed. Here's fifty-six channels of it. Watch these pituitary retards bang their fuckin' skulls together and congratulate yourself on living in the land of freedom. Here you go, America! You are free to do as we tell you! You are free!'

Hicks worked at a tremendous rate, pounding away at the absurdities of American culture with short jabs of wit and following up with a flurry of counterpunches. 'Ever notice how people who believe in creationism look really unevolved?' he said. 'Their eyes real close together. Eyebrow ridges. Big, furry hands and feet. "I believe God created me in one day." Looks like he rushed it.' Later, near the end of the evening, Hicks drew one final lesson. 'The world is like a ride at an amusement park,' he said. 'And when you choose to go on it, you think that it's real. Because that's how powerful our minds are.' A young Englishman three seats away from me shouted 'Bollocks!' And, without missing a beat, completely caught up in the dialogue he was having with his audience, Hicks said, 'There is a lot of denial in this ride. The ride, in fact, is made up of denial. All things work in Goat Boy's favor!' Thrilled by the improvised insight, the audience burst into applause, and then Hicks guided the rest of the show smoothly to its conclusion, which, for all its combativeness, ended on the word 'peace.'

Hicks came to my house the next day for tea. He was tired and a little distracted, and was wondering out loud which way to take his quirky talent. 'Once this stuff is done, it's over with – I'm not married to any of it,' he said. 'Goat Boy is the only thing that really intrigues me right now. He's not Satan. He's not Evil. He's Nature.' Hicks paused and added, 'I'm trying to come up with this thing about "Conversations with Goat Boy."' Then, suddenly, the interrogator and, Goat Boy started a conversation at my tea table:

'You don't like America?'

'I don't *see* America. To me, there is just a rapidly decreasing wilderness.'

Hicks stopped and smiled. 'That is Goat Boy. There is no

America. It's just a big pavement now to him. That's the whole point. What is America anyway – a landmass including the Philippines? There are so many different Americas. To him, to Nature, it's just land, the earth. Indian spirit – Indians would understand randy Pan, the Goat Boy. They'd probably have a mask and a celebration.'

My son wandered into the kitchen and lingered to eavesdrop on the conversation. At one point, he broke in. 'I don't know how you have the courage to say those things,' he said. 'I could never talk like that in front of people.'

Hicks smiled but had no response. Saying the unsayable was just his job. He analyzed the previous night's performance, which had been filmed for an HBO special. (It was broadcast in September to good reviews.) 'People watch TV *not* to think,' he said. 'I'd like the opportunity to stir things up once, and see what happens. But I've got a question. Do I even want to be part of it anymore? Show business or art – these are choices. It's hard to get a grip on me. It's also hard for me to have a career, because there's no archetype for what I do. I have to create it, or uncover it.' To that end, he said, he and Fallon Woodland, a standup from Kansas City, were writing 'The Counts of the Netherworld,' a TV comedy commissioned for England's Channel 4 and set in the collective unconscious of mankind. Hicks was doing a column for the English satire magazine *Scallywag*. He was planning a comedy album, called 'Arizona Bay,' a narrative rant against California with his own guitar accompaniment. Should he stay in England, where he was already a cult figure, or return to America? He recounted a joke on the subject by his friend Barry Crimmins, another American political comedian. '"Hey, buddy," this guy says to him after a show. "America – love it or leave it!" And Crimmins goes, "What? And be a victim of our foreign policy?"'

As Hicks was about to go, he said, 'We are facilitators of our creative evolution. We can ignite our brains with light.' The line brought back something his high-school friend Kevin Booth had told me: 'Bill was the first person I ever met whose goal was to become enlightened.' At various times in his life, Hicks has meditated, studied Hindu texts, gobbled hallucinogens, searched for

U.F.O.s – anything to make some larger spiritual and intellectual connection. His comedy takes an audience on a journey to places in the heart where it can't or won't go without him. Through laughter, Hicks makes unacceptable ideas irresistible. He is particularly lethal because he persuades not with reason but with joy. 'I believe everyone has this fuckin' poem in his heart,' he said on his way out.

II

My *New Yorker* profile about Bill Hicks – Part I of this foreword – sat unpublished at the magazine for nearly four months. Hicks' ban from the David Letterman Show and his subsequent thirty-one-page hand-written screed to me (see "Letter to John Lahr", pages 300–323) provided the impetus to get the profile into print by November 1st. 'The phones are ringing off the hook, the offers are pouring in, and all because of you,' Hicks wrote to me the following week, signing himself 'Willy Hicks'. 'I've read the article three times, and each time I'm stunned. Being the comedy fan that I am, I've ended the article every time thinking, "This guy sounds interesting."' Hicks continued, 'It's almost as though I've been lifted out of a ten-year rut and placed in a position where the offers finally match my long held and deeply cherished creative aspirations . . . Somehow, people are listening in a new light. Somehow the possibilities (creatively) seem limitless.'

Re-reading Hicks' letter now, ten years later, the parentheses in the last sentence hit me like a punch to the heart. Hicks was suddenly, to his amazement, no longer perceived as 'a joke blower', his word for the kind of pandering stand-up he hated. In the two months following the publication of the *New Yorker* profile, seven publishers approached him about writing a book; 'The Nation' asked him to write a column; Robert DeNiro met with him to discuss the possibility of recording his comedy on his Tribeca label; and Britain's Channel 4 with Tiger Aspect green-lighted Hicks's 'Counts of the Netherworld' ('Channel 4 wants our first show to somehow

tie in with their celebration of the birth of Democracy two thousand years ago,' Hicks wrote to me. 'Democracy may have been
born then, I just can't wait till it starts speaking and walking'). The
creative possibilities may have seemed limitless to Hicks, but, even
as he was writing me letters about 'the hoopla' and his newfound
calm ('I'm very grateful for it'), he knew that he was dying.

In June, touring Australia with the comedian Steven Wright,
Hicks had begun to complain to his manager and girlfriend Colleen
McGarr about horrible indigestion. He hadn't had a proper physical exam in ten years; so when they returned, later in the month,
to West Palm Beach for a week's engagement at the Comedy Corner,
McGarr booked a check-up for Hicks. On June 15th, his first night
at the Comedy Corner, Hicks came offstage clutching his side. 'The
physical had been set up for the following Thursday,' McGarr recalls.
'But when I took a look at him, I said "We gotta get you in tomorrow."' Hicks was thirty-one. Because of his relative youth, the doctor,
William Donovan, seemed convinced that the swelling on Hicks'
side was a gall-bladder problem. He sent Hicks for an ultrasound.
'The ultrasound guy said, "We have to get him over to the hospital. We have to do a biopsy because this isn't gall bladder,"' McGarr
says. 'They looked very grim at the time.'

On the night of his liver biopsy, Hicks slept at the Good Samaritan
Hospital. 'He was really digging it,' McGarr says. 'I was going out
to get him his favourite treats – grilled-cheese sandwiches and soup.
It was like an enforced rest after all the touring. He was kind of
chipper.' At five the next morning, William Donovan phoned her.
'Colleen, it's the worst news possible,' he said. 'You've got to get
down here now. We have to talk to him.' In person, Donovan
explained to McGarr that Hicks had pancreatic cancer; he had only
about three months to live. At 7.30, they went into see Hicks, and
Donovan told him that he had stage-four pancreatic cancer and that
there was very little that could be done about it. At first poleaxed
by the news – 'He looked like he'd been shot,' Donovan is reported
as saying, in Cynthia True's *American Scream: The Bill Hicks Story*
– Hicks finally said, 'What's the battle plan?' What had to be decided,
Donovan explained, was how Hicks wanted to live the time he had
left. Aggressive treatment would leave him mostly incapacitated.

Since Hicks felt 'at the peak of his powers,' according to McGarr, a compromise treatment was arranged, so that he could continue to write and to perform. 'There was no crying. There was no going nuts,' McGarr says. 'It was really, really calm.' She adds, 'He'd known for awhile, I'm sure, that something was wrong. I mean people don't have indigestion for six months.'

The following Monday, Hicks started chemotherapy. A network of doctors around the country was set up so that Hicks could get treatment wherever he happened to be touring. Hicks responded well to the therapy. 'No one knew about his illness,' McGarr says. 'The only people who knew were my business partner, Duncan Strauss, and Bill's immediate family. Nobody else. We didn't tell anyone. That was also Bill's decision. He had a lot to do – he was finishing the record "Arizona Bay" and he had a ton of gigs.' She adds, 'He wanted the work to get out without the taint of any sentimentality.'

In the months that remained to him, by all accounts, Hicks seemed to inhabit the world in a different way. Instead of scourging it, he beheld it. 'Things became a lot more meaningful than he'd ever given them credit for,' says McGarr, who saw him 'growing on a spiritual level.' 'Flowers. The beach. He started swimming in the ocean for the first time, splashing around like a dolphin which is not really Hicks-like – at the beach, when he was dragged there, he was always the guy dressed head-to-toe in black.' Hicks referred to his cancer as a 'wake-up call'. Where, in the past, Hicks had styled himself as an outlaw onstage and a loner off it; now he sought out people and engaged them. His spirit and his wardrobe started to lighten. 'He was astounded by how much love came around him as a result of this,' McGarr says. 'He realized that people really did care about him and that he didn't have to be alone.' For a time, he moved into McGarr's West Palm Beach apartment, and he 'began to take some actual joy' in domestic life. 'This is a guy who had been on the road for about fifteen years,' McGarr says. 'He's used to eating crap – spaghetti sauce out of a jar. "I need you to get me some Ragu", he'd say. I'm like, "We don't have jarred spaghetti sauce in this house, we have homemade." Fun stuff like that. It was a revelation to him.'

Before returning to Little Rock, Arkansas, for his birthday –
December 16th – and for Christmas with his family, Hicks cele-
brated his own unofficial Yuletime with McGarr in Florida. They
brought a Christmas tree and decorated it with homemade orna-
ments. Hicks drew a reindeer on a card and tied it to the front
bough of the tree. He told McGarr to open it. 'Will you marry me?'
it said. The question was academic. By late December, according
to McGarr, Hicks was 'really, really bad.'

'On a work level, everything was done,' she says. 'He'd recorded
"Arizona Bay", performed his last complete sold-out set at Igby's in
Los Angeles on November 17th, pitched the TV show at Channel
4.' In just four months, Hicks had acquired what had eluded him
for fifteen years – a receptive American audience. But on a physical level he was now fading. Nonetheless, after Christmas, he
insisted on meeting McGarr in Las Vegas to watch Frank Sinatra
and Don Rickles in concert. 'I almost passed out, he looked so bad,'
McGarr recalls. The day after the Sinatra show, they flew back to
West Palm Beach. The doctors wanted to admit Hicks to the hospital; he refused to go. 'Things got very tense,' says McGarr, who had
to enlist the help of hospice nurses and of Hicks' mother, Mary.

On 5 January, 1994 – against McGarr's wishes – Hicks did the
eight o'clock show at Caroline's Comedy Club, in New York. In her
attempt to prevent Hicks from doing the gig, McGarr rang Dr
Donovan. 'Colleen, Bill is ready to die. He just won't lie down,'
Donovan told her. She hung up on him. Hicks was about thirty
minutes into his set when he looked up over the microphone and
scanned the crowd. 'Colleen, are you out there?' he said. From the
back of the room, McGarr called out, 'Bill, I'm right here.' 'I can't
do this anymore,' he said. McGarr rushed to the side of the stage.
Hicks glanced over at her, paused, then put the mic back in its
stand, and stepped into the wings. It was his last performance.

On 26 January, McGarr put Hicks on a plane to Little Rock.
'Bill always wanted to die with his parents at their house in Little
Rock,' she says. 'He wanted the circle complete – that was very
important to him.' On Valentine's Day, after making a few calls to
old friends, Hicks announced that he was finished with speaking.
Although he hardly uttered another word, except to ask for water,

he wandered around the house, according to his mother, almost every night. On 26 February, at 11.20 p.m., Hicks died with his parents at his bedside. His radiant comic light had burned for thirty-two years, two months, and ten days.

When a great comedian dies, the culture loses a little of its flavour. The world rolls on, of course, but without the comedian to both witness and illuminate the deliria of his moment. In Hicks's case, the loss is even more piquant, given that the American public discovered him largely after he'd departed it. 'This is the material by the way, that's kept me virtually anonymous in America,' Hicks joked in his last complete set, after a detour into philosophy. 'You know, no one fucking knows me. No one gives a fuck. Meanwhile, they're draining the Pacific and putting up bench seats for Carrot Top's next Showtime special. Carrot Top: for people who didn't get Gallagher.' He continued, '*Gallagher!* Only America could produce a comic who ends his show by *destroying* food with a sledgehammer. Gee, I wonder why we're *hated* the world over.' At the end of the set – in an inspired moment that was captured on film – Hicks came back on stage for his encore with a large paper bag, from which he extracted a watermelon. He put it on a stool, grabbed the microphone, raised it high above his head and brought it down on the side of the stool. He'd missed the melon but hit the target. The audience howled. As Rage Against the Machine's 'Killing in the Name' blared over the loudspeakers – '*Fuck you, I won't do what you tell me*' – Hicks shouted in unison with the lead singer: '*Motherfucker!!!!!!*' Hicks made his exit, flipping the finger wildly with both hands to the room, to the world, to the cosmic order that his jokes frequently invoked.

The revenge that Hicks took with laughter – his almost infantile glee at getting even for the credulity of the republic ('You're a moron!' 'You suck Satan's cock!' he frequently yelled to the idiots in his mind and in the audience) – marked him as the genuine comic article. 'Listen to my message, not the words,' Hicks told his mother. Composed in equal parts of scepticism, scatology, and spirituality, Hicks' humor gave off a very special acrid perfume. 'Prolifers murdering people,' Hicks heehawed. 'It's irony on a base level, but I like it. It's a hoot. It's a fuckin' hoot. That's what fundamentalism breeds, though – no irony.' To the spellbound and the spellbinders, Hicks bequeathed a heritage of roaring disgust. If he wanted to force the public to descry a corrupt society, he also wanted it to descry the low standard of commercial American comedy, which raised laughs but not thoughts and, in his eyes, hawked 'fucking beer commercials,' while leaving the public 'without any kind of social fucking awareness.'

The white heat of Hicks' fulminations was meant, in part, to purify comedy itself – a notion explicitly stated in a film script he developed in the last year of his life, which told the story of a serial killer who murders hack comics. 'I loved those who gave their lives to find the perfect laugh, the real laugh, the gut laugh, the healing laugh. For love, I killed those comedians,' the murderer explains when he's finally caught. Hicks wanted to play the serial killer; his act was part of the same search-and-destroy mission.

Hicks came of age when the sitcom showcase was king. At a time when the romance of the road was over for American comedians, and the goal was to get a development deal – your own show and a big payday – Hicks returned comedy to its essential atmosphere of challenge and unpredictability. In a riff about 'Tonight Show' host Jay Leno doing Dorito commercials ('What a fucking whore!'), Hicks said, 'Here's the deal folks. You do a commercial, you're off the artistic roll-call. Forever. End of story. You're another fuckin' corporate shill . . . Everything you say is suspect, everything that comes out of your mouth is like a turd falling into my drink.'

As the Letterman incident and his reaction to it dramatized, Hicks was as hungry as the next comedian for mainstream success, but only on his own terms. He was not prepared to sacrifice the emotional integrity of his material for popularity. 'There's dick jokes on the way,' he'd say to his listeners when he raised ideas that flummoxed them, then he'd put on his cracker accent: '"This guy better have a big-veined purple dick joke to pull himself out of this comedy hole".' As a comedian, Hicks was never soft and cuddly. For the first-class members of the next generation of American comedians, such as Jon Stewart of 'The Daily Show,' the purity of Hicks' comic quest was inspirational. 'Hicks was one of the guys fighting the good fight,' says Stewart, who considered Hicks 'a legendary figure' and who worked with him a couple of times on the road. 'He was the guy you looked to. He wasn't trying to be mediocre; he wasn't trying to satisfy some need for fame; he wasn't trying to get a sitcom; he was trying to be expert.' Stewart adds, 'Hicks was an adult among children.' Among the daring lessons that Hicks's comedy taught Stewart and other comedians of the next generation was 'to walk the room' – if Hicks didn't think that the room was worthy of him, he would 'walk it', that is, drive his comedy further than even he might normally think of doing. 'The audience's apathy spurred him on,' Stewart says. For instance, at one gig, as Hicks was launching into a bit about the Zapruder film, a drunken blonde called up to him, 'You suck!' Hicks rolled the words around in his mouth, stepped downstage, and pointed to the woman. 'Get out! Get out, you fucking drunk bitch! Take her out! Take her fucking *out!* Take her somewhere that's good. Go see fuckin' Madonna, you fucking idiot piece of shit!' Hicks began to imitate her voice – '"You suck, buddy! You suck!"' – and ended up skipping around the stage in her persona. '"I got a cunt and I'm drunk. I can do anything I wa-aant! I don't have a cock! I can yell at performers! I'm a fucking idiot 'cause I got a cunt!"' He knelt down. *'I want you to find a fucking SOUL!!!!'*

As a performer, Hicks was not short on soul or on charisma. In front of the paying customers, he was powerful, unpredictable, and thrilling. 'He was bigger than the room,' Stewart says. A great comedian is by definition inimitable. Nonetheless, since his death, and even before it, American comedians like Dennis Leary have made a good living reworking his lines and faking his bad-ass attitude. The indicators of posthumous longevity for Hicks are good. A biography has been published ('the most outspoken, uncompromising and famous unknown comic of all time,' the jacket says); Hicks' record sales are bullish; in a recent TV documentary about censorship, for which Hicks' expletives were deleted, his name was added to the short list of comic martyrs.

Since his death, history has caught up with his comedy. In the early nineties, he was already talking about Iraq and the first President Bush. 'If Bush had died there,' he said, in a bit about why we should kill Bush ourselves instead of launching twenty-two

Cruise missiles at Baghdad in response to his alleged attempted assassination, 'there would have been no loss of innocent life.' In a culture made increasingly woozy by spin-doctors, Hicks' straight-talking about political chicanery was a few years ahead of its time. If Hicks didn't pave the way for comic civic disobedience in such popular TV shows as 'Politically Correct' and 'The Daily Show', he was an immanence of subterranean rumblings. 'When they were putting together "Politically Incorrect,"' Colleen McGarr says, of controversial American TV show, 'they were actually considering Bill as the original host instead of Bill Maher.'

A dream is something you wake up from. It is compelling and significant that the final words on Hicks's last record, 'Rant in E-Minor', are a prayer: 'Lift me up out of this illusion, Lord. Heal my perception, so that I may know only reality.' Hicks mocked society's enchanters – advertisers, TV networks, rock-and-roll icons, religious fanatics, politicians – with the sure knowledge that as in all fairytales only the disenchanted are free. He made that show of freedom by turns terrifying, exhilarating, and hilarious. He was what only a great comedian can be for any age: an enemy of boundaries, a disturber of the peace, a bringer of insight and of joy, a comic distillation of his own rampaging spirit.

– John Lahr
January 2004

Good evening ladies and gentlemen. My name is William Melvin Hicks. Thanks Dad.

Austin, Texas, 1983

Part 1: 1980–91

Climbing Up to Center Stage, *The Oracle*, Stratford High School Newspaper (1980)

by Julia Joseph

Los Angeles has 'The Comedy Store'. New York has 'Catch A Rising Star'. Now in Houston, up and coming comedians have a place to launch their careers. The Comedy Workshop is now in session.

Since its start a few years ago, the Comedy Workshop has become one of Houston's most popular night spots. Houston comedians, both amateur and professional, go to the Workshop to try out new material, improve on established material, and receive inspiration for future material.

Senior Bill Hicks is one of the Comedy Workshop comedians who has aspirations for a career in comedy and entertainment. He has been doing comedy since he was in the 7th grade. Bill and a former Stratford student, Dwight Slade, who is also interested in a career in entertainment, went to the Workshop two years ago and performed on amateur night. Dwight has since moved to Oregon, but plans to return to Houston. He and Bill are going to form a comedy team. As a team Bill says that he and Dwight have 'something special that will make us the two who become famous.' 'There is a rapport with Dwight that makes me come up with things quickly,' said Bill.

'It used to be just amateur night,' said Bill of the format in the Annex of the Workshop. 'They started having stand-ups about two years ago.' Bill has been hired as one of the regular stand-up comics.

The Comedy Workshop is now divided into two parts, the Cabaret and the Annex. The Cabaret houses satirical revues Wednesday through Sunday, and the Flipped Side of the Comedy Workshop – the touring company – Thursday and Sunday. The Annex houses an open stage for stand-up comedians and specialty acts every night, along with regular paid Stand-ups Friday and Saturday.

Bill is the youngest comic at the Workshop and for him to have gotten this job is no mean feat. 'Two of the comics were in the National Laff-Off,' said Bill. He explained that this is a contest held to determine the five best comedians in the United States. Several celebrities, both local and national, also perform at the Workshop. For example, Gary Richardson, a Burt Reynolds look-alike, has opened Charo's show in Las Vegas. He is also renowned in Houston for the local TV commercials that he does for a weight reduction clinic.

Stand-up comedy requires as much preparation as any stage performance does. 'You've got to be your best supporter,' said Bill. 'Sometimes you feel in control and it's great, but sometimes you just don't feel in control and you really have to struggle to get laughs.' He said that he does not have a specific place or situation from which he gets his material. 'It just comes to me.'

Bill is having increasing success with his career. Besides working at the Comedy Workshop, he has performed with other comedians at the University of Houston. Private groups are able to arrange with the Workshop for a group of the comedians to perform at a special function or gathering.

Since working at the Workshop, Bill has had only one bad experience. 'There was a bad audience; half of them were asleep and the other half was insane. One guy hated my guts, I don't know why. We started arguing back and forth,' he explained. Bill said that he tried to continue with his routine but soon gave up as the heckler continued. 'I totally fell apart. I wasn't funny at all. He (the heckler) pulled a gun.' The episode ended as Bill left the stage and the heckler was subdued and led away by the managers of the Workshop.

There are over 2000 comedians trying to make it and Bill explained that the road to stardom is long and hard. 'Think of Rodney Dangerfield; he's what, 50, and it took him about 20 years to make it.' The competition at the Comedy Workshop is also keen. 'Any comic that's there feels threatened by another comic,' said Bill, but added that they remain, for the most part, friends.

'You wonder if you're going to be that one that makes it, like Steve Martin,' mused Bill. Well, it's a one in 2000 chance.

Late Show with David Letterman (1985)

T hank you. Thank you very much. How many of y'all feel this is probably the peak of the party right here? (*laughter and applause*) Me too. I am a comedian. I like my job, it's a good job, I like the hour and ah . . . it's a tough job and I'm here to do it. I feel good about it. I can't do anything else: I have what is called a bad attitude. Got any bad attitudes out there? (*audience clap*) I'm also not a team player. Ooooh. So my principal told me, 'Bill, I'm sorry, son, but you're just not a team player.' Oh, there's a couple of sleepless nights I spent. What am I gonna do with all these jerseys I bought, you know? I mean . . . you know. I was born alone, not with an end field, all right? So. Yeah, I got a hostile attitude. I got it from a hostile family. It was pretty rough. Kids would come up to me when I was younger and go, 'My Dad can beat up your Dad.' I'd go, 'When? Take the man out, you know. He's cutting the lawn Saturday, pick him off then, why don't you? While he's got on that Bermuda jumpsuit he found somewhere in Oklahoma' . . . I think . . . I don't know where he sends away for that.

I just got back from Oklahoma, I'm on my way to San Antonio: my career continues to wobble unevenly. Yeah, Oklahoma, that's a great place. Impression of Oklahoma. (*audience member shouts 'All right!'*) You like Oklahoma? Here's an impression for those who've never been before. (*makes noise of wind whistling and a dog howling*) That was inside the club I was playing. People in Oklahoma think the Marlboro man is effeminate, OK? And the women make him look that way, so I was glad to get out of that place. It was strange. You see signs by the road in Oklahoma, signs saying 'Dirt for sale'. Aww, I'd like to get inside that guy's mind and look around for an hour. This guy sees opportunity at every glance, man. I don't know why he didn't open up an air dealership while he was there. As long as you're selling the elements here. 'Thinking of startin' your own planet? Come on down to Bo Jim's Landland.' I checked him out. He had a great rap. Came up to me and goes, 'I don't wanna pressure you now, but we got a family of worms lookin' at this.' They were here first. Yeah, I like Oklahoma. They got all those southern evangelists down there too. I like southern evangelists. Real powerful dudes. See stuff in the TV Guide on Sunday like 'Brother Dave heals the deaf. Show close captioned.' How powerful's Brother Dave here? So we got out of there quick. Even though warnings beside the road saying 'Speed limit is enforced by unmarked vehicles', we figured we were speeding in an unmarked vehicle. How they gonna know it's us? So I'm feeling pretty good.

Been dating the same girl now for seven years. Think I'm finally ready to pop the question: 'Why are we still seeing each other?' It's gotten kinda ugly. She freaked out on me, she really freaked out. Calls me up in the middle of the night going, 'I don't know who I am.' 'How did you know to call me?' Some pretty heavy odds there. Tells me she's thinking about jumping in front of a bus and I'm not being very helpful . . . so I sent her a bus schedule. 'Yeah, look honey, there's one every hour.' 'Why do you tease me?' 'I'm too old to pull your hair, all right?' I'm glad. I don't want to be that wrapped up in anyone. I look what it does to other guys. I was reading about Vincent van Gogh. Whoa! The guy cut off his ear and sent it to this girl, man. Makes a dozen roses look like a booger jack. Wow! I can hear his friends going, 'Are you sure you love her, Vince?' He's going, 'What?' I think Vince likes this chick, man.

So I don't know, I'm glad to be here. I would like to be a rock star. What a great job. I *am* a rock star. I'm just waiting to get my band together and learn how to play an instrument and I'm on the road. I'm watching *Entertainment Tonight*. They came out and announced Paul McCartney makes ten million dollars a month. That kind of puts our lives in perspective there. I'm watching that, going, 'Ten million a month!' This guy next to me goes, 'Yeah, but taxes eat that up.' Yeah, Paul's out there scrambling for rent right now, huh? Every time I think I'm partying too hard, I just keep in mind that Keith Richards is still alive and breathe a sigh of relief, huh? Makes that pack of Marlboro a day look pretty mediocre compared to this guy's lifestyle, man. But he outlived Jim Fixx, the runner and health nut . . . so I'm stating facts, make your own connections there. I picture a nuclear war – two things are gonna live: Keith and bugs. 'Where did everybody go? I saw a bright light; I thought we were on.' Hey folks, thank you. Have a [. . .]

Quotes and Lyrics

I f you are living for tomorrow, you will always be one day behind. Any organization created out of fear must create fear in order to survive.
A living philosophy is not a belief – it is an act.

22 October 1986

I want to be happy. I want to be at peace.
I want to be creative, joyous and complete.
I want to be whole and I want to be aware.
I want to be strong and healthy and to care.

December 1987

I believe the cost of life is Death and we will all pay that in full. Everything else should be a gift. We paid the cover charge of life, we were born.

February 1988

I need to be reminded where I'm going
I need to be reminded why I'm here
I need to be reminded where I came from
I need to be reminded not to fear.

15 April 1988

New Happiness
(28 January, 1986)

I'm done with excuses
I've run out of time
I've wallowed in sorrow
And spent the night cryin'
I've floundered in darkness
in sight of the light
If I am to live, then now is the time.

Oh you knew I knew you
I'm crying out to be led through
the valleys of darkness
these pits full of fears.
I only know one thing for sure, I know
I don't belong here.

When I was younger things went untold.
I built up a hard front, I acted quite bold.
My feelings were strangers, interpreted none,
I felt treated more like a daughter and less like a son.

I was only a youngster when I fell in love
My heart touched another's outside of my home
My passion was fragile, obsession quite real.
I followed my lover's dream till the end.

My chasm of darkness needs to be filled
Recovered feelings from long ago years
No one was there to understand,
Though as a child
I thought like a man.

Now I feel both – so young and so old
My body more tired and desperate, not bold
I've run from the shadows into the night
If I am to live, then now is the time.

I've Been Waiting For the Day

I woke from this dream
There was no tomorrow

And no sign of day

I woke from this dream
At a lovely hour
No one to hold onto tonight
No stars are shining through my window
No sign that day will ever light.

I woke from this dream
There was no tomorrow

The clock was ticking but there was no day.

Interview
by Allan Johnson
(14 September 1989)

W hen you first see Bill Hicks, you immediately think of a college scholar: studious and intelligent-looking, especially when he wears a pair of glasses. Here's a person you might think is very serious-minded. You probably would never associate Hicks with stand-up comedy.

And then you see him on stage:

'Jimi Hendrix died in a pool of his own vomit,' Hicks says. 'Do you know how much you have to puke to fill a pool?'

Or: 'Flag-burning really brought out people's true colors. People were like, "Hey, buddy, my dad died for that flag." Well, that's weird, 'cause I bought mine.'

Or jokes on sex, nonsmokers, former President Reagan and singers Rick Astley, Tiffany and George Michael. And you won't believe Hicks' theory on who the anti-Christ is (hint: think 'oldest teenager'[1]).

Hicks, 27, has always seemed to tell jokes that will bring a start to audiences. His first stand-up performance was at the tender age of 13, at a Baptist camp talent show. Hicks based his act on mostly Woody Allen jokes.

Hicks was 'this little WASP kid, but I was talking about how rough my childhood was, because that was the angle Woody Allen took, right? But I did that joke . . . "I was breast-fed from falsies." And they went "Whooaaa, he said breasts."

'They were thrilled to have me,' Hicks remembers.

Hicks, who is indeed very serious-minded and thoughtful offstage, says that it's not his intention to offend anyone. He just wants to do an intense brand of comedy and hopefully convey some messages along the way.

'Here's what I try and do,' Hicks explains. 'To me, there are so many comedians out there. And they're so prevalent, and they (audiences) see it constantly. I try and give them a twist on it. One way that I do it is by being intense.'

Hicks has a comedy album coming out, taped 'Caroline's Comedy Hour' for Arts & Entertainment, and recently appeared on 'MTV's Half-Hour Comedy Hour.' He has performed on 'Late Night with David Letterman' four times and was featured on a Rodney Dangerfield HBO special. Hicks is working at the Funny Firm through Sunday, at 318 W. Grand Ave.

Hicks started professionally in 1979. He was part of the original Houston-based Outlaws of Comedy, which was headed by Sam Kinison.[2]

Kinison, rightly or wrongly, has been lumped in with a growing breed of 'shock comics,' a group that will say anything, no matter how raunchy or offensive. One might get the impression that Hicks may belong in that bunch, but he doesn't see things that way.

'I don't wanna be lumped in with anybody,' Hicks states firmly. 'I mean, I'm sorry that people have to have a label so they can feel better about their description of the world.'

Hicks stands out from shock comics in that his routines contain intelligent humor, whereas others will just sputter anything that they feel will get a laugh.

Performing earlier this week in Chicago was Andrew 'Dice' Clay, who has drawn criticism for his material on women and gays, among others. How does Hicks feel about Clay?[3]

The man who explains in no uncertain terms what hotel house-keepers will find if they jerk open his door when the 'Do Not Disturb' sign is out simply says, '"Dice" Clay is not my cup of tea.'

Bush
(1990)

Hello, I'm Bill Hicks, and I'm standing at one of the foot of one of the halls of justice of our great country. You know, when the producers of this video asked me to discuss my opinions on the George Bush administration, I was struck by the very cynical thought, 'What is the fucking point? People still love Ronald Reagan.' After eight years of lies and hypocrisy, people love this guy. Leads me to a very disturbing question: how far up your ass does this guy's dick have to be before you realize he's fuckin' ya? Ha, people are just, 'I like Ronald Reagan. He looks good on TV, he made the country stronger, patriotism's at an all-time high. Hold on a minute, something's slappin' my ass. Hey, he's fuckin' us!' What's the point of George Bush? Reagan-lite. No one cares that he was the ex-head of the CIA, now elected president. The CIA – political assassinations, overthrowing governments, death squads, drug-running. Let's give them more power! Let's put 'em in the White House! No one cares that George Bush's first two executive decisions were to name a vice-president who's whiter than Arsenio Hall. I guess you could commission Ted Turner to colorize Dan Quayle later. Bush's second decision was to name a secretary of defence who would begin every unilateral arms agreements off with 'Hi, I'm John and I'm an alcoholic.' Now, people love him. What is the point? People are already saying, 'I like George Bush. He looks good on TV, he brought back family values, he's fighting the war on drugs. Wait a minute, something's slappin' my ass. Hey! He's fuckin' us!'

Recorded Live at the Village Gate, NYC, and Caroline's Seaport, NYC (1990)[4]

T hank you. Anyway, it's good to be here. I ah . . . what? Recording an album tonight and tomorrow, so you're on the album. If you could make a little more noise than *that*, that would be (*audience laughs*) There you go. That's what we want to hear on the fucking album. Ha ha ha ha ha ha! Don't worry: funny material and laughter will be dubbed in later, so. Hey, you know, why pressure ourselves?

It's good to be here. I'm from ah Houston, Texas, originally, and moved up here a year ago, and ah . . . thank you. Ah, there's that warmth I've come to know on the island. It is my object to be stared at like a dog that's just been shown a card trick, you know what I mean? So . . . it's good. First thing I noticed when I came up here was of course the *homeless* situation. Now, I'm no bleeding heart, OK? *But* . . . when you're walking down the streets of New York City and you're stepping over a guy on the sidewalk who, I don't know, might be dead . . . does it ever occur to you to think, 'Wow. Maybe our system doesn't work?' Does that . . . question ever bubble up out of ya? I mean, if there was only a couple of bums, I'd think, 'Well, they're fuckin' bums.' But there's THOU-SANDS of these fuckin' guys. I mean, I'm running like a bum hurdle down the fucking st— The hundred-yard bum hurdle. Watch out, guys. There we go. 'Hey, you got any money, hey, you got any money, hey, you got any money?' Ooh, woah, I tipped that last guy, but it's OK – I didn't tip him over. That hurdle counts. And I had no idea there was *thousands* of these guys,[5] you know what I mean? So when I first moved here, I'm walking down the street, and all I get is, you know, ten/fifteen guys per block: 'You got any money?' I was like, 'Yeah, I do. Thanks for reminding me. It feels great. Shit.' I thought they were like asking about my wealth. You know, 'You OK? You got money? You callin' your mom? Your health all right?' Yeah, boy, people in New York are so friendly.

Man! Some of these guys though, they look healthy. I don't get it. They're just fuckin' bums, you know what I mean? Very idea they want me to just give them the hard-earned money my folks send to me every week. Fuck! You leech, get a *job*, man. My dad works eight hours a day for this money. Goddamn it, I'll get on a soapbox right on the street. I will. The nerve of these people. I mean, I had to cut the lawn every Saturday for fifteen years for a fucking quarter. This guy comes out from behind a *dumpster* and wants a cut of my action, you know? Shit, where were you when I was edging?

You ever have the one that flips on ya, that turns psycho on ya? Cos I give 'em quarters and sometimes I don't have any fucking change, and I'm not gonna break a twenty for a bum, OK? I've got a life. And, you know, they're the one that turns on ya.

> 'Hey, could you help me out?'
> 'Sorry, don't have anything.'
> 'MOTHERFUCKER!'
> 'Woah, woah, where's my chequebook, hold on. Is that Mr Bum? How do I make it out? [. . .] What? . . . Didn't know you were a psycho. Definitely wasn't your personality that put you on the street, was it?'

Jesus. They got balls, man. One of 'em said to me, you know, I said, 'Sorry, I don't have any money, man.'

> 'Thanks for nothing, buddy! You don't know what it's like to be broke.'
> 'Well, yeah I do. That's why I work. I know *exactly* what it's like: you sleep on the pavement, you dig through the garbage for food, and you bum money from strangers. Am I right?'

'That *is* what I do.'
'See ya.'

I feel very sorry for these guys, cos I don't know *why* they're bums. Do you know *why* they're bums? No one asks. When the guy's digging through the garbage, no one ever goes up and asks, '*What* the fuck you doing? *Why* you digging the garbage?' They're just psychos. You know, and some of them: 'Have you got any money? You got a quarter?' Hey, for the same quarter I can get that bum to squeegee my window, you know what I mean? I wanna comparatively bum shop, I want . . . I want the most from my bum quarter, goddamn it, and I want a receipt. That's how you get rid of 'em: get a receipt, you know (*snorts*) 'Here. Thanks.' Or some people: 'Oh, don't give him any money. It's probably for drugs or alcohol.' Well, yeah. You've never been a fucking drug addict then. Drugs are pretty important to a drug addict. (*chuckles*)

> 'Goddamn right, it's for drugs, lady. And if I don't get
> 'em I'm gonna cut your fucking heart out and eat it in
> front of ya.'
> 'Well, you put it that way . . . ding!'
> 'Thank you.'

See, I feel very sorry for these guys, cos I was an alcoholic. I quit drinking two years ago. I coulda been a bum. Anybody could be a bum. All it takes is the right girl, the right bar and the right friends, man. You are well . . . oh, your buddies'll see you off, goddamn it. They'll *christen* your dumpster for you.

Embarrassing drinker I was. I'd get pulled over the by the cops, I'd be so drunk, I'd be out dancin' to their lights, thinkin' I'd made it to another club. Turn the music up! Hey, what is this, a leather bar? Hey, hey, hey, hey, hey. I'm not into this, you faggots. Oh, *shit*! You guys go all out.

Man, I don't even wanna chance that, too. The attitudes change . . . little too serious. Remember ten years ago if you got pulled over and you'd been drinking, a cop came up to your car:

> 'Son, you been drinking?'
> 'Yeah.'

'Oop, sorry to bother ya. Hope I didn't bring your buzz down any. All right, get on outa here and have a good time. Bye-bye. Back in the car, Tommy, it's just a drunk guy behind the wheel of an automobile. Come on.'

Been on what I call my Flying Saucer Tour, which means, like flying saucers, I too have been appearing in small Southern towns . . . in front of handfuls of hillbillies lately, and ah . . . been doubting my *own* existence. I've noticed a certain anti-intellectualism in this country. Have you noticed that? Ever since around 1980,[6] coincidentally enough. Last week I was in Nashville, Tennessee. After the show I went to a waffle house. I'm not proud of it, but I was hungry . . . and I'm sitting there, and I'm eating, and I'm reading a book, right? I'm alone, I don't know anybody, I'm eating, and I'm reading a book. Fine. Right? Waitress comes over to me: (*chewing*) 'What you readin' for?' I said, 'Wow, I've never been asked that. Goddang it, you stumped me. Not what am I *reading*, but what am I reading *for*? I guess I read for a lot of reasons, but one of the main ones . . . is so I don't end up being a fucking waffle waitress. Yeah, that'd have to be pretty high on the list.' Then this trucker in the next booth gets up, stands over me and goes, 'Weell, looks like we got ourselves a reader.' What the fuck's going on here? It's like I walked into a clan rally in a Boy George costume or something, you know? This is a book. I read. Am I stepping out of some intellectual *closet* here? There, I said it. I feel better.

I'm telling you, man. Tennessee. You know, in many parts of our troubled world, people are yelling, 'Revolution. Revolution.' In Tennessee they're yelling, 'Evolution . . . We want our thumbs!' The thing is, they see people with thumbs on TV all day. Boy, that's gotta drive them hog-wild, huh? (*makes chimp noise*) It's a thumb, goddamn it. I can't say enough about the thumb. I'm tellin' you, man. There are some serious pockets of humanity out there. Go to some of these truck-stops the middle of nowhere, order a coffee. The guy behind the counter goes:

'You want the 32 ounce or the large?'
'Ah, shit, how big is that large?'

'You gonna want pull yer car round back. I'm gonna start the pump.'

Boy, that sounds like a lot of coffee, man. I don't know if I want to be *awake* that long in Tennessee, you know? They're nice people. They are. What would you describe them as? Rural? Backwoods? Hicks? After the show, one of them came up me real excited. 'Man, you're great. You're cracking me up. I was about to spit.' 'Sorry.' He said, 'No, I loved it. I'd like you to meet my wife and sister.' And there was one girl standing there . . . not a thumb between 'em.

So . . . 'Smokers, thank you. Thank you, guys. Just smoke away, huh? Don't worry about us.' Hokay. How many smokers do we have here tonight? Smokers? (*a few claps from audience*) Oh boy, listen to that energy they can pump out at will, huh? (*wheezy coughs by Bill*) Thank you, guys. That was a *valiant* effort on your parts. Listen to this: how many non-smokers do we have here tonight? Non-smokers? (*lots of audience applause*) Hear that? Bunch of whining little maggots, aren't they? Aren't they? Obnoxious, self-righteous *slugs*. I'd quit smoking if I didn't think I'd become one of them. The worst kind of non-smoker's the one where you're smoking and they just walk up to you and (*coughs affectedly*). I always say, 'Shoot. You're lucky you don't smoke. That's a hell of a cough, dude. I smoke all *day* and don't cough like that. Maybe you were conceived with a weak sperm. Maybe your dad was jacking off and your mom sat on it at the last second.' Did I over-react? Didn't, did I? I think that's kinda cruel: I'm smoking and you come up coughing at me. Jesus! You go up to crippled people dancin', too, you fucks? 'Well, hey Mr Wheelchair, what's your problem? Come on, Ironside. Race ya.' You fucking sadist. *I'll* smoke, *I'll* cough, *I'll* get the tumours, *I'll* die. Deal? Thank you, America. People say, 'Well, it's not that, i-i-i-i-it's the secondary smoke. It's not just the smoke that you smoke but the smoke that comes out of you. That's called secondary smoke. And that's not good smoke, just cos it came out of you.' Shut the fuck up, right now. Goddamn it, if I don't smoke there's gonna be secondary *bullets* coming your way. D'you understand this? I'm fuckin' tense! All right? Thank you!

I been on a fucking flying saucer tour for three months, OK? Thank you. Hope you don't mind if I just enjoy my cig.

I love when people in New York City complain about your smoking. Isn't that great? Yeah. These people are standing ankle-deep in dog links, straddling a dead guy, you know. Apparently my cigarette's fucking up the delicate balance of nature here. 'Oh, this is bothering you? Ohhhh. I'm sorry. Let me go over here to this pile of bum dung and put this out. There we go. Restore New York to that pristine state we know it exists in . . . if it weren't for my godawful cigarette.' Jesus. How much do you smoke a day, dude?

Man in audience: Pack an' a half.

Bill: Pack an' a half? You little puss. Get a little— why don't you just put a dress on and swish around for us. (*singing*) 'Pack an' a half. I smoke a pack an' a half.' Makes me ill. I go through two lighters a day, dude. Yeah. And I'm startin' to feel it. Eurgh, shit. But I do have this big fear, right? Doing smoking jokes in my act? Showin' up five years from now, going (*in monotone*), 'Good evening everybody. Remember me? Y'all were right. Smoking's bad.' Ewwwww. You ever seen that? Does that . . . let me tell you something: if you're smoking out of a hole in your neck . . . *I'd* think about quittin'. I would. And that's just *me*, you know. See, once again I'm not being stringent with the rule of thumb. See, what's cool is every pack has a different Surgeon-General's warning. Isn't that great? Mine say: 'Warning: Smoking may cause foetal injury or premature birth'. Fuck it! Ha ha ha! Found my brand. Just don't get the ones that say 'lung cancer', you know. Shop around, man. 'Yeah, give me a carton of low birth weights. What the fuck do I care?'

'Cigarette smoke contains carbon monoxide.' Well, so does my car and it still fucking runs, so. Ah, shit. See, I smoke, I don't drink, I don't do drugs, you know. Can I smoke? Can I? Like a fucking fiend I can.

The fact that we live in a world where John Lennon was murdered, yet Barry Manilow conTINues to put out fucking albums. Goddamn it. If you're gonna kill somebody, have some fucking taste. I'll drive you to Kenny Rogers' house, all right? Get in the car, I know where Wham! lives. (*singing*) 'You gotta have faith, da da da da. (*makes sound of two gunshots*) No, George, you've gotta have *talent*, dude. (*three gunshots*). New rule. *And* you can shave that two-day growth of beard off, buddy. Cos you're fooling no one, you big girl. (*gunshot*) For the record . . . and let's not mince words, because our very lives depend *only* upon truth: George Michael is . . . a . . . big . . . girl. *If* you ladies like him, you're dykes. End . . . of . . . fucking . . . story. This is not a matter of opinion, this is not a matter of taste, or perception. I can prove this on a home computer. These aren't idle thoughts. The guy's such a big girl. Have you seen this? He's hawkin' Diet Cokes now. Ewwww. Diet Coke. Even *Madonna* fucking hawked *real* Coke. You little puss. 'Diet Coke. I'm George Michael. I drink Diet Coke so my heinie doesn't get too big. We don't like big heinies, do we girls? Hee hee hee. Diet Coke.' Why don't you just put the fucking skirt on and get it over with, that's what I say.

These are our like our music representatives. These are our rock stars. What kind of fucking Reagan wet dream *is* this world, man? Rock stars hawking Diet Cokes! What real rock star would do something like that, you know?

> 'It's Keith Moon for Snickers!'
> 'Sometimes I'm doing a drum solo, and I haven't eaten
> for like three fucking weeks. I eat a Snickerrrrrsssssssss.'

That's a rock star.

> 'It's John Bonham for Certs.'
> 'Threw up blood in me sleep last night. I got a date with
> two thirteen-year-old twins. I suck a Certs.'

That's a rock star. 'Diet Coke!' Boy, I tell ya, if money had a dick, George Michael's would be a flamin' faggot. 'Oh, Diet Coke? Ohhhhhhhh, oh boy, ohhhh. Mm-mmm, I love that Diet Coke, ohhhhhhhhh, god damn that, oh god *damn* that Diet Coke. Ohhhhhh! Drink it every day! Ohhhhhhh.' He's a demon . . . set loose on the earth to lower the standards. *End* . . . of fucking story. Everyone, though. Everyone is hawking products. That's like the highest thing you can achieve now, isn't it? Become some *barker*. Sinatra hawks beer; he doesn't have enough money, does he? No. Nothing's sacred to these fucks, man. I'm waitin' to see:

'It's Jesus for Miller.'
'I was crucified, dead for three days, resurrected, and
waited 2,000 years to return to earth. It's Miller time.'
'You know, Jesus, it doesn't get better'n this.'

You don't see the imminent danger, do you? You're staring at me
like, 'Bill, they're just musicians, and they're, you know, and they're
just doing their thing, and' NO! They are DEMONS SET LOOSE
ON THE EARTH TO LOWER THE STANDARDS FOR THE
PERFECT AND HOLY CHILDREN OF GOD! Which is what
we are. Make no mistake about it. What's *happened* to us? After
eight years of Ronald Reagan and Yuppies we live on like the third
mall from the sun now, you know? Come *on*, man. Is it fuckin' me?
Debbie Gibson[7] *had the number one album* in this country, y'all.
Now, if this doesn't make your blood fucking *curdle* . . . I mean,
who buys that shit, you know? Is there that much babysitting money
being passed around right now? Have you seen that little mall crea-
ture at work? (*singing*) 'Shake your love.' What love are you shak-
ing, Debbie? You're twelve. You got no titties . . . you look like
Johnboy, and your music SUCKS. Go back to the mall that spawned
you. This is not a matter of *perception*, this is not a matter of *taste*,
I can prove this on an Etch-A-Sketch. Go babysit Tiffany.[8] That's
what you should be doing. Spank her little bottom till it's bright
red, then lick it all over. There's a video I'll fuckin' watch of yours.
Wouldn't you love to see those two little hairless peach fishes locked
in a sixty-nine?

'Oh, Debbie.'
'Oh, Tiffany.'
'Oh, baby what have we been waitin' for, honey?'
'Oh, no. Oh, Lord.'

For God's *sake*, keep their mouths busy so they can't sing. *Anything*.
Number one album. Sorry. I find that . . . hard to believe, but . . .
then again Reagan was elected twice. Ha ha ha ha ha! I should be
used to disappointment, I guess. 'Get over it, Bill!'
   Man, Rick *Astley*?[9] Have you seen that little incubus at work?
(*singing*) 'Don't ever wanna make you cry. Never wanna break your

heart.' Ha ha ha, I wouldn't worry about it without a *dick*, Rick.
You got a corn-nut, you got a clit, you're not even a guy. You're an
Aids germ that got off a slide. They're putting music to Aids germs,
putting a drum machine behind 'em, and Ted Turner's colorizing
them, goddamn it. These aren't even really people. It's a CIA plot
to make you think malls are *good*. It's all in *Omni*[10] next month.

You're still staring at me. You just don't feel the fire cos you just
been anaesthetized, right? You just, 'Come on, Bill. Debbie Gibson,
she's just a little girl.' NO! 'You know Debbie Gibson writes all her
own songs?' No! Fucking just pull me up a chair. 'Yeah, she writes
all her own songs about her own real-life experiences.' Yeah, what's
her next one called? 'Mom, Why Am I Bleeding?' *When* did we
start listening to pre-pubescent white girls? I musta missed that
meeting. We have on our fingertips the greatest minds of all time,
the knowledge and history of the greatest thinkers of ALL FUCK-
ING TIME, but no, what's that little white girl sayin'? Let's go
put Debbie Gibson's thoughts on a fucking compact disc so they'll
never be destroyed. Is it me? I mean, goddamn it, I remember I
think – and maybe I'm romanticizing the past – but I remember
when music had a conscience, and music had soul, and music
had balls, man. Does anybody remember that at all? Jimi Hendrix?
Any question about that guy? (*singing*) 'Stand by the mountain/
Chop it down with the edge of my ha-ay-and.'(*Boom . . . Whoo*)
This guy had a dick . . . like an anaconda . . . blowing in the wind,
man. (*singing*) 'Don't ever wanna make you cry, never wanna break
your heart, Diet Co-o-oke for ever.' 'SCUSE ME! I would love to
have seen the Jimi Hendrix/Debbie Gibson album. (*laughs*) I bet
he could shake her love right in half. Boozch! (*imitates opening to
'Foxy Lady'*)

> (singing) 'Foxy!'
> (screaming) 'MUMMY!'
> (singing) 'Foxy lady!'
> (screaming) 'MUMMY!'
> 'Debbie, you wanted to be a rock star, honey, remem-
> ber? You gotta hang with the big boys, sweetie.'
> 'I wanna go back to the mall! I suck! I suck! Get him

away! HE'S GOT THE BIGGEST DICK!'
(Boom crash) (singing) 'Voodoo Chile, baby!'

Just a dick like a buzz-saw. (*makes buzz-saw noise*) Cut her into little mall cordwood, man. Save a pair of bloody panties for George Michael to slip on. Boom! He's a woman; she's dead. Jimi's still fucking jamming, goddamn it.

I don't do drugs . . . any more. Ha ha ha ha ha! Haven't done drugs . . . today. Oh, god. Used to do lots of drugs. Not ashamed of it. You know. Had no luck with drugs. One time me and three friends dropped acid, drove round in my dad's car. He has one of those talking cars. We're tripping, and the car goes, 'The door is ajar.' We pulled over, thought about that for twelve hours, man.

> 'How can a door be a jar?'
> 'Well, why would they put a jar on a car?'
> 'Oh man, the freeway's melting.'
> 'Put it in the jar.'

Hours. (*makes sound of crickets chirruping*) 'But if it's a jar . . .' (*crickets chirruping*) '. . . for what kind of car?' (*dog howls*)

Got pulled over tripping once, too. Whoo, there's a dream come true. I'll match that with any drunk's story you've ever *heard*. Man, a cop was tapping on this window. We're staring at him in this mirror over here.

> 'How tall are you?'
> 'Ambush!'
> 'Big one and a little one. Twins.'

George Bush[11] says we are losing the war on drugs. You know what that implies? There's a war being fought, and people on drugs are winning it. Ha ha ha ha! What does *that* tell you about drugs? Some smart, creative people on that side. They're winning a war, and they're fucked up! Ha ha ha! Are we winning? It's like, they fight the war on drugs like the colonials fought the Indians, right? They're walking in a straight line and red coats; drug users are like Indians. They're up in the trees, going, (*inhales smoke*) 'Are they fighting us? (*exhales smoke*) We're not even in that fucking field. (*inhales smoke*) I guess we're winning by default. Ha ha! No combat; we're ahead.' (*inhales smoke*) Drugs– you know, war on drugs. Hey, I don't get it, because alcohol and cigarettes are drugs, so the war is definitely taking a ceasefire here, isn't it? Yeah. Alcohol and cigarettes kill more people than crack, coke and heroin . . . *combined*.

You never see a positive drugs story on the news, do ya? No. Always negative. News is supposed to be objective, isn't it? Supposed to be? *The* news? But every drugs story is negative? Well, hold it. I've had some killer times on drugs. I'm not promotin' it, but I'm not denyin' it. Let's hear the whole story. Same LSD story every time: 'Young man on acid, thought he could fly, jumped out of a building. What a tragedy.' What a dick! Don't go blaming acid on this guy. If he thought he could fly, why didn't he take off from the ground first to check it out? He's an idiot. He's dead. Good. You mean there's one less doorknob in the world? Whoo! What a tragedy! 'Why so down, Bill?' We're missing a moron. Ha ha ha ha ha. We're missing a moron.

I'd like to see a positive LSD story. Would that be newsworthy? Just once? Hear what it's all about?

> 'Today a young man on acid realized that all matter is merely energy condensed to a slow vibration, that we are all one consciousness experiencing itself subjectively. There's no such thing as death, life is only a dream, and we're the imagination of ourselves. Here's Tom with the weather.'
> 'Wow! Did you see the news?'

You know it's not gonna— it's not a war on drugs, it's a war on personal freedom is what it is, OK? Keep that in mind at all times. Thank you. They lump all drugs together. It's not gonna work. *Pot* and *crack*? Hey, hey, hey, dude. Don't put pot in the drug category. It's an *'erb*, man. Like *tea*. Not only do I think pot should be legalized, I think it should be mandatory. Think about it. You get in traffic behind somebody:

(*makes sound of truck horn*)
'Shut up and smoke that. It's the law.'
'Oh sorry, I was taking life seriously. Ha ha ha ha . . .
oh, man, who's hungry?'

That'd be a nice world, wouldn't it? Mellow, hungry, quiet, fucked up people everywhere. Dominos' pizza trucks passing each other on every highway. Parades of Dominos'. (*truck horn*) Let *them* get stuck in traffic: all our pizzas will be free. Come on. 'Drugs are so bad, drugs are so bad.' Yeah, yeah, well how come Keith Richards still walks? *Explain that*, Mr Surgeon-General. You never hear the Surgeon-General mention Keith, do ya? Ahh, little hole in the theory there. Surgeon-General says, 'Drugs are bad! Drugs are EVIL! . . . 'Cept for that guy. Ha ha ha ha. They work real good for him. But the rest of ya.' It's like that commercial – the guy with the skillet?[12] This is your brain: schhhhhhhh. 'Here's Keith's brain: schhhhhhhh. Here's Keith's brain on drugs: (*opening notes to 'Satisfaction'*) Hey, that sounds pretty good. That's him on drugs? Well, let's give him some more. Ha ha ha ha ha. 'Here's Keith almost dead: (*opening notes to 'Jumping Jack Flash'*) It's good. Let's kill him. Ha ha. Get some hits. This guy *defies* the edge, man.

Keith Richards outlived Jim Fixx,[13] the runner and health-nut dude. The plot thickens. You remember Jim Fixx? This human cipher. What a dark period in our country's history, too: the health years. Remember that? Everyone was trying to make up for all those cocaine disco bashes. 'I guess I should jog—' Anybody love watching people jog in New York? It's 110 degrees, they're they're they're dead and . . . they're in traffic. 'I gotta get skinnier, I gotta be thinner.' Hey dude, you're gonna get hit in the fucking head with a car. You're gonna look real good like a *puddle*, OK? Wow, what a thin-looking healthy puddle that is. 'I'm still, I'm still not good enough . . . I'm still not good enough.' Sorry. I was born perfect. Been that way ever since. Sorry. I have an *unscrappable* faith.

Remember Jim Fixx, though? This guy used to write *books* about jogging. What do you *jot down* about jogging, you know? 'Right foot, left foot . . . faster, faster mmm, go home, shower.' OK. Thanks, Jim, for putting that literary mind to the jogging issue. But I know how to jog . . . being the biped that I am. Then this doofus goes out and has a heart attack and *dies* while jogging. Ahh-ha ha ha ha ha! There *is* a God. 'Right foot, left foot, haemorrhage.' Yeah, Jim, we're gonna need a happier ending, buddy. What is this 'Right foot, left foot, blood spurts out nose, Jim?' You having troubles at home, son? Keith Richards is shooting heroin into his eyeball and still touring, all right? I'm getting mixed signals. I picture nuclear war, two things surviving: Keith and bugs. 'Where'd everybody go? I saw a bright light, I thought we were on.'

Too weird, man. I think the world's falling apart out there. You feel that way? Do you watch this shit? Did you watch the flag-burning thing?[14] Wasn't that great? Boy, if everyone showed their true colours then, didn't they? Re*tarded* nation that we are. Scary. People just . . . people acted as though the Supreme Court *approved* of flag-burning, you know what I mean? 'Does that mean we have to burn our flags? What did they— they said that we had to—' No! No! NO! That's not what they said. They said that perhaps if somebody wants to burn a flag, he perhaps doesn't need to go to jail . . . FOR A YEAR. Pretty harsh on their part, huh? 'Does that mean we have to burn the– they said we should burn—' They didn't say that, they didn't say that, they didn't say that . . . they didn't say that. 'Does that mean I have to go out now—' No, no, no, no, NO! *Listen. Read. Think.* Calm down, relax, shut the FUCK up! 'Well, I don't get it. I don't wanna burn my flag—' Then DON'T! People snapped over this. Did you watch that? People were just: 'Hey, buddy. Let me tell you something . . . my daddy died for that flag.' Really? Wow, I bought mine. (*chuckles*) Yeah, they sell 'em, you know, at K-mart and shit, yeah. 'Yeah, he died in the Korean War for that flag.' Oh, what a coincidence: mine was made in Korea. Wow, the world is that big.

No one, and I repeat *no one* has ever died for a flag. A flag is a piece of cloth. They might have died for *freedom*, which – by the way – is the freedom also to burn . . . the fucking flag. You see, burning the flag doesn't make freedom go away; it's kinda like *freedom*. And also this case . . . they've had four of these cases in the country's 200-year history, so don't think it's that big and scary of an issue, do you? One of the hotter smokescreens these people

have put down the pipe for us. 'Rampant flag-burning, hurrrrrrrr.'
I tell you, the only way – and I don't approve of flag-burning. I
don't *wanna* burn a flag, but if somebody wants to burn a flag, what
business is it of mine? Is it my business if someone wants to burn
a flag? Is it? No. No, it's not. Is it my business what other people
read or watch on TV? NO, IT'S NOT! Thank you! You see, when
you talk these things out they come a little clearer, don't they? They
do. That's called logic and it'll help us all evolve and get on the
fuckin' spaceships and GET OUTA HERE! Let's go! (*chuckles*)

And the abortion thing, you know. Unbelievable. I'm not a girl, you
know, I'm a guy, but at the same time, I'll tell ya how you can solve
this abortion thing right now: those unwanted babies that women
leave in alleys and in dumpsters? Leave about twelve of them on
the Supreme Court steps. Ha ha ha. This is over . . . like that. 'You
guys said we have to have 'em, well then you guys FUCKIN' RAISE
'EM! Raise 'em then. *You* fucking raise 'em. *You* raise 'em. You say
I had to have it, then it's yours, fuck! It's yours. Take it!'

I generally love my job. You know what's great about being a comic?
It's I have no boss. There's a definite plus in a lifestyle, huh? Isn't
it? Aren't bosses something? They're like gnats on a camping trip,
aren't they? (*makes sound of gnats whining*) Get the fuck out of
here, buddy. It's just a job. It doesn't mean a thing, all right? I
smoked a joint this morning, you're lucky I showed, bud, all right?
My bed was like a womb.
    I always used to get from bosses: 'Hicks, how come you're not
workin'?' I'd go, 'There's nothing to do.' And they'd go, 'Well, you
pretend like you're workin'.' 'Yeah, why don't *you* pretend I'm workin'?
You get paid more than me. You fantasize, buddy. Hell. Pretend I'm
mopping. Knock yourself out. I'll pretend they're buying stuff; we
can close up. Hey, I'm the boss now – *you're* fired. How's that for
a fantasy, buddy? If you're gonna pretend, go ahead and [. . .]'
    I can't have a job: I need my sleep. You know what I mean? I
do. I need eight hours a day, you know, and about ten at night
(*sniffs*) and I'm good . . . I'm good, I am.

I look just like my dad. That scares me to death. I'm afraid I'm gonna wake up one day and start *acting* like my dad, you know? I mean, I love him, but he is a goober, man. All dads are goobers. They are. You become a goober, I don't know why. Life just breaks ya, man, and one day you just go, 'Screw it! I don't care what people think of me any more. I'm gonna wait for the paperboy in my underwear. I'm gonna go to the mall in a Bermuda jumpsuit. I'm gonna walk about the house in a robe that won't quite close. Who wants sausage with breakfast? I'm fixing sausage!' 'Dad, put some shorts on. You're a *goober*.'

You guys ever find yourselves . . . sitting around the house like that? That goober moment is almost upon you. When that sock starts dangling and you don't care, you got some serious fucking questions you better start askin'. You're about to start worrying about your lawn.

> 'I wonder how the lawn is? Let me just go out and stand
> naked in my lawn and survey my goober domain.'
> 'Dad, what the FUCK IS IN YOUR EAR?'

Something very vital is in my dad's ear. He's always— something's in there. Could be my college money. (*laughs*)

I never got along with my dad, man. When I was a kid, other kids would come up to me: 'My dad can beat up your dad.' I'd go, 'When? . . . He cuts the lawn on Saturdays. Nail him out there . . . when he's got those Bermuda shorts, red tennis shoes and sock garters on.' Brrrrrrrrrrrr. 'Go pop him in the head with a rake.' (*pop*)

I got an older brother who's a genius. Certifiable genius. As though an older brother enough is not enough to cause you havoc, right? A *genius* on top of it. Boy, that sucked. When I was younger we used to fight, you know, and I'd go, 'I don't have to do anything if I don't want to.' He'd go, 'Yeah, you do. You gotta take up space.' . . . 'Oh yeah?' Even then I was king of the comebacks, you know. (*whistles*) Ohhhh, boy. Remember summer vacations with your folks? Does anybody get the concept behind that? We did not get along together in a five-bedroom *house*. Dad's idea was to put all of us in a *car* . . . and drive through the desert at the hottest time of the year. Pffft! Good call, Dad! Let's confront our tensions. Remember that? *Stressful*, they weren't fun, you weren't vacating, it wasn't leisure. 'We're gonna get up at 2 a.m. I wanna be on the road by

2.05. We don't have time to stop at restrooms; we're passing Dixie cups around the car. We're gonna drive for fourteen-hour stretches in no direction whatsoever. The sun will always be shining through your window, Bill, figure that out.' I have seen the sun take *turns* with our car before . . . to beam through my window. I'm in the back-seat like an ant under a magnifying glass.

> (*desperately*) 'Dad, turn the air-conditioning on, please.'
> 'Nope, it eats up gas.'
> 'Then Dad, you take my college money and you turn that goddamn AC on, buddy. I'm not gonna be a sunstroke mongoloid so you can save two cents A FUCK-ING MILE!'
> 'Hush . . . Heavens, have a plum.'
> 'I don't wanna plum! I wanna be freeze-dried and mailed home. I'm not having fun on our vacation.'

Being in the car with my mom for fourteen hours, man. She's just talkin', talkin', talkin', just talkin', talkin', talkin'. I just wanna go, 'Mom, (*wearily*) I been listening to you for about ten hours now, and I got a really serious question I wanna ask ya: do you know ANYONE WHO DOESN'T HAVE A FUCKING TUMOR! *Everyone*. 'Got a tumor, gotta see it, you know that tumor started to swell like a melon, and er . . .' Who has swelling tumors? Don't talk about them! I'm trying to eat a fucking *plum* back here, mom. Plum/tumor – do *you* get the similarity at all?

That's one thing about travelling, man. I stay in hotels all the time. Anybody stay in hotels on a regular basis? Can you help me with something? Does 'Do Not Disturb' mean 'Knock Immediately' in Spanish? Or ah . . . what's the fucking problem here? Do . . . not . . . disturb: fairly clear. Then again, I'm a reader. Put that on your door, within five minutes they're there. 'Housekeeping.' (*knocking*) That's not too disturbing, is it?

> (*knocking*) 'Do you need fresh towels?'
> 'Yeah, I'm gonna need to wipe up your blo-ood. If you keep KNOCKIN' on that fucking door!'

They'll even walk in with a pass key. Have you ever had that? Your room, you're in it, 'Do Not Disturb' on the fucking door! Housekeeping *strolls* right in. You're sitting there going, 'Hey, hey, HEY!'

> 'I'm here to change the sheets, hu-huh.'
> 'Yeah, come back in five minutes. You're gonna be work-
> ing overtime on this crusty pillowcase. I'm young, too:
> you'd better check the ceilings, baby.'

Like there's anything to jack off to in a hotel room. There's another symptom of the third mall from the sun, man. They got this thing in hotel rooms now. Instead of cable TV, they got a thing called Spectravision. You know what that is? Where you *buy* the movies. They got these movies on there, it says right there on the movie card: adult feature. Movies called *Sex Kittens*. Adult feature, it's on after twelve, costs $6.35. Well, look . . . I'm an adult, I got $6.35 and oop! I'm up after twelve. Ha ha ha ha. Let's see the fucking film. Have you ever seen one of these? It's a pornographic movie *but* the pornography *is cut out of it*. Ahhh-ha ha ha ha ha ha! Ooo-hoo hoo hoo hoo! *There* is a frustrating hour. You wonder why people run through malls with automatic weapons these days, you know? 'I almost saw the pussy!'(*gunshot*) 'I need to see the pussy!' (*gunshot*) Now, I don't wanna seem shallow . . . but I don't think the plot and dialogue alone are enough to carry these films, y'all. I'd leave those fucking scenes in, if I were you . . . for continuity.

And they got all these weird cuts where you don't see the woman at all. But, what do they leave in? Ah! The guy's hairy ass.

> (*singing*) 'Ding ding ding ding ding ding ding ding ding
> ding ding.'
> 'Housekeeping.' (*knocking*)
> 'GO AWAY! I'm looking at a guy's hairy ass!' (*makes wah-
> wah pedal sound*)

Where are the sex kittens? Two guys make these movies. One guy films his own ass, the other guy has a wah-wah pedal and comes up with titles. These guys are making a fortune!

'Let's call this one *Stewardesses in Heat.*'
'Good title, Timmy. Film my butt!'
(*singing*) 'Ding ding ding ding. Ding ding ding. Ding ding ding ding. Ding ding ding.'

Where are the stewardesses?

'Let's call this one *Waitress Daisy Chain.*'
'Great, get a close up.'
(*singing*) 'Ding ding ding ding. Ding ding ding. Ding ding ding ding.'

Hey, where are the fucking chicks? I gotta pay for these movies! The guy at the [. . .] is going:

'Hey, you the guy who bought all the hairy bobbing man-ass films?'
'It didn't say that! It said *Pink Librarians!*'
'Yeah, buddy. Right.'
'If it had said *Hairy Bobbing Man-Ass* I'd have never bought the motherfucker!'

Goddamn it! Is it me?

And they have these . . . on the movie card it says, 'If you have any suggestions for our films, please write.' Eh, I wrote 'em a letter, and I said, 'Yeah: come shots.' It's not an adult feature unless at the end someone's gooey, OK? Arcing ropes of jism hitting chins. *That* is an adult feature. Women licking up semen like kittens under a cow udder. *That* is an adult film. That's a hairy bobbing man-ass. I don't know who that's for. I don't know *who* watches that. I mean, I've got that kind of time, but ah . . .

Boy, the pornography industry. They're such pompous fucks, huh? You ever look at a hardcore pornographic magazine? They have this disclaimer that says, 'All of our models are eighteen years and older.' Uh! These are *models* all of a sudden. Yeah, tell me something Miss Model: how is jism being worn this year? Is it being worn back, or in bangs, or off the chin? Yeah, these are *models*. Yeah, here's Dusty modelling a fourteen-inch cock up her ass. Come on down, Dusty. This is how cocks are worn in Europe, you know. Yep, and here's

Dallas with a penis ensemble. These are *models*. Yeah, I'm an amusement engineer, OK?

Adult features . . . with no sex in 'em. Does that sound like the throwback to Aids? Is that what that is? Call it Aids, man. What other generation had anything comparable to Aids, you know? The fifties: rug burn. Pffft. I don't know how much Aids scares y'all, but I got a theory: the day they come out with a cure for Aids, guaranteed one-shot, no-problem cure – on that day there's gonna be fucking in the streets, man. 'IT'S OVER! Who are you? Come here. What's your name? No, it's over! YEAH! WHOOOOOO-HOO!' Man, there's gonna be news cameras on every corner. 'They're fucking everywhere! This is Dan Rather and you're not gonna *believe* this shit.' Course, all you're gonna see on the news is: (*singing*) 'ding ding ding ding. Ding ding ding.' That's right: the hairy bobbing man-ass. The one adults know and love.

You know what? Here's my actual true . . . I've had a vision. And what it is, is although this is a world where good men are murdered in their prime, and mediocre hacks thrive and proliferate, I gotta share this with ya, cos I love you and you feel that. You know all that money we spend on nuclear weapons and defence every year? Trillions of dollars? Correct? *Trillions*. Instead, if we spent that money feeding and clothing the poor of the world, which it would pay for many times over, not *one* human being excluded, not *one*, we could, as one race, explore outer space together in peace for ever. You've been great, thank you. (*three gunshots*)

Recorded Live at the Vic Theatre, Chicago (November 1990)[15]

CHICAGO! YEEAH! OH YEAH! All right. Good evening, brothers and sisters, friends and neighbours, vibrations in the mind of the one true God whose name is love. It's warm in here; I don't know how you deal with these winters here, man. I don't get it. I was here last winter; one of the days I was here it was three below zero, no wind chill. A little nippy. It's kinda fun though in that weather, goin' outdoors and watching smokers pass out, cos they don't know when they're done exhaling. Just good cheap American fun, you know. Smokers cracking their heads open on the icy sidewalk, blood steaming . . . we laughed and laughed. How many smokers do we have here tonight?[16] Smokers? (*applause and hooting from the crowd*) That's a lot of energy for you fuckers, that's good! Usually you get . . . (*coughs six times*) Thank you guys, thank you. Next time I need you, just hawk up a chunk of lung for me, all right? Rear back, launch a flim-jim towards the stage. BUT! Listen to this; how manyyyyy *non*-smokers do we have here tonight? (*louder applause and hooting from the crowd*) Bunch of whining little maggots. You obnoxious . . . self-righteous . . . slugs. Don't take that wrong. I'd quit smoking if I didn't think I'd become one of you. You are the worst advertisement for non-smoking, you know that. Tell you, the worst kind of non-smokers is the kind where when you're smoking and they just walk up to you . . . (*coughs affectedly*) I always say, 'Shit. You're lucky you don't smoke. That's a hell of a cough you've got there dude. I smoke all day and don't cough like that. I'm smoking, you're coughing, wow.' That's kind of cruel man, going up to a smoker and coughing at him. Shit! Do you go up to crippled people dancing too? You fucks? 'Hey Mr Wheelchair, what's your problem? Come on Ironside, race ya!' Fucking sadist! Obnoxious, self-righteous sadist. Don't take that wrong.

But you've got to understand something. First of all, I don't do anything else, all right? Now I don't drink . . . now a lot of you non-smokers are drinking. OK, I'm a non-drinker and I smoke. Now to me, we're trading off vices. That seems fair to me. Yeah, lying fuck. 'No it's not, no it's not. Why should our lives be threatened by your nasty habit, nyah, nyah, nyah, nyah, nyah.' Yeah, well, you know what? I can't kill anyone in a car cos I'm smoking a fucking cigarette, all right? An' I've tried! Turn off all the lights, rush 'em, they always see the glow. 'Man there's a big firefly heading this way. Shit it's knocking over *shrubs!*' It's me coming in for the kill. Like I say, I don't drink . . . any more. I had to quit cos I *really* drank. K? K. And I was really fucking pathetic, K? K. Shit, man, I'd get pulled over by cops, I'd be so drunk I'd be out dancing to their lights thinking I'd made it to another club. It does not look good on the arrest report, man. You ask a State Trooper to do-si-do, they tend to remember you. So I don't drink, I don't do drugs . . . any more. I used to take drugs and I quit, but I tell you something . . . I have nothing against drugs whatsoever. That's kind of weird, huh? You've never heard that one. 'Used to take drugs, quit, and have nothing against them. Wow, never heard that, let's hear more.' OK. I'll tell you something else. I know this is not a very popular idea, you don't hear it very often any more, but it's the truth. I have taken drugs before and ahh . . . I had a *real* good time. Sorry! Didn't murder anybody, didn't rob anybody, didn't rape anybody, didn't beat anybody, didn't lose . . . mmmm . . . one fucking job. *Laughed* my *ass* off . . . and went about my day. Sorry! Now, where's *my* commercial? Shit, I'll be the guy holding that skillet in that commercial, man. 'That ain't a brain, that's breakfast! Let's eat! What, have we been up five days now? I'm fucking *starving!*' Tshhh . . .

I find that commercial a tad insulting to my intelligence, you know, the one 'here's your brain'. I've seen a lot of things on drugs, but I have never, ever, ever looked at an egg . . . and thought it was a fuckin' brain, not once. I have seen UFOs split the sky like a sheet, but I have never looked at an egg and thought it was a fucking brain, not once. I have had seven balls of light come off of a UFO, lead me on to their ship, explain to me telepathically that we are all one and that there's no such thing as death. *But* . . . I've never looked at an egg and thought it was a fuckin' brain. Now . . . maybe I wasn't getting good shit, but ahh . . . That's what I hate about the war on drugs, I'll be honest with you, it's what I can't stand is all day long when we see those commercials: 'Here's your brain, here's your brain on drugs', 'Just say no', 'Why do you think they call it dope?' And then the next commercial is: 'This Bud's for you.' Come on everybody, let's be hypocritical bastards. It's OK to drink your drug. (*laughs*) We meant those *other* drugs. Those *untaxed* drugs. Those are the ones that are bad for ya. Nicotine, alcohol . . . good drugs. Coincidentally, taxed drugs. Oh, how does this fucking work?

Thank God they're taxing alcohol, man . It means we've got those good roads we can get fucked up and drive on. 'Thank God they're taxing this shit, man . . . we'd be doing doughnuts in a wheat field right now. Thank God we're on a highway. Whoooo, this is a *good* drug.' Cos I'll tell you something, I'll be honest, man. If I were going to legalize a drug, it sure wouldn't have been alcohol. Sorry, there's better drugs, and better drugs for you. That's a fact. You may stop your internal dialogue. 'Hmm, but Bill, alcohol's an acceptable part of . . .' Shut the fuck up. You're wrong. K? K. Shit man, not only do I think marijuana should be *legalized* . . . I think it should be mandatory. I'm a hardliner. Think about it, man. You get in traffic behind somebody like: huuuh, huuuh. (*making car horn noises*)

'Shut up and smoke that: it's the law.'
'Oh sorry, I was taking life seriously. Oh, man! Who's hungry?'

That would be a nice world, wouldn't it? Quiet, mellow, hungry, high people everywhere. Just Dominos' pizza trucks passing each other. Every single highway, parades of Dominos'. (*car horn*) Let them get stuck in traffic: *all* our pizzas will be free. I'm a fucking dreamer, man! But I'm not the only one. (*audience cheers*) Dreamers, man. Pot is a better drug than alcohol – fact! Fact. Stop your internal dialogue. 'But Bill, alcohol's a blah blah blah—' Shut up! You're wrong, get over it. K? K. I'll prove it to you, man. You're at a ball game, or a concert and someone's really violent and aggressive and obnoxious. Are they *drunk*? Or are they smoking pot? Which is it?

Audience: Drunk!

Bill: They're drunk. I have never seen people on pot get in a fight because it is *fucking* impossible.

> 'Hey buddy!'
> 'Hey what?'
> 'Hey.'
> 'Hey.'

End of argument. Say you get in a car accident, and you've been smoking pot . . . you're only going four fucking miles an hour. (*makes skidding, then crashing noise*)

> 'Shit, we hit something.'
> 'Oh, uh-uh, uh-uh. We got rear-ended by a Dominos' truck, man.'

Just a better world. I'm *not* promoting the use of drugs. I'm just telling ya, I've had good times on 'em. That's the truth. I've also had bad times on 'em too, OK? But I've had good and bad relationships, and I'm not giving up pussy.

> 'Hi, I'm Bill and I'm a pussyholic. I like the way it smells . . . I like the way it tastes, and uh . . .'
> 'Keep coming back, man. Keep coming, you're in the right place.'

I'm not proud of this moment, all right? It happened; I moved on. You know what I mean though, we need a new enemy? Cos uh we're so miserable in our own lives we've got to keep pointing fingers and blaming. 'Drugs, yeah, drugs are the enemy. Hoo, yeah, what were we thinking?' People forget about drugs, man, people forget. People think drugs don't do anything good for us. How many people here believe drugs don't do anything good for us? Someone must. Chicken shits! Yeah I know, cos now they've got a beer, I know. If you believe drugs don't do anything good for us, do me this favour will you? Go home tonight, take all your albums and tapes, K? And burn 'em. Cos you know what? The musicians who made all that great music . . . *reeeeeeal* fucking high on drugs. Shit, the Beatles were so high they let *Ringo* sing a couple of tunes. Tell me they weren't a partying. (*sings*) 'We all live in a yellow submarine, a yellow submarine . . .' We all live? You know how fucking high they were when they wrote that song? They had to pry Ringo off the ceiling with a rake to record that, man.

> 'Get Ringo, John, he's got a great tune. Pull him down
> to the mic.'
> 'John, get Ringo. He's got a great song about we all live
> in a yellow tambourine or something, I don't know.'
> 'Fuck John, get off the ceiling.'
> 'Ah fuck, let's bring the mics up here. We'll sing from
> up on the clouds.'

They were real high. Great music, they were high, drugs had a positive effect. Shall I walk you through it *again*? Aaaah! Gotta have an enemy though. Cos we're so miserable we've got to keep blaming something, right. Let's blame some more stuff. Drugs, good. Rock'n'roll. Every few years rock'n'roll becomes the big enemy doesn't it? Like this Judas Priest trial, did you follow this? You know the story? Two kids, big fans of Judas Priest, listened to this album and then went out and killed themselves. And the parents sued the band, Judas Priest. OK, first of all two kids, big fans of Judas Priest,[17] commit suicide. Wow! . . . Two less gas station attendants in the world. I don't want to sound cold or anything, but ah . . . we didn't lose a cancer cure here. And hey, most stations are self-service now anyway so; we saved them a long troublesome job search. BUT! They tried to prove there were subliminal messages on this album telling you to kill yourself. Now, I may be naive, but ah, what performer wants his audience dead? I'm having trouble with the whole fucking theory. What are these guys in the band doing?

> 'I'm fucking sick of it, I am fucking sick of it. I'm sick
> of the touring, I'm sick of making 400,000 dollars a fuck-
> ing night. I'm sick of the free drugs, the free booze and

the groupies blowing me dawn to fucking dust. I'm in
a rut and I want out.'
'We've got all those concerts coming up.'
'I know, it sucks. *Unless* . . . Ian, Nigel, come here. I
just had a fucking idea, man. What if, Ian, what if, let's
just say what if . . . open your mind real wide now. What
if we kill the fucking audience? Could I go back to my
day job? I could sell shoes again.'

It just doesn't make a lot of sense. When you talk it through. But
every few years these little . . . they try and nail rock'n'roll.
Remember this shit: if you play certain rock albums backwards
there's satanic messages? Let me tell you something, if you're sitting
round your house playing your albums backwards, you *are* Satan.
You needn't look any further. And don't go ruining my stereo to
prove a fucking point either.

'Come here, come here, listen. (*makes snorting, growling noises*) Can you hear that? Listen.'
'Hey cut it out. That's brand new, man. What the fuck
are you doing?'
'No, shut up. Listen, real close. (*growling*) Can you hear
that? It's crystal clear. "Satan is lord, Satan is lord." It's
like he's in the room.'
(*makes growling noises again*)
'Oh my God, *you're* Satan! Aargh!'

Satan! Ruiner of stereos, destroyer of needles! Because, listen, I've
got an idea. It's time to make a bold admission, all right? Because
for the last ten years we've seen the rise of conservatives and fundamentalists and other forms of (*takes deep gasp*) *fascist*, OK? Who
try and tell us what to believe and what to think. I've got a bold
admission if you're one of those people, are you ready for it? They
say rock'n'roll is the devil's music. Well, let's say that we know for
a fact that rock'n'roll *is* the Devil's music. And we know that it is
for sure, OK? At least he *fucking* jams! If it's a choice between
eternal hell and good tunes, or eternal heaven and New Kids on
the fucking Block . . . I'm gonna be surfin' on the lake of fire,

rocking out. Do you know if you play New Kids on the Block albums backwards, they sound better? Gives them that edge they're missing, ya know, puts some hair on their balls.

But we've got to have an enemy. Rock? Drugs? We're so miserable, what's the enemy? Got it. Pornography, that's it. Yeeeeah, tremor through the room. Uh . . . the problem with pornography, basically, is this. No one knows what it is. Other than that, we've got a real good grasp on the situation. We know it's bad, we just can't figure out what the fuck it is. The Supreme Court says pornography is any act that has no artistic merit and causes sexual thoughts.[18] That's their definition. No artistic merit. Causes sexual thoughts. Hmmmmm. Sounds like almost every commercial on TV to me. You know when I see those two twins on that Double Mint commercial? I'm almost embarrassed to tell you this. Aaaah . . . I ain't thinking about gum.

(sings) 'Double your pleasure, double that fun.'
'Yeah honey, where's the Wrigley's? I feel like chewing on something.'

Every commercial. Here's a commercial they'd like to do. If they could, they'd do it. Here is the ultimate television commercial. We might see it one day yet. Here's the woman's face, beautiful. Camera pulls back, naked breast. Camera pulls back, she's totally naked, legs apart, two fingers right here, and it just says: 'Drink Coke'. Now I don't know the connection, but I'm drinking lots of fucking Coke! Snickers! Dr Pepper! . . . No I don't know the connection. Yes, I'm buying these fucking products. But you know, what does that say about us, man? Causes sexual thoughts is the subject of *fear*? Causes sexual thoughts. Yeah? . . . so? . . . and? . . . what? When did sex become a bad thing? Did I miss a meeting? *Playboy* – pornography – causes sexual thoughts. *Penthouse* – pornography – causes sexual thoughts. You know what causes sexual thoughts when it's all said and done? Let's cut to the chase; I'm tired of the debate, OK? I'll clear it up for ya mmm right fucking now. Here's what causes sexual thoughts . . . having a dick. End of story. I can speak for every guy here tonight, aaaand, OK I will. In the course of our day ANYTHING can cause a sexual fucking thought. You can be on a train, and it's rocking kinda nice. Pants

are a little tight. Oh my God, I've got a woody! I got a woody on the
El train. What are we gonna do, ban public transportation? I find it
ironic that people who are against sexual thoughts are generally these
fundamentalist Christians who also believe you should be fruitful and
multiply. It seems like they would *support* sexual thoughts, you know,
perhaps even have a centrefold in the Bible. Miss Deuteronomy. Turn
offs: floods, locusts, smokers. I actually did that joke in Alabama,
right. These three rednecks met me after the show, man. 'Hey, buddy!
Come here. Hey, Mr Comedian! Come here. Hey, buddy, we're
Christians, we don't like what you said.' I said, 'Then forgive me.' It
seemed so obvious. You know? But we've gotta have an enemy, man.
I'm tired of enemies; I'll be honest with you. I'm sick of enemies. I
got no fucking enemies, K? K. It's just a strange world; I don't know
what we choose, why we choose the things we do as a collective. You
ever wondered that? You know what I mean, the fact that we live in
a world where John Lennon was murdered, yet Milli Vanilli walks the
fucking planet. You know? Bad choice. Just from me to you, it wasn't
a good one. But isn't that weird, we always kill the guys who try and
help us. Isn't that strange, that we let the little demons run amok,
always? John Lennon: murdered. John Kennedy: murdered. Martin
Luther King: murdered. Ghandi: murdered. Jesus: murdered. Reagan
. . . wounded. You know. Bad fucking choice.

But even though that's the case, where we live in a world where good
men are murdered and little demons run amok, I'm sorry I still believe
it isn't; in fact I had a *vision* of a way we could have no enemies
ever again, if you're interested in this. Anybody interested in hearing
this? It's kind of an interesting theory, and all we have to do is make
one decisive act and we can rid the world of all our enemies at once.
Here's what we do. You know all that money we spend on nuclear
weapons and defence every year? Trillions of dollars. *Instead*, if we
spent that money feeding and clothing the poor of the world, which
it would pay for *many times over*, not *one* human being excluded . . .
not *one* . . . we could as one race explore outer space together in
peace, for *ever*. Thank you very much. You're great.

(sound of three gun shots)

Recorded Live at Funny Bone, Pittsburgh, PA (20 June 1991)[19]

Good evening, ladies and gentlemen. Hope you're doing well tonight. I'm glad to be here. I been on the road doing comedy now for ah ten years, so bear with me while I plaster on a fake smile and plough through this shit one more time . . .Teasing, it's magic every show.

Ah, fuck. Summertime . . . summertime *blues* is what I have. You know why? Don't like the fucking summertime, K? Think it sucks. Hot – sticky – sucks; hot – sticky – sucks. K? K. People love the summertime, cos people are (*makes bleating noise*) sheep. Good! Good answer, sir. Thank you. 'It's summertime and it's so good. It's hot and sticky, uh-huh.' I don't fucking get it, man. Gotta retire all my cool jackets for another fuckin' season, you know. I don't *have* to do that, but I don't wanna be, you know, hanging out in a leather jacket . . . in 90 degrees. That ain't cool, it's . . . HOT AND STICKY! Yes, sir, thank you. Good answer. Everyone goes to the beach. What is the— what is the— I don't get the bea— 'Where you going, the beach? God, I love to go the beach. Man, we could just go to the beach. God. What you wanna do? Go to the beach? Yeah! Uh, if I could live at the beach. *Could you imagine that? Living at the beach?*' What's the fucking deal with— it's where dirt meets water, all right? Chill out. That's it. End of fascination. I gotta bathtub and an imagination. I'm staying indoors this summer, all right? That way I can listen to music *I* like.

I don't know, maybe I'm jealous. Everyone at the beach is perfect:

tan, white teeth. I got white skin, tan teeth, you know. Not my environment. You put me under a neon beer light, I look pretty fucking cool. Particularly if it's one of those blinking ones – whoo! *Stud* muffin. The fucking beach.

I'm so pale, man, I take my shirt off at the beach, it's like a prism. People are just: 'Bill, put your shirt back on! We can't find our towels!' All these moths are bumping into me. Boy, moths are weird. You ever wonder what moths bumped into before electric lightbulbs were invented? Boy, the lightbulb really fucked the moth up, didn't it? First lightbulb ever turned on – *billions* of moths (*makes banging noise*). What, I don't get the appeal. What's the fucking deal with that, huh? What did they do before light– are there moths on the way to the sun right now, going, 'It's gonna be worth it.' It's a *hell* of a commute, man . . . and I don't wish that upon my little MOTH BUDDIES!

I just don't feel well, man. I had to set my alarm for this show, so it gives you an idea what kind of excitement I lead during the day. I just don't . . . I don't fit in anywhere, man. I really don't. I don't agree with anything either, not even with what I just said, so I think you see the fucking problem here. I'm stranded without a fucking clue, and I'm gonna say 'fuck' 8 million times, so keep, keep track . . . somebody. My dad: 'Bill, do you have to say the 'f' word in your act, son? Bob Hope doesn't need to use the 'f' word in his act.' 'Yeah, well, dad, guess what, Bob Hope doesn't play the *shit-holes* I play, all right? You put him in some of these joints, he'll have Emmanuel Lewis[20] and Phyllis Diller sixty-nining as his closer . . . just to get out of there alive.'

I smoke ah . . . if this bothers anyone, I recommend you looking around the world in which we live and shutting your fucking mouth. Take that home with ya. I got some news to tell you tonight. Very exciting news. For non-smokers? Oh, I can't wait to tell y'all this cos I know you don't know this . . . and I feel it's my duty to pass on information at all times so that that way we can all evolve quicker. Non-smokers, you ready? This, by the way, is a *fact* too. Non-smokers, ready? Drum roll. Brrrrrrrrrrrrrrrrrrrrrrrr. Non-smokers die every day. Ha ha ha ha ha ha ha! O-ho, sleep tight. Oh, the truth which shall set you free. I know that you non-smokers entertain some type of eternal life fantasy because you don't smoke cigarettes. Well let me be the first to (*makes exploding noise*) pop that fucking bubble and send you about your way with some little truth: you're gonna fucking die. OK? OK. Love ya! Shut the fuck up. And you know what doctors say: 'Shit, if only you'd smoked. We'd have the technology to help ya.' It's you people dying from nothing that are screwed. I got all sorts of neat gadgets waiting for me. Iron lung, oxygen tent, it's like *Christmas*.

S'weird man. People say the dumbest things, too. 'Hey, you quit smoking, you get your sense of smell back.' I live in New York City. I don't want my fucking sense of smell back. (*sniffs*) Is that urine? (*sniffs*) I think I smell a dead fella. Where's that coming— look, honey, a dead fella. I found him. Thank God I quit smoking: I can find dead fellas in urine puddles. (*sniffs*) Oooo, I love living in New York.

I know, it's a weird– does anyone remember this: when Yul Brynner *died* and came out with that commercial after he was *dead*? Does anyone remember that? 'I'm Yul Brynner, and I'm dead now.' What the fuck's this guy sellin'? Guy crawled through the earth to get a residual cheque here. 'I'm Yul Brynner, and I'm dead now cos I smoked cigarettes.' It's pretty frightening, you know. But they coulda done that with anybody. They coulda done it with that Jim Fixx guy just as easily.

> 'I'm Jim Fixx, and I'm dead now . . . an' I don't know *how* the fuck it happened. I jogged every day, ate nothing but tofu, swam 500 laps every morning; I'm dead. Yul Brynner drank, smoked, and got laid every night of his life; he's dead . . . shit. Yul Brynner's chain-smoking, drinking, fifteen-year-old girls sitting on his cueball noggin every night of his life; I'm running around a dewy track at dawn. We're fucking both dead. Goddamn it.'

I know it's a nasty habit, but guess what? Drum roll. Brrrrrrrrrrrrrrrrrr. I'm addicted. Ha ha ha ha ha ha ha! Tried to quit. You ever tried to quit, sir? I love it. Ever smoker, I love it. You ever try an' quit? 'Mmm-hmm? Oh yeah, I'm trying right now.' Did you try cold turkey? No, what did you try?

Man in audience: Didn't last long.

Bill: Didn't last long. But you did try stopping?

Second man in audience: [. . .]

Bill: Cold turkey? Thank you, sir. I haven't . . . believe I've entered you into the show yet. I'm talking to the smoker cos he's smoking. When I start talking about *goofballs*, you get ready. When the word '*goofball*' comes up, you sit up and take a sip of coffee, cos you're on. Listen, folks, the audience participation part of the show is limited to this and this only: direct 'yes' and 'no' answers to my questions, laughter, applause, and a blowjob from all the women afterwards. That's it. You can all relax within those parameters, I believe. Good. Glad we know the fucking schedule.

So you did try? Cold turkey's hard. It's the most– it's really aggravating. What I'm gonna do is I'm gonna quit gradually, and what you do to quit gradually is, I'm gonna lose one lung . . . and then a little while later I'm gonna lose the other one. And that's it. I feel better having a plan. So, I smoke a lot. How much do you smoke a day, sir?

Man in audience: Two packs.

Bill: Two *packs*? Pussy. (*laughs*) I go through two *lighters* a day, dude, all right? So . . . two packs, you're like a health nut to me. You're like the Jack LaLanne[21] of smokers, man. You could tie a piano to your back, you could swim the English fucking Channel with a cigarette. Two lighters a day is a bit much. Oyy . . . the only good thing about smoking now is every cigarette pack has a different Surgeon-General's warning. That's kinda neat. Mine say: 'Warning: smoking may cause foetal injury or premature birth.' Fuck it. (*laughs*) Found my brand. Just don't get the ones that say 'lung cancer', you know. Shop around. It is your body. 'Yeah, give me a carton of low birth weights. I think I can live with low birth weight, line 'em up, goddamn it. I'm here to take the low-birth-weight challenge. Let's go. One, two, three. Come on.' 'That's good, Willie. Do your little smoking jokes while you still got the breath left in you to do 'em, son.' That is my big fear in life: doing smoking jokes in my act, and showing up five years from now: (*in monotone*) 'Good evening everybody. Remember me? I was wrong. Smoking is real fucking bad for ya. No joke!' Oh my god, man. I've seen people *do* that. You ever seen someone do that? Is that unbelievable? Man, if you're smoking out of a hole in your neck, *I'd* think about quittin'. Wouldn't ya? I mean, at that point? Chew some gum, or something, I . . . I'm not trying to tell you how to live, I'm sayin' . . . that just shows a commitment I cannot fucking relate to, man. I mean, we're beyond image at that point, you know. Jesus, what's next for that guy, you know? 'I just can't stop. It gets worse and worse every year. I'm telling you, man, I cannot quit. I can't quit smoking! They're starting to taste like shit, but I . . .' Dude, you got a cigarette in your *butt*, man. Chew some fucking gum or something. You got a stogie[22] in your heinie, buddy, I'm tellin' you. Chew some gum, get a mint, get a toothpick, there's other ways. (*quietly*) Yeah, we're done with that shit there, I'm done with that shit. I'm just really tired, man.

You know what's bumming me out? I realize what bums me out: I watch too much news, man. It's depressing. You ever watch CNN for longer than say . . . twenty hours in one day? I gotta cut that out. Watch CNN: it's the most depressing thing you'll ever see, man. 'WAR, FAMINE, DEATH, AIDS, HOMELESS, RECESSION, DEPRESSION, WAR, FAMINE, DEATH, AIDS.' Over and over again. Then you look out your window: (*makes crickets chirruping sound*). Where's all this shit going on, man? Ted Turner is making this shit up. Jane Fonda won't sleep with him, he runs to a typewriter: 'By 1992 we will all die of Aids. Read that on the air. I don't get laid, *nobody* gets laid.'

The war (*clears throat*) the war was a very stressful time for me,[23] the war. Yeah. I was in a very unenviable position of being for the war but . . . against the troops. (*makes crickets chirruping sound*) First of all, and this needs to be said, cos it isn't said enough, and in fact it was *never* said. There NEVER was a war. A war is when *two* armies are fighting. Right there, I think we can all agree.

Boy, Bush turned out to be a real demon, didn't he? Remember when Bush was first President? He was the *wimp* President. You remember that? Cover of *Newsweek*: 'WIMP President!' Apparently, this stuck in that guy's craw a little bit. Guy turned into a fucking demon, man.

'We surrender!'
'Not good enough.'
'We run away!'
'Too little, too late. We're havin' *way* too much fun.'

Kidding me? Those guys were in hog heaven out there, man. They had a big weapons catalogue opened up.

'What's G12 do, Tommy?'
'Says here it destroys everything but the fillings in their teeth. Helps us pay for the war effort.'
'Well, shit, pull that one up.'
'Pull up G12, please.'

Yeah, everyone got boners over the technology. And it was pretty amazing, you gotta admit, watching a missile *fly down* an air vent. Pretty unbelievable. But couldn't we feasibly use that same technology to *shoot food* at hungry people? You know what I mean? Fly over Ethiopia. 'There's a guy that needs a banana.' Schhhh (*explosion noise*). Schhhhhhh (*explosion noise*). Schhhhhhhh (*explosion noise*). The Stealth Banana. Smart Fruit. (*quietly*) I don't know. (*clears throat*)

Guess the most amazing thing about the war to me was the disparity in the casualties, man. Iraq: 150,000 casualties. We had . . . seventy-nine. A hundred and fifty *thousand*. We had . . . seventy-nine. Does that mean if we had sent over eighty guys, we still woulda won this fucking thing, or what? One guy in a ticker-tape parade:

'I did it! Hey! You're welcome!'
'Good work, Tommy, how d'you do it?'
'I pulled up G12. It was in the catalogue. Worked like a charm.'

Seventy-nine. After we had a war – we killed 150,000 people, we lost seventy-nine, mostly to friendly fire – did those army commercials even need to be *aired* any more? 'We're the army and we're look-ing for a few good – fuck, we got enough good men. Screw it! We need eighty of ya, that's it. Eighty of ya and that weapons catalogue.'

Y'all are about to win the election as the worst fucking audience I've ever faced. Ever . . . ever . . . ever! S'all right. S'all right. No, listen folks. Here's the deal. I know you're getting concerned. Let me *assure* you right now – there are dick jokes on the way. Relax, I'm a professional. Here's the deal: I editorialize for forty minutes. The last ten minutes we pull our 'chutes and float down to dick-joke island together, OK? And we will rest our weary heads against the big, purple, thick-vein trunks of dick jokes, and we will sit in our comfy beanbag scrotum chairs, and giggle away the dawn like good American audiences, K? Penis jokes are comin' up. Relax. I understand what country I'm in. (*sighs, then whistles*)

The media: once again, watching too much news really bummed me out. Remember how it started? They kept talking about the *Elite* Republican Guard? You know, the *Elite* Republican Guard. These were like the bogeymen of the war, the first couple of months. 'Well, we're doing good now, but we have yet to face the *Elite Republican Guard.*' Like these guys were ten-feet-tall desert warriors. (*makes crashing footstep noise*) 'Never lost a battle.' (*crashing footsteps*) 'We shit bullets.' (*crashing footsteps*) Well, after two months of bombing and not one reaction from these people they became simply . . . the Republican Guard. Ha ha ha ha ha! Not nearly as elite . . . as we may have led you to believe. After another month of bombing, they went from the *Elite* Republican Guard, to the Republican Guard, to the Republicans made this shit up about there being guards out there. We hope you enjoyed the fireworks show. 'Boy, it was pretty.'

People said, 'Uh-uh, Bill, Iraq had the fourth largest army in the world.' Yeah, but let me tell you something: after the first three largest armies, there's a rrrreal big drop off, OK? The Hare Krishnas are the fourth largest army in the world – fifth largest – and they've already got our airports. *I* am the sixth largest army in this world. Just to give you a numerical perspective.

I'll tell you, the people that bug me are people that say, 'Oh, the war made us feel better about ourselves.' Who are these people with such *low self-esteem* they need a *war* to feel *better* about themselves? I saw them on the news, waving their flags. Could I recommend instead of a war to feel better about yourself, perhaps . . . sit-ups? Maybe a fruit cup? A walk around the block at dusk – I always find that cheers me up. (*chuckles*)

What's the phone for, man? Are you guys drug dealers? What's that for? You gonna call somebody or what? Huh? What do you do?

Man in audience: Dentist.

Bill: You're a dentist, and you need to be ready at all times . . . It's not your phone? Whose phone is it?

Man in audience: Gentleman behind.

Bill: Gentleman behind you? And who— and what do you do?

Man in audience: He's the drug dealer.

Bill: He's the drug dealer. I see. You fuck their teeth up, you get 'em hooked, and we *rock* in the nightclubs all night long. (*laughs*)

Woman in audience: He's my doctor.

Bill: He's your doctor? Are you kidding? What kind of doctor? You're lyin'. Are you kidding me? Yeah, you are. (*sighs*) Fucking hell, man. What? Are y'all from some outpatient clinic that I need to know? 'Bill, we are all on Thorazine. Your stuff is quite humorous; we are drugged beyond belief. We are this close to palpitating and releasing our souls through the tops of our heads . . . at which time you will ah . . .'

Man in audience: We can call anyone.

Bill: What?

Man in audience: We can call anyone—

Bill: We can call anyone. Well, how about my fucking agent and let's fire him together:

> 'Pittsburgh, you bastard. Good crowds. They stared at
> me like a dog that's just been shown a card trick.'
> 'Bill, maybe they're all on Thorazine.'
> 'Well, let me check. Fuck, you were *right*!'
> 'It's why I been in this business three months, boy.'

Watch too much TV. TV'll— I can't watch TV longer than five minutes without praying for nuclear holocaust. Really. On my hands and knees, wishing it upon every one of *you*. That's how much I love TV. (*chuckles*) Think it's great. I watched *The Love Connection*. That's gotta be the most depressing show I've ever seen in my life. ADULT human beings on national television, *grovelling* for dates. Have some self-respect: stay home and jerk off, man. Guys, buy a *Hustler*, toss off a load, go about your fucking day, all right? Have some dignity. Ladies, get in the tub. Get under the spigot. Come, and go about your business. Have some self-respect. Show makes jerking off look like a spiritual quest. 'At least I'm not on *The Love Connection*. I can hold my head high. There is pride in my family, pride!'

I don't get along with anything, I really don't. I'm just . . . I'm, I'm, maybe I'm just a, you know, incredibly tasteful human being. I think that's absolutely true, but . . . like this, I'll give you a 'for instance'. I live in New York City. New York – anyone here know about New York? This thing called Channel J? Is anyone familiar with this at all?

Man in audience: Sure.

Bill: Channel J. One person's all it takes. Channel J is a channel that shows pornography commercials for ah . . . escort services and phone-sex lines. All night long they show commercials. Now, first of all, phone sex. I have never called phone sex up, and I never could. 'Why Bill?' Well . . . I just would be embarrassed, you know. I couldn't do that, have some woman on the other end of the line:

> (*whispering*) 'Oh, you got me so hot. I'm so wet. Your
> cock is so big, I've never seen a cock that big in—'
> 'I think I got the wrong number.'

You know what I mean? I couldn't deal with that. You know what I mean? And maybe it's . . . I'm a realist. And they also have these numbers for escort services, and once again I just don't agree, you know what I mean? I'm watching these commercials: (*deep voice*) 'Call 970-SLUT, and the girl of your dreams will come to your house.' Well, I got news for ya, folks. The girl of my dreams doesn't blow fifty different guys a day, OK? Maybe I'm out of fucking line here . . . ah, the girl of my dreams, I don't feel like eating a trucker's come out of her pussy, it's weird, I'm weird that way, and the girl of my dreams does not have stretchmarks around her mouth, all right? Sorry. I know you're going, 'Bill, you're too inflexible here, you're gonna have to get off your high horse, son.' The girl of my dreams, you can't play Connect the Dots with the herpes sores around her anus. D'you understand? The girl of my dreams, I'm putting on a pedestal so that I can . . . do nasty, nasty things to her, but . . . 'The girl of your dreams.'

Ooooooo doggy! Actually, I'm kinda seeing a young lady right now, very young, an' ah, I kinda feel ill that I'm seeing someone this young. It's ridiculous, but . . .

Man in audience: Fifteen?

Bill: A little bit older than that. Between fifteen and ah nineteen, something like that. I can't help myself, man. I'm weak. I'm weak. I'm sorry, you get down between her legs, and it's, there's this, it's, it's like a wisp of cotton candy framing a paper cut, you know? I ah . . . it's really, really nice, and ah . . . (*laughs*) Sick? That's sick? What are you – like these coalminer women with pussys so big you find dead canaries in 'em? I mean . . . 'scuse me, but ah . . . fifteen-year-old girls ARE NOT SICK. Oop, I gave it away, fifteen, all right – between fifteen and nineteen.

Man in audience: Gerbils!

Bill: Gerbils? That man just leapt out of the closet during our show tonight. Sir, this is not a big [. . .] meeting, we're not sharing right now, all right? Believe or not, somehow there's gonna be a joke involved on my part. 'I like gerbils, Bill!' Thank you, sir. Thank you. Thank you. Ohhhhhhhhh! This is a really, really awful night for me.

Woman in audience: What?

Bill: What? It's really an awful night for me.

Audience members: Why? Oh, come on. Why?

Bill: I don't know, I don't feel like y'all are laughing, man. You don't, you're just staring. Are y'all all right? Is it me?

Man in audience: Whooooooo!

Bill: That's not laughter, sir. This ain't the fucking Arsenio Hall[24] Show either. Shut the fuck up. Fucking . . . I wanna see Arsenio come out on rollerskates with a big cigar in his mouth one night, that would be more apropos, I think. Have him do backflips during this monologue. That would crack me up. Doesn't need a band, he needs an organ grinder. Hokay. I'm teasing. He's a great talent . . . and I am a liar. OK. He is. And I pray for nuclear holocaust . . . in five minutes.

Maybe it's my face. I got one of those faces, man, I'm just– People come up to me I don't even know, come up out of the blue and go:

'What's wrong?'
'Nothing.'
'Takes more energy to frown than it does to smile.'
'Yeah, you know it takes more energy to point that out than it does to leave me alone? (*laughs*) Get the fuck away from me.'

The world confuses me. Why is the first guy at the light always the last to see the light change to green? Can somebody explain that? Are there any physicists here tonight can possibly explain this fucking phenomenon to me? Wouldn't you think speed of light distance, the first guy would be, I don't know, the *first* to see the fucking light change? Wrong. It's always the last guy, who has to go through nineteen other cars. Go, go, go, go, go, go, go, GO! It's green! That's as green as it ge-ets. I'm gettin' older, GO! Finally this guy snaps and putters through the yellow. 'Oh, shit.' Brrrrrrrrrrrrrr. I'm stuck at the same fucking light, and I'm thinking, 'I hope that guy *dies* on the way home. I hope he's cut in two by a train in front of his kids. They can watch both halves of their moron daddy wiggle like worms on a hot pavement. You're too stupid to fucking drive, you shoulda been a blowjob. Fucking idiot.' Then behind me, I hear, 'GO!' I never said I was perfect. We all have our little problems. I don't know. So I smoke . . . I smoke too much. You know you smoke too much when other *smokers* tell you to please put it out, you know. That's a lie.

So ah, maybe I'm just sick of doing this. What do you do for a living? . . . If you could answer within five minutes of the question, it would really help the timing of the show, cos once again I already pre-planned comedy answers, hokay? Sorry to pop the spontaneity fucking bubble. I'm str—

Woman in audience: I work in a law firm.

Bill: You work in a law firm. Was that fucking difficult? Move on. Something more funny than that. What do you do, sir? This is the like the *Thirtysomething* . . . you were in mourning when *Thirtysomething* got cancelled, weren't you, this whole table? *That* show makes me want to nuclear holocaust in two minutes. Fucking whining white pieces of shits. 'Life is so difficult.' Like you wanna know how to make life a little less difficult? Come here. (*makes sound of three gunshots*) There we go. There's one less whiner in the fucking world. Kill all white people: that is my theme. Oh . . . I'm seeing sparks, stars in front of my eyes, doc. What kind of doctor are you?

Man in audience: Me?

Bill: NO, HIM! I'M FUCKING CROSS-EYED, YA GOOF-BALL! IF I'M LOOKING AT YA AND TALKING, LET'S GO AHEAD AND ASSUME IT'S *YOU* I'M FUCKING TALKING TO! You're a professional what?

Man in audience: I manage professional wrestling.

Bill: You manage profess— oop! I want outa comedy, now how did I do? I could pin those fucking— they're fairies, one an' all, aren't they? ADMIT IT! ADMIT IT! They put on their little pantie tights and they all have circle jerks. And they all have all the kids come back for autographs.

> 'Come here, sit on Hulk's lap, young man.'
> 'Hey, what kinda hold is this, Hulk?'
> 'It's called Hulk's special love hold, young 'un.'

Swear to God, I woke up in the best mood. Happened to be eight p.m., but . . . you really manage professional wrestlers? Why the thumb? Is there a *meet* going on right now, a match? You waitin' to hear the latest on the Hulk Hogan steroid . . . travesty? 'What are we gonna do if all these athletes . . . are using steroids?' Hulk Hogan –

another reason I pray FOR NUCLEAR HOLOCAUST WITHIN ONE MINUTE! BECAUSE THIS FUCKING PITUITARY RETARD WALKS THE FUCKING PLANET I want you all to die. I know it doesn't make a lot of sense, but work *with me* on this. 'I'm the Hulk.' You're a fucking retard, OK? Case closed. 'He's a retard that makes more money than you. Uh-hoo hoo hoo hoo hoo hooo!' (*sighs*) IS THAT ALL IT IS, FUCKIN' MONEY TO YOU PEOPLE? Sorry. I don't know where this came from. Sorry. Later on we're gonna play put-put golf up here, so get ready. I'm going to be the windmill.

(*singing*) 'These boots' – what do you do, sir? Are you from Pittsburgh? Very beautiful town. What do you do here? Student! Very good. And where do you stude? Cornell? Cool. What're you majoring in?

Student: Psychology.

Bill: (*laughing*) Psychology. Bet you're having a *field* day watching this shit, aren't ya. 'See, he talked about fucking young kids in the ass, he smoked twenty cigarettes in a row. I think I'm gonna do a *thesis* on this guy. Fuck it. Can I get some more napkins, waitress? I'm writing something here.' Psychology's an interesting topic, I must have missed at college. Freud had an interesting theory: the Oedipal theory, you know that? All men, he said, wanna sleep with their moms. I thought that was bullshit, till one day I saw a picture of Freud's mom. Owwwwwww! Hot tub! Yeah! In a *minute*. Whoo! I woulda done her over the dryer. Oww! Mama! But he obviously wasn't looking at my mom when he came up with that theory.

Well, I respect anyone who could go to school. I went to college for three weeks, so ah, I could not get up for that eight o'clock class, as hard as I tried, man. You know that feeling? Yeah. I was going to night school, though. University of Houston, Texas, and Los Angeles Community College where I took karate with the East LA gangs, who had swastikas tattooed on their forehead, thank you very much. These were my *classmates*. Ha ha ha, OK. Swastika tattooed on their foreheads. Ta*ttooed*, no less. OK, great . . . Hoy, shabadoom . . . I had no luck in school. I'll tell ya my luck, man. You tell me if this sucks. One day in first grade our teacher left the room for like a minute. And we started playing 'keep away' from this girl with her pencil. We're all in first grade, we're laughin'. 'Y'all quit it. Give me my pen— would you quit it? I need my pencil.' Pencil came to me, I throw it . . . goes in this guy's eye. Blinds him for life. Everyone in class goes, 'Jesus, Hicks. It's a game. What *are* you, a psycho or something?' Now suddenly I'm Henry Lee Hicks here . . . cos this guy can't catch a number two pencil like a normal human, you know.

'I got it! Ugh.'
'Good move, you dork. I'm an *assassin* now.'

Teacher came back in the room. 'Hicks stabbed him.' Oh, suddenly I *went* for the guy. Come on! It was a childhood game. It went askew.

One time I was late for class, but it's not late, it is . . .
Audience: Tardy.
Bill: Tardy! That is a school word that means absolutely *nothing* on the streets, I hope you realize that. If you don't realize that, try showing up late to work tomorrow and run in:

'Hey, am I tardy?'
'No, you're fired.'
'Not what I thought it meant.'

But I'm late/tardy – whatever. I'm sitting down, guy next to me yanks my chair out from under me, right when I sat. I hit the floor, even the teacher cracks up. 'That's what you get for being tardy!' Later on that year, that guy was late, class had started, he's sitting down, I yank his chair out from under him. Boom! Middle of class. Breaks his fucking back. 'Shit, get up. Try harder.' That guy was in every one of my classes the next five years. 'Real funny, Hicks.' The guy with one eye pushing him around. What am I supposed to say? 'Well, you guys can park closer to the school now. No more tardys. (*chuckles*) Look on the bright side.' Took his fucking bright side out. Boy, am I embarrassed.

So, what do you go to college, too? Cornell? Penn *State*. And what are you majoring in? Huh? Education. OK, yeah. What are you majoring in?

Woman in audience: Physical Therapy.

Bill: Physical Therapy? (*inhales*) How d'you meet that dude? (*laughs*) What do you do? Majoring in? Economics? Dude. Wrestler, huh? Do you see it? Come on, man, how about the pissed-off fucking economist, man. Like here's what we'll do. We'll do a whole thing where he wins, and then he gets the purse, right? And it's like 'This is not what I expected.' Then he goes fucking bezerk. (*makes crashing noise*) Kids'll go crazy for that. I'm trying to help us all, man.

I envision a world where we all make money doing NOTHING. There's not enough . . . there's not enough, you know– people are 'Uh, wha, what? We *like* our jobs, Bill. We like the gruelling in and out, eight hours a day, setting the alarm clock, traffic, Bill – traffic! We love it!' You know what I hate about working? Bosses. That's what I fucking hate. First of all, let me tell you something real quick. The very idea that *anyone* could be my boss, well . . . I think you see the conflict. Not in this lifetime, Charlie. A few more incarnations, we'll sit down and chat. But I used to always get harassed. 'Hicks, how come you're not workin'.' I'd go, 'There's nothing to do.'

> 'Well, you pretend like you're workin'.'
> 'Well, why don't *you* pretend I'm working? Yeah, you get paid more than me, *you* fantasize. Pretend I'm mopping. Knock yourself out. I'll pretend they're buying stuff; we can close up. I'm the boss now, *you're* fired. How's that? I'm on a fuckin' roll. We're all millionaires and you're rich. I'm pretending shit, I'm just, I'm wacky, I can't be stopped.'

I don't know if I have the right attitude for the workplace.

I don't drink ah . . . I don't do drugs. I wanna thank management for offering . . . but, oh yeah, *huge* pile of that shit right up there, yeah. Ever seen it so big it had a ski lift on it? Really, it's unbelievable. Right up there. But ah . . . no, actually, I, I, I, I quit doing drugs. I used to take drugs and I quit. But I'll tell you something honestly about drugs, and I don't think this is said enough any more

– I mean, it's the truth: I had a great time doing drugs. Ha ha ha ha ha! Sorry. Never murdered anybody, never robbed anybody, never raped anybody, never beat anybody, never lost a job, a car, a house, a wife, or kids, laughed my *ass* off, and went about my day. Sorry. Now where's *my* commercial? How come *I* don't get a fucking commercial? I'll be the guy holding that skillet on that commercial, man. That ain't a brain, that's breakfast. Let's eat! Pschhhhhhhhh. What, have we been up five days now? I'm STARVING! Get the plates and forks out, boys, the brain's almost ready. Whoooooo! Pschhhhhhhhh. It is that very commercial that tells me how completely unhip and unintelligent our fucking government is, that commercial. 'Here's ya brain. Here's ya brain on drugs.' And you seen the guy in that commercial. Guy's got a beer gut: 'Here's ya brain. Here's your brain. Here's your brain on drugs.' I've seen a lot of weird shit on drugs, but I have never ever ever looked at an egg . . . and thought it was a fucking brain, man. I have seen UFOs split the sky like a sheet, but I have *never* looked at an egg and thought it was a fucking brain, not once. I have had seven balls of light come off of a UFO, lead me on to their ship, explain to me telepathically that we are all one and there's no such thing as death, but I have *never* looked at an egg and thought it was a fucking brain, not once. Now, maybe I wasn't getting good shit. I admit it, I see that commercial, I feel cheated. Hey, where's the stuff that makes eggs look like brains? Did I quit too soon? What is that? CIA stash? I'm in. CIA: biggest drug runners in the world.[25] FACT! I'm teasing. Our government's great. Liar! No, they are good people. Suckers of Satan's cock. No, they are good.

The guy in the commercial's got a beer gut. 'All right, this is it. Look up now. See that? That's ya brain. All righty? There it is: your brain. There it is. See it? That's a brain. Your brain.' The guy is fucking drunk doing this commercial, man. 'Here's your brain.' That's an egg! That's a frying pan, that's a stove, you're an alcoholic, dude . . . I'm tripping right now, and I *still* see that is a fucking egg, my friend. I see the UFOs around it, but . . . there's an *egg* in the middle. There's a hobbit eating it, but goddamn it that hobbit is eating a fuckin' egg. He is on a unicorn . . . but they're eating *eggs*! How dare you have a wino tell me not to do drugs. And that is what I hate about the war on drugs. All day long you see those commercials: 'Here's your brain', 'Just say no', 'Why d'you think they call it dope?' And the next commercial is: 'This Bud's for you.' Come on, America. Let's be hypocritical bastards. Come on! 'It's OK to *drink* your drug. *(gulping sound)* We meant those other drugs. Those *untaxed* drugs. Those are the bad ones.' I think you see that.

Thank God they're taxing alcohol, man. It means we have those great roads we can get fucked up and drive on. Thank God they're taxing this shit, huh? We'd be doing doughnuts in a wheatfield right now. Thank God we're on a pretty good, smooth freeway. Whoo! Party time. Cos I have some more news to tell you, folks, and it's not popular news, but once again it's the *fucking truth*! Ready? It's a two-parter. It's a two-parter, ready? Drum roll. Here's number one. Drum roll. Brrrrrrrrrrrrrrrrrrrrrr. Alcohol's a drug. Ha ha ha ha! OK. And here's number two, and this is the one that hurts. Brrrrrrrrrrrrrrrrrr. Alcohol kills more people than crack, coke and heroin combined each year. Ha ha ha ha ha ha! *(singing)* 'Na na na. Na na na.' So thanks for inviting me to your little alcoholic drug den here tonight. You hypocritical scum-sucking pieces of shit, you. Ha ha ha. I'm teasin'. No, I'm not. I'm filled with hate. What does that mean, psychologist? Have you gotten that far yet? A man FILLED TO THE FUCKING BRIM WITH PURE, WHITE HATRED! Do I fall under the fucking Manson category yet? Who will be my Squeaky Fromme[26] tonight? Who will join me on a spree of bloodcurdling horror? Who *is* the girl of my dreams? Call 970-ASSASSIN and she will come to your house. She will bring sharp kitchen knives and— OK, sorry. 'The girl of your dreams.'

Man in audience: Butcher knives.

Bill: Butcher knives – that's better. Hey, man, I'm improvving this shit, dude. Drugs . . . I'll tell ya, man, if I were going to legalize a drug, it would not be alcohol. You know why?

Woman in audience: Why?

Bill: There's better drugs and better drugs for ya. That's a *fact*. So you can stop your internal dialogue. 'Wait a minute, Bill. Alcohol's an acceptable form of social interaction, which for thousands of years has been an accep—' Shut the fuck up, man. Your denial is beneath you . . . and thanks to the use of hallucinogenic drugs, I see through you. Oh yes, I do. I'm cursed with vision. And I love those pants!

Not only do I think marijuana should be legalized . . . I think it should be mandatory. Think about it, man, you get in traffic behind somebody.

> (*makes sound of truck horn*)
> 'Shut up and smoke that – it's the law.'
> 'Sorry, I was taking life seriously. Oh man, who's hungry?'

That'd be a nice world: quiet, mellow, hungry, high people everywhere. Just Dominos' pizza trucks passing each other. Every single highway: parades of Dominos'. (*truck horn*) Let them get stuck in traffic: all our pizzas will be free, you see. 'I'm a dreamer, I'm a fuckin' dreamer, I'm a dreamer, Tommy. Tommy, join the band, I'm a fuckin' dreamer.' What?

Pot is a better drug than alcohol. FACT! I'll prove it to ya. You're in a ball game or a concert and someone's really violent and aggressive and obnoxious. Are they drunk or are they smoking pot?

Audience: Drunk!

Bill: Drunk would be the one and only correct answer, thank you very much. Drunk would be the ONE and only correct answer. I have *never* seen people on pot get in a fight because it is fucking impossible.

> 'Hey, buddy!'
> 'Hey, what.'

End of argument. Kind of hard to hold a resentment when you can't remember 'em. You know. 'I'm supposed to hate you, but I don't know why. Ah, forget it.' Say you get in a car accident and you've been smoking pot. You're only going four miles an hour. (*laughs; makes sound of car crash*)

> 'Shit, we hit something.'
> 'Uh-uh, we got rear-ended by a Dominos' truck. That's
> his fault. That means it's free. Tommy, get the coupon.
> We will feast on the turnpike.'

It's just a better drug.

I have never heard one reason that rang true why marijuana is against the law. Never heard one reason that *rang true* why mari-juana is against the law. Marijuana grows all over the world, serves a thousand different functions, ALL of them positive. To make marijuana against the law is like saying God made a mistake. You know what I mean? It's like God on the seventh day looked down on his creation, and he said, 'There it is, my creation. Perfect and holy in all ways. Now I can rest . . . Oh my Me! I left fucking pot everywhere. I should never have smoked that joint on the third day, shit. Boy, if I leave pot everywhere, it's gonna give people the impres-sion they're supposed to *use* it. Shit! Now I have to create Republicans.' So you see, it's a *vicious* cycle. And one we're paying for dearly daily. Ha ha! Dearly daily. OK. Little pun there. Little fun. Fun time. I'm amusing people one at a time here tonight: this is unique. I'm amazed at the restraint of the rest of you till your time comes up. You're really patient. 'That one wasn't for me. I'll wait till mine comes around the corner.'

I am not promoting the use of drugs, I'm just saying if you're gonna have a war against drugs, have 'em against all drugs includ-ing alcohol, the number one offender, or shut the fuck up. And oh, by the way, my simple pleasurable advice would be: shut the fuck up. Ha ha ha ha ha. Just shut up. Your ways are tired, your point of view is meaningless, and you live hollow fucking lives. Shut up, and learn from your master . . . that guy. (*laughs*) He is the master.

I've had good times on drugs, that's a fact. I've had bad times on drugs, too, OK? But I've had good and bad relationships . . . an' I'm not giving up pussy.

> 'Hi, I'm Bill. I'm a pussyholic. I like the way it smells,
> I *love* the way it tastes.'
> 'You're in the right place, man, keep coming back. We
> are all powerless over pussy here.'
> 'Cool, y'all have any literature?'
> 'Yeah, here's a *Penthouse*.'

You ever read those *Penthouse* letters? Those are pretty weird. *Penthouse* forum?

> 'I never believed your letters were true till I attended a large, mid-Western college in the south-east. On the first day of class, I went to my first ah class, and ah, the class was me and . . . thirty other girls. Thirty girls. Thirty girls and me, and the teacher was a woman. And me. And class began normally when the bell rang, and ah right after that . . . they all started blowing me. Yeah, they were all blowing me, they got in a big line, and they all blew me, then they got in a big daisy chain, and I shot on their tits, and they ate each other off each other's tits. Name and address withheld.'

Guys, we all know if that happened to us, we'd put our fucking *names* on that letter. Bill Hicks, New York, New York, name and address *not* withheld. Bill Hicks . . . thirty girls blew me – *Bill Hicks*. Big daisy chain – *Bill Hicks* was in the middle. *Bill Hicks* shot on their tits, *Bill Hicks* watched them eat it off, *Bill Hicks*. Name and address not withheld – *Bill Hicks*. Jiminy Crickets, man. You guys are tighter than . . . that girl I'm seeing. Ha ha ha ha! Like a wisp of cotton candy surrounding a paper cut. Ohhh, I'm proud of that image. That's poetry, friends. Get off your high horses, join young Willie in this trench.

I have had bad times on drugs. One time me and three friends dropped acid, drove round in my dad's car. He's got one of those talking cars. We're tripping. The car goes, 'The door is ajar.' We pulled over and thought about that for twelve hours.

> 'How can a door be a jar?'
> 'Shit, I don't know, but I see it.'
> 'I see it, too.'
> 'Shit, why would they put a jar on a car?'
> 'Shit, I don't know. What's that?'
> 'That's an egg! Oh great, we're not that high yet. When this turns into a brain, we're getting a hotel room. I'll

drive in the jar-car – that brain-egg, that's way too fucking high, man. I've never seen that. I've *never* seen that.'

K, I'm not proud of this moment in my life, but you know what
my point is? My point is I was not a *criminal* when I did drugs,
no more 'n you're a criminal cos you're drinking a beer. People who
do drugs are not *criminals*. They might be *sick*, but I don't think
jail is gonna heal 'em. 'Yep, thank God they caught me. What was
I doin' ruinin' my life with that marijuana? I wanna thank Bubba,
my rehabilitator back there.' I would not come out of jail wanting
to do less drugs, I would wanna come out mainlining heroin into
my fucking eyeball. I don't know the case yet that jail healed
anybody. K? K, America? Wake up from your law enforcement fucking fantasy, and shut up. It ain't gonna work, K? It's not gonna
work. So let's move on to a plan that *might* work. Isn't that simple?
Feels good too, don't it?

George Bush has filled up all the jails with drug users. The jails
are overcrowded. I guess he wants to make sure there's no room
for Neil.[27] A true criminal of humankind, by the way. I'm kidding,
he's a great kid. Liar! No, he is. He's a good man. Sucker of Satan's
cock. No, I'm teasing. He's a great kid, and George Bush is really
an American. Come on, wink with me. Join me on the sarcasm
slide: it's a big fucking amusement park. Let's get on the sarcasm
slide, whoo-whoo-hoo-hoo!

I was almost arrested that same night we got pulled over tripping on acid. Longest night of my life. Cops were tapping on this
window. We're staring at him in this mirror.

'How tall are you?'
'Look, they're little biddy coppers, look at them!'
'How do they drive that big fucking car?'
'Shit, I think I got one in my hair.'
'What are we gonna do?'
'Let's put him in the jar! Put him in the jar! Poke some
holes in the lid, leave him by the road. You'll never get
us, copper. You'll never get us!'

I'm not proud of every moment in my life, all right?

Thank you, Daddy. Thank you, Daddy, thank you, Momma. That's another thing. I don't understand America. I DON'T UNDERSTAND AMERICA!

Why do families go— remember going on summer vacations with your family as a kid? Wasn't that the most nightmarish, hellish experience? Packing up in the car, driving fourteen hours, no direction whatsoever . . . *hating* with all of your heart every member of your family. 'I'm going to kill them all at the Holiday Inn tonight. I'm going to be a little mass murderer.' Why don't families, instead of doing that – instead of taking that summer trip – take acid and stay home and trip together? It would be much more fun and edifying, and the home movies would be infinitely more amusing. Just twenty minutes of someone's thumb. Rrrrrrrrrrrrrrrrrrrrrrrrrrrrrrr. 'You notice, son, the thumb is opposable, and thus we can grab and grasp things and use tools.' Rrrrrrrrrrrrrrrrrrrrr. 'I think I see, Daddy. I think I see.' It would be a lot more edifying than . . . a Stuckey's[28] diet for ten days. (*a few titters from audience*) I stand alone with these theories. You know how *lonely* it is being me? Can you imagine everything you say, the reaction is this? (*silence*) Everything you say, people go . . . 'Are *you* the Devil?' No, I'm not the Devil. Look, it's two sixes and a nine. I'm bluffin'. Trying to get eighteen the hard way . . . Let's see, which one's the right one? (*laughs*) Trying— it's like a Three Card Monte[29] game? OK. Another joke that *just didn't go*, did it? Just 'Bill, shut up with your little jokes. Do mime.'

One more thing about drugs and I'm gonna quit the drug topic, and we're *that* much closer to the dick jokes. OK. Ahm . . . and you don't hear this enough either, and I gotta say it: drugs have done . . . *good* things for us. Yeah. And if you don't believe they have, I want you to do me a favor. Go home tonight, take all your albums, your tapes and your CDs, and *burn* them. Cos you know what? The musicians who made that great music that has enhanced your lives throughout the years? Rrrrrrrrrrrrrreal fucking high on drugs. Yeah. Man, the Beatles were so high, they let Ringo sing a coupla tunes. Tell me they weren't partyin'. (*singing*) 'We all live in a yellow submarine, a yellow submarine, a yell—' We all live in a yell— you know how fucking high they were . . . when they wrote that? They had to pull Ringo off the ceiling with a rake to sing that fuckin' song. 'John, get Ringo. He's in the corner. Pull him down. Wow, look at him scoot! Grab him, John. He's got a song he wants to sing us. Something about living in a yellow tambourine or something. Ringo, Yoko's gone! Come down. We can party again.' They were real high, they wrote great music, drugs had a positive effect. End of story – no, let's don't end the story. Let's extend the theory one more step. Feel the more proof, the better acceptance I might get for my little theory. These musicians today that don't do drugs, and in fact speak out against them? 'We're rock against drugs.' Boy, they suck. Ha ha ha ha ha ha! 'Big ol' ball-less soulless suck-jobs, every one of 'em, aren't they? Corporate little bitches, one an' all. Suckin' Satan's cock every morning when they wake up. (*makes snorting, snarling noise*) 'I'm a rock star who sells Pepsi Cola products.' (*snorting, snarling noise*) 'I'm an artist who also sells Taco Bell.' (*snorting, snarling noise*) I will lay down the law right now: anybody that sells Taco Bell products is immediately and for all time eliminated from any artistic endeavours. Case . . . fucking closed. You may shit *Mona Lisa*s out yer ass as a party trick, you're a fucking evil piece of shit. End of story. The end. The story just ended. There'll be no further discussion. Dude, is it me? You're the only guy giggling during the whole show, dude. Show 'em your pants, maybe that's it. You're tripping, man. YOU'RE TRIPPING! Oooooooooooo. (*laughs*)

(*whistles*) Taco Bell. Let me ask ya a quick question: why does Taco Bell have a fucking menu? Do ya need this? I mean, just go up to the counter. The guy should go:

> 'How do you want your beans and flour arranged?'
> 'I want mine to look like a taco.'
> 'I'd like mine to look like a churrito.'

It's like the Playdo of fast food, they just have this . . . thing with different little forms. (*makes squirting sound*) 'Get the taco mould out.' (*squirting sound*) It's like the Playdo. If you ever had a Playdo factory as a child, you'd know that it's the same Playdo but it comes out different, and ah . . . and I don't know, herein might be a humorous or nostalgic view of childhood, and thus tying it in with the caring God, I'm gonna need lots of good dick jokes, I'm in a fuckin' hole here, dude. Diggin' the hole deeper and deeper. You know, people are heckling in Chinese right now. (*in Chinese accent*) 'Why you not just start with dick joke? Why you have to . . . why you have to change people's minds and beliefs? They don't want to stand out. They want to be in the crowd. They don't want to have beliefs.' Oh, OK, thank you. The ancient wisdom of the Chinese. (*Chinese accent*) 'They don't want to rock the boat. They just want to hear dick jokes and go home.' Well, fuck it, you know.

I am available for children's parties, by the way. I know some of y'all might have a young 'un coming of age, and not wanna go the traditional clown/balloon animal route this year. Might wanna look me up: Beelzebozo. Clown from hell. It's in the phone book under 'B' and 'H'.

> (*singing*) 'It's Beelzebozo time.'
> 'Hi kids, it's Beelzebozo time! Tell me something, who here out of you young 'uns has never smoked a ciga-rette. Come here! What's your name?'
> 'Tommy.'
> 'Tommy. How old are ya?'
> 'Five.'
> 'Five years old. And you mean to tell Beelzebozo you're not smoking cigarettes yet? Come here, Tommy.'
> (*coughing*) 'Mummy!'
> 'Hold it in!'
> (*coughing*)
> 'Hold it in, Tommy!'
> (*singing*) 'It's Beelzebozo time.'
> 'Tell me something, who here out of you young 'uns has *never* . . . watched a skin flick. Come here, kids. Rrrrrrrrrrrrrrrrrrrrrrrrrrrrrrrr. See them, them's titties, hu-huh.'
> 'Mummy!'
> 'That is yer mummy. Hu-huh!'

I'm kiddin' ya. (*singing*) It's Beelzebozo time. (*makes sound of crick-ets chirruping*)

Skin flicks. Or as Jesse Helms calls it, 'POE-NOGRA-PHA. POE-NOGRA-PHA.' I don't think you should be against something till you can pronounce it. Am I being too strict? What is pornography? Forget what poe-nogra-pha is, and no one will ever figure that out, but pornography – what is it? No one knows. Supreme Court says pornography is any act that has no artistic merit and causes sexual thoughts. That's their definition. No artistic merit; causes sexual thoughts. Hmm. Yeah . . . and . . . so . . . what? When did . . . sex become a bad thing? Did I miss a meeting? 'Bill, we had a big vote: fucking's out. You were asleep.' *Wake* me for that vote! I might be a *swing* vote. '*Playboy* – pornography – causes sexual thought. *Penthouse* – pornography – causes sexual thought. Madonna video – pornography – causes sexual thoughts!' You know what causes sexual thoughts? I'm gonna clear the air for ya tonight. I'm so tired of this debate. It's beneath us, and there are real issues that go undiscussed because of this . . . *horseshit*. Ready? Here's what causes sexual thoughts. Drum roll. Brrrrrrrrrrrrrrrrrrrrrrrrrrrrr. Havin' a dick. Hokay. End of fuckin' story. Case closed. (*makes sound of door creaking shut*) I can speak for every guy here tonight – you know what? Think I will – in the course of our day *anything* can cause a sexual thought, all right? You can be on a bus, a train, it's rockin' kinda nice . . . pants are a little tight . . . oh my God, I got a woody! I got a woody on a bus! Now what are we gonna do? Ban public transportation? Before *Playboy*, before *Penthouse*, before pornographic movies ever existed, people still had sexual thoughts, OK? 'How do you know that, Bill?' Well . . . we're here. Ha ha ha ha! Somebody's been fuckin'. Yeah. You follow your family tree back at every branch . . . fuckin'. Yeah, true. What caused it way back then? Well, maybe the wagon train ride out West.

> (*singing 'I Wish I Was In Dixie Land'*)
> 'I don't know what she has under that gingham skirt,
> but when we stop for water, we're fuckin', baby. (*singing*)
> 'I got a woody on the trail. I got a woody on the trail.'

You see, they're getting the cart before the horse on this pornography issue. *Playboy* does not create sexual thoughts: there *are* sexual thoughts. And *thus* there is *Playboy*. You see? What came first, the hard-on or the Madonna video? Ah . . . it's a big philosophical question. And if a hard-on falls in the forest and no one's around . . . will you go blind? I don't know what the fuck that means, but . . . I'm proud to be a part of my own act.

Dude, can I bum one from you, man? I'm tryin' to quit buyin'. Man! Newports. Menthol, I like that. It's like smoking a Certs. Hey, you're smoking, your breath tastes great, fuck it! Amazing – science! (*singing*) 'Do do do do do do.'

And I know pornography is a sticky topic, you know, but ah . . . my girlfriend *hated* those porno movies. Sometimes I'd bring 'em home, cos sometimes they get mixed up in the boxes at the video stores . . . for a dollar extra.

> 'Hey, this isn't *Bambi*.'
> 'Shut up, her name *is* Bambi. Pay attention, maybe you'll learn something, honey. See, that's not hurtin' *her*.

They're liars, one and all. D'you see that? See what I'm up against? 'What's he talkin' about? That doesn't hurt her . . .'

> 'Why would you wanna do that to me? If you loved me, you wouldn't wanna do that.'
> 'Well, it's because I love you that I wanna do that.'
> 'But it'll hurt?'
> 'Hey man, life fuckin' hurts. I live it, all right? Goin' to work, pleasin' the kids hurts, K? But it's Beelzebozo time and I'm off. Now put on your little green booties and be my fuck elf. Let's go.'
> (*singing*) 'It's Beelzebozo time.'

But she hates those movies. I'll be watching one, she'll come home: 'That woman's not enjoyin' that. She is not enjoyin' that.' I'm going, 'Well, honey, she's got a *pretty* big grin on her face, and we know she's not a good actress.' (*chuckles*) But her attitude – I guess a lot of women's attitudes – is that those movies are *degrad-*

ing to women. And I say, 'Pff, look at the *guys*. Are they *exalted*? I couldn't make a face like that if a car ran over my foot. She looks *great*. He looks like a *doofus*.' Tell ya what, if I had my way, there wouldn't be any men in pornographic films.

Man in audience: Great idea, Bill.

Bill: Yeah, I always felt it was, too. Cos, you know, the only thing more beautiful than a woman . . . is two of 'em. That's right. Two women together in bed is God's way of showing how much he loves us. Two men together in bed is evil. Two women together in bed is a miracle bestowed upon God's children . . . to give us hope and joy. Two men together in bed is satanic. You know, a lot of people think that is a double standard. Ha ha ha ha! Poor misguided fools exist on this planet.

(*sighs*) Oh, fuck. Well, folks, I want to thank you for being here for the recording of my live comedy album. Funny material and laughter will be dubbed in later. Why pressure ourselves? I did a little longer than I was supposed to do. The reason is I always do long shows when I'm in Pittsburgh, cos I know for a fact . . . there's nothing else going on here, so. Thank you very much. Good night. (*singing*) 'Hallelujah! Hallelujah!'

Salon Interview
(October 1991)

You know, I don't think mass murder is funny at all. Probably the opposite. But I just have this weird theory. The best kind of comedy to me is when you make people laugh at things they've never laughed at, and also take a light into the darkened corners of people's minds, exposing them to the light. I thought the whole point of it was to make you feel un-alone. Many thoughts I do have are not my own thoughts. You know what I mean? They're not secret thoughts.

Recorded at Laff Stop, Austin, TX (14–17 December 1991)[30]

Thank you! How you doin', folks? Me too. You gotta bear with me ah, I'm very tired of, very tired of ah travelling, and ah . . . very tired doing comedy, and ah . . . very tired of staring out at your vacant faces looking back at me, wanting me to fill your empty lives with humour you couldn't possibly think of yourselves. Good evening. It's been a while since I've been here. It's great to be back. Wherever I am, I always love it when I'm here. A lot's happened, I guess. (*laughs*)

Hey, man! That Clarence Thomas[31] thing, I guess you watched that, hey? Boy, I tell you something. I learned something very important watching that Clarence Thomas hearing, and d'you know what I learned? I don't stand a fuckin' chance. (*laughs*) Don't even call the committee to order. It'd be a real short hearing.

> 'Mr Hicks, are you familiar at all . . . with the video series called *Clam-Lappers*, volumes one through ninety?'
> 'All of them? I don't recall.'
> 'Uh-huh. And Mr Hicks, are you familiar at all with a man named Manuel who works at the Show-World Adult Video Parlour?'
> 'Manny!'
> 'Mr Hicks, they subpoena me! They subpoena me!'
> (*quietly*) 'Shit.'

But I tell ya, after the Pee-wee Herman[32] thing and then after the Clarence Thomas hearings, pornography's gotten a really bad name in our country. And I'd like to state for the record right now . . . I *love* pornography. Love it. I have tapes that are pure fuckin' art, I'm telling ya. People fuckin', suckin', every imaginable position, the finest-looking women, fuckin', suckin' . . . I love it. For the record.

> 'Mr Hicks, thank you for your testimony. I don't know if we have a place for ya right now on the Supreme Court, but boy, you ever thought about becoming a senator? Come 'ere, boy! Bring some of them tapes over here. Look at that. Whoar . . . bring them over to Teddy's[33] house. Yeah, look at that there. Whoo! She go to that like a duck to water. Look at that there. How! How! How!'

That is one of my big fears in life – that I'm going to die, you know? And my parents are gonna have to come clean out my apartment . . . find that porno wing I've been adding on to for years. They'll be two funerals that day . . . Just see my mom going through my stuff:

> 'Look, honey. Here's Bill when he was a Cub Scout. Look how cute my baby is! His little short pants and his little hat. Look how cute my baby was. I wonder what's in this box over here? *Rear Entry*, volume one through forty?' (*makes crashing noise*)

I'll be the only guy going through the gates of heaven with his mom spanking him.

> (*makes slapping sound*) 'Mom, they were on sale!'
> (*two slaps*) 'Someone named Manny called.'
> 'Oh, shit!' (*two slaps*)

I don't understand anything, so there you go. You know my problem? I watch too much news, man. That's my prob— that's why I'm so depressed all the time. I've figured it out: I watch too much CNN, man. I don't know if you've ever sat around and watched CNN longer than say . . . twenty hours in one day? I don't recommend that. Watch CNN headline news for one hour. It's the most depressing thing you'll ever fucking do. 'WAR, FAMINE, DEATH, AIDS, HOMELESS, RECESSION, DEPRESSION, WAR, FAMINE, DEATH, AIDS, HOMELESS.' Then you look out your window: (*makes crickets chirruping sound*). Where's all this shit happening? Ted Turner's making this shit up, man. Jane Fonda won't sleep with him, he runs to a typewriter: 'By 1992 we will all die of Aids. Read that on the air. I don't get laid, *no one* gets laid.' I'm writing Jane Fonda: 'Will you fuck this guy so we can get some good news, please?' I wanna see a well-laid Ted Turner newscast. 'Hey, it's all gonna work out! Here's sports.'

So, it's good to be here, wherever I am. Gosh, since I was here we had a war. That's pretty fucking weird, huh? A *war*? Wasn't really a war, you know. A war's when *two* armies are fighting. So . . . I don't know if you could call it a war exactly, you know. The Persian Gulf Distraction is more like it, I think. Pretty amazing thing, really. Bush turned out to be a major fucking demon – who woulda guessed? Remember when he was first President,[34] he was the *wimp* President. D'you remember that? Cover of *Newsweek*. Cover of fucking *Newsweek*! '*Wimp* President.' Apparently this stuck in this guy's craw a little bit. The guy was a dynamite waiting to go off.

> 'We surrender.'
> 'Not good enough.'
> 'We run away.'
> 'Too little, too late. Call me a wimp – come on, fuckers! Come on!'
> 'Hold him back.'

Those guys were in hog heaven over there, man. They had a big weapons catalogue opened up.

> 'What's G12 do, Tommy?'
> 'See, it says here it destroys everything but the fillings in their teeth. Helps us pay for the war effort.'
> 'Well, fuck, pull that one up.'
> 'Pull up G12, please.'
> Shhhhhhhhhhhhhh (*makes explosion noise*)
> 'Cool. What's G13 do?'

Big Sears weapons catalogue. 'Weapons for all occasions.'
 You know. See, everyone got boners over the technology, and it

was pretty incredible watching missiles fly down air vents. Pretty unbelievable. But couldn't we feasibly use that same technology to shoot food at hungry people? Know what I mean? Fly over Ethiopia. 'There's a guy that needs a banana.' (*makes sound of missile*) The Stealth Banana. Smart Fruit!

I don't know. Once again I was watching the fucking news and it really threw me off. It depressed *everyone*. It's just so scary watching the news, how they built it all out of proportion, like Iraq was ever, or could ever, possibly, under any stretch of the imagination be a threat to us . . .*whatsoever*, but watching the news you never woulda got that idea. Remember how it started? They kept talking about the Elite Republican Guard in these hushed tones? Like these guys were the bogeyman or something. 'Yeah, we're doing well now, but we have yet to face the Elite Republican Guard.' Like these guys were twelve-feet-tall desert warriors. (*makes crashing footstep noise*) 'Never lost a battle.' (*crashing footsteps*) 'We shit bullets.' (*crashing footsteps*) Yeah, well, after two months of continuous carpet bombing and not *one* reaction at all from them, they became simply the Republican Guard. Ha ha ha ha ha ha! Not nearly as elite as we may have led you to believe. And after another month of bombing they went from the *Elite* Republican Guard, to the Republican Guard, to the Republicans made this shit up about there being guards out there.

> 'We hope you enjoyed your fireworks show.'
> 'It was so pretty, and it took our mind off of domestic issues.'

The Persian Gulf Distraction.

People said 'Uh-uh, Bill. Iraq had the fourth largest army in the world.' Yeah, maybe, but you know what? After the first three largest armies, there's a *real* big fucking drop-off, all right? The Hare Krishnas are the fifth largest army in the world. And they've already got our airports, OK? So. Think that's the greater threat right now. Mr Onion-head in Terminal C is scaring the shit out of me. Get him away from me.

Isn't that an amazing thing, though? And you know, the amazing thing, obviously the disparity in the casualties. Iraq: 150 *thousand* casualties; USA: seventy-nine. Iraq: 150 *thousand*; USA: seventy . . . nine. Does that mean if we had sent over eighty guys we still woulda won that fucking thing or what? One guy in a ticker-tape parade.

> 'I did it! Hey! You're welcome, hu-huh.'
> 'Good work, Tommy. How'd you do it?'
> 'I pulled up G12. It was in a catalogue. Worked like a charm, hu-huh.'

You know, my biggest problem with the whole thing was the blood lust that everyone, that came out of everyone, you know? This blood lust, man. It's really unbelievable. Like I was over in England – you ever been to England anyone? Been to England? No one has handguns in England, not even the cops. True or false? True. Now! In England last year they had fourteen deaths from handguns. Fourteen. Now! United States, I think you know how we feel about handguns. Whoo! I'm getting a warm, tingly feeling just saying the fucking word to be honest with you. I swear to you, I'm hard. 23,000 deaths from handguns. Let's go through those numbers again cos they're a little baffling at first glance. England, where no one has guns: fourteen deaths. United States – and I think you know how we feel about guns; whoo! I'm gettin' a stiffy – 23,000 deaths from handguns. But there's no connection . . . and you'd be a fool and a communist to make one. There's no connection between having a gun and shooting someone with it, and *not* having a gun and *not* shooting someone. There've been studies made, and there is no connection at all there. Yes. It's absolute truth. You know, fourteen deaths from handguns– probably American tourists, too.

> 'Call this a sandwich? (*three gunshots*) You don't boil pizza.' (*two gunshots*)
> 'That's the way we eat here! S'way we eat here!'
> (*three gunshots*) 'This food sucks!' (*three gunshots*)

And boy, does it suck. OK. Great. If I'd had a gun, I would have been number fifteen on that fucking list. You know, fourteen— OK, though admittedly last year in England they had 23,000 deaths per soccer game. All right. OK, OK. Not saying every system is flawless, I'm saying if you're in England, don't go to a goddamned soccer game and you're coming home, OK?

It's weird. They don't have guns in England, but they have a very high crime rate, which tells you how polite the fucking English are.

'Give me your wallet.'
'All right.'

At least no one was hurt. (*laughs*) How d'you have a crime rate and no weapons, man? Does the guy walk into a bank:

'Give me all your money . . . I've got a soccer ball!'
'Shit, Ian, that's a Spalding. He's serious. Hand over the pounds!'

I just don't understand this blood lust cos, you know, I know the world seems really frightening at times, but I think we're gonna do OK. I'll tell you a true story, a true fucking story, man, about blood lust. I was down in Alabama, and I was playing a town called Fyffe, Alabama, last year. And they wanted me there to host their annual Rickets Telethon or something, I don't know what the fuck it was, but anyway . . . it was great to be there and ah . . . *anyway*, this is absolutely true: last year in Fyffe, Alabama,[35] they had all these UFO sightings. And apparently everyone in this town saw these UFOs. All right? Which really pissed me off, cos when I was there . . . about *forty* people saw me. But there was no advance advertising, no publicity. That's a *big* market for me. *Anyway*, I'm curious about UFOs, so I ask people there what it was like. And this guy said, 'Oh, man, it was incredible. People came from miles around to look at 'em. Lotta people came armed.' People are bringing *shotguns* . . . to UFO sightings. Kind of brings a whole new meaning to that phrase 'You ain't from around here, are ya, boy?' I said to the guy, 'Why did y'all bring shotguns to UFO sightings?' Seems to me there's gonna be a point in our development or evolution when you put your guns aside. You know what I mean? Don't you think that would happen just fuckin' once? The guy said, 'Well, we didn't wanna be abducted.' I'm thinking, 'Yeah, and leave all this?' (*chuckles*) Dude, if I lived in Fyffe, Alabama, I'd be on my hands and knees praying for abduction every goddamn morning, all right? And believe me, I would not be picky. Greyhound. Abduct me. But I said, 'What do you mean, abducted?' He said, 'Well, they abduct people and they perform scientific and medical experiments on 'em.' I said, 'Well, maybe we'll be lucky and it's some kind of sterility/dentistry programme they got going. Maybe they come down here, castrate ya, straighten your teeth and split. Sort of a clean-up-the-universe pact.' He said, 'Huh?' I was almost sure I was talkin' to that dude.

I tell you, too, that's starting to depress me about UFOs. The fact that they cross galaxies, or wherever they come from, to visit us, and always end up in places like Fyffe, Alabama. Maybe these are not super-intelligent beings, man. Maybe they're like hillbilly aliens. Some intergalactic Joad family[36] or something. 'Oh, we don't wanna land in New York or LA. Nah, we just had a long trip – we're gonna kick back and whittle some.' Oh my God, they're *idiots*. 'We're gonna enter our mother ship in the tractor pull, hu-huh.' My God, we're being invaded by rednecks. My biggest fear.

Last thing I wanna see is a flying saucer up on blocks in front of some trailer, you know? Be depressing? Some bumper sticker on it: 'They'll get my ray gun when they pry my cold, dead, eighteen-fingered hand off of it.' See, in England, man, they had these crop circle things. Did you hear about that? These crop circles that show up, you know? Which two guys have since claimed they were responsible for, but I believe they're aliens too. But they think aliens actually landed around Stonehenge and take off, and I asked people what it was like over there. And they said, 'Oh, it's incredible. People came from miles around. Lot of them brought soccer balls.' Would you let the aliens land, please? They might be here to pick me up.

I don't care what you believe, but you've got to admit beliefs are odd. You know what I mean? You *have* to admit that. A lot of Christians wear crosses around their necks. You think when Jesus comes back he ever wants to see a fucking cross? Kind of like going up to Jackie Onassis with a rifle pendant on, you know?

> 'Just thinkin' of John, Jackie. Just thinkin' of John . . .
> Just thinkin' of John, baby. We love him.'
> 'Don't love me that much.'

Hey man . . . killer idea. You guys like going to the movies? You, you, you do? Three of you do? I, I love the fucking movies. Love 'em. Now, I'm watching *Terminator 2* – d'you ever see that movie? Well, I'm watching, and I'm thinking to myself, you know what? There's no way they're ever going to be able to top these stunts in a movie again. You cannot *top* this shit . . . unless . . . they start using terminally ill people as stuntmen in pictures. Well, hear me out. Cos I know to some of ya this may sound a little cruel. 'Aww, Bill, terminally ill stuntpeople? That's cruel.' You know what I think cruel is? Leaving your loved ones to die in some sterile hospital room, surrounded by strangers. Fuck that! Put 'em in the movies! What? You want your grandmother dying like a little bird in some hospital room? Her translucent skin so thin you can see her last heartbeat work its way down her blue veins? Or do you want her to meet Chuck Norris?

> 'Hey, how come you've dressed my grandmother up as
> a mugger?'
> 'Shut up and get off the set. Action! Push her towards
> Chuck.'
> (*fight noises*)
> 'Wow, he kicked her head right off her body. Did you
> see that? Did you see my Grammy?'

She's out of her misery; *you've* seen the greatest film of all time. I'm still feeling some resistance to this here. What's up? 'Ugh ugh.' You and your *fake* fuckin' sympathy. OK, how about these guys are being executed? Don't do *that*. Poison, electrocute – how cruel? And unimaginative. Put 'em in the movies! 'Jeffrey Dahmer,[37] for your crimes against humanity of which you've been found guilty, I sentence you . . . to Wes Craven's next picture. Ha ha ha ha ha!' (*screams*) OK, not one of my more popular theories. But just do me a big favour: don't ever say you love film as much as I. I think we've found your limit.

So what else, folks? I smoke ah . . . (*clears throat*) if this bothers anyone, I recommend you looking around the world in which we live and . . . shutting your fucking mouth. Either that or suffer a facial burn – your choice. After all, this is America, Land of Freedom, so you have that option ahead of you. I now realize I smoke for simply one reason, and that is . . . spite. I hate you non-smokers with all of my little black fuckin' heart . . . you obnoxious, self-righteous, whinin' little fucks. My biggest fear if I quit smoking is that I'll *become* one of you. Now don't take that wrong.

How many non-smokers do we have here tonight by round of applause? Non-smokers? (*big round of applause*) Few of ya. Good, cos I have something to tell ya. I do. I have something to tell you non-smokers and this is for you and you only . . . because I know for a fact that you don't know this. And I feel it's my duty to pass on information at all times so that we can all learn, evolve . . . and get the fuck off this planet. Non-smokers – this is for you and you only. Ready? Non-smokers die . . . every day. Sleep tight. You see, I know you entertain some type of eternal life *fantasy* because you do not smoke cigarettes. May I be the first to (*pop*) pop that little fucking bubble of yours? And send you hurtling back to the truth? You're dead too. Ah-ha ha ha ha ha! Ah! Ah! Have a good evening. Ah-ha! And you know what doctors say? 'Shit, if only you smoked – we'd have the technology to help you.' It's you people dying from nothing that are screwed. I got all sorts of neat gadgets waiting for me, man. Oxygen tent, iron lung. It's like going to Sharper Image[38] . . . Major rationalizations. (*laughs*)

We live in such a weird culture, man. Does anyone remember this? When Yul Brynner *died* and came out with that commercial *after* he was *dead*? 'I'm Yul Brynner, and I'm dead now.' What the fuck's *this* guy sellin'? I'm all ears. 'I'm Yul Brynner, and I'm dead now cos I smoked cigarettes.' OK, pretty scary. But they could have done that with anyone. They could have done it with that Jim Fixx guy, too. Remember that guy? That health nut who died while jogging? Ho, I don't remember seeing his commercial.

> 'I'm Jim Fixx, and I'm dead now . . . an' I don't know *what* the fuck happened. I jogged every day, ate nothing but tofu, swam 500 laps every morning – I'm dead. Yul Brynner drank, smoked and got laid every night of his life – he's dead. Shit! Yul Brynner smokin', drinkin',

girls are sittin' on his cueball noggin every night of his life. I'm runnin' around a dewy track at dawn . . . and we're both fuckin' dead. Yul used to pass me on his way home in the morning. Big long limousine. Two girls blowin' him. Cigarette in one hand; drink in the other. One day that life's gonna get to you, Yul.'

They're both dead. Yeah, but what a healthy-looking corpse you were, Jim. Look at the hamstrings on that corpse! Look at the sloppy grin on Yul's corpse! Yul Brynner lived his life. Sure, he died a 78-pound stick figure, OK. There are certain drawbacks. Oh, man.

People say the stupidest things sometimes, too. 'Hey man, you quit smoking, you get your sense of smell back.' I live in New York City, I got news for you: I don't want my fucking sense of smell back.

(sniffs) 'Is that urine? (sniffs) I think I smell a dead guy. Honey, look at *that* guy! Covered in urine – check this out! Someone just *peed* on this guy – that's fresh! Just think, if I'd been smoking I never would have found him. (sniffs) A urine-covered dead fella. What are the odds? Thank God I quit smoking. Now I can enjoy the wonders of New York, honey. Look! (sniffs) Ahhh.'

I'm Bill Hicks and I'm dead now . . . cos I smoked cigarettes. Cigarettes didn't kill me, a bunch of non-smokers kicked the shit out of me one night. I tried to run, they had more energy than I. I tried to hide, they heard me wheezing. Many of them smelled me.

(sniffs) 'There he is! Get him!'
(wheezes)
'Oh, he's hardly fucking moving. This is pathetic!'
(wheezes)
'Look, he's still trying to get away. He's like a roach. Step on him!'
(wheezes)
'Squash him!'
(wheezes)
'Let's kill him and pee on him. Yeah!'

Man in audience: You got a bad attitude.

Bill: (*singing*) 'We've only just begun.' I got alllll sorts of new dark shit for *you*, my man. You ever danced with the Devil in the moonlight? I don't know what my attitude is. I'm trying to work on it all the time, you know. I'm drinking water tonight. That's pretty amazing. Water. It's really weird how your life changes, you know what I mean? Water. Four years ago – opium. Ha ha ha! Isn't that weird? I mean, really . . . night and day. Night and fucking day!

Some of y'all may remember me as a drinker, ah . . . I was a weekend drinker, you know. I'd start on Saturday, end on Friday, and ah . . . thought I was controlling it there, but. I don't drink any more. I don't do drugs any more either than . . . I'd say the average touring funk band. If I had to add it up. I don't do drugs any more, either.

But I'll tell you something about drugs – I used to do drugs – but I'll tell you something honestly about drugs – honestly – and I know it's not a very popular idea, you don't hear it very often any more, but it is the truth. I had a great time doing drugs. Sorry. Never murdered anyone, never robbed anyone, never raped anyone, never beat anyone, never lost a job, a car, a house, a wife, or kids . . . *laughed* my ass off, and went about my day. Sorry. Now, where's *my* commercial? Why don't *I* get a commercial? Why's it always that other guy that gets the commercial? 'I lost my job, then my house, then my wife, then my car, then my kids. Don't do drugs.' Well, I'm definitely not doin' them with you. Fuck! Man, you're bumming me out. Get him out of here. Who invited Mr Doom over? Get that guy outa here! That guy by the dip – he's bumming everyone out. He hasn't stopped talking– I wish he'd lose his fucking *voice*. I mean, I've lost my car before, OK. Found it the next day, you know, no biggy. I don't think that warranted a commercial. 'I lost my car and ah . . . no, there it is by that dumpster. Ha ha ha! Forget it! See you tomorrow!' (*makes sound of truck horn*) Rrrrrrrrrrr. You know, I've lost stuff. I'm not saying that.

I knew we were in trouble when that damn that . . . egg commercial. I knew. That was the government's take on drugs, you know, we're *fucked*, believe me. 'Here's ya brain.' I've seen a lot of weird shit on drugs. I've never, ever, *ever*, *ever*, *ever* looked at an egg and thought it was a fucking brain. Not once. All right? I have seen UFOs split the sky like a *sheet*, but I have never, ever, ever looked at an egg and thought it was a fucking brain . . . not once. I have had seven balls of light come off of a UFO, lead me on to their *ship*, explain to me telepathically that we are all one and there is no such thing as death, but I have never, ever, ever, *ever* looked at an egg and thought it was a fuckin' brain. Now . . . maybe I wasn't getting good shit. I admit it, I see that commercial, I feel cheated. Hey, where's the stuff that makes eggs look like brains? That sounds neat. Did I quit too soon? What is that? CIA stash? You see the guy in that commercial, the guy's got a beer gut. 'All right, this is it. Look up, man. This is ya brain. I ain't doing this again. That's ya br–' The guy's drunk doing the fucking commercial, man. 'Here's ya brain.' That's an EGG! That's a frying pan, that's a stove, you're an alcoholic. Dude, I'm tripping right now, and I still see that as a fucking egg, all right? I see the UFOs around it, but that is a goddamned *egg* in the middle. There's a hobbit eating it, but goddamn it, that hobbit is eating a fucking *egg*. He's on a unicorn, but that no, that ah, oop, that's a fucking egg. Yeah. How dare you have a wino tell me not to do drugs.

Woman in audience: Why did you quit?

Bill: Why did I quit? Because after you've been taken aboard a UFO it's kinda hard to *top that*, all right? You know, they have Alcoholics Anonymous, they don't have Aliens Anonymous. Tell you what, though, going to AA meetings – which I have to do – but ah going there and hearing people talk about their fucking booze stories, you know. I'm sitting there.

> 'You know, I love the taste of gin, it's just so good.'
> 'Fuck you, I've been on a UFO. Fuck off! I went *drinking* with aliens, you fucker! Shut up!'
> 'I lost my wife.'
> 'I LOST AN ALIEN CULTURE WHO WANTED TO TAKE ME TO THE PLANET ARTURUS.[39] FUCK YOU!'

I mean, I don't know if I've gotten the resentment, you know, forgiveness part down in the programme, but . . . (*singing*) 'One day at a time.'

No, I just cannot, you know, believe in a war against drugs when they have anti-drug commercials on TV all day long, followed by 'This Bud's for you.' I got news for ya, folks: a1) alcohol is a drug. b2) And here's the rub: alcohol kills more people than crack, coke and heroin . . . combined each year. So, thanks for inviting me to your little alcoholic drug den here tonight . . . you fine, upstanding citizens, you. Wink, wink. Nudge, nudge. Now! You know what? If I was gonna have a drug be legal it would not be alcohol. You know why? There's better drugs and better drugs *for* you. That's a *fact*. So you can stop your internal dialogue. 'Oh, wait a minute, Bill. Alcohol's an acceptable form of social interaction, which for thousands of years has been the norm under which human beings have congregated and formed social (*drops to a mumble*) . . .' Shut the fuck up. Your denial is beneath you, and thanks to the use of hallucinogenic drugs . . . I see through you. Pot is a better drug than alcohol – *fact* – and I'll prove it to you. You're at a ball game, you're at a concert, someone's really violent, aggressive and obnoxious. Are they drunk or are they smoking pot?

Audience: Drunk!

Bill: The one and only correct answer. Tell 'em what they won, John. I've *never* seen people on pot get in a fight because it is fucking impossible.

> 'Hey, buddy.'
> 'Hey, what.'

End of argument. Say you get in a car accident and you've been smoking pot. You're only going four miles an hour. (*makes sound of crash*)

> 'Shit, we hit something.'
> 'Forgot to open the garage door, man.'
> 'Got to get the garage door open so Dominos knows we're home.'

But I'll tell you the truth. I have never heard one reason that rang true why marijuana is against the law. That rang *true*, now. I'm not talking about the reasons the government tells us, cos – I hope you know this; I think you do – all governments are lying cocksuckers. Hope you know that. Good. All right.

I mean, marijuana grows everywhere, serves a thousand different functions, all of them positive. To make marijuana against the law is like saying God made a mistake. You know what I mean? It's like God on the seventh day looked down on his creation. Said:

> 'There it is: my creation. Perfect and holy in all ways.
> Now I can rest . . . Oh my Me . . . I left fucking pot
> everywhere. I should never have smoked that joint on
> the third day. Shit! If I leave pot everywhere, it's gonna
> give people the impression they're supposed to *use it*.
> Shit! Now I have to create Republicans.'

So you see, it's a vicious cycle.

And I'm not promoting the use of drugs, believe me. I'm not. I've had bad times on drugs, OK? I mean look at this haircut – fuck! I tell ya, I live in New York now, man. I tell you, man. The war on drugs has definitely taken a ceasefire there, it's . . . I mean, it's incredible. They sell drugs out loud on the streets. 'Heroin! Heroin! Heroin! Coke! Coke! Coke! Smoke! Smoke! Heroin! Heroin!' Those guys bug the shit out of me. I'm walking down the street one day. This guy's walking ahead of me, passes one of those dealers. He looks at 'em, he goes, 'Heroin! Heroin! Heroin!' I pass him, he looked at me, goes, 'Glue!' 'I can afford heroin, you fucker. I'm doin' laundry right now. As soon as my shirt's out of the cleaners I'm coming back and buying some of that shit from you.' He embarrassed me to death, all right? I was mortified. Glue. *Fucker*. Where's a bank machine? Come 'ere. Come 'ere Mr Dealer, come 'ere! I'm gonna show you my balance. Then I'm gonna buy heroin from that little kid across the street. Fuck you! New York's a rather tense town.

See, I think drugs have done some good things for us, I really do. And if you don't believe drugs have done good things for us, do me a favor. Go home tonight, take all your albums, all your tapes, and all your CDs, and burn 'em. Cos you know what? The musicians who made all that great music that's enhanced your lives throughout the years . . . rrrrrrrrreal fucking high on drugs. Man, the Beatles were so high they let Ringo sing a coupla tunes. Tell me *they* weren't partyin'. 'We all live in a yellow submarine, yellow submarine . . .'

We all live in a— you know how fucking high they were when they wrote that? They had to pull Ringo off the ceiling with a *rake* to sing that fucking song.

> 'John, get Ringo. He's in the corner.'
> 'Put him— ooh, look at him scoot. Grab him!'
> 'Hook his bell bottom! Hook his bell bottom!'
> 'He's got a song he wants to sing us. Something about living in a yellow tambourine or something. Ringo! Yoko's gone. Come down! We can party again!'

They were real high, they wrote great music, drugs did have a positive effect.

OK, and I'll tell you what else. I'm gonna extend the theory to our generation now, so it's more applicable. The musicians today who don't do drugs, and in fact speak out against it? 'We're rock against drugs.' Boy, they suck. Ha ha ha ha ha ha! Suck. Ball-less, soul-less, spiritless, corporate little bitches, suckers of Satan's cock, each and every one of 'em. (*makes snorting, snarling noise*) (*singing*) 'Suckin' Satan's pecker.' Suck it! Put that big scaly pecker down ya gullet. 'We're rock against drugs, cos that's what George Bush wants.' (*snorting, snarling noise*) That's what we want, isn't it? Government-approved rock and roll? Don't you want to be in a concert one night, look to your right and see Dan fucking Quayle right next to you, man? You *know* you're partying then, you *know* you're on the edge. 'Fuck it, the Quayle monster's here. There ain't *no* coming back. We might be up to *eleven* tonight. Fuck this!' 'We're rock stars who do Pepsi Cola commercials.' (*snorting, snarling noise*) Luckily Satan's dick has many heads, so all these little demon piglets can nuzzle up and suckle all at once. Here comes a fella named Vanilla Ice. (*snorting, snarling noise*) Here comes MC Hammer. (*snorting, snarling noise*) Here's Madonna with *two* heads. (*snorting, snarling noise*) (*singing*) 'Suckin' Satan's pecker.' Suck it! It's only your dignity – suck it! It's only your dignity – suck it!

MC Hammer – oh, I'm sorry, it's *Hammer*. He dropped the 'MC'. I can't wait till he drops the 'Hammer' too. How 'bout this? Drop it all. Good.

I am available for children's parties, by the way. I know some of y'all might have a young 'un coming of age, and not want to go the traditional clown/balloon animal route this year. Might wanna look me up: Beelzebozo. Clown from hell.

> 'Hi kids. It's Beelzebozo time. Tell me something: who here out of you young 'uns has never smoked a ciga-rette? Come 'ere, kids. What's your name?'
> 'Tommy.'
> 'Tommy. How old are ya?'
> 'Five.'
> 'Five years old. And you mean to tell Beelzebozo you're not smokin' cigarettes yet? Come here, Tommy.'
> (*sucking, then wheezing sound*)
> 'Hold it in.'
> (*sucking sound*) 'Mummy!'
> 'Nope, it's Beelzebozo time. Tell me something: who here out of you young 'uns has never watched a skin flick? Come here, kids.'Brrrrrrrrrrrrrrrrr. 'See them, them's titties. Hu-huh.'
> 'Mummy!'
> 'That *is* your mummy. Come on! It's Beelzebozo time. Clown from hell.'

See, I don't know. I'm just different, you know. Like, remember those summer trips you'd take with your folks, growing up? Remember those nightmare fucking excursions, you know? Instead of doing that . . . why don't families take mushrooms? Stay home and trip together. It'd be a *much* better trip. The home movies would be *tonnes* more fun. Just twenty minutes of someone's thumb. Rrrrrrrrrrrrrrrrrrrrrrrrrrrrrr.

> 'You see, son, the thumb is opposable. That's why we can use tools and live indoors.'
> Rrrrrrrrrrrrrrrrrrrrrr.
> 'Speaking of indoors, you get the impression the walls are breathing?'
> 'I do, Mom.'
> Rrrrrrrrrrrrrrrrrrrrrrrr.

'It's like we're all one consciousness experiencing itself
subjectively.'
Rrrrrrrrrrrrrrrrrrrrrrr.
'There is no such thing as death,[40] son. It's only illusion
that we are separate beings. In actuality we are all one
kind.' Rrrrrrrrrrrrrrrrrrrrrrrr 'God is love and love is all
there is, and if that's all there is there can be no opposite.'
'Cool, Dad.'
Rrrrrrrrrrrrrrrrrrrrrrrrr.

I think that'd be such a neat trip . . . in a way, with your parents.
I think it might be more of an . . . eye opener. Perhaps a *third*-eye
opener. Ha ha ha ha!

That's the problem with this country. Ah, one of them. There are
many. But this whole issue of sexuality and pornography, which I
don't understand what pornography is, I really don't. To me pornography is, you know, spending all your money and not educating the
people in America, but spending it instead on weapons. That's
pornographic to me. That's totally filthy, and etcetera, etcetera,
down the line . . . you all in your fucking hearts know the goddamn
arguments. OK, good. But no one knows what pornography is.
Supreme Court says pornography is any act that has no artistic
merit and causes sexual thoughts. That's their definition essentially.
No artistic merit. Causes sexual thought. Hmm. Sounds like *every*
commercial on television, doesn't it? You know, when I see those
two twins on that Double Mint commercial . . . I'm not thinkin'
of gum. I am thinking of chewing. Maybe that's the connection
they're trying to make. What? You've all seen that Bush beer
commercial? The girl in the short hotpants opens the beer bottle
on her belt buckle, leaves it there, and it foams over her hand and
over the bottle. And the voiceover goes, 'Get yerself a Bush.' Hmm.
You know what that looks like? Nah, no way.

   I'll tell you the commercial they'd like to do if they could, and
I guarantee if they could they'd do this right here. Here's the
woman's face – beautiful. Camera pulls back – naked breast.

Camera pulls back, she's totally naked . . . legs apart. Two fingers right here. And it just says 'Drink Coke.' Now, I don't know the connection here . . . but goddamn if Coke isn't on my shopping list that week.

'Dr Pepper.'
'Snickers satisfyin'.' (*sings opening notes to 'Satisfaction'*)

Damned if I'm not buyin' these products. My teeth are rotting out of my head, I'm glued to the television, I'm as big as a fucking couch. 'More Snickers, more Coke.'

That's what I find ironic, too, is that people who're against these things that cause sexual thoughts are generally fundamentalist Christians . . . who also believe you should be fruitful and multiply. Boy, they walk a tightrope every day, don't they? (*singing*) 'Da da da da da da da.' How do we be fruitful and multiply and not think about it? Ha ha! We could sing hymns during it. (*singing*) 'One stroke at a time, sweet Jesus. One stroke at a time, sweet Lord.'

I did that joke in Alabama in Fyffe and these three rednecks met me after the show. 'Hey, buddy! Come here! Mr Funny Man, come here! Hey buddy, we're Christians. We don't like what you said.' I said, 'Then forgive me.' Later, when I was hanging from the tree . . .

Here is my final point. Oh thank you, God. About drugs, about alcohol, about pornography – whatever that is – what business is it of yours what I do, read, buy, see, or take into my body, as long as I do not harm another human being on this planet? And for those of you out there who're having a little moral dilemma in your head how to answer that question, I'll answer it for ya. *None* of your fucking business! Take that to the bank, cash it and go fuckin' on a vacation out of my life. But see, here's their argument to that each and every time: 'But we have to protect the children, we have to protect the children.' Let me tell you something: children are smarter than any of us. You know how I know that? I don't know one child with a full-time job and children. Yeah. They're *quick* these kids, man. They're fucking *quick*.

But where did this veneration of childbirth come from? I missed that meeting, I'll tell ya that. 'Oh, childbirth is such a miracle. It's such a miracle.' Wrong. No more a miracle than eating food and a turd coming out of your ass. You know what a miracle is? A miracle's raising a kid who doesn't talk in a fucking movie theatre. *That, that . . . there's* your goddamn miracle. If it were a miracle then not every nine months any ying-yang in the world could drop a litter of these mewling fucking cabbages on the planet, and in case you have not checked the single-mom statistics lately, the miracle is spreading like fucking wildfire. Hallelujah! Trailer parks all over America. Fillin' up with little miracles. Thunk! Thunk! Thunk!

'Look at my little miracles.'
Thunk!
'Fillin' up my trailer like a sardine can. Look at them.'
Thunk!
'You know what'd be a real miracle? If I could remember your daddy's name, goddamn it.'
Thunk!
'I guess I'll have to call you Trucker Junior. That's all I remember 'bout your daddy, was his fuzzy little pot belly riding on top of me, shooting his caffeine-ridden semen into my belly to produce my little waterhead miracle baby child.'
Thunk!
'There's your brother: Pizza Boy Delivery Junior.'
Thunk!
'There's your other brother: Exterminator Junior.'
Thunk!
'There's your other brother: Will Work For Food Junior.'

Thank you very much. Good night!

Interview with Funny Man Bill Hicks
By Jimmy O'Brien
(November/December 1991)

A comic's comic is a rare commodity. Bill Hicks fits this description wonderfully, from his on target assaults on the injustices perpetrated by a government, to his not too genteel solution of the problem of an aging America.

We caught up with Bill at a local recording studio while he was putting the finishing touches on his second album, scheduled for release on 15 January [1992] for Invasion Records.

FM: When did you first realize you wanted to be a comic?

BH: I was 13 years old when I decided to do comedy.

FM: Was there a triggering incident?

BH: Yeah, there was. I was watching late night TV and a Woody Allen movie came on, and there was something about it that made me laugh so hard and it just struck me. So the next day I was in a bookstore and I picked up a copy of *Without Feathers*, by Woody Allen and I just fell on the floor. I couldn't get out of the bookstore, I was screaming and laughing so hard. I don't know why I related to Woody Allen. I'm not Jewish. I'm not short. I'm not a schlemel. But I really related to him comically. I started writing jokes like him. Although, thinking back, I could relate to his women problems.

FM: How long did you do open mics before your first paying gig?

BH: Five shows.

FM: Five shows!

BH: Yeah! (laughs) I tell ya man, it was a unique situation in Houston (where I grew up), comedy wise. I mean, I literally walked in and said, 'How do you do this?' And they said, 'Can you work this weekend and we'll split the door?' Nobody knew what it took for 45 minutes of material, certainly not the audience, not like now. This was back in '78, before everything broke loose.

FM: We're talking about a group at the Comedy Workshop who became known as 'The Outlaws.'

BH: Yeah, it was myself, Sam Kinison, Riley Barber, Ron Shock, Steve Epstein, Jimmy Pineapple, a lot of guys.

FM: A lot of readers saw your HBO special earlier this year. How'd that work? Did you have to temper your set?

BH: No, they let me do everything I wanted except at the end where I do this beautiful speech and then you hear a gunshot and I fall to the stage. I wanted it to fade to black and roll the credits. They didn't want that because their statistics show that the viewer will change the station within 30 seconds if left with a black screen. So I had to get up while the credits rolled to show everybody that it was 'just a little joke.' God knows we need those fucking marketing people out there working for us.

FM: Has your career changed much as a result of the HBO special?

BH: No! (laughs)

FM: Bill, in your act you reveal that you no longer drink and drug.

BH: Right.

FM: Do you feel you're a better comic as a result?

BH: Definitely! My whole life is better because of that. Not to disparage drugs, because I tell ya, some drugs that I took either: a) opened my mind, or b) confirmed several things in my mind. Since I quit drinking, because I did drugs so I could drink more, I'm much, much better.

FM: What makes comedy good for you?

BH: Good question. First, wit. Someone once described wit as finding similarities in things that are different, and finding differences in things that are similar. I like that a lot as far as wit.

As for humor, I think it has to ring true emotionally, coupled with justified anger at how the world is, and how you know in your heart how the world can be. In that lies humor, and the word 'fuck' (laughs).

FM: Where does your comedy come from, anger?

BH: Well, not just the anger. I like to offer information on how I'd rather see the world. I'm not just yelling in the wind, I hope. So I guess I'm just trying to share the message of love, and hope more people will think that way, thereby validating my lifestyle. (laughs) The more people Bill works, the less work Bill has to do.

FM: Bill, with regards to today's comics, the public seems to think we're a bunch of misfits; pissed off at the world. I'd be curious to hear what kind of a read you're getting on the road.

BH: Well, I think comedy should be enlightening, and that's the reaction I get. As far as how the public perceives us. I'm glad they think we're misfits. We don't need more people saying. 'You can make how much? I'm in! I'm in!' (laughs)

FM: You're regarded as a comic's comic. Do you feel pressure from that?

BH: No, not really. I love comics and I think they're very smart. To me they're like the last bastion of free speech in the country. But nobody takes us seriously because we're comics. Actually, I guess that's a blessing.

FM: What's your opinion of comedy in Texas?

BH: In Texas, all you guys are really philosophical, conscientious and very moral people. San Francisco had a comedy era, but it wasn't like this. Boston is very political. You guys do this socialist kind of humor. I love Texas. Everybody has this image of cowboys and shit like that. To me, Texas is Austin, a bunch of cool people trying to make a difference.

Part 2: 1992

Hicksville UFO, *New Musical Express* (18 January 1992)

Whoop! Whoop! Warning! Warning! Danger approaching! Danger! Quick, Will Robinson, into the ship!

And what will young Will find in that spaceship? Well, if the man in front of me is to be believed, it could well be an American comedian in a black suit. Yes, BILL HICKS, recently seen on telly in his own one-hour comedy special and gen-u-ine BIG American name at last year's Edinburgh Fringe, has actually been in a spaceship. And not just some tacky theme park version of the Space Family Robinson's Jupiter, but a *real* spaceship, with *real* aliens!

'Without going into too much detail, me and two friends had a shared vision, while not being together physically, of being taken up in a UFO,' he says in calm, rational, measured tones not at all like a madman.

'When we got back together, none of us remembered it and one friend said, "Do you get the impression that we're meeting a lot of new friends tonight?" And all three of us remembered the experience. Ever since then I've been looking over my shoulder . . .'

Not surprisingly, Bill Hicks is now fascinated by UFOs, and the possibilities they offer to point out to people that they need not think the way the 'authorities' say they should.

'I like to use aliens in my act to point out a fear of strangers, xenophobia. Aliens landing in Alabama – like Alabamans hate everybody but I had to use aliens to make it a more universal thing – and they're afraid of these aliens. What are you afraid of? Are you afraid they're going to take your jobs? "We've come to work at the Sonic Burger! C'mon!"

'And these people, they hear about a UFO sighting and they all take off to see the UFO carrying guns. *Why*? What are they going to do with them? These creatures have travelled millions of miles and you've got a shotgun? When are you going to *stop*?'

Born, already jaded, in Georgia about 30 years ago, Hicks moved with his parents to Texas and later based himself in New York, along the way becoming a chain smoker ('How many do I smoke? I'm a two-lighter a day man') and rabid campaigner against intolerance and banality ('I hate it when people come up to me and say. Bill, it takes less energy to smile than frown'. Yeah? Well it takes less energy for you to leave me alone . . .).

The self-styled King Of Rationalization, Hicks claims not to be a political comedian, though almost everything he deals with can be traced to an acute awareness and amazement at how political systems rule our lives, tell us how to think and teach us not to question.

'Comedy is a double-edged sword; on one hand no-one gives you any flak because you're a comedian and it's all a joke, on the other hand it's not a joke – I'm serious about what I'm saying but they think it's a joke.

'For instance, when Reagan got elected, that was when all this comedy boom started, and all these comedians all over America are getting on stage and saying, "Have you seen what this guy is doing, he's a *demon*." And the crowd laugh and go, "He's a demon, hahaha!" "No! *Listen*, he really IS a demon, we're serious." "A demon, hahaha!" And you'd run down exactly how this guy was a liar and an idiot and they laugh and go and elect him again. Same with your Mrs Thatcher.'

By now Bill, who tends towards a Van Morrison silhouette although he is a good six feet tall, has worked up a head of sweat and is not about to relinquish the floor. He is a serious comedian. What follows is all off the top of his head, not part of his act . . .

'Look at Reagan, the guy's a moron. His IQ was like 100. You know why he was elected president? The average American IQ is 100 – it's like an idiot, right? Isn't that like a *moron*? And then this weasel Bush came in, he's a sleazebag, they're all sleazebags.'

Could Elvis have been elected president?

'These guys all do commercials and they have f— ing publicists, it's all showbiz, so maybe Elvis could have been president. What strikes me as funny about Elvis is that all the impersonators choose to do the Vegas Elvis; not the young, cool guy, always the bloated fool.'

Worshipping Elvis seems to be an excuse for Americans to be fat and stupid.

'Probably, probably, they love vulgarity. Look at McDonald's. You have a McDonald's in Moscow now, and that's something I really don't care for – the Americanization of the world.' Hicks continues. He's off on a tangent but it all makes seamless sense to him. 'Yeah! (*Holds out his hand with fingers splayed like an advertising exec showing a client the new campaign slogan*) The Americanization of the world – Bad Products Served Rudely, hahaha!

'But I'm an American who loves an America which doesn't exist, which is a land of freedom and free ideas. The business of America is not business, to me it's the creation of ideas.'

But isn't the American dream all the money you could want and a condo by the beach – money that buys your freedom? Considering how laid-back a man Bill Hicks is, he nearly explodes.

'Nah, that's a lie! Money doesn't buy you *anything*, it's an illusion. If there was no money on this planet there wouldn't be any less food. It's a big cocksuck, man, money's time is up. That's what people are realizing, hopefully. The grossest thing about poor people is that they crave money. Everyone should wear blue jeans and three T-shirts and eat beans and rice and break every f—ing company, *break* 'em. Don't buy McDonald's – we're gonna break your ass Big Mac, OK? Quit makin' such shit.' He pauses, looking more startled than out of breath. 'Where the f— did all THAT come from, Jeeeezus!'

It's no surprise that you're also not a great believer in organized religion. Did you have a previous bad experience?

'Well, my whole philosophy in life,' he starts in top Tapesque manner, 'is that we are all one and the minute you call yourself one thing you immediately separate yourself from all the other things. And yes, I had a bad experience.'

What, were you beaten in a coven as a child?

'Well, with a five minute UFO experience I got a taste of holiness I never got in 20 years of religion. All the things I talk about are foils to point out perceptions, so I really don't have anything I'm against so much as I'm for, and that's what I think my material keeps pointing at – deflating balloons, deflating fantasies and trying to find some element of truth.

'Ah, that's pretty pompous, but I have to have somethin', some kind of belief. 'Til that f— in' ship comes back anyway.'

Roll over Jimmy Swaggart, and tell the Venusians the news . . .

'We are the perfect and holy children of God, and I don't see, being the perfect and holy children of God, how any limits could possibly be put upon us . . . not at all. That's the point of my act. I just want to be free of the fears and anxieties of death and the superstitions of religion. Being raised in a Baptist . . . with an avenging God, a God who created hell for his children. I'm sorry, but . . . no. Wrong. You're wrong. That's an insane God and therefore not mine. Because, see, God would be very sane, don't you get it? That's my act. Everything branches off from that.'

Mr Malcontent
By Robert Draper, *Texas Monthly*
(June 1992)

Perhaps the most talented American comedian working the circuit these days is a native Houstonian who looks about as funny as a death in the family. Bill Hicks is a pallid, limp-haired, sad-faced, hostile thirty-year-old with a taste for black clothes, black humor, and musicians who die before their time. He tells his audiences, 'People like to come up to me and say, "Takes more energy to frown than it does to smile!" I say, "Yeah, and it takes more energy for you to tell me that than it does for you to shut up and leave me alone."'

Hicks gets his laughs the way Lenny Bruce (to whom he is often compared) did: by attacking conventions of every sort, including those that govern what should and should not be fodder for humor. During last year's flush of national patriotism for Desert Storm, Hicks proclaimed on *Late Night With David Letterman*, 'I'm for the war, but I'm against the troops. I'm sorry, I just don't like those young people. Don't get me wrong, though – I'm all for the carnage.' Despite his provocations, or because of them, Hicks's reputation as a comedian of ferocious passion and intellect has led to ten appearances on the Letterman show, as well as a spotlight segment on CBS's *48 Hours* and his own HBO comedy special. More important, his success has earned him the ultimate compliment in a cutthroat business: a rash of lesser competitors who pattern their acts after his.

'I only wish that the people who think I'm so worthy of imitation had production companies,' says Hicks, who, after fifteen years of live performances, has begun to wonder if his resentful demeanor is too forbidding for those who parcel out movie deals and TV series. Such offers have gone to comedians like Roseanne Arnold and Andrew Dice Clay, who are punchier, raunchier, louder, fatter, and possess a more camera-ready wardrobe than Hicks. Yet what Bill Hicks lacks in these areas he makes up for in sheer comic inspiration.

The titles of Hicks's two live albums – *Dangerous* and the recently released *Relentless* – tell something about his bombing-raid approach. The ground he strafes is familiar enough: Bush, Baptists, the National Rifle Association, his parents, his ex-girlfriends. But his humor gets its edge from the punishing force of truth behind it, whether he is belittling the war in the Persian Gulf or the farmers in Fyffe, Alabama, who saw a UFO and immediately scrambled for their guns. Between bits, he paces the stage, grimacing and scratching violently at his scalp while the audience, mindful of his talent for eviscerating hecklers, maintains a respectful silence. At times Hicks will solicit an audience reaction, such as when he asks, 'How many nonsmokers do we have tonight?' After taking stock of the applause, Hicks will light a cigarette. 'I hate you nonsmokers with all my little black heart.'

'The richest kind of laughter is the laughter in response to things people would ordinarily never laugh at,' says Hicks, whose own laugh recalls the impudence of Eddie Haskell in *Leave It To Beaver*. In person he is engaging, though there is an unease about him, as if at any moment he expects to be asked to leave. Hicks gives the impression that his search for humor is a mission to avoid despair. That Hicks grew up idolizing Woody Allen, a comedian with an entirely different style and range of targets, is not surprising – 'The connection is a low self-esteem,' says Hicks.

Hicks was a fourteen-year-old introvert living in the suburbs of west Houston when he first saw Allen in *What's New, Pussycat?* It was the funniest movie he had ever seen, and the notion of its nebbish screenwriter having cast himself as a hero rang all the right bells. Hicks began to write comedy stories. One morning while reading the newspaper, he noticed that a downtown club called the Comedy Workshop was sponsoring an amateur night. Hicks called and asked to perform, and the manager said he could. Hicks' parents forbade him to do so, but he was undeterred. He sneaked out of his second-story window, crawled across the garage, and ran to a nearby church parking lot, where a friend with a car ferried him to his first gig. That night he earned $8 with such rehearsed lines as, 'My girlfriend is very small – she's a stewardess on a paper airplane.'

Gradually, as Hicks continued his clandestine pilgrimages to the Comedy Workshop, his material advanced from the merely absurd to the poignant: 'I've been with the same girl for five years now, so I finally popped the question: "Why are we still seeing each other?"' His popularity grew. He performed his first solo show at the age of fifteen, at a church camp. His first major fee was $150, earned at a breakfast party at Sakowitz at six-thirty in the morning. 'There was a huge buffet,' he recalls, 'and they said, "We don't have time to do the show. Just be funny while we get our food." I stood between the ham and the powdered eggs.'

The management and the older comedians at the Comedy Workshop adopted Hicks as a talented apprentice. His teachers and classmates at Stratford High School began to show up to see him perform, and before long Bill Hicks was accorded outlaw celebrity status among his peers. One night after a football game, he showed up at the local Wendy's and was goaded into what became ninety minutes of stand-up before a packed house of hamburger-eating students. When word spread at school one afternoon that Hicks would be doing his routine in a nearby vacant field during lunch, more than two hundred students flocked to see the free show. Not everyone was enamored of the campus rebel. 'You're pathetic,' he remembers one of his principles telling him. 'You have the sense of humor of a third-grader.'

Hicks knew a setup when he heard one. 'Well, then,' he replied, 'you must have the comprehension of a second-grader.'

Following his graduation in 1980, Hicks and three other Houston comedians – including the late Sam Kinison – moved to Los Angeles, hoping to find work at the burgeoning Comedy Store nightclub. They did, but Hicks grew bored with the scene, the city, and the very act of telling jokes for a living. He enrolled at Los Angeles Community College and on his first day got his nose broken in karate class. Taking that as a sign, Hicks returned to Texas and signed on at the University of Houston.

'It was the Great Postponement,' Hicks admits of his stint at the university. 'I figured that if I hung in there for four years, something would strike me. I started off taking public speaking and philosophy. I thought it would be good to start off my college career with a couple of A's. The public speaking guy tried to turn me into a Rotary Club speaker, with all the right gesticulations. I did my speech – muttered and paced and smoked and yelled at someone. And the philosophy professor wanted us to prove David Hume's there-is-no-God thesis right at a time when I'd just taken mushrooms for the first time. He turned purple every time I raised my hand. I failed both classes.'

Sulking, Hicks returned to the Comedy Workshop, where he knew he could get free drinks. It was 1982, and for reasons Hicks now insists have something to do with Reagan's presidency, the American comedy scene was exploding. The nightclub's booking agent urged Hicks to rejoin the circuit. 'It literally went like this: "Bill, we have a gig for you in Victoria, Texas. Oh, and while you're there, a club just opened in El Paso." It happened in every state.'

Hicks and his menacing stage act became much in demand. In 1983, at 21, he opened for a hot New York comic named Jay Leno in an Austin nightclub. 'What're you doin' down here?' Leno demanded after seeing Hicks' performance. 'Why aren't you on TV?' A few months later, Leno arranged to get Hicks on David Letterman's show. Subsequently, Hicks appeared several times, on the third visit incorporating an attack on the Reverend Jerry Falwell that greatly displeased Letterman's producers. Hicks was not invited to hurry back. His defiance only fueled his renegade image – a reputation that included an overt fondness for alcohol and drugs.

'Rock and roll would not exist without drugs,' he delighted in pointing out in his shows, adding, 'The Beatles were so high they even let Ringo sing a couple.' But drugs, especially alcohol, were slowly getting the best of Hicks, who would later tell crowds, 'I was a weekend drinker – started on Saturday, ended on Friday.' His routines became more meandering, his words less comprehensible. By the mid-eighties, Hicks began to see in the faces of the audience the sentiments of his former principal: 'You're pathetic.' This time around he began to believe it.

One night was particularly grim. Hicks spent the entire evening on a binge, then had to do a radio show at seven the next morning. 'I was up all night with the most satanic thoughts,' he said, 'thinking, "I have chosen evil." Somehow I did the radio show – and was really funny. But my heart was pounding and I thought I was gonna die. I went back to the hotel. And this guy I was working with who used to have a problem also, he was up whistling and looking peaceful. I said, "Man, you going to one of those AA meetings today?" He said, "I've been waiting three years to hear you ask that. There's a meeting in fifteen minutes. Let's go."'

Going straight was not easy for Hicks, who had come to think of the whiskey shots as stage props. He wondered if he would be funny without drugs. 'But I also realized,' he says, 'that I wouldn't be funny if I was dead.' That Hicks' shows are now more sharply focused is a matter of personal pride for him. Yet Bill Hicks does not sell his sobriety either as a story or as a stage sermonette – beyond telling his audiences, 'I admit I've had bad experiences with drugs; I mean, look at this haircut.' He continues to insist that hallucinogens changed his life for the better, maintaining, with deadly seriousness, that he was taken aboard an alien spacecraft during a mushroom trip. He says that Debbie Gibson and Hammer are proof of what a lack of drugs does to rock and roll and that 'marijuana should not only be made legal, it should be made mandatory.' If anything, his own misadventures have strengthened his convictions. 'People from AA come up and say, "Bill, I loved the show." If reformed addicts aren't offended, why should anyone else be?' he asks.

In 1988 Hicks moved to New York, in large part to redeem himself with Letterman's people. He quickly did, and in January of this year, he again packed his bags and returned to Los Angeles. There he hopes to increase his exposure. He also wouldn't mind if he happened to gain the favor of the *Tonight* show, soon to be hosted by his old friend Jay Leno and those elusive Hollywood producers. Until then, he remains one of the few comics in America popular enough to pick and choose where he performs.

Which is not to say that Bill Hicks has it easy. Unmarried and forever on the road, he's living a life that's hellish-lonely, anyway. But as with everything he has survived, Hicks has managed to turn bad karma into good material. 'All this travelling, all this moving from town to town, living out of a suitcase,' he murmurs to his audience, affecting a pout. 'You know, it's a hard life for anyone to comprehend. It's really going to take one very special woman . . .' The crowd ponders this with him. Then the silence is broken by Hicks's cackle. 'Or a lot of average women,' he says.

THE QUESTIONNAIRE
(SUMMER 1992)

1. What is your idea of perfect happiness?
Playing music – Performing – Creating.

2. What is your greatest fear?
Answering introspective questions about myself.

3. With which historical figure do you most identify?
Don't identify with anyone historically, but there are several people in the future who I am a dead ringer for.

4. Who do you most admire?
All the poets, all the prophets.

5. What do you most deplore about others?
Ignorance, dishonesty.

6. What vehicles do you own?
A left foot and a right foot.

7. What is your greatest extravagance?
My guitars.

8. What do you always carry with you?
My guitars.

9. What makes you most depressed?
Human suffering – especially my own.

10. What do you most dislike about your appearance?
My receding hairline.

11. What is your favourite smell?
Women.

12. What is your most unappealing habit?
Smoking.

13. What is your favourite word?
Release.

14. What is your favourite building?
My home.

15. What is your favourite journey?
The inner journey or my home, whichever comes first.

16. What or who is your greatest love?
Laurie, Pamela, Jennifer, Robin, Massie, Lisa, Sue, Jessica . . .

17. Which living person do you most despise?
Every politician, no exceptions.

18. Which words or phrases do you most overuse?
Cool, later dude, look!, a pumpkin!

19. What is your greatest regret?
Laurie, etc.

20. When and where were you happiest?
March 6, 1986, 3.30 p.m., Raleigh NC.

21. How do you relax?
Playing guitar.

22. What single thing would improve the quality of your life?
Quit smoking.

23. Which talent would you most like to have?
To be able to sing.

24. What would your motto be?
Let go and let God.

25. What keeps you awake at night?
Loneliness and fear.

26. How would you like to die?
Rich, happy and very old.

27. How would you like to be remembered?
Rich, happy and very old, but serious as an artist who was true to himself.

Intro to Scotland
(Summer 1992)

H ello. My name is Bill Hicks. I am a comedian from the USA, and I'll be appearing soon at the Edinburgh Festival. This will be my first trip to Scotland, so the promoter of my show thought it would be a good idea for me to write an article as a way of introducing myself to you, while also procuring him some free publicity. So here goes . . .

I've been a comedian for most of my life. I feel I was destined to be a comedian, as I started very young and have done little else by way of work. My love of comedy and my dedication have paid off handsomely. Through years of touring and performing my hilarious, hard-hitting comedy, I have become what's known in the states as a 'BIG STAR'. I'm so big, in fact, that this isn't even me writing to you now. This is Lars, Mr Hicks' tireless and loyal man Friday. Mr Hicks is currently indisposed, confined on doctor's orders to a hot tub with his tireless and loyal nurses Heather and Dusty. (I hear giggles now, where earlier I heard groans. I feel confident a full recovery is imminent.) To be on the safe side, I will suggest Mr Hicks bring his young, nubile healers with him on his trip to your fair country. They may also come in handy during Mr Hicks' shows, in case someone passes out due to oxygen loss to the brain brought about by excessive laughter. This has posed a considerable problem here in the States. It was how, in fact, during just one of these crises that I came to be in Mr Hicks' employ.

Years ago, I was living in Poteet, Texas, under the name of Larry Sloman. Poteet was a small, mean town that God never heard of, and the Devil found uncomfortably hot. You couldn't buy a breeze in Poteet, which explains why most of the townspeople spent their nights in the relative cool of Stumpy's Strip Joint and Bait Shop, hoping the sweat on the girls would make their panties fall off. (This never happened, although I did see several runny tattoos.)

One night, the disc jockey interrupted our half-hearted ogling to announce a comedian was going to perform, and we should all shut up and listen and not cause a stink. It was too hot to argue, and the only stink being raised was coming from the bait shop (at least I hope it was coming from the bait shop), so Bill Hicks bounded onstage and began his show.

Suddenly the place came alive. People were howling and screaming with laughter. I knew then I was in the presence of a great man, 'cause I didn't understand a word he was saying. One by one, people started passing out around me, until the only folks left standing were myself, and two of Stumpy's best looking girls – Heather and Dusty.

After the show, Mr Hicks walked over to me, stepping carefully over the still unconscious audience. He told me he was on a world tour that could take him as far as Louisiana, and he might need someone to help with the driving. He was impressed by the fact that I had stayed conscious during his show, and he felt I was a man he could trust with his life. He would gladly take me along under one condition – that I shorten my name to Lars. Well, I had nothing but a string of debts holding me in Poteet, and the collection agency was looking for a fellow named Larry Sloman. I told Mr Hicks Lars was at his service. Later that night as I drove through the vast desert of Texas, with Heather, Dusty, and my new boss giggling in the backseat, I wondered what could make a man so funny that he causes an entire audience to pass out laughing. Aw, Hell! It was probably just the heat . . .

The Counts of the Netherworld (July 1992)

TREATMENT

Beethoven's 9th begins playing softly.
Close-up – glass bauble filled with water and little figurines of Big Ben and Tower Bridge, which when shaken makes snowfall scene. Behind bauble we see warm fire flickering in fireplace.

Bill (v.o.): Mankind's Unconscious Mind must be awakened. That Unconscious Collective Mind in which we share . . . memory of Hope's ember burning there.

Close-up – warm crackly fire in fireplace.

Bill (cont.): Round which the Voices of the Soul commune . . . A starfilled twilight and radiant moon . . .

Shot of dazzling milky way and full moon, then close-up of feathered plume in someone's hand, scribbling furiously.

Bill (cont.): Calling for the spark in every brain . . . To recognize it is the same . . . As the spark in everyone . . . And in joining to become . . . From an Ember, to a Sun.

Close-up of Bill's enraptured face as he ends the poem. We pull back to reveal Bill sitting in french window looking out at the stars and the moon. Fallon sits at desk, feathered plume in hand, reviewing what he has just written.

They are the Counts in their beautiful salon – bookshelves lined with leather-bound classics. Red velvet furniture sits atop plush Persian rugs. An ornate mahogany desk, littered with reference books and baubles and curiosities such as the snowfall scene of Big Ben and Tower Bridge. Old World globes and maps, and a telescope placed about the room give the easy impression there are minds at work here. The whole salon speaks of extreme warmth, safety, and comfort.

Bill: Did you get all that?

Fallon (looks up from writings): Hmmm? Get all what?

Bill (incredulous): The Poem!

Fallon: Sorry, no. I was just writing to this girl I met who works at the fishmongers.

Bill glares at Fallon, then leaps up from the french window and storms over to the red velvet couch where he plops down boredly.

Fallon(cont.): I think she works at the fishmongers . . . either that, or she likes me a whole lot more than I first imagined.

Bill is holding a book of Carl Jung's work, which he is leafing through thoughtfully.

Bill: You see, Jung had this idea of a Collective Unconscious which mankind shared . . . and I agree. But! I think this Collective Mind is supposed to be conscious, not unconscious! And that is our job as the Agents of Evolution to enlighten – to bring light into the dark corners of that Netherworld and thus awaken our Mind to Truth and complete the circle that was broken with the dream of our fall from Grace.

As Bill is saying this, he is leafing through a copy of the Madonna 'Sex' book, which sits on the coffee table before him.

Bill: Did you get all that?

Fallon looks up from what he's just written.

Fallon: Hmmmm?

Bill: Don't tell me you weren't writing that down.

Fallon: Sorry . . . I'm writing to the girl I love so when I finally meet her all the paperwork will be in order.

Bill (disgusted): As the Scribe and Recorder, I'd like to know exactly what you think is important to get down here.

Fallon: Sorry.

Fallon puts away his personal correspondence. Bill continues leafing through the Madonna book, finally focusing on what he's seeing.

Bill: Say, what is this?

Fallon: That's the Madonna 'Sex' book. It's been out a while . . .

Bill: Cool! She's naked squatting on a dog's face!

Fallon begins scribbling again with his feathered plume. Bill looks up.

Bill: What are you writing now?

Fallon (reading): 'Cool! She's naked squatting on a dog's face!'

Fallon looks up.

Fallon: Is that right?

Bill: Yes . . . perfect.

Bill continues to flip through the book. He yawns and throws the book aside.

Bill: Surely this isn't what passes as risqué these days.

Fallon: It's caused quite a stir actually. Some people even consider it pornographic.

Bill and Fallon look at each other and burst out laughing.

Bill: Good God! I wonder what those people would think of that special Anniversary Edition of the Kama Sutra I own?

Fallon: You mean the Director's cut?

Bill: Exactly. You'd think people would know by now that pornography, like beauty, is in the eye of the beholder.

Fallon: Exactly.

Bill: And this to me is pure tripe. I've been more aroused by soda ads and less offended by snuff films.

Fallon: Yes, sex is in the mind, and that book's vision is the product of a child, to be sold to children. At least intellectually.

Bill: Yes. Penis and breast size notwithstanding, there is no sense of proportion here. The one picture that displayed promise is never again explored.

Fallon: Perhaps the Canine Union has stricter laws than we imagine.

Bill (disgusted): Probably. And of course all in the name of 'progress'.

Bill shakes his head sadly.

Fallon: Say, what was the fellow's name who wrote that book
            you liked?

*Bill motions to the bookshelves sagging under the weight of thousands
of books.*

Bill: Uh, could you be more specific?

Fallon: The one you were reading to me from the other day.
            About money.

Bill: Oh, yes! 'Money.' Martin Amis wrote that.

Fallon: Yes. Didn't you say Mr Amis fancied himself a porno
            connoisseur?

Bill: Well, the character in the book did.

Fallon: Maybe we could talk to him and see if he can shed
            any light on this subject?

Fallon begins scribbling furiously.

Bill: An excellent idea! Let's invite him at once!

Fallon: It's done!

*Fallon seals an envelope then writes 'Mr Martin Amis' on the front.
He hurls the envelope into the fireplace where it bursts into flames,
causing sparks to fly up the chimney.*
   *Close-up – chimney outside as sparks fly up into mankind's dark-
ened mind. Beethoven's 9th crescendos.*

INT. – SALON.

Martin Amis and Bill sit in red velvet chairs in front of fire. Fallon remains at the desk. Martin is reading a scene from his book 'Money'. It is a raucous, hilarious scene. When he finishes, Bill and Fallon laugh and applaud. Bill asks him what he thinks of the Madonna 'Sex' book. A conversation ensues covering pornography, censorship, fantasy, love, death, gardening, and anything else that comes to these philosophers' minds. This spontaneous conversation is filmed at our leisure, then edited to its most exciting kernels to get the full breadth and depth of our beloved guest's intellect and worldview. If the guest is an actor, perhaps a scene from current work will be acted out with Bill and Fallon playing the supporting roles. A singer might sing acoustically, a painter might paint during the interview. A dancer might dance to an old-fashioned wind-up Victrola playing classical music. In other words, we will remain true to the time period of the salon, and true to the integrity of the salon – a place where interesting people came to discuss the ideas of the day, socialize, and entertain one another and themselves by exercising the formidable skills of their imaginations.

As always, Bill and Fallon celebrate the talents and intellects of their guests, who have enlightened the Counts, who in turn wish to pass on to others from their inner space ship – the Salon.

In the course of our conversations, brief visual interludes take place in which a black and white film scene unfolds. As the conversation continues over it, the visual interlude can be a literal, cinematic, or subconscious bearing on whatever we're talking about. Most interludes take place outside the salon. All the world outside the deep, colorful salon is in black and white. Perhaps the Counts are telling Martin Amis about some beautiful nude sculpture they've seen at a museum. While this description is going on, we see Bill and Fallon in black and white film looking at the nude sculpture in the museum, or the camera just goes up and down the nude as the Counts describe it in glowing terms. (This is obviously a literal rendering of the dialogue.) The use of the interlude is infinite and obviously will be sparked by whatever has come up in our conversations with our guests, or from something the Counts have set up in their opening. Black and white film will add to the surreal and dreamlike quality of the Count's existence, while heightening the richness and glory of the salon. As the filmed interludes won't have matching sound, we think this will be a cheap, as well as artistic, way to get us out of the salon and prevent a sense of static and inaction in our talks. The interludes provide their own commentary on our conversations, or can be sparked by something someone has said – giving evidence of the multi-dimensional consciousness the Counts believe mankind shares.

The Counts – being Awake in the Dream – are not bound by convention, linear time, nor sense of place like the 'real' world appears to be. The salon should be as safe and warm and comforting as a favorite pair of slippers, providing stark contrast to the (black and white) sombre, restricted world outside us. From the salon comes the hum of excited voices, for it is here – around the glowing embers of Hope that the voices of the Soul commune. A place where Anything can happen.

As the conversation continues the interludes may get more and more frantic, or perhaps the conversation fades as the music gets louder, and a series of surreal scenes unfold inside and outside the salon. The Counts fencing. A beautiful woman undressing. Fallon sculpting. Bill and Martin Amis playing darts. Bill and Martin fencing in the museum, surrounded by statues of nudes. The chimney with sparks fling up into the dark. Finally, we see Martin Amis' eyes as he looks at himself in the mirror of his bathroom at home.

It's the middle of the night. A voice calls from the bedroom asking if he's all right. Distractedly, he answers . . .

Martin: Yes . . . I just had the weirdest dream.

He turns off the bathroom light, and Beethoven's 9th punctuates dramatically. We hear the Counts' laughter and watch as more sparks fly up into the darkened mind.

The Counts of the Netherworld
(July 1992)

MANIFESTO

I. LE MANIFESTE DES COMTES

The time has come to air the Voice of Reason,
In a world gone mad, adrift on banal seas,
For all who feel that lies have had their season,
And whose Hearts Cry Out, instead, for Honesty,

For all the weary souls grown bored with dreaming,
Whose thirst for Knowledge and for Beauty goes unslaked,
For all who long to wake from what is seeming,
And know what's Real, and what is Real, to embrace,

For all who've sat and watched with mounting horror,
Evil's reign upon this world grow ever-clear,
For all who've sought in vain, Emancipators,
Wielding Swords of Truth, and laughing without fear.

For all who've ever asked themselves in reference to the world. 'Is
it just me, or does this suck?' Take Heart!

It *does* suck, but you are not alone in thinking so. Behold the
Counts! Beacons encouraging the spark in every mind to join them
in illuminating the Netherworld of our Collective Unconscious.
Sleeper Awaken to the cry of players as they call for the Voice of
Reason in every mind to come forth in choir and sing hymns to
Beauty and Truth.

II. THEATRE DES DAMNES

The Counts are Bill Hicks, a misanthropic humanist, and Fallon Woodland, a humanistic misanthrope. Two opposites who have overcome their differences, and live in self-imposed exile from modern times and popular culture.

A Victorian era salon is their refuge from the shrieking idiocy of our times. It is here they revel in a world of ideas, surrounded by the Arcana of the Wizard – a globe, a telescope, a giant dictionary on a stand, and bookshelves sagging under the weight of the greatest thoughts from the greatest minds in human history.

Count William lounges in decadent repose upon a red velvet couch, dressed all in black and adorned with a rapier that shines as bright as the light of his intellect. Count Fallon hunches over a desk, scribbling furiously with feathered plume, an indictment against the enemies of Truth and Good Taste. A discussion about advertising has inspired Fallon's savage treatise. William leaps up and refers to the dictionary, looking for synonyms for the word Satan, in order to help Fallon, who's bogged down in a particularly tricky passage.

Typically, it was a specific egregious assault against Reason that has inspired this swift and vigorous counter attack by our two defenders of the Truth. In this instance, the culprit was an ad for a popular soda pop that featured a moribund and emasculated pop star singing one of his hits from yesteryear, only now using the name of the soda in place of the original lyric. This affront to the Count's sense of decency, has spooked their indefatigable minds on a wild discourse ranging from mankind's shameless worship of Money, to the dubious merit of hair weaves, and paying particular attention to the substance of our diet and its connection with the ever growing instances of illiteracy and sterility in the masses. Whereas Count William passionately advocates the probability of a government conspiracy involving the soda, the pop star, and illiteracy, Count Fallon begs to differ, and proposes, instead, an impressive theory connecting the hair weave, sterility, and the Prince of Darkness himself. It is at this point Count William leaps to the dictionary to find synonyms for Satan, to aid Fallon in further developing his remarkable hypothesis. It is just another day in the life of the Counts.

If all the world's a stage, and we but actors upon it, the Counts have taken this idea to its logical extreme playing characters who are themselves, in a Victorian era salon set in the present, in an empty turn-of-the-century theatre – The Theatre of The Damned.

In the world but not of it, the Counts explore the beliefs that rule our lives; celebrating ideas which free the human spirit, and skewering unmercifully those which chain us.

In the set but not of it, the Counts are able to roam freely through this metaphorical theatre – the world – perhaps even to venture outside in a horse drawn carriage, parading through the streets of London, where they can view the activities of modern man with their contemptuous glare.

But always they return to their safe haven, the salon, to discuss the affairs of the world, which they view with a critical eye and the sentiments of the Aesthete. It is in the salon where the Counts exult in the virtues of their misanthropy, and their complete rejection of popular opinion. It is only their irresistible humanism that keeps them from coming off as vicious cads. A great part of their charm is in watching them explore their dichotomous natures and defend the conclusions they have come to regarding mankind.

It is here in the salon where their inner voices are trusted and given vent to the passions of their minds. In this salon, all minds are invited to join them in celebrating a *new* philosophy for the world – the Philosophy of the Counts, which can be summed up very simply in this way: 'The Means and the End are the Same'. Herein lies Salvation.

III. MISANTHROPES UNIS!

The Counts' salon serves the purpose salons and their likenesses (i.e. the jazz clubs in the 50s, the coffee houses of the 60s) have served since time immemorial as bastions of free thinking, where ideas are explored that are alternative to the established belief, the party line, or popular opinion, during times of Revolution and of Renaissance.

In the Counts – Bill Hicks and Fallon Woodland – we have two eloquent satirists who, in their conversations on the topics of the day, offer a charming, enlightened, and highly dangerous take on mankind's troubled evolution. Whether it be discussions on Gun Control, Religion, Pornography, Advertising, Consumerism, Rationalism, Political Correctness, Relationships, Patriotism, Arms Dealing, Imperialism, or the Mass Media itself, one can rest assured their comments will ring with the resonance of Truth, or at least emotional honesty – a commodity in great demand by the young and young at heart the world over. That great number of souls who long to shake their fiery individuality in the face of convention; those long suppressed masses who seek heroes who give voice to the decency, common sense, and love of freedom that exists in us all. These heroes are the Counts – Spokesmen for the Damned.

The silent quests of the salon – the Audience – are privy to the over-the-top pomposity of these two free souls, as they give voice to every thought that excites them – no matter how profound or profane, ridiculous or sublime, in their never-ending love affair and courtship with the Truth.

Are they Angels, or are they Devils?

Precisely.

Be forewarned, the Counts will offer no apology or explanation, for in this Spiritual Odyssey, ultimately, all is forgiven. With this in mind, one can relish the antics of our heroes as they try nobly to illuminate mankind's collective unconscious, and act as a catharsis for this world's troubled soul. With Style, Wit, and Grace, the Count's philosophy unfolds with invitation for all to join them in making this odd, bittersweet journey called Life a glorious and satisfying end unto itself. In this we are committed,

Now, let us Embark . . .

CAPITOL HILL
(31 October, 1992)

Come November 3, it's odds-on that America will have a rock 'n' roll President in the White House. But if Bill Clinton takes the oath, the deal involves PMRC head-babe Tipper Gore too. Top US funnyman BILL HICKS casts a dry eye over the election circus . . .

With the presidential election currently taking place here, it has become more and more obvious that there is one political party in America, and that is – *THE BUSINESS PARTY.*

And, in order to placate the masses with the illusion of democracy, they hold a purely ceremonial election every four years while their propaganda arm – the corporate-owned mainstream media – obediently and even gleefully plays it to the hilt, as though there was actually a choice and you, the American people, were the ones getting to make that choice.

In looking over the current field of presidential hopefuls, I want you to tell me (and without laughing) that these men represent the best our country has to offer in the way of leadership and nobility (OK, you can laugh now)?

Who are these men? And who do they represent? Could it be they are the best the Business Party has to offer in the way of maximizing profits for the few, while pacifying the childlike masses with flag-waving, jingoistic rhetoric? Well? Is the choice between Democrat and Republican really a choice? There may be two sides to every coin, but what connects them is the coin.

Before going any further, you must understand one thing about my personal philosophy. I do not believe making money in order to consume goods is mankind's sole purpose on this planet. (If you're wondering what I believe our purpose on this planet is, I'll give you a hint . . . it has to do with creating and sharing.)

As you may have noticed, this idea is so far outside the allowance spectrum of debate that it is not even considered, much less voiced. Instead, this idea is relegated to the ash heap of history along with other radical fringe philosophies such as Gandhi's non-violent resistance and Christ's sermon on the mount.

It has been accepted, and without argument, that America's foremost problem is the economy. All the candidates have stated repeatedly the need to 'put America back to work'. Simultaneously, all the candidates have come out in support of the Free Trade Agreement with Mexico. Which will allow US corporations to shift their operations south of the border where they can hire a peasant workforce willing to work long hours for low pay without insurance or health benefits (retirement being a moot point, as the lack of environmental controls will return the average life span to what it was during the Jurassic period).

This begs the question – if there are no jobs in America, what exactly will Americans work at? Is it impossible to imagine, in the not too distant future, Americans sneaking into Mexico, en masse, seeking regular employment and a better way of life?

CANDIDATE-PRESIDENT

George Bush, in an effort to buy votes from an understandably nervous workforce, has made three decisions recently involving the military industrial complex. Decisions that will no doubt make the other nations of the world, particularly those nations not featuring a white majority, rest peacefully in their dungheaps at night.

The first is authorizing the go-ahead for the production of 30 new Stealth Bombers - the invisible fighter jet. Apparently, to help America defend itself against the invisible countries that threaten us daily. Looking around the world, I'm hard pressed to find any country that could possibly threaten us in any way, by any means, or by any stretch of the imagination (I'm speaking, of course, only of those countries we haven't armed first).

All the candidates soberly maintain that, even though the cold war is over, the world is still a very dangerous place, and I couldn't agree more. As long as war turns a profit for the elite oligarchy that rules this planet, you may rest assured those Stealth Bombers won't be gathering dust for long, but will be used to defend America in the event that some unanticipated, unforeseen, totally unexpected war might break out, say, for instance, around election time.

In a similar view, Bush OK'd the sale of 164 F-14 fighter jets to South Korea. This sale inspires two questions. First, what the hell does South Korea, or any country for that matter, need 164 fighter jets for? Secondly, how many fighter jets does it take to defend against 30 brand new Stealth Bombers?

If this line of questioning seems paranoid to you, you're wrong. It's cynical. I have no illusions that I, by myself, pose any threat to the current status quo. They who have effectively neutered and marginalized the population so greatly, that a coffee-table book of Madonna's twat constitutes a greater threat in Americans' minds than does a 150 billion dollar defence budget during peace time (more on Madonna's twat later.)

The third decision by Bush, and supported heartily by the other candidates, was the sale of 236 desert assault tanks to Kuwait, to be used by those notoriously dedicated, no-nonsense Kuwaitis. What an awesome spectacle they will make on Saturday night, parked outside the disco of the Cairo Hilton (remember the days when an Alfa Romeo was enough to impress the chicks?)!

The point I'm trying to make is this – regardless of where the candidates say they stand, or whose interest they say they represent, one very important issue seems to be beyond debate, and that is, the re-arming of the world in order to control it. Yes, America wants you to be free . . . as long as the choices offered can in no way effect real change or threaten the status quo. For all the lip service being paid by our candidates for the need to change, it looks like Business As Usual here in America.

So, who am I supporting? Which candidate best represents my interests?

As for me, I'm voting for Madonna's twat.

Recorded Live at the Dominion Theatre, London (November 1992)[41]

You're in the right place . . . It's Bill. I'm living out in Los Angeles now so, you know, I like coming over here, you know, for the weather. You guys *have* weather. Cool. Los Angeles, every day: hot and sunny; today: hot and sunny; tomorrow: hot and, for the rest of the . . . hot and sunny, every single day, hot and sunny. And they love it. 'Isn't it great, every day, hot and sunny?' What are you, a fucking lizard? Only reptiles feel that way about this kind of weather. I'm a *mammal*, I can afford coats, scarves, cappuccino and rosy-cheeked women.

LA is the home of the pedestrian right of way law. What this law is, is if a pedestrian decides to cross the road, anywhere or any time on the road, every car has to stop and let this person cross the road. Yes, cos only in LA does common courtesy have to be legislated. Ha ha ha. Every car has to stop. Pretty ludicrous in light of the city we're in now, right? If someone steps in front of your car here, you speed up and turn your wipers on, you know.

> (*makes sound of windscreen wipers*)
> 'Bad call, brother. Rrrrr.'
> 'Must've had a bad day. I don't know.'

Stupid law. How many of y'all wondered, like I did, during the LA riots,[42] when those people were being pulled out of their trucks and *beaten* half to death . . . how many of y'all wondered, like I did: step on the fucking *gas*, man!? They're on foot, you're in a truck . . . I think I see a way out of this! It's that pedestrian right of way law. People are driving home, a gang of youths stepped in front of their truck, Molotov cocktails, clubs in hand, everyone of these idiots: (*makes noise of car braking*). I guarantee you that Reginald Denny, that truck driver? . . . Never gonna stop again as long as he lives. Could be an old woman with a baby carriage crossing the road, he's: (*makes truck horn noise*). 'Not today, baby.'

Not a time to quit smoking, kids. (*laughs*) But I fucking did it. And yes, I miss 'em. It is hard to quit smoking. Every one of 'em looks real good to me right now. Every cigarette looks like it was made by God, rolled by Jesus . . . and moistened shut with Claudia Schiffer's pussy right now. (*makes heavy breathing sounds*) Golly, that looks tasty.

Every time I'm here something weird happens. This time, Bush lost . . . cool! People ask me where I stood politically, you know. It's not that I disagree with Bush's economic policy or his foreign policy . . . but I believe he was a child of Satan here to destroy the planet Earth. Yeah, I'm a little a little to the left there, I was. I was leaning that way, I think. Yeah, you know who else is gone? Little *Quayle boy*. Little *Damian*. Is that guy *Damian*? Tell me those blank empty eyes aren't gonna glow red in the very near future.

> 'Stop making jokes about meee. (*makes satanic snorting, growling noise*) I'll spell potato any fucking way I want. (*snorting, growling*) Rioters in LA – let's nuke them. Bush was a pussy. (*snorting, growling*) He held me back.'

Frightening people, man. Bush tried to buy votes towards the end of the election. Goes around, you know, selling weapons to everyone, getting that military industrial complex vote happening for him. Sold 160 fighter jets to Korea and then 240 tanks to Kuwait, and then goes around making speeches why *he* should be commander-in-chief, because, 'We still live in a dangerous world.' Thanks to you, you fucker! What are you doing? Last week Kuwaitis had nothing but rocks! Quit arming the fucking world, man. You know we armed Iraq. I wondered about that too, you know, during the Persian Gulf War those intelligence reports would come out: 'Iraq: incredible weapons – incredible weapons.' How do you know that?

'Uh, well . . . we looked at the receipt.[43] Ah but as soon as that cheque clears, we're going in. What time's the bank open? Eight? We're going in at nine. We're going in for God and country and democracy and here's a foetus and he's a Hitler.[44] Whatever you fucking need, let's go. Get motivated behind this, let's *go!*'

Oh, oh, looks like Mr Major's on the hot seat there for a second too. Little Iraq-gate,[45] little rapscallion he is. 'Did we send, did I do . . . did . . . I'll have to check Maggie's old calendar.' What's funny about this, every one of your papers says that you guys sold Iraq *'machine tools'* . . . which Iraq then *converted* . . . into military equipment. I have news for you, folks: a *cannon* . . . is a machine tool. Your Orwellian language notwithstanding, it's a fucking machine, it's a tool. Our papers in the States have the same thing. We sold Iraq *'farming* equipment' which Iraq then *'converted'*. How did they do this?

'Simsalabim, simsalabim, oooh salabim, sim sim sim salabim.'
'Wow! It was a chicken coop; it's now a nuclear reactor!'
'This war's for Aladdin.'

Farming equipment which they converted into military, OK, you got me, I'm curious, exactly what kind of farming equipment is this?

'Oh! OK, well, it was stuff for the farmers of Iraq.'
'Yeah? What?'
'Ooh OK, ahhh well, ooh, one of the things we gave them was for the farmer. It's a new thing we came up with called ah, the ah, flame-throwing rake. No it was for the farmer, see. He would rake the leaves and then just turn around. (*makes explosion noise*) But you know what the Iraqis did with that?'
'There's no trees in Iraq, what are you sending them rakes for, you asshole?'
'We could have done our research better perhaps, yes.'
'What else did you sell 'em?'

'OK, ah one of the other things we gave 'em was a new thing . . . for the farmer. The, ahh, armoured tractor. No, see, farmers when they farm would look over their shoulders at times and ah they won't see a tree and they'll hit it maybe and there'll be a wasp's nest in the tree and the wasps will come in and sting 'em. So we put four inches of armour all over the tractor. And a turret to shoot pesticide on the wasps. Yeah, but you know what the Iraqis did with that? Can't trust 'em.'

I'm so sick of arming the world and then sending troops over to destroy the fucking arms, you know what I mean? We keep arming these little countries, then we go and blow the shit out of 'em. We're like the bullies of the world, you know. We're like Jack Palance in the movie *Shane* . . . throwing the pistol at the sheep herder's feet:

'Pick it up.'
'I don't wanna pick it up, mister; you'll shoot me.'
'Pick up the gun.'
'Mister, I don't want no trouble, huh. I just came down town here to get some hard rock candy for my kids, some gingham for my wife. I don't even know what gingham is, but she goes through about ten rolls a week of that stuff. I ain't looking for no trouble, mister.'
'Pick up the gun.' (*three gunshots*)
'You all saw him. He had a gun.'

Kennedy. I love talking about the Kennedy assassination, because to me it's a great example of, ah, a totalitarian government's ability to, you know, manage information and thus keep us in the dark; anyway they . . . oh sorry, wrong meeting . . . ah, shit. That's the meeting we're having tomorrow at the docks. I love talking about Kennedy. I was just down in Dallas, Texas. You know you can go down there and, ah, to Dealey Plaza where Kennedy was assassinated. And you can actually go to the sixth floor of the Schoolbook Depository. It's a museum *called* . . . the Assassination Museum. I think they named that *after* the assassination. I can't be too sure of the chronology here but . . . Anyway, they have the window set up to look exactly like it did on that day. And it's really accurate, you know, cos Oswald's not in it. 'Yeah, yeah so . . . wow, that's cool.' *Painstaking* accuracy, you know. It's true, it's called the Sniper's Nest. It's glassed in, it's got the boxes sitting there. You can't actually get to the window itself, and the reason they did that of course, they didn't want thousands of American tourists getting there each year going, 'No fucking WAY! I can't even see the ROAD! Shit, they're *lying* to us. FUCK! WHERE ARE THEY? THERE'S NO FUCKING WAY.' Not unless Oswald was *hanging by his toes*, upside down from the *ledge*. Either that or some pigeons grabbed on to him, flew him over the *motorcade* . . . surely someone would have seen that. You know there was rumours of anti-Castro pigeons seen drinking in bars . . . Someone overhead them saying, 'Coup, coup. Coup.' Unbelievable. And you know what's wild, people's, ah, attitudes in the States about it. Talking about Kennedy, people come up to me: 'Bill, quit talking about Kennedy, man. Let it go. It's a long time ago, just forget about it.' And I'm like:

> 'All right, then don't bring up Jesus to me. As long as we're talking shelf life here.'
> 'Bill, you know Jesus died for you.'
> 'Yeah, well it was a long time ago. Forget about it! How about this. Get Pilate to release the fucking files. Quit washing your hands, Pilate. Release the goddamn files. Who else was on that grassy Golgotha that day?'
> 'Bill, it was just, you know, ha ha, taking over of democracy by a totalitarian government, let it *go*.'
> (*snorts*) 'OK, sorry.'

That's another good thing about Bush being gone, man, cos for the last twelve years with Reagan and Bush, we have had fundamentalist Christians in the White House. Fundamentalist Christians who believe the Bible is the exact word of God, including that wacky fire and brimstone *Revelations ending*, have had their finger on the fucking button for twelve years. 'Tell me when, Lord, tell me when. Let me be your servant, Lord.' Fundamentalist Christianity: fascinating. These people actually believe that the Bi— ah, the world is 12,000 years old. Swear to God. Based on what? I asked them.

'Well, we looked at all the people in the Bible and we
added 'em up all the way back to Adam and Eve, their
ages? 12,000 years.'
'Well, how fucking scientific, OK. I didn't know that
you'd gone to so much trouble there. That's good. You
believe the world's 12,000 years old?'
'That's right.'
'OK, I got one word to ask you, a one-word question,
ready?'
'Uh huh.'
'*Dinosaurs.*'

You know, the world's 12,000 years old and dinosaurs existed, and
existed in that time, you'd think it would have been mentioned in
the fucking Bible at some point:

And O, Jesus and the disciples walked to Nazareth. But
the trail was blocked by a giant brontosaurus . . . with
a splinter in his paw. And O, the disciples did run a
shriekin': 'What a big fucking lizard, Lord!' But Jesus
was unafraid and he took the splinter from the brontosaurus's paw and the big lizard became his friend. And
Jesus sent him to Scotland where he lived in a loch for
O so many years, inviting thousands of American tourists
to bring their fat fucking families and their fat dollar
bills. And O, Scotland did praise the Lord: 'Thank you
Lord, thank you Lord. Thank you Lord.'

But get this, I actually asked one of these guys, 'OK, dinosaurs
fossils – how does that fit into your scheme of life? Let me sit
down and strap in.' He said:

'Dinosaur fossils? God put those here to test our faith.'
'Thank God I'm strapped in right now here, man. I think
God put you here to test my faith, dude. You believe that?'
'Uh huh.'

Does that trouble anyone here? The idea that God might be . . .
fuckin' with our heads? I have trouble sleeping with that knowledge.

Some prankster God running around: 'Huh huh huh ho ho ho ho. We will see who believes in me now, ha ha . . . I am God, I am a prankster. I am killing Me. Huh ho ho ho.' You know, you die and go to St Peter:

> 'Did you believe in dinosaurs?'
> 'Well, yeah. There was fossils everywhere. (*makes sound of trapdoor opening*) Aaaaaaarhhh!'
> 'You fuckin idiot. Flying lizards, you're a moron. God was fuckin' with you!'
> 'It seemed so plausible, ahhhh!'
> 'Enjoy the lake of fire, fucker!'

They believe this. You ever noticed how people who believe in Creationism look really unevolved? You ever notice that? Eyes real close together, eyebrow ridges, big furry hands and feet. 'I believe God created me in one day.' Yeah, looks liked he rushed it. They believe the Bible is the exact word of God, *then* they *change* the Bible! Pretty presumptuous, huh? 'I think what God meant to say . . .' I have never been that confident. Next we have a Bible out called The New Living Bible. It's the Bible in updated and modern English. I guess to make it more palatable for people to read. But it's really weird, when you listen to it. 'And Jesus walked on water. And Peter said, "Awesome!"' Suddenly we got Jesus hanging ten across the Sea of Galilee. Christ's Bogus Adventure, you know. Deuteronomy 90210, you know.

Such a weird belief. Lot of Christians wear crosses around their necks. You think when Jesus comes back he's gonna want to see a fucking cross, man? 'Ow.' May be why he hasn't shown up yet.

> 'Man, they're still wearing crosses. Fuck it, I'm not goin', Dad. No, they totally missed the point. When they start wearing fishes I might show up again, but . . . let me bury fossil heads with you Dad, fuck 'em, let's fuck with 'em! They're fuckin' with me now, let's get 'em. Give me that brontosaurus head, Dad.'

You know, it's kinda like going up to Jackie Onassis with a rifle pendant on, you know. 'Thinkin' of John, Jackie. We love him. Just tryin' to keep that memory alive, baby.' Back and to the left, back and to the left, back and to the left, back and to the left. Which, by the way, that action you see Kennedy's head do in the Zapruder film – caused by a bullet . . . comin' from up there, ha ha. Yeah, I know it looks to the layman or someone who might dabble in physics . . . This action here would have been caused by a bullet coming from . . . well . . . up *here*, did you see that? Did everyone see that? Yeah, but no. What happened was Oswald's gun went off, causing an echo to echo through the buildings of Dealey Plaza, and the echo went by the limo on the left, up into the grassy knoll, hitting some leaves, causing dust to fly out, which fifty-six witnesses testified was a gunshot, cos immediately . . . Kennedy's head went over. But the reason his head went over is cos the echo went by the motorcade on the left, and he went 'What was that?'

'So there, we have figured it out, go back to bed, America: your government has figured out how it all transpired. Go back to bed, America: your government is in control again. Here, here's *American Gladiators*. Watch this! Shut up! Go back to bed, America: here's *American Gladiators*. Here's fifty-six channels of it. Watch these pituitary retards bang their fuckin' skulls together and congratulate you on living in the Land of Freedom. Here you go, America. You are free – to do as we tell you. You are free – to do as we tell you.'

'Oh good. Honey, I heard on the news that they've figured out that the gun, what happened is, is that there was an echo and Kennedy was, ah, asking ah Jackie what it was, and that's why his head flew u— Honey what time's *Gladiators* on? Are we missing it? Wooo, I'm so glad we're free, honey.'

This was just a few weeks ago. All these articles in the paper. 'Is *Gladiators* too violent? And what are we doing watching this? Is it really good for us to watch? Is it too violent?' NO! Fuck it! Give these guys chainsaws! Let them fuck each other up good. It's not violent enough. Let these fuckin' morons *kill* each other in that goddamn pit! Give them chainsaws an' . . . I want to see a fuckin' railway spike go through their eyeballs. How about this? Give everyone in the audience a pistol. 'There, you fuckers! (*makes sound of gunshots*) See who comes out alive! (*gunshots*) You know, I'm tired of this false fuckin' sanctimonious morality about *life*. 'Ain't life keen, ha ha. Let's pat ourselves on the back.' FUCK you! They want to kill each other, I'm filming it. You know?

I, I had a great idea for the movies. No one wants to fucking hear it, I don't know why. I was watching *Terminator 2*, and I'm thinking to myself, these are the most amazing stunts I have ever seen. A hundred million dollars it cost to make this film. *How* are they ever gonna top these stunts in a movie again? There's no way. Unless . . . they start using terminally ill people . . . hear me out . . . as *stuntmen* in pictures. OK, not the most popular idea ever, but I prefaced it with that. What? You know, some of you probably think that's cruel, don't you? 'Ooh, it's cruel, terminally ill stuntpeople? Biiill. How cruel.' You know what I think what cruel is? Leaving your loved ones to die in some sterile hospital room surrounded by strangers. Fuck that! Put 'em in the movies! Whaaat? Do you want your grandmother dying like a little bird in some hospital room? Her translucent skin so thin you can see her last heartbeat work its way down her blue vein? Or do you want her to meet Chuck Norris? Why be so selfish as to deprive her of that thrill?

> 'Doc, how come you dressed my grandmother up as a mugger?'
> 'Shut up and get off the set. Action! Push her towards Chuck.'
> (*sound of karate kick*)
> 'Wow, he kicked her head right off her body! Did you *see* that? Did you see my grammy? She's out of her misery. I just saw the greatest fucking movie of my life. Cool!'

OK, not the most popular idea ever. All I'm saying is people are dying every day, and movies are getting more and more boring. I am the weaver. I don't know . . . (*whispers*) 'Is *American Gladiators* too violent? Ooh, I don't know.' Watch the fucking news, man; it's frightening. What could be worse? You watch the news these days, you know, it's unbelievable. You think you just walk out your door, you're immediately going to be raped by some crack-addicted, Aids-infected pitbull, you know. Horrible news stories, you know.

> 'Honey, I'm gonna check the mail . . .'
> (*makes sound of pitbull savaging something, then door slamming*)
> 'Whaddya say we stay inside tonight, baby? Let's let the pizza delivery guy deal with that shit out there. Hello? Pizza delivery, could you send another car over please. I know that's your third one, that last guy almost made it. I can almost reach the pizza box with the broom handle. How come those pitbulls are eating your driver but they're not touching that fucking pizza? What do they know that we don't know, *hellooo*?'

Pretty soon we're all gonna be locked inside our homes with no one on the street but pizza delivery guys and armoured cars with turrets shooting pizzas through the mail-slots of our front doors. Every house will glow with *American Gladiators* beamed in. 'We are free – keep repeating, *we are free.*' The news is just apocalyptic. Didn't you think with the Cold War being over, things should have gotten better? How many of y'all were as stupid as I was in believing that? Wow, it's over, forty years of threat of nuclear weapons, it's over, cool, cool . . . WRONG! Now twelve different countries have nuclear weapons, it just got twelve times as bad, fuck you! Life is harder now. Work more – oop, jobs are scarce, fuck you! Ha ha ha ha ha ha.

By the way, if anyone here is in advertising or marketing . . . kill yourself. Thank you, thank you, thanks. Just a little thought. I'm just trying to plant seeds. Maybe, maybe one day, they'll take root – I don't know. You try, you do what you can. Kill yourself. Seriously though, if you are, do. Aaaah, no really, there's no rationalization for what you do, and you are Satan's little helpers. OK? Kill yourself, seriously. You are the ruiner of all things good, seriously. No, this is not a joke. You're going, 'There's going to be a joke coming', there's no fucking joke coming. You are Satan's spawn filling the world with bile and garbage. You are fucked and you are fucking us. Kill yourself. It's the only way to save your fucking soul, kill yourself. Planting seeds. I know all the marketing people are going, 'He's doing a joke.' There's no joke here whatsoever. Suck a tailpipe, fucking *hang* yourself, borrow a gun from a Yank friend – I don't care how you do it. Rid the world of your evil fucking machinations. Machina– Whatever, you know what I mean.

I know what all the marketing people are thinking right now, too: 'Oh, you know what Bill's doing? He's going for that anti-marketing dollar. That's a good market, he's very smart.' Oh man, I am not doing that. You fucking *evil* scumbags! 'Ooh, you know what Bill's doing now? He's going for the righteous indignation dollar. That's a big dollar. A lot of people are feeling that indignation. We've done research – huge market. He's doing a good thing.' Goddamn it, I'm *not* doing that, you *scumbags*! Quit putting a goddamn dollar sign on every fucking thing on this planet! 'Ooh, the anger dollar. Huge. Huge in times of recession. Giant market, Bill's very bright to do that.' God, I'm just caught in a fucking web. 'Ooh, the trapped dollar, big dollar, huge dollar. Good market – look at our research. We see that many people feel trapped. If we play to them, and then separate them into the trapped dollar . . .' How do you live like that? And I bet you sleep like fucking babies at night, don't you? 'What did ya do today, honey?' 'Oh, we made ah, we made ah arsenic ah childhood food now, good night. (*snores*) Yeah we just said, you know, "Is your baby really too loud?" You know. (*snores*) Yeah, you know, the mums will love it.' (*snores*) Sleep like fucking children, don't ya? This is *your* world, isn't it?

But, you know, I saw this movie this year called ah, *Basic Instinct*. OK now. Bill's quick capsule review: piece of shit. OK now. Yeah, yeah, end of story, by the way. Don't get caught up in that fevered hype, phoney fucking debate about that piece-of-shit movie. 'Is it too sexist? And what about the movies? Are they becoming too blah, blah, blah, blah.' You're, you're just confused, you don't get, you've forgotten how to judge correctly. Take a deep breath (*breathes in*), look at it again. 'Oh it's a piece of shit!' Exactly, that's *all* it is. Satan squatted, let out a loaf, they put a fucking title on it, put it

on a marquee, Satan's shit, piece of shit, walk away. 'But is it too
. . . what about the lesbian connota– blah, blah, blah, blah .' You're,
you're getting really baffled here. Piece of shit! Now walk away.
THAT'S ALL IT IS; IT'S NOTHING MORE! Free yourself folks,
if you see – piece of shit, say it and walk away. You're *right*! *You're*
right! Not those fuckers who want to tell you how to think! YOU'RE
FUCKING RIGHT! Sorry, wrong meeting again. I keep getting my
days mixed up. Tomorrow it's the meeting at the docks. Tonight it's
comedy entertainment with young *Bill*! Horrible film. And then I
come to find out after that film, that all the lesbian sex scenes, let
me repeat that, *all* . . . all the lesbian sex scenes were cut out of
that film, because the *test* audience was turned off by them. Ha!
Boy, is my thumb not on the pulse of America.

I don't want to seem like Randy Pan the Goatboy, but ah . . . that
was the only reason I went to that piece of shit. If I had been in that
test audience, the only one out front protesting that film would have
been Michael Douglas demanding his part be put back in, all right?

'I swear I was in that movie. I swear I was.'
'Gee Mike, the movie started. Sharon Stone was eating
another woman for an hour and a half. Then the credits rolled. I ah, I don't remember seeing your scrawny
ass, Mike.'
'Was Bill Hicks in that test audience?'
'Ha ha ha ha ha ha ha ha ha. Goatboy called it like he
saw it, Mikey. You made your 14 mill., now hit the fucking road. Goatboy has invited some people over to see
the video premiere of the *Goatboy* edited version. Ha
ha ha. I am Goatboy.

'What do you want, Goatboy? You big old smelly, shaggy
thing?'
'Ho ho ho. Goatboy is here to please you.'
'How?'
'Ha ha ha ha ha. Tie me to your headboard, throw your
legs over my shoulders and let me wear you like a feed-
bag.' (*makes snorting, sucking noise*)
'Aaargh!'

'Hold on to my horns.'
'Goatboyyyyy!'
'Yes, my love?'
'You're a big old smelly thing.'
'Ha ha ha ha ha.'

I need professional help at this point I think I need a priest at this point.

'Forgive me Father for I have sinned.'
'What have you done, my son?'
'Well, I said the word "fuck" gratuitously.'
'Yes and what else, my son?'
'Er . . . (giggles) I lied.'
'Yes, and what else my son?'
'That's about all – oh, oh, one thing: I keep thinking I'm
a randy goat, fucking everyone. Ha ha ha. Baaaaaa baa
baa.'

Unless of course it's a woman priest, in which case it'll go like this: forgive me, Father, for what I'm about to do. (sings) 'Ding ding ding ding.' People ask me what I think about that woman priest thing, you know. What, a woman priest? Women priests. Great, great. You know, now it's priests of both sexes I don't listen to. Fuck, I don't care. Have a hermaphrodite one. I don't fucking care. Have one with three dicks and eight titties, I don't, I don't . . . you know, have one with gills and a trunk. That would be cool. I might go see that, you know, but . . . You know, I appreciate your quaint traditions and superstitions. I, on the other hand, am an evolved being who deals solely with the source of life, which exists in all of our hearts. Ha ha ha ha ha. That middle man thing, it's *wacky* and I appreciate it . . . gotta run, there's a voice a-callin' me. Ha ha ha ha ha. Now, *you* guys are totally weird sexually. Here's why. Oh yeah, coming from Goatboy, oh boy. 'Yes Bill, and how is that? That we have *human* sex? Does that bother you, Bill?' Goatboy finds that disgusting. Where is the fun in that? Ha ha ha ha ha. Goatboy loves young girls. Sixteen years old, ooh Goatboy, hello.

'Hi Goatboy you big old smelly thing. Ooh, you smell like an old boot.'
'Ha ha ha ha. I don't see you running away.'
'I'm not scared of you . . . besides, your eyes are really kind and peaceful. Except for that fire that burns real far deep inside of 'em.'
'Ha ha ha ha.'
'Oh, Goatboy, what's that?'
'That is my purple wand and my hairy sack of magic.'
'You do tricks?'
'Ha ha ha ha.'
'What can you do with that?'
'Goatboy can make a bell ring in your stomach.'
'What does that bell mean?'
'It calls Goatboy to dinner, ha ha ha ha.' (*snorts*)
'Goatboy! Aargh!'

'OK Bill, stop with the Goatboy thing, we get it all right. It's kinda amusing but . . . OK.' You don't like Goatboy? Goatboy is hurt by your indifference. He wanted you to come dance with him in the pastures. Ding ding ding ding. Goatboy wants to string flowers through your hair, and on your head. Do do, do do, do do, do do de do.

'Why do you like young girls, Goatboy?'
'Because, you are beautiful. There's nothing between your legs, it's like a wisp of cotton candy framing a paper cut. Ha ha ha ha. (*snorts*) And turn you around and open your cheeks, it's like a little pink quivering rabbit nostril. Oh how cute! I bet your asshole tastes better than most girls' *pussies*. Come here.' (*snorting, sucking sound*)
'Goatboyyy!'
(*snorting, sucking*)
'Shaggy old thing. I'm not going to kiss you, I don't know where your mouth's been.'
'Do you want me to tell you?'

'OK, Bill, seriously, this Goatboy thing, quit it, it's getting weird.' Except for some of my goat children. (*makes bleating sound*)

'Morrrre, Faaather, morrrre, more Goatboy, Faather. We are your goat children. We, too, lay in the forest waiting for young virgins to come.' But you guys are weird – get this, man. I'm walking down through the West End one day, right, and this busload of tourists from Iowa gets off the bus. These big cow people, right? Bump into me and I go *flying* into this adult bookstore, OK? And my hands were in my pockets and I took 'em out and money *flew* out of my hand and wafted down on to the cash register, and this guy hands me a magazine. How embarrassing. I go home *immediately* to the hotel and throw it away. Towards the garbage, it breaks open, face up, on the bed. Give me a BREAK, Lord. But I'm looking at your British hardcore pornography, which I just spent HARD-core fucking dollars for. And I'm going, 'Something's wrong with this. Goatboy will figure it out!' I realize it's porno, yeah, just what we know and love, but there's blue dots covering all the good shit! What, whaaat's going on? There's a guy standing there like this. There's a woman kneeling, well . . . I believe she was like this. And there's this big blue dot right here. What the fuck! This comes off, I hope . . .What, you gotta buy the blue dot eraser separately? *What the fuck?* I'm an adult. Don't protect me. Let's *go*! Goatboy wants his money back. You know. And then I see a club in the West End that has this marquee sign, says 'Live Sex Show On Stage'. I thought, what a bummer actually to have to be the guy that holds the blue dot. All right, but what's weird is that's your hardcore porno, then you go home, turn on Channel 4 late at night, there's people fuck-ing, yeah, they're right there. No blue dot, just people fucking right there. Free, no money, people fucking. It's a foreign film: it's art all of a sudden. Hey! Put some subtitles in there. Here's your pussy, here, you got it. Everyone happy? There you go, it's art, goddamn it. All right, I see. You pay, you get ripped off – free, you get it all. Dig it, love it! . . . I am available for children's parties, by the way.

'Mommy, I want Goatboy to come play at our house.'
'Ha ha ha ha ha ha.'

But, you know . . . Pot! Right. They lie about marijuana. Tell you pot-smoking makes you unmotivated. *Liiie*. When you're high, you can do everything you normally do, just as well, you just realize it's not worth the fucking effort. There is a difference. (*inhales, as if from spliff*) Sure I can get up at dawn (*inhales*) go to a job I hate, that does not inspire me creatively whatsoever, (*inhales*) for the rest of my fucking life. (*inhales*) Or I can wake up at noon, and learn how to play the sitar! (*in monotone, repeatedly*) 'Now ning now ning ning ning now.' Pretty simple when it's spelled out in black and white, isn't it? You know. Only thing I've ever heard about pot is that pot might lower sperm count. *Good*! There's too many fucking people in the world. Someone needs to say that, by the way. Tired of this, 'Hey hey aren't we the coolest? Humans are so neat.' Too many of yer. Quit rutting, just for a fucking day. Let's work out this food/air deal. Then go back to your rutting.

But I'll tell you this. Where'd this idea that childbirth is a miracle come from? Ha, I missed that fucking meeting, OK? 'It's a miracle, childbirth is a miracle.' No, it's not. No more a miracle than eating food and a turd coming out of your ass. It's a chemical reaction, that's all it fucking is. If, you know, you wanna know what a miracle is – raisin' a kid that doesn't talk in a movie theatre. OK, there, there, there is a goddamn miracle. It's not a miracle if every nine months any yin yang in the world can drop a litter of these mewling cabbages on our planet. And just in case you haven't seen the single mom statistics lately, the miracle is spreading like *wild-fire*. 'Hallelujah!' Trailer parks and council flats all over the world just filling up with little miracles. Thunk, thunk, thunk, like frogs laying eggs.

> 'Thunk. Look at all my little miracles, thunk, filling up my trailer like a sardine can. Thunk. You know what would be a real miracle, if I could remember your daddy's name, aargh, thunk. I guess I'll have to call you Lorry Driver Junior. Thunk. That's all I remember about your daddy was his fuzzy little pot-belly riding on top of me, shooting his caffeine-ridden semen into my belly to produce my little water-headed miracle baby, urgh, thunk. There's your brother, Pizza Boy Delivery Junior.'

'Hallelujah!' Hold on for a minute, let's figure out this food/air deal, OK? K. I'm just weird, you know? How about have a neat world for kids to come *to*? Ha ha, OK, it's me, OK. Drop 'em like fucking flies, boom. Just fill up the world with 'em. I just don't get it, you know. I mean, I'm sorry man, you know, kids are fine, just keep 'em away from me. All right? There. All right?'

Now, get this: I've been travelling all over the country on British Air. No smoking on British Air. Now let me get this straight: no smoking, right, *but* they allow children. Little fairness, huh? 'Well, smoking bothers me.' Well guess what? I was on this one flight, right, I'm flying, I'm sleeping on the plane, I'm fucking 'knackered'. Very tired, right, and I feel this tapping on my head. And I look up, and there's this little kid . . . *loose*! On the fucking plane, he's just loose. It's his playground in the sky. And he has decided that his job is to repetitively tap me on the top of the head. I look across the aisle at his mom. She's just smiling, you know. Guy next to the mom goes, 'They're so cute when they're that small.' Isn't that amazing, letting your kid run loose on a fucking plane? And then the kid runs over to the emergency exit, and he starts flipping that handle to the door. And the guy next to the mom starts to get up, and I go:

> 'Wait a minute . . . we're about to learn an important lesson right here. (*makes sound of explosive decompression*) Boy, you're right: the smaller he gets, the cuter he is. God, I wish I had a camera right now. With a telescopic lens. Love to get a picture of his face when his pudgy little legs hit that farmhouse down there. Aah, aah, kids. Ha ha ha. Stewardess, since we got a breeze in here can we smoke now? Fairly well circulated at this point.' (*breathes in*)

True story. But, you know.

Why is marijuana against the law? It grows naturally upon our planet. Doesn't the idea of making nature against the law seem to you a bit . . . paranoid? You know what I mean? It's *nature*. How do you make nature against the fucking law? It grows everywhere. Serves a thousand different functions, all of them positive. To make marijuana against the law is like saying *God* made a mistake. You know what I mean? It's like God on the seventh day looking down on his creation:

'There it is, my creation, perfect and holy in all ways. Now, I can rest . . . Oh my Me . . . I left fucking pot everywhere . . . I should never have smoked that joint on the third day . . . shit . . . That was the day I created possums. Ha ha ha. Ohhh, still gives me a chuckle . . . If I leave pot everywhere, that's gonna give humans the impression they're supposed to . . . *use* it. Now I have to create Republicans.'

'And God wept' . . . I believe is the next verse. You know what I mean? I believe that God left certain drugs growing naturally upon our planet to help speed up and facilitate our evolution. OK, not the most popular idea ever expressed. Either that or you're real high and agreeing with me in the only way you can right now. 'I forgot the code – is it two blinks "yes", one blink "no"?' Do you think magic mushrooms growing atop cow shit was an accident? Where do you think the phrase, 'that's good shit' came from? Why do you think Hindus think cows are holy? Holy shit! Why do I think McDonald's is the Anti-Christ? That's God's little accelerator pad for our evolution. Let's think about this, man.

For billions of years – sorry, fundamentalists – we were nothing but apes. (*makes chimp noises*) Probably too stupid to catch a cow, you know . . . (*chimp noises and mime ending in laughter*). 'I think we can go to the moon.' (*hums theme tune from* 2001: A Space Odyssey) That is exactly how it fucking happened. Except for the marketing people, whose belief is, 'No, it was proven that ah it might be a good market on the moon and aah and a lot of people went up there, good numbers, good space numbers . . .' Urgh. Save your story of creation, please.

Not all drugs are good, now. OK? Some of 'em are great. Just gotta know your way around 'em is all. Yeah, I've had good times on drugs. I've had bad times on drugs, too. I mean, shit, look at this haircut. There are dangers. Think some of y'all have tripped here before perhaps, yeah? I used to love tripping, man. There's always one guy when you're tripping who wants you to do something to enhance the trip. You know what I'm talking about.

'You're tripping? Oh *duuude*, you gotta play miniature golf.'

'Ha ha ha ha ha, yeah, that's exactly what I was thinking, man. I'm just sitting over here watching the pyramids
be built by UFOs right now, but get me to that fucking
golf course. I'm watching Jesus flying around on a unicorn,
but I bet that little miniature golf would be just the thing
to make this trip . . . peak. So you guys can use your legs,
huh? No, it's just that I'm turning into a fish right now
and ah . . . how 'bout I meet you there later? . . . Thanks,
I'm pretty fucking high right now. Thank you.'

You know. You just gotta be careful. I don't know what you gotta
be, fuck it. We got pulled over tripping on acid one night, pulled
over by the cops. Don't recommend it. Cops don't appreciate *fish*
driving around. They *frown* on that. Long night, man. Cops were
tapping on *this* window. We're staring at him in *this* mirror.

'How tall are you?'
'It's a liddle cop, look at him!'
'How does he drive that big fucking car?'
'Urr, there could be thousands of them, shit!'
'What are we gonna do?'
'Let's put him in the jar.'

Made perfect sense at that moment. Put him in a jar, poke some
holes in the lid, leave him by the road.

'You'll never get us, copper. Ha ha.'
'We'll send some little firemen to let you out.'
'Hey, I bet they know where the miniature golf course
is!'
'Boo! Ha ha. *Fuck* it, they scared us.'
'Son, d'you wanna stand up, please?'
'I just found the driver.'
'We don't need a driver, we're playing miniature golf.'

True story. *Now*, later, when I was released . . . I mean spiritually
. . . I feel . . .

'I need to see some ID.'
'I'm me, he's him, you're you.'

'Put your hands against the car, please.'
'Which one? The UFO, the unicorn or your cruiser?'

Drugs have done good things for us. If you don't believe they have, do me a favor – take all your albums, tapes, and CDs and burn 'em, cos you know what? The musicians who made that great music that has enhanced your lives throughout the years? *Rrrrreal* fucking high, ha ha ha ho ho ho ho. OK And these other musicians today who don't do drugs, and in fact speak out against them? Boy, do they suck! What a coincidence! Ball-less, soulless, spiritless, corporate little bitches, suckers of Satan's cock, each and every one of them. (*makes snorting, snarling noise*) 'We're rock stars against drugs, cos that's what the President wants.' Aw, suck Satan's cock. That's what we want, isn't it? Government-approved rock 'n' roll?   Whooo, we're partying now!

'We're rock stars who do Pepsi Cola commercials.'
(*makes snorting, snarling noise*) 'Suck Satan's cock. Put that big scaly pecker down your gullet. Drink that black worm jism. Drink it! Fill your little bellies. Ha ha haaaaa. Send in Vanilla Ice. Hello Vanilla. Says here on your application you have no talent, and yet you want to be a star. I think something can be arranged. (*Whoosh, crash!*) Suck Satan's cock. (*makes snorting, snarling noise*) I will lower the standards of the earth. (*snorting, snarling*) I will put fifty-six channels of *American Gladiators* on every TV. I will put all the money in the hands of fourteen-year-old girls. They will think you are charismatic, deep and edgy. (*snorting; makes sound of screaming orgasm*) Send in MC Hammer on your way out. Hello Hammer. Back again, huh?'

Boy, that Hammer. There was another boat that left me on the island, man.

'Bill, are you gonna get on the Hammer boat with us?'
'No, I'd rather stay here and eat my own flesh.'
(*makes boat horn sound*)

Totally mystifying, I mean, you know, you could sit and explain it to me from now until, well, the end of time, and I'll go, 'Fucking don't get it, man.' I, I, I, it . . . it's geni— it's geni— it's con . . . genital? It's, err, genetic! Maybe it is genital, hey, wait a minute. Freud, come here! 'Hammer's a great dancer.' Whaaat? The guy's gotta sand crab in his knickers. He's not dancing – he's having a fit! That's Satan's sperm eating its way through the lining of his stomach. (*makes snorting, snarling noise*) Fifteen minutes almost up, Hammer! (*snorting, snarling, then crashing noise*) Ha ha ha ha ha ha ha ha. Send in Marky Mark. And the beat goes . . . yeah. I don't know, it's good for the voice. Hey, don't fuck with me, man. You know what I mean though – am I the only one that's fucking lost here?

You never see positive drugs stories on the news, do ya? Isn't that weird? Cos most of the experiences I've had on drugs, were rrreal fucking positive. Ah. Who are these morons they're finding, that's what I wanna know. I used to want to call the news:

> 'Come over to our house! Watch Tommy, he's a pig –
> film him!'
> 'Oink oink, oink oink.'
> 'Hee hee, he's been doing that for hours. He's killing us.
> You getting all that?'

You know what I mean? Always that same LSD story; you've all seen it. 'Young man on acid, thought he could fly, jumped out of a building. What a tragedy.' What a dick, fuck him! He's an idiot. If he thought he could fly, why didn't he take off from the ground first? Check it out. You don't see *ducks* lining up to catch elevators to fly south. They fly from the ground, you moron. Quit ruining it for everybody. He's a moron, he's dead – *good*. We lost a moron – fucking celebrate. Boy, I just felt the world get lighter, we lost a moron. Put on the Hammer album, I'm ready to dance! . . . 'We lost a moron.' I don't mean to sound cold or cruel or vicious, but I *am*, so that's the way it comes out. Professional help is being sought.

How about a positive LSD story? Wouldn't that be newsworthy, just for once? To base your decision on information rather than scare tactics and superstitions . . . and lies? I think it would be newsworthy:

'Today, a young man on acid realized that all matter is merely energy condensed to a slow vibration. That we are all one consciousness experiencing itself subjectively. There is no such thing as death, life is only a dream and we're the imagination of ourselves. Here's Tom with the weather.'

You've been fantastic and I hope you enjoyed it. There is a point – is there a point to all of this? Let's find a point. Is there a point to my act? I would say there is. I have to. The world is like a ride at an amusement park. And when you choose to go on it, you think that it's real because that's how powerful our minds are. And the ride goes up and down and round and round. It has thrills and chills, and it's very brightly colored, and it's very loud and it's fun, for a while. Some people have been on the ride for a long time, and they begin to question – is this real, or is this just a ride? And other people have remembered, and they come back to us. They say, 'Hey! Don't worry, don't be afraid, ever, because, this is just a ride.' And we . . . *kill* those people. Ha ha ha. 'Shut him up! We have a lot invested in this ride. SHUT HIM UP! Look at my furrows of worry. Look at my big bank account and my family. This just has to be real.' It's just a ride. But we always kill those good guys who try and tell us that, you ever notice that? And let the demons run amok. But it doesn't matter *because*: it's just a ride. And we can change it any time we want. It's only a choice. No effort, no work, no job, no savings and money. A choice, right now, between fear and love.

The eyes of fear want you to put bigger locks on your doors, buy guns, close yourself off. The eyes of love, instead, see all of us as one. Here's what we can do to change the world, right now, to a better ride. Take all that money that we spend on weapons and defence each year, and instead spend it feeding, clothing and educating the poor of the world, which it would many times over, not one human being excluded, and we could explore space, together, both inner and outer, for ever, in peace. Thank you very much, you've been great. I hope you enjoyed it. London, you were fantastic, thank you, thank you very much.

(*three gunshots*)

Recorded Live at the Oxford Playhouse, UK (11 November 1992)[46]

I t's great to be here, wherever I am. I always love it when I'm here. (*sighs*) If I've never been here before, it's great to be back, and ah . . . Pardon the way I'm dressed. I just got back from my wedding in Cowley and ah . . . I'd like you to meet my new bride, but she's . . . hurling in the toilet right now, and she'll be out later, soon as she's done. (*shouts from audience*) All right, one at a time now. Let's go now. Gonna have to take a number.

People often ask me where I stand politically. It's not that I disagree with Bush's economic policy or his foreign policy, it's that I believe . . . he was a child of Satan here to destroy the planet Earth. Little to the left. And it's weird – politics does make strange bedfellows, man. You know, when the dust settles, to see what side you're on. It's really odd, you know what I mean? I was reading in the paper on ah Tuesday, Wednesday, after the elections were over, and there was a quote from Saddam Hussein, going: 'We have nothing against America. We just want to see George Bush beheaded, and his head kicked down the road like a soccer ball.' I'm thinking, 'That's what *I* wanna see. Cool, me and Hussein! We're like *this*, man! Saddam!' You know Hussein is just still laughing in some basement bunker somewhere when that fucking election came around and he lost, huh? That's what bugged me– Hussein's still in power, that's the crack-up of all time to me, you know. CIA has a plot to get rid of him. It's a plot they've used before to get rid of world leaders. Only problem they're havin' is convincing Hussein, you know . . . to fly to Dallas . . . and ah, yeah. I think, once there, the plan is fairly, you know, we got it. It's pretty operable. Can't say Dallas doesn't love you, Saddam. (*laughs*)

But ah, see, you know what bugged me about the whole election? Was that they made it, you know, they totally reduced it to this worship of money, and that's what they made the whole election about, was *taxes*, you know? Voting with your *wallet*, you know what I mean? People would say to me, 'Bill, you vote for Clinton, he's gonna raise your taxes, OK? I mean, he'll tell you he's not . . . but he's gonna. A vote for Clinton is a vote for higher taxes, Bill.' See, I have news for ya, folks: there's other reasons not to vote for George Bush than taxes, OK? I don't know what's happened to us as a world – maybe twelve years of Republicanism has made us think this way. But the reason I didn't vote for George Bush is because George Bush, along with Ronald Reagan, presided over an administration whose policies towards South America included *genocide*.[47] (*laughs*) So, yeah, you see . . . the reason *I* didn't vote for him is *cos he's a mass murderer*. Yeah. I, yeah. OK. Yeah. Yeah. I'll . . . I'll pay that extra nickel on, you know, a litre of petrol just knowing little brown kids aren't being clubbed to death like baby seals in Honduras so Pepsi can put a plant down there. I'll pay the extra nickel. And Bush, looking horrible the last few days, was wonderful to watch. Just little– he was just whiney and little– he looked terrible. He looked like Skeletor, man. For Hallowe'en they put a candle in the back of his throat, and he went out as a jack-o'-lantern. 'Heh, heh, heh, heh.' But he's trying to buy votes, you know. He sells 164 fighter jets to South Korea, he sells 240 tanks to Kuwait, and then he has these speeches where he goes, 'We still live in a dangerous world.' Thanks to *you*! Fuck, before that Kuwait had *rocks*, man.

He authorizes the production of more Stealth Bombers. The invisible fighter jet: I guess to help us defend ourselves against the invisible countries that threaten us every fucking day . . . to be named later. I'm looking around the globe – there's no one that can threaten America ever again. It's over. We know Russia was a fucking lie, anyway. There's nothing there. There's nothing anywhere. How does it feel to find out *we* are the evil empire? Ha ha ha! There's no one who can threaten us, man, and I'm talking now only of countries we don't arm first, OK? So if you wanna argue on that level, you have a point. We keep arming these little countries and then going blowing the shit out of 'em. We're like the bullies of the globe. We're like Jack Palance in the movie *Shane*, throwing the pistol at the sheep herder's feet.

> 'Pick it up.'
> 'I don't wanna pick it up. You'll shoot me.'
> 'Pick up the gun.'
> 'I don't want any trouble, mister. I just came into town to get some hard rock candy for the kids and some . . . gingham for my wife. Let me get back to my sheep farm, mister. I don't want no trouble.'
> 'Pick up the gun.(*three gunshots*) You all saw him. He had a gun.'

(*singing*) 'America.' That's my little Western skit.

You know, find out Bush has sold weapons to Iraq since '86. Some of your fuckers have been selling weapons to 'em too, huh? That's what bugged me about Bush, man, this whole thing about him being a foreign policy expert, you know what I mean? 'Yeah, well, you know, when it comes to foreign policy, George Bush is the man I trust. He's got the . . . you know, experience and the . . . look at the coalition against Iraq. Incredible. Incredible, that *huge* coalition, that *giant* coalition that included . . . England.' Yeah, that must've been hard. The two predominantly white nations going blowing the shit out of this little brown nation. What a hard sell that must have been for John Major, huh?

> 'John, George Bush. How are ya? Good. We have disgruntled masses getting really bored here. How about a little fireworks? Well, let's go through the Rolodex. No, Noriega – got him. Oh, here's one – Saddam Hussein. That'll look good. Let's go kill some sand niggers, yeah?'
> 'Brilliant, brilliant. We'll be there. Right, right. We'll be there. Brilliant. Yes, we've already armed them, too. It's brilliant. We know exactly what we're up against. It's brilliant.'

What a *huge* coalition it was, you know? 'Oh, France had a coupla planes in there.' Yeah, yeah. We told 'em, 'Put a few fucking planes in or Mickey Mouse leaves the country.' 'Hurry, let's get back in line . . . for the rollercoaster. We have done our duty.'

Selling weapons since '86 to Iraq, and I wondered about that. During the Persian Gulf War, those intelligence reports before it all started:

> 'Oh Iraq, they have incredible weapons, incredible weapons.'
> 'How do you know that?'
> 'Well . . . we looked at the receipt . . . but as soon as that cheque clears, we're goin' in. What time's the bank open? Eight? We're going in at nine . . . for God 'n' country 'n' . . . here's a flag. Whatever symbol y'all need. Let's go! Come on, we're killing sand niggers. Let's go!'

'He's a Hitler. He's a Hitler. Saddam Hussein is a Hitler.' What does that make you – Goebbels? Quit arming him. 'He's a Hitler.' He was your friend last week. 'He's a Hitler now.' Trying to motivate people, you know. It's unbelievable how they got 'em. People were just like:

> 'He's a Hitler – yeah, Bush. Get real, man.'
> 'You like dogs, don't ya?'
> 'Yeah, we love dogs.'
> 'Well, we have an intelligence report that says here Saddam Hussein likes to fuck dogs in the ass and then take their spine out and use it as a toothpick.'
> 'You're shittin' me. Let's go *kill* this guy. I had no idea he was that much of a maniac. This is for Rover!' (*crash*)
> 'That's what intelligence reports say. He's a Hitler. He fucks dogs. Mm-hm.'
> 'I don't know. You're sure that's true?'
> 'You like kittens?'
> 'Yeah, I like kittens. They're cute.'
> 'He boils 'em and eats 'em.'
> 'Fucker. This is for Fluffy!' (*three explosions*)

They say anything they want, you see, and you'll follow them, cos we are the docile masses. (*singing*) 'We're the puppet people! Ho, put it on our TV, it's true. Put it on our TV, it's true. We're the puppet people! Hey, guide us, you fuckin' scum! Hey, we're the puppet people.' And we are.

I was here during the riots. That was weird. That was the last time I was here. This time there's an election. Last time, a riot. I came over the day the riots happened, too. That was what was so weird about it. I left LA:

> 'Bye Bill, enjoy England.'
> 'I will, y'all have fun while I'm gone.'
> 'We will, Bill. Bye. Bye. Bye. See you. Bye-bye.'

Land at Heathrow Airport eleven hours later, pass a newspaper stand: 'LA Burns to Ground.' Shit, did I leave a cigarette lit? How much are these? See if my picture's in here. Right, and I'm over here, trying to get news of the riots, right? You got four channels, all four are playing *snooker* for no fucking apparent reason. What is this? Different angles of the table? 'For north/south coverage of snooker, turn to BBC2. For east/west coverage of snooker, turn to BBC1. For the overhead view, turn to BBC3. For a look under Jimmy White's left arm, turn to Channel 4.' You're going, 'Duh, how much longer are you gonna continue that impression, Bill? Any more in the act?' (*laughs*)

Who is this guy Jimmy White? Last time I was here: riots. I turn on the TV; there was snooker: Jimmy White. Nine months earlier, the last thing I saw when I left the hotel room, turned the TV off before I did, what's that? Jimmy fucking White. Does this guy have a bad home life or something? Let's get him *home*. Let's iron that vest. I mean, I like snooker, don't get me wrong, you know. I think it's a little slow, you know. Perhaps could use ah some livening up. You know what snooker could use? Riot. That'd be cool, cues . . . But I've figured out why it's so long, man. It's cos this little fucking old guy – not the two players – this little old guy keeps taking the balls out of the pockets and putting them back on. 'Hey, you asshole. He got it in. Let's go! The game's almost over. He has to come over again . . . It's gonna take all fucking night.'

So I'm trying to get news of the riots. Nothing but snooker on, right, and ah all my friends here trying to sympathize with me. 'Oh, Bill, crime is horrible. If it's any consolation, Bill, crime is horrible here too.' 'Shut up. This is Hobbiton and I'm Bilbo Hicks, OK? You live in a fairyland. Fucking crime. I was reading the papers here. You have crimes like: "Yesterday some hooligans knocked over a dustbin in Shaftsbury." The hooligans are loose. The hooligans are loose. What if they become ruffians? I would hate to be a dustbin in Shaftsbury tonight. (*singing*) No one knows what it's like to be a dustbin . . . in Shaftsbury . . . with hooligans.' It's such a stupid word, you know? Hooligan. Very unthreatening word. I don't even know what a hooligan is. I think I could take twenty or thirty of 'em. I picture these real pale guys in penny loafers and no socks. 'We're the hooligans.' *Pop!* Ow, you fucker. Come here. 'No, have to catch us. You corner me, I might become a scallywag. I'm a ne'er do well.' There was something in the paper yesterday: 'Some hooligans caused a rumpus.' Not quite the same as Crip and Blood[48] . . . that's a little more cutting. Little more telling. Blood. Hooligan. Bloods versus the hooligans.

> *Pop!*
> 'Hey man, what you doin' motherfucker. Come 'ere.'
> 'Got to catch us!'
> 'Yeah, I'm trying that now. (*gunshots*) There . . . catch your skinny pale ass. How's that?'
> 'Ow, he got me in the rumpus. The Blood hit me in the rumpus.'

You know, Crip, Blood, rumpus. No, I don't know. You do not have crime like we have, and you should be very grateful. Our crime is like: 'Yesterday a student beheaded his teacher. Named "Best in the Class".' Holding up the head.

I love talking about the Warren Committee. I love talking about the Kennedy assassination. I really love it, man. I was just down in Dallas, Texas . . . and ah you can actually go . . . to the School Book Depository on the sixth floor. It's a museum . . . called the Assassination Museum. And they have the window set up to look exactly like it did on that day. And it's really accurate, cos . . . Oswald's not in it. Incredible, painstaking detail. I don't know who did the research, but I applaud them. But it's true. It's called the Sniper's Nest, and you know, the boxes are set up, it's glassed in, you can't actually get to the window. And the reason they did that, of course, is they didn't want thousands of tourists every year, you know, coming through to the window, going, 'No way.' Yeah, that would have started this *truth* inertia happening. Who knows when it would've stopped. But there's no way. I mean, you can get to the window next to it, and you look down, you go, 'I can't see the fucking *road* from here, man.' There's a tree right here. There's no way, unless Oswald was hanging by his toes . . . upside down from the window ledge. *Surely* someone woulda *seen* that? Either that or some pigeons grabbed on to him and flew him over the motorcade. You know, there was rumors of anti-Castro pigeons seen drinking in bars . . . the week before the assassination. Someone overhead them saying, 'Coup, coup. Coup.'

People say, 'It's so weird.' You wouldn't believe the attitude in America. 'Bill, quit talking about Kennedy, man. Let it go. K? It was a long time ago. Would you just forget it?' I'm like, 'All right. Then don't bring up Jesus to me . . . Well, long as we're talking shelf life here.' 'Bill, you know Jesus died for you.' Yeah, yeah, it was a long time ago. Let it go. Forget about it. How about this: let's get Pilate to release the fucking files. Quit washing your hands and release the piles, Filate. Piles, Filate? Piles, Filate. Don't worry, don't worry.

I want you to know this is the longest I've ever gone without a cigarette in my fucking life, and ah, no. Actually I quit smoking, so ah . . . (*audience complain*) Hey, hey! This ain't Dylan goes electric. Chill out, all right? 'Judas! Traitor!' People ask the weird— 'Why d'you quit smoking?' Is that a weird question only to me? 'Why d'you take your mouth off the exhaust pipe, man? You were almost there. Traitor! Judas!' I'm far from reformed, all right? I mean, I mean, they look good to me, I tell ya. It's hard. It's really hard. After you eat at a restaurant, people light up around ya. Man, they look good. Everyone one of 'em looks like it was made by God, rolled by Jesus, and moistened shut with Claudia Schiffer's pussy right now. (*sucking sounds*) 'Golly, that looks tasty.' It's very hard. I don't know how to quit. My friends recommended this thing called a patch. I don't know if you get this here? The patch. It's like a nicotine Band-Aid you wear, and I don't see how it works, you know, unless you wear it over your mouth. (*makes muffled noise*)

> 'What's he saying?'
> 'I think he wants a cigarette.'
> (*makes muffled noise*)
> 'Put it up your nose?'
> 'I don't think the patch is helping him any.'
> 'Least he's not gaining weight.'

I was walking through Central Park and I saw an old man smoking. Nothing makes a smoker happier than to see an *old* person smoking. This guy was ancient, bent over a walker, puffing away, I'm just, 'Dude! You're my hero! Guy your age smoking, man. It's great.' He goes, 'What? I'm twenty-eight.'

I was worried for a while, man, the polls, you know? I was over here when you went through the Labour/Tory poll situation.[49] That was . . . I was so afraid that was gonna happen back home, man. Labour ahead, Labour ahead, Labour ahead, Labour ahead, cool, it looks like it's Labour ahead! FUCK YOU! WRONG! WRONG! DEATH TO YOUR DREAMS AND HOPES! THE RAMPAGING ELEPHANT HAS FRIENDS! (*trumpets like an elephant*) See, I wonder how real this whole thing is, man. You know, did people actually get in there, vote with their fucking wallets again? Or did they *vote* for Labour, and then that fucking old guy from the snooker game go over and take their votes? 'There will be no changes. Your hopes will remain just that.' The polls – I'm sick of the polls. Cut 'em out. They're not funny. Quit it. You know, and they're, they're so misleading. I saw one on CNN one time: How many people disapprove of George Bush's handling of the country? Seventy per cent. Of these same people, how many will vote for him again in November? Seventy per cent. What the fuck? Where did they take that at? Some S&M parlour? 'Ow! More. Ow, keep going. Ow, don't stop.' I've never been in an S&M parlour. You get the fucking point. It's my white-boy, suburb fucking impression of S&M. Requires bending over, I don't know. (*laughs*) I'm just so . . . right on the money.

But these polls, you know, they get the answers they want by how they ask the questions, you know what I mean? Like during the Persian Gulf War, we would hear questions like:

> 'Do you think George Bush, a good Christian white man
> . . . should send troops to Iraq to stem the brown, Islamic
> tide from coming over here and fucking your daughter?'
> 'I'd like to say I'm *for* this war.'
> 'Ninety-eight per cent of all Americans support the war.
> This just in!'

Guess who was in that two fucking per cent?

Actually, I was for the war, I was just against the troops, and ah . . . I didn't like those young people. I was all for the carnage, don't get me wrong, I *am* an American. Americans love carnage, we love death, folks, it's a – what do they say? An ecstasy and violent fucking dream America is. NRA – National Rifle Association – love the LA riots. They *love* the LA riots. You shoulda seen them on TV. Oh, man, during the riots they're on TV: 'Ah! A-ha ha! Yeah! Uh-huh! Ha ha!' That's about as literate as they can be, but . . . I think what the fine, Neanderthal, redneck fella was trying to get across in his own inimitable grunting way . . . I actually heard one of 'em say, 'See, yeah! See, now how do you feel? The mob comin' at you – no gun. Ah? Ha ha! Here come the mob: you . . . no gun. How does *that* feel?' See, before I bought a gun, I'd try to figure out what it is about me that keeps track of the fucking mobs, man. That's the way I'd work the problem. After all, I might run out of ammo one day. Have to talk to these fellas.

Our last export was the Madonna Sex Book. Did you see that? Did you have the same effect it had on me as you? Almost a jaw-breaking fucking yawn? (*yawns*) (*sleepily*) That's it? That's the whole book? OK, Bye-bye. Bye-bye. It's pretty good? Yeah, it's OK.

Twenty-five pounds for that thing? Man, for twenty-five pounds you can actually *have* sex. *Twice* if you're in Cowley. I don't know why I keep mentioning that. I had to do a radio show over there, and I just started . . . I just . . . found Alabama of the fucking Britain, sort of, you know. Wow! 'This is where Oscar Wilde went to school.' Cowley? 'No, across the river.' Oh, OK.

I was down in London and ah I don't know where the fuck I was. I was in London one time, and ah . . . this like busload of Iowa tourists got off. These cow people, right? And ah they bumped into me, and I went *flyin'* . . . into this adult book store. My hand was in my pocket, and I went, 'Shit, I got to get outa here', and money *flies* out of my hand, on to the counter. This guy hands me a magazine. I'm just . . . embarrassed. I'm beet red, and I . . . I'd better get home to the hotel and throw this away. *Instantly*. Get to the room, throw it towards the garbage can, it breaks open on the garbage can, and opens face up . . . on my bed. But I'm looking at your English porno, and I'm chuckling to myself, wondering what the fucking joke is here. There's these blue dots over everything. OK, yeah. I'm the only one here with the fucking fetishes, right? 'Bill, we really don't read porno. We're in college. We read poetry and art and science . . . while you frequent the seedy, sticky-floored porno theatres, we're planning your future and the future of the entire world.' Great. Well, anyway, I'll tell you what it's like, save you a field trip. There's these blue dots over all the– I mean, like there's a guy standing here naked like this. There's a woman lean– kneeling naked like this. And there's a blue dot right here. Hmmm. Wonder what you're doin'? It's very strange, I mean to go *that* far, then put a blue dot over it. I don't get it. And then I saw a club that said 'Live sex show on stage' down in the West End, and I wondered what a bummer that must be to have to be the guy that *holds* the blue dot.

By the way, if anyone here is in marketing or advertising . . . could you do me a favour . . . and kill yourself? So sick of the idea of marketing, man. You know what they do to movies now? Do you know what they do? It's unbelievable. They show movies to a test audience before the movie is released, then change the movie depending on how these 200 random *yahoos* liked it or did not like it. As though we are all the same. As though we share the same taste. I think a quick perusal of my video collection will tell you . . . many of us walk to the beat of our own drummer. I saw this movie this year, *Basic Instinct*. How many of y'all saw this piece-of-shit film? Horrible film. Like a bad *Streets of San Francisco* episode. I kept waiting to see Karl Malden show up in drag as one of Sharon Stone's lesbian lovers. He looked the part, lacked only the lumberjack shirt. He would have been perfect, but no. Anyway, come to find out all the lesbian sex scenes were cut out of this film – all the lesbian sex scenes were *cut* out of this film – because a test audience . . . was turned *off* by them. (*laughs*) Man, is *my* thumb not on the pulse of America. I don't wanna seem like Randy Pan the Goatboy, but ah . . . the only reason I went to that piece-of-shit film, you know. If I had been in that test audience, the only one out front protesting that film woulda been Michael Douglas demanding his part be put back in. 'I swear I was in that movie. I swear I was. Was Bill Hicks in that test audience?' Hur hur hur hur hur hur. Goatboy called it like he saw it, Mikey. (*makes snorting and snarling noise*)

Horrible film. Just like Madonna's Sex Book, all it's meant to do is titillate the completely neutered and docile fucking consumer community which we have become. What do people say about that film? 'It's great.' Why? 'You get to see Sharon Stone's pussy.' Ooh, the hallmark of art. Yeah, you get to see her pussy for one-eighth of a second. I timed it. Don't blink, you might miss the plot. That's how bad this film is. Forty minutes into it, you're going, 'What a piece of shit.' She goes [. . .] .

> 'Did you see her pussy?'
> 'No, I was reaching for my coke. What happened?'
> 'Dude, you missed it, man. We gotta watch this again.
> This could be the greatest film all year!'

God, are we that fucking *neutered*? Maybe you don't know this. Maybe . . . you know there's movies you can rent? *Nothing But Pussy* – did y'all know that? Swear to God, one-eighth of a second of plot, the rest of the film: pussy. The numbers are exactly reversed.

One line of dialogue: 'I'd like to see your pussy.' Boom. Did y'all know that? Yeah, yeah, you can. I really, I'd prefer if people did that instead of paying for this Hollywood titillation horseshit that comes out . . . that's supposedly for adults. Save payin' Joe Eszterhas any more money for these scripts, that fat, no-talent fucking whale who needs to die in front of his children on the kitchen floor with a blood bubble coming out of his left nostril and . . . etcetera, etcetera. He *wrote* that. Remember the ad for *Basic Instinct*? '*Basic Instinct* – from the writer of *Flashdance*.' (*laughs*) When did *Flashdance* become a literary barometer in our culture? I missed that meeting. 'Honey, the guy who wrote *Flashdance*, he's pumped out some more literary magic. Call a babysitter. We're not gonna miss this. You *know* it's good.' How do you write *Flashdance*, first of all, you know?

> '*Flashdance, Flashdance* (*drops to a mumble, then clicks his fingers*). Young girl shows titties. (*sound of zip fastening*) There.'
> 'That's fucking brilliant, Joe. Can we give you a million dollars for that? Oh, that's brilliant. Genius. *But* can you top yourself in *Basic Instinct*?'
> 'Young girl shows pussy.' (*zip fastening*).
> 'He's a *genius*. Can we give you *three* million dollars for that? Now, we'll give you six million if you can top yourself . . . in *Basic Instinct 2*.'
> 'Young girl shows titties and pussy.' (*zip fastening*)
> (*whispers*) 'God Almighty, he's a fucking genius.'

Yeah, I'm just a sick guy, man. I don't know what's going on. People hate me back home. I was in Oklahoma, lady yelling at me, 'You goin' to hell, boy.' Fuck it, I'm already in Oklahoma, lady. Fuck it, man. Say something that might scare me, like my return ticket is cancelled. Aargh! 'You're going to hell.' I wish, I wish I could meet a Christian who would proselytize to me. They keep running away from me. I wanna *talk* to y'all. They bolt when they see me, like bunny rabbits in car headlights. Dong! Dong! Come back, Christian, come back! I wanna ask you some questions. You know, Christianity is such a weird religion. Lot of Christians wear crosses around their necks. Do you think when Jesus comes back he's gonna wanna see a fucking cross, man? Ow. That may be why he hasn't shown up yet. 'Shit, they're still wearing crosses. Fuck it, I'm not going, Dad.' They totally missed the point. When they start wearing fishes I might show up again. Look at that big gold one on that rap dude. Uh-uh.' It's kind of like going up to Jackie Onassis with a rifle pendant on, you know. 'Just thinking of John, Jackie. We love him. Just trying to keep that memory alive, baby.'

'Back and to the left. Back and to the left. Back and to the left.' Which, by the way, that action you can see Kennedy's head doin' in the Zapruder film was caused by a bullet . . . coming from up there. Yeah, I know it looks to the layman or anyone who might dabble in physics that this action here . . . was caused by a ah . . . well, hell, let's . . . up here. Did you see that? Up here – the right front, or grassy knoll area, I think I've heard it referred to. Look back in the Rolodex. Yeah, grassy knoll area. But no, it was caused by a bullet up here. See, what happened was when Oswald's gun went off in Dealey Plaza, the gun echoed all over the place. Echoes went everywhere, and the echo went by the limo on the left, it went up into the trees and the grassy knoll, and hit some leaves, causing some dust to fly up, which fifty-six witnesses testified was a gunshot, but it wasn't, even though Kennedy's head at that very moment went over. But it was dust, caused by an echo, and the reason Kennedy's head went over, cos the echo went by the car on the left, and he went, 'What was that?' Yeah, on very clear versions of the Zapruder film you can actually see him say the words, 'You hear something to the left? It sounds like a gunshot but could be an echo.' Yeah, it's very . . . You have to get a microscope and . . .

> 'Go back to bed, America. Go back to bed. It is all explained to you now. There should be no question about your government's legitimacy. Go back to bed. Here – here's *American Gladiators*. Watch that and shut up. Go back to bed, America. Here's fifty-six channels of horse-shit. Watch that. You're in the Land of Freedom now. Go back to bed, America. Here's a flag . . . Go back to bed.'

Lot of people are confused. There was an execution in California, and there was a lot of Christians out front *supporting* the death penalty. A lot of people found that ironic, particularly people who, you know, know the *words* of Christ. Ah . . . yeah, I didn't know 'Thou shalt not kill' had a footnote . . . but apparently, again, it's 'Thou shalt not kill asterisk' – oh, unless you really want to. Yeah, so, it's a lot of flexibility in the religion, which I love. Very yoga-like. But ah . . . I didn't find it ironic at all – Christians for the death penalty – cos after all, if it weren't for capital punishment, you know . . . we'd have no Easter. (*laughs*) So, fuck it, that's a three-day weekend where I came from. Tie these people up.

They actually have a Bible out called The New Living Bible. It's a Bible in updated and modern English . . . I guess to make it more palatable for people to read. But it's kinda strange listening to 'And Jesus walked on water, and Peter said, "Awesome".' Suddenly we got Jesus hanging ten across the Sea of Galilee, Christ's Bogus Adventure. 'Goin' to hell, boy.' Yeah, well . . . at least that's where all the good music's gonna be, so . . . 'God created the world 6,000 years ago, and he put dinosaur fossils in the earth to test our faith.' Yeah, I'll get back to you in a bit with that theory. We'll, we'll go toe to toe with ya. I can't *talk* to you. The idea of God *fucking with my head* scares the shit out of me. Believe me, the *fossil* is the least of the little pranks that are fucking with me right now. (*laughs*) There's someone actually said that: 'He did that to test our faith.' Yeah, cos there is no mention in the Bible of dinosaurs. What happened there? I think he woulda fucking noticed that, you know. I mean, you know, walking on water – cool. But what's that big serpent? You ever noticed how people who believe in Creationism look really unevolved? You know, you always get the eyebrow ridges and the big furry hands and feet. 'I believe God created me in one day.' Man, it looks like he rushed it.

I think it's interesting the two drugs that are legal – alcohol and cigarettes, two drugs that do absolutely *nothing* for you at all – are legal, and the drugs that might open your mind up to realize how you're being *fucked* every day of your life? Those drugs are against the law. (*laughs*) Coincidence? See, I'm glad mushrooms are against the law, cos I took 'em one time, you know what happened to me? I laid in a field of green grass for four hours, going, 'My God, I love everything.' Yeah, now if that isn't a hazard to our countries . . . How are we gonna justify arms dealing if we know we're all one? See the conflict between love . . . and the Tory administration. Wrong crowd? What?

> 'Bill, we are at Oxford. We happen to have some dough. Hmm? Fine and dandy your little peace tactics, but taxes are a more pressing need to us. Hmm? Don't force us to sic the Cowley hooligans upon you.'
> 'We're the hooligans. Yes we are.'

These musicians today who don't do drugs and instead speak out against 'em? 'We're rock against drugs.' Boy, they suck. Ha! Ball-less, soulless, pieces of shit, suckers of Satan's cock, each and every one of 'em. Corporate little bitches. (*makes snorting, snarling noise*) Sucking Satan's pecker is what they're doin'. They have their little fucking careers.

> 'I am Satan. I give away fifteen-minute careers. Send in Vanilla Ice. Hello Vanilla. We'll have to do something about that hair. Says here on your application you have no talent . . . and you want a career in show business. Is that right? Hur hur hur hur hur. (*makes unzipping, then crashing noise*) Suck Satan's cock. (*makes snorting, snarling noise*) I will lower the standards of America. (*snorting, snarling*) I will give all the money in the hands of twelve-year-old girls. (*snorting, snarling*) You will be their star. (*snorting, snarling*) Leave. Send in MC Hammer.'

MC Hammer – there's another boat that left me on the fucking island, man.

> 'Bill, you comin' aboard? It's nice.' (*laughs*)
> 'I'll stay here and eat my own flesh.'
> (*makes noise of boat horn*) 'Bye Bill.'

MC Hammer, I never . . . what is the deal with him? 'He's a great dancer.' What? It's like a fucking sand crab in his knickers. He's not dancing, he's having a fit. Satan's semen burning a hole in the lining of his stomach, that's what . . . (*makes snorting, snarling noise*) Big fucking worm inside of him. (*snorting, snarling*) Ha ha ha ha! It's part horror film. Just hang with me, all right? 'What is this, Satan's semen? What is this? What *is* he doing?' (*snorting, snarling*) I think that's the perfect response for comedy, right there. Ha ha ha ha ha!

I love film, and I was watching *Terminator 2*, and I was— incredible. It is a good movie, incredible special effects, unbelievable stunts, right? And I'm thinking to myself, hundred-million-dollar budget . . . unbelievable stunts, man. A guy flies out of a building, through glass, on a helicopter and lands – I mean, through – oh no, hold on, on a motorcycle and lands on a fucking helicopter. Unbelievable. *How* are they gonna top this stuff in a movie ever again? How can you *top* this? There's no way! Unless . . . they start using terminally ill people . . . hear me out . . . as stuntmen in pictures. OK. I know to some of you this perhaps sounds a little *cruel*, maybe. 'Oh God, Bill, terminally ill stuntpeople? That's terribly cruel.' You know what I think cruel is? Leaving your loved ones to die in some sterile hospital room surrounded by strangers. Fuck that. Put 'em in the movies. What? You want your grandmother dying like a little bird in some hospital room? Her translucent skin so thin you can see her last heartbeat work its way down her blue veins? Or do you want her to meet Chuck Norris? She'll be *thrilled*.

> 'Doc, how come you've dressed my grandmother up as a mugger?'
> 'Shut up and get off the set. Action! Push her towards Chuck.'
> (*makes fight noises*)
> 'Wow, he kicked her head right off her body. Did you see that? Did you see my Grammy? They add sound effects later.'
> 'Give me all your money. I've got a gun. I'll cut your fucking head off.'
> 'It's not Grammy – they added that later.'

OK, not the most popular theory ever professed. Terminally ill– all I'm saying, folks, is movies are getting more and more boring each year, and people are dying all the time. I'm a weaver.

I ah . . . this abortion issue in the States is dividing the country right in half. You know, and even amongst my friends – we're all highly intelligent – they're totally divided on the issue of abortion. Totally divided. Some of my friends think these pro-life people are just annoying idiots. Other of my friends think these pro-life people are evil fucks. How are we gonna have a consensus? I'm torn. I try and take the broad view and think of them as evil, annoying fucks. Yeah. But I'm a diplomat. And a weaver. I'm Earl Weaver.[50] I'm McCloud. You know what bugs me about abortion, though? Is people – even people who are pro-choice – waffling on the idea of abortion. You know what, pro-choice people like 'We're not pro-abortion, we're pro-choice. We just don't believe the government has a right to tell us what we can or cannot do with our own bodies. We're not pro-abortion, we're pro-choice.' Hey, just say it. Just fuckin' say it. People *suck*, there's too many of 'em, and they're easier to kill when they're foetuses than when they're grown up. Just say it. People suck! . . . Sorry. The mask came off there. I'll put it back on.

See, America's all screwed up, and American airlines? American planes? They don't allow smoking, right? *But* they allow children. Hey. Let's be *fair*. I was on this flight from LA to New York, I'm asleep on the plane, right? All five seats were empty, cool, I was laid down, going to sleep, and I feel this tapping on my head, and I look up, and there's this little kid loose on this fucking plane. He's just loose. This is his playground in the sky. And he's decided the funnest thing he could do is repetitively tap me on the top of the fuckin' head. The ONE PERSON WHO WANTS NOTHING TO DO WITH THE FUCKING KID. Everyone else: 'Hey, come here, little boy! Come here, little kiddy! Oh, yeah, you're so cute.' No! No! He comes right to me – na! Na! Na! Na! Na! Na! I look across the aisle at his mom. She's just smiling, you know. 'Mmmm.' This guy next to the mom goes, 'They're so cute when they're that small. Huh, huh, huh, huh.' Isn't that amazing? Just letting your kid run loose like that on a fucking plane? And the kid runs over to the emergency exit, and he starts flipping that handle to the door. The guy next to the mom starts to get up, and I go:

> 'Wait a minute. We're about to learn an important lesson right here. (*makes sound of door opening*) Oh, you're right. The smaller he gets, the cuter he is. Ah, wish I had a camera right now . . . with a telescopic lens. *Love* to get the expression on his face when his pudgy little legs hit that farmhouse down there. Stewardess, since we got a breeze in here, can we smoke now? Fairly well circulated.'

True story. In these days and times, only the death of a child will amuse me.

I saw a lady today, a kid on a leash. You seen these people? Kid on a leash? How *horrible*. Put him in the pound where he belongs. 'Oh, you don't mean that, Bill.' That's why my girlfriend and I broke up. She wanted kids, and I (*laughs*) oh, well. She wanted kids. (*laughs*) I had no idea her philosophy was that flawed. She goes, 'Wouldn't it be nice to have a kid, to have this fresh, clean slate, which we could fill, and a little clean spirit, totally, you know, innocent, and to fill it with good ideas.' Yeah, yeah, how about this? If you're so fucking altruistic, why don't you leave the little clean spirit wherever it is right now? OK? Horrible act, childbirth. It's a nightmare. Bringing– I would *never* bring a kid to this fucking planet.

(*laughs*) I'm not usually doing shows at this hour. This is usually back when I'm in my room calling the States, going, 'I don't know if I can go on. I don't know if they like me, or they're laughing *at* me. I can't tell. They seem nice enough, but they stare. I . . . I . . . and I can't understand a word they say, yet we're all speaking English . . . I . . . I . . . I . . . they all sound like little birds tweeting to me.' I think I've been over here a lot, cos suddenly the food tastes good, so ah . . . I think I'm getting used to it here. When I came over first of all, I was pretty stunned. First of all, you don't *boil* pizza. Now . . . no, no listen to me. *I* think. And this fascination with fucking chips – french fries. You call 'em chips; they're french fries. I love fries, don't get me wrong. If you leave here tonight going, 'Bill doesn't like fries' . . . you'll be wrong. But every single fucking time you eat? Come on! You're having too many *fries*! You're *over* your spud quota. *Everything* has these. I saw hookers on London streets going, 'Head and chips!' You may think you've gotten good head before, but unless you've had it with a big, hot, piping plate of fries in front of you . . . Very civilized. We could learn a lot from you. You're an ancient culture. We, a young, upstart nation . . . exporting *American Gladiators*, so instead of us having to grow, we'll bring you to our fucking level. Ha ha ha ha ha!

I'm trying to get this show on Channel 4, right? We came up with this show. I think it's real good idea for a show, and I'm like, you know, going to all these meetings with Channel 4 (*whispers*). Then I picked up the paper, and I read Channel 4's TV listings. (*laughs*) Ah, fuck you. '*Scooby-Doo, Get Smart, Blossom, Who's the Boss?, Full House.*' Aargh! Same country where George Bernard Shaw used to jot things down? Why are you exporting our American horseshit? Why do I get off the plane and see Kentucky fuckin' Fried Chicken? Why am I yelling at *you* about it? 'Bill, we didn't do– we had nothing to do with it. Giant corporate conglomerate that has tentacles all over the world. We are like you, Bill, merely the puppet people. They tell us where to go and what to do.'

Open a McDonald's in Moscow and everyone's backslapping each other. It's depressing to me. 'Oh, it'll help the economy. McDonald's, it'll supply forty-five new jobs there in Moscow.' Yeah, twenty dentists and twenty heart specialists. It's shit. Don't eat it.

I need to get laid, that's ah . . . I just realized what it is. I just realized I'm starting to have that kind of draggy, pale, wan, jacking off a little too much for my own good. I am, I'm going for some kind of masturbation record right now. It's not pretty at all. Is it a bad sign when you come and nothing but air comes out? I know, I mean, even I, failing biology, understand the ramifications . . . and implications . . . of tossing air, you know? Uh, uh. Oh, room service, could you send some milk up here, please? Think I lost all my bodily fluids. I am merely a shell of my former shadow. I am so pale and so wan.

But it's hard to have a relationship in this business, you know? I mean, no really, I'm not looking for sympathy, but you're always travelling, keeping weird hours, you know, it's gonna take a very special woman, you know? Or a bunch of average ones. Again . . . I ah, far be it from me to set some type of demarcation zone on the qualities I look for in a woman – breathing . . . is ah, for me, you know, 99 per cent there. Breathing and no fuckin' Hammer albums. That's it, I'm in love. Hammer. 'He's a good dancer.' Think we need a Priest to this guy's concerts, he's ah . . . I think he's possessed. (*sighs*) But my girlfriend left me, and ah, years ago, and ah (*laughs*) I'm still talking about it, because . . . I loved her. Oh, me? She's got five guys since me. 'Tell us about your ex, your true love. Oh, you mean Hank? Tony? Don? Tim? . . . Bill?' (*laughs*) Yeah, five back! Me! Goatboy! Randy Pan the Goatboy. (*bleats*) She loved me. I know she loved me, man. Cos I am Goatboy. I am here to please women, that is my only job, I worship them. Tie me to your headboard, ladies. Let Goatboy wear you like a feedbag. (*makes snorting, sucking noise*) So it's really weird, I'm askin', I'm talkin' to Martin, my tour— my factotum tour manager, Martin. I'm goin', 'Martin, why is it after every show the only people that wanna meet me are about five to seven pale young guys?' (*laughs*) And he goes, 'Well Bill, could it be perhaps the subject matter of your show?' I don't know. All I talk about is how much I like eating pussy. You'd think there'd be five to seven lovely young women going . . .' Carrots in each hand. 'Hello goat.' (*bleats*) But no, I always get five to seven pale guys. 'We jack off too till we're almost dead.' 'Nice to meet you.' Grips on them.

But my girlfriend left me and I was very depressed for ah seven years, and I drank my body weight in Jack Daniels whisky every fuckin' night, and ah . . . and ah . . . then it occurred to me: you can't get down, man. You gotta let it go, you know, I mean, it's, look, you know, you gotta, all right, you have to look on the bright side, you know? You *have* to, there's no other way, and as small as that bright side may be, you gotta look at it, and that's all, that's all you got, you know? So I think on the bright side it helped my career that she left me. Well, I mean cos now . . . I'm driven . . . by a fantasy . . . that one day this girl who I loved more than anything in the world and she said she loved me then left? One day she's gonna be living in a trailer park . . . somewhere in Oklahoma. She's gonna have nine naked little kids with rickets that bring home dead animals from the side of the road for them to eat at night. Birds in their hair, mud on their face, rats laying babies in their ears at night . . . she's gonna live with this ex-welder, 600 pounds, fur all over his back, drinks warm beer, farts, belches, beats the kids, watches *American Gladiators* every fuckin' night, and has to have it *explained* to him . . . yeah. One night he's gonna be making love to her and his heart's gonna explode, and she's gonna be trapped under 600 pounds of flaccid fish-belly cellulite shifting like the tides of the ocean . . . as blood and phlegm and bile and a chaw of tobacco pours out of his mouth and nose . . . into her face. And just before she drowns in that tepid puddle of afterbirth . . . she turns to the telly, and I'm gonna be on it. So you see, I'm not bitter and ah . . . the important thing is to live and let live. Hoh, I'm hangin' by a hair. Hangin' by a hair to sanity.

So you guys in college? Is that the deal? College? Oxford? No? Cowley High? Where are you? 'I'm takin' Assembly Line and Nuts and Bolts 101, and How to Clean the Ashtray.' I'm an elitist scum. Welcome me to your hearts. I only like readers. Sorry! No time for hooligans. Readers and artists, those are my kind. But you ladies keep fuckin' the Conservative guys, yeah, keep fuckin' the Tories, fuckin' the Republicans. These bullneck, bulging vein, fuckin' burr-cut, waterhead fuckin' idiots, you keep fuckin' 'em. Two-inch piggly-wiggly dicks, probably can't even put 'em in you one time before they come. 'Eurgh, ahhh. Sorry honey.' (*snores*) Yeah, and then we see ya on *Donahue* and *Oprah*, you know, years from now, going, 'I wish my husband would eat me more, make love to me better.' Right, fuck it, you chose him. Sorry, you had the artist who wanted to eat your *butthole* for dinner, but no. You chose Conservative Mr Bank Account. Well, fuck off! Get in the tub and fuckin' raise your legs under the water – there! There! There's your fuckin' love. Let the poets jack off in circles in the woods. You get stuck with piggly-wiggly, burrcut, two-inch pecker. Fuck it. Fuck the artist! That is your job. Fuck artist! Find a flute player, someone who can use his fingers and his tongue! Fuck artist . . . only! 'I'm an accountant at Western and Western, I'm a lawyer.' NO! You're now a jack-off gang. 'I'm fuckin' the street musician over you . . . guy who I can reside my buttocks on his face.' Do I seem shallow? 'No Bill, you have a great emotional depth.' 'I'm scared for your soul, Bill.' Don't worry – I don't have a soul. Hey. 'Send in Bill Hicks.'

Is there a message in all this? Cos I know all y'all gonna remember is the dick jokes, I know *that*. I do two hours, the last seven minutes are dick jokes, everyone goes, 'He's so dirty.' And with Madonna it's all fuckin' *pussy* on every page, and you go, 'She's making a political statement.' I can't WIN! Do I have a message? Yes, I do. Here's my message: as scary as the world is – and it is – it is merely a ride . . . in the amusement park of the universe it is merely a ride. It has its thrills, it has its chills, it has its ups, it has its downs . . . my factotum Martin, getting ready for the pale young men to line up. Either that or I get women – weird women with their poetry.

> 'Here Bill, I think you can relate to this: The hooved beast rode me like the incubus bitch I was.'
> 'Thanks, I . . . I don't . . . I'm not in the mood to read right now. I *appreciate* your thoughts . . . on the hooved beast who rode you like the incubus bitch you were, but your poem?'
> 'No, those are your notes. They fell out of your pocket.'
> 'Thanks.'

The world is just a ride, and some people have known it. We think it's real, cos that's how powerful our minds are, but it's not, it's a ride. And some people have known it, and they've come here an' told us: 'It's just a ride.' And we . . . have killed those people. (*laughs*) Cos we love the fuckin' ride. You ever noticed that? We always kill the good guys and leave these *demon*s just running amok on the planet – you ever noticed that? Jesus – murdered. Martin

Luther King – murdered. Gandhi – murdered. Malcolm X – murdered. Reagan – wounded. But it's just a ride. And since you know it, and some people are tired of the ups and downs and the thrills and chills, and prefer instead the quiet – they have to be told it's just a ride. Thank you very much. You've been fantastic, I appreciate it, I hope you enjoyed it. Oxford, you've been great! Thank you! Thank you very much.

UK TV Interview

Female Interviewer: **Do your audiences get upset sometimes by what you say? I mean . . . in America, any way.**

Bill: Occasionally there are some members of the audience who don't find it funny. And therefore they've paid money, therefore they get upset, you know. What am I supposed to do when half the people are going, 'That was great', and the other half are going, 'You're evil'? Is it my job to go into their lives and try and please them? I actually had a woman say, 'Why can't you do things that appeal to everyone?' That's impossible! What a burden! (*laughing*) No one's done that yet! That would be a challenge. I will please all people. And I also got . . . you know, someone made a comment, going, 'We don't come to comedy to think.' Well, gee, where do you go to think? I'll meet you there! We don't have to do this here!

Female Interviewer: **Isn't there a sort of halfway between?**

Bill: But . . . but . . . but my way is halfway between. I mean, this is a nightclub and, you know, these are adults, and what do you expect? What you're gonna see on TV? No! This isn't TV live. And also it's my show. What am I supposed to do? Change my . . . my . . . my own outlook and my beliefs? To be what to them? I try to talk to the audience the same way I talk to my friends, to take away the artifice of show business and actually have a feeling of a conversation going on. If some of the audience gets offended, then they're saying to me, 'I don't want to be your friend any more.' And that's fine.

Female Interviewer: **But what's your background? Where do you come from?**

Bill: I come from a Southern Baptist household. Does that make sense?

Female Interviewer: **What do your mum and dad think of it?**

Bill: They don't like it at all.

Female Interviewer: **They don't.**

Bill: No.

Female Interviewer: **And it offends them.**

Male Interviewer: **Would you let . . . would you mind them going to see it?**

Bill: Not at all. No. They come to see me all the time. They still . . . they don't get it, you know. My dad: 'Bill, do you have to use the F word in your act? Bob Hope doesn't need to use the F word in his act.' Yeah well Dad, Bob Hope doesn't play the dives I play.

Male Interviewer: **Yeah, right. So you don't so much give them what *they* want, you give them what *you* want. (*laughs*)**

Bill: Sure. You know why? Cos I honestly believe that we're all the same, and I think to go, 'Well, I'll give them what *they* want,' is very condescending. And I don't try to condescend to people, you know? And that's why I treat 'em like my friends. And I guess that's a shocking way to behave in this world . . . for some people.

Male Interviewer: **I think that's admirable, actually.**

Bill: For some people. But I don't sit there and go, 'Well, you're all a bunch of idiots so I will do things I don't believe in to amuse you!'

Female Interviewer: **But they want to be entertained, don't they! I mean, they want to laugh. They don't wanna think.**

Bill: Well, when did thinking not become entertaining?

Female Interviewer: **They don't wanna think.**

Bill: You think they don't wanna think?

Female Interviewer: **No, they want to laugh.**

Bill: Well, what am I supposed to do? Am I supposed to go out and tickle them individually? We have to express an idea here.

Male Interviewer: **Well, this is why we want to put some-thing on TV that does question these . . . where one draws the line. What is . . .**

Bill: There are no lines.

Male Interviewer: **. . . acceptable and what . . .**

Bill: There are no lines. I say erase all the lines. Erase–

Female Interviewer: **Yes, but that's what our programme is all about. It's–**

Male Interviewer: **Well, it's all very well for you to say , but . . .**

Female Interviewer: **It's where you *can* draw the line. It's where you *can* draw the line**.

Bill: Can . . . can I recommend some jugglers you might like?

Thoughts on Love and Smoking (November 1992)

(My first love was like smoking – both bad habits and both totally seductive – and as time goes by, my addiction to both lingers until they intertwine, interchange, become inseparable in my mind – forming a nostalgia on the brain, for which there is no cure.)

Autumn in New York. Spring in the step. Rosy-cheeked women dressed in black go bouncing down the avenues. Their coolest coats and jackets hunched against the whipping winds. Their brightly colored scarves dancing under the slate-grey sky. They threaten to turn the clock back to 1964, and everywhere you look is like the cover of a Dylan album – pre-Jesus, post-folk, ultra-cool. This is why I smoke.

A cafe spills out into the street. It's warm, roasted light and cappuccino steam drawing mods and spectres and VAMPIRE QUEENS with the promise of fresh-brewed blood from the bean. On the sidewalks nearby, the multitudes flow by. Red lips giving cigarettes a tug, making embers flare like lightning bugs. Fir and woodsmoke fill the sparkling air, the breath exhaled just hanging there like some frozen joyous scream. And all the girls evoke the dream of Autumn in New York.

It's on nights like this I think of her the most . . . When we first met, I was a roaring drunk. I was twenty-six years old and in a grave deep rut. She was a southern girl, which is the same as saying she was insane. All southern women are insane. Some are cold blooded killers and some are harmless eccentrics, but the best of the breed exhibit both of these characteristics and always the one you expect the least at the time you least expect it. She was the best of the breed and the best I've ever had. The night of our third date, I grabbed her by the neck and punched holes in the wall around her head, then tried to hurl her off the balcony of my 22nd floor apartment. That was the night she fell in love with me. She liked my style. See, she was an addict too, just like me . . . Later, we smoked and had a good laugh over it all.

I flipped her every which-a-way, like a cat batting around a half-dead mouse, for its own amusement, staving off the kill. She whimpered and cried and begged for mercy until I found her hot pulse throbbing and bit down deep. Closest to the bone is the sweetest meat. Her hands grabbed my hair and her feet fluttered against my back as I gulped all the life in her greedily down my throat. Then she lay very still. I rolled away and stood swaying next to the bed, letting the blood rush from my head, trying to remember where the hell my cigarettes were. I crashed about in the dark, knocking over tables and lamps and chairs, finally finding my pack in the pocket of the shirt I was wearing. I smoked a few while strumming my guitar, then I wrote a song and sang it at the top of my lungs. A baby cried next door, and a fire truck thundered down the street, its sirens wailing. And all the while she never stirred.

In the morning I awoke, curled next to her like a spoon, feeling her bottom pushing repeatedly against my lap while she whispered breathlessly to some dream lover. I got up and put some water on to boil, then sat at the kitchen table, smoking, my back to the bed. Suddenly, her arms were around me and I was smothered in her charm. Her need was ferocious and I lay helplessly on the floor as she exacted her sweet revenge, biting down deep again and again until the shriek of the steam and the sound of my screams was all that filled the room.

New York is where we moved when Texas got too small. It was summer time. New York in July is hotter than I care to describe, but I will try. Imagine, if you will, the hottest part of hell. The place where advertisers and marketing executives go to dwell. And now try to think of even hotter still, where bankers and landlords and like-minded swill, go to spend all the profits that they've made, eternally. And now, if you can, go even one step further into the furnace, back where the coals glow white with rage, where child molesters, bureaucrats, and arms dealers play, and even further still, where the guy who stole my stereo will spend his lonely never-ending night. Picture a heat that hot, only now add to it ninety-eight percent humidity. This is New York in July. We had a ball, living in an unair-conditioned railroad flat whose kindling walls bulged under the weight of the infernal heat.

I'd come to in the worst part of the day, gasping, and kicking away non-existent sheets and covers. She'd already be up, pressing a cold water jug to her forehead, leaning naked against the fridge. My dry voice croaked for her to bring me the water. As she walks towards me, I feel her heat cut through the New York summer, and her wetness damper than the July air. She sees the look in my eye but reacts too slowly, stupefied by the temperature in the little wood oven we called home. The water jug falls to the floor, forgotten, as I pull her down on top of me and drink from her, long and slow.

As the days grew longer, the heat gave birth to some truly inspired inventions. More than once the blistering sun found us lounging in a tub of water, while a fan blew through the cool material of a moistened sheet draped over us from head to toe. Voila! An air conditioner! Rather primitive, to be sure, but that embodied its allure, we were immigrants, setting about exploring our new love, filling the places where others had things, with simple pleasures and ecstasy's screams, from where in the tub we reflected the glare of the sun. Smoking away the heat of the day. Our lighter flicking repeatedly, fighting fire with fire until the sun would retreat.

At night we'd crawl through the streets of the city, tracking the shy breeze that had poked its nose through our open window, then withdrawing with an almost imperceptible tug on our threadbare curtains, all the 'oomph' of an inaudible sigh. People lolled about in doorways and on stoops, half-dressed and blinking stupidly. The women fanned themselves through damp see-through blouses, their legs apart and skirts hitched high above the knees. Inviting our shy breeze to poke its nose anywhere it likes. The neighborhood crazies were out in force. The Man-with-no-nose oozed by, eyeing me conspiratorially. I wonder if he heard us earlier? Me yelling 'I love you' as I drove my point home, again and again? Ah, who cares? We're all nasty, rutting beasts and those who aren't are dead. It was too hot to care or to think, so we just walked along smoking, absorbing whatever hope the night could bring.

Once, a careless drunk staggered into the traffic and got sent airborne by a tourist bus late in leaving this freak show of a city. The tourists' cameras started flashing in hope of capturing the drunk as he sailed through the intersection ahead of the bus and finally coming to rest in the gutter he'd just left as the bus trundled on down the street. Everywhere a stillness, a quiet broken only by the sporadic moaning coming from the drunk. 'Shaddup!' the Man-with-no-nose ordered, and sniffed disgustedly. Then the stillness would return and everyone sat smoking, lazily pondering their existence. She and I would hold onto each other tightly and come to no conclusion other than IT'S TOO DAMN HOT. We'd buy ice cream and return to the tinder-box. We'd play chess in our underwear, smoking, eating ice cream. She moves. I move. She moves. Check. She looks innocently up at me, licking the last of the ice cream from the spoon. The sun starts to rise behind her. I start to rise in front. She chooses me over the sun, and we tumble into bed where I make my final move. MATE.

It all ended rather quickly. One day I came home and found her gone. She'd cleaned the place and baked a cake which sat next to a note on the kitchen table. I ate the note with a glass of milk, then tore the cake into a thousand little pieces. Her dresser drawers were empty as was the clothes hamper. I was hoping she'd overlooked a pair of knickers from which I could inhale her scent again before beginning the arduous task of tracking her down to the ends of the earth and . . . and . . . and what? I had no idea. There was nothing I *could* do, except fall into bed with my guitar, which I banged away on for a month. Playing what was left of my heart out, and crying what was left of my tears, and smoking all the cigarettes North Carolina had exported that year. Classic withdrawal. Finally, I reached the end. I stumbled into the bathroom and a tub of hot water, where every ache and pain was left running down the drain. I smiled rudely to myself, feeling like a new man. It would be hard of course, but I'd make it. This was life, my friend, get used to it. Buckle up! You'll be fine. In the mirror I gave myself a self-mocking scowl, then I reached up on the shelf for a towel, and a pair of her knickers wafted down, landing crotch first on my face. That night, the hunt began . . .

Years later we bumped into each other at the club. She was waiting for me, really, but I didn't mind. There will always be something about her that just kills me, and she knows it. Is that why she'd come? What do I care? I'd been lonely for too long. When she saw me, she took a final puff from her cigarette, then stamped it out and looked up at me – hopefully and a little afraid. So I said 'hey', as though nothing had gone down. As though we'd parted only moments ago. As though . . . As though . . . As though . . . I said 'hey' and she smiled and breathed a slight sigh of relief and then she said 'hey' back to me. Then arm-in-arm we marched right to my bed. God, how I loved her. I thought there must be some hope, some way, some future we could share. I thought of fate and destiny, past lives and tea leaves, of black magic and voodoo and anything else that might explain our recurring rendezvous, as we went about the serious business of washing my sheets in tears and sweat. As usual. God, how I loved her then. I was addicted to her, and she to me. And we always found ourselves rather easily lowering ourselves into each other's hottest fires. Fearlessly leaping into the abyss, mouths locked together in a kiss that killed us long before we ever hit the ground.

Afterwards, we lay there smoking, legs entwined. She spoke softly everything that came to mind, avoiding only that which was real, and the thousand pieces of my heart each broke again, into a million, leaving a fine layer of bittersweet dust on my tongue which then burned away with every inhalation of my hot smoke.

She could still have me, if she'd only let me go. But she won't, ever, and even now she holds me tight with her milky-white thigh and her flat stomach pressed against my hip and her soft, firm breasts pushing against my chest. And I just wanting to die, to disappear behind my cloud, and listen to her prattle on forever and ever . . .

EPILOGUE

London, England, November. I sit staring at the phone and my pack of smokes which sit side by side on the table before me. The cold grey skies bring out the veteran Heathcliff complex which resides in me, near the surface, always ready to rise. She'd never been to England. She would love it here. My hand reaches towards the table, tentatively rests on the phone. She's a call away, waiting. Pain is one plane flight away. Ecstasy on delivery. My hand leaves the phone and swoops up my pack of cigarettes. I light one up and inhale deeply. No, I won't call. I must drop these bad habits one at a time.

And I must start now, with her. 'Goodbye, Catherine,' Heathcliff whispers from the thickening cloud of smoke that surrounds him to this day.

Touch Me, I'm Hicks!
(14 November, 1992)

Following BILL HICKS' recent 'it doesn't matter who you vote for, the government always gets in' rant against the American presidential campaign in these pages, we invited him to sit in a room on election night with STEPHEN DALTON and explain why he's mellowed to the idea of Clinton

'Is this making any sense or am I just jetlagged?' Erm, no, please carry on. Could you repeat the bit about the insect-headed aliens gazing down from the spinning globules of light?

'That night we had a lot of insect realizations. The crickets were not just rubbing their f— ing legs together, it had deep meaning there were these balls of light and inside were these little insect-like beings . . . I don't know what all this means.'

Earth calling Bill Hicks, your signal is breaking up. You may well be America's funniest stand-up surrealist on a whistle-stop tour of Britain. But here in this London hotel, detailing your UFO abduction anecdotes with a perfectly straight face, you are starting to sound like a fruitcake from Planet Drugs.

'I should perhaps first say that I was tripping.'

Ah.

'That's what bugs me about the experience. That's why I quit tripping, but it opened a door and I believe there will be another time. People are starting to realize what is real, what is imagined what's the difference? It's very tempting to go into the desert with a bag of mushrooms right now, but I'm not going to because I want the experience to be real.'

Were these extra-terrestrial insects trying to tell you anything, Bill?

'We're just bugs!'
Of course. It all makes sense now.

Bill Hicks has been almost as ubiquitous in our media during recent weeks as Bill Clinton. Usually, the former has been talking about the latter. Whether snuggling up to Cindy Crawford on TV-AM, riffing madly on late-night comedy shows or dissecting the US electoral circus in these very pages. Hicks displays a rare gift of extracting informed humor from randomly assembled streams of bemused observation.

We meet as the first polls are coming in, but Hicks is rightly confident of a Clinton landslide. 'It's like voting for your dad or for your wacky cool uncle who plays the sax. It's a generational thing, a big deal. Both him and Gore smoked dope, or said they did. They might be lying . . .'

But in the article he wrote for NME two weeks back. Bill was understandably cynical about the whole two-party farce. Why is he getting so affectionate for Clinton now?

'I am cynical, but I believe he offers a very small, narrow, tiny window of opportunity. The rhetoric alone will open people's hearts. It already has. It really is the difference between hope and fear.'

Hope and Fear's crazy bus, maybe (top '70s joke for Pulp and Denim fans). So what does that make Ross Perot?

'Perot is just some screaming bat out of hell. If it's a choice between your dad and your cool uncle, Perot is your grandad who wants to take us all back in time and harness us behind mules!'

Surely Clinton's presidency will be a double-edged sword for comics like Hicks? Who can possibly replace barn-door-sized targets like Bush's evil drawl and Quayle's retarded ramblings?

'They should give Quayle his own network and just ask him questions, that's the show. He's *brilliantly* funny, there's *nothing* there, he's a cypher. And it's just wonderful he has to feign emotions, he has to be *coached* on emotions. When he does anger he *smiles*!'

Hicks traces the explosion which created America's current comedy network back to Reagan's first election victory in 1980, 'which is no coincidence, all this propaganda bullshit being shoved down our throat.' So how will Bill and his fellow dissidents react to a presidential team who can spell the names of major vegetables?

'Obviously a Clinton victory will be bad for comedians. Comics have had the greatest punchbags and been the antidote to 12 years of Republican rule. Now the enemy's all deflated and dead. I feel like all my friends and all the artists were like little pygmies and we've been trying to kill this elephant all these years with little arrows, and finally tonight . . . CRUNCH! Now what? We've got to go hunting again.'

You won't have too long to wait. No doubt Clinton will soon be as shit as every previous president: breaking promises, screwing up the economy, stomping on small countries.

'You're right; even when Kennedy was in office we were under-taking policies that were absolutely horrible, unknown to Americans, as they still are. So what does it all mean? But also during that time there was Martin Luther King and the music and everything. There was hope. My theory is we're going into this horrible down-ward spiral and Clinton is a poor imitation of Kennedy, Madonna's a poor imitation of Marilyn. If they hook up and Clinton is assas-sinated, it's just going to be too *corny*.'

In his new live video, *Relentless*, Hicks plays a boggle-eyed Pied Piper leading several hundred frightened Canadians into a customized universe inhabited by hillbilly aliens, imaginary Iraqi soldiers and moths who fly all the way to the sun. There are no actual jokes. It is hilarious.

Bill stepped into this personalized galaxy aged 13 and hasn't yet emerged. That was when he started writing routines. Five years later, in 1978, he joined the Comedy Workshop in his native Houston and stumbled upon a motley team of like-minded souls.

'All the guys there are still my friends, still totally cool comics, and I think one day the Houston influence will be a chapter in the development of comedy. We really believe in what we're doing, we believe it has a meaning other than making money or that it's a cool showbiz job. Which it's not. We have a philosophy that's very overt. You talk about everything, don't care if you provoke people, there's no rules, it's very free-form. Life can be good if you choose to make it that way, you should tell the truth, expose lies and live in the moment. It's a very Eastern philosophy . . .'

Bill explains his philosophy a bit more. It seems to involve space, peanuts and a stoic refusal to believe in past or future time. It does, at least, sound refreshingly optimistic.

'Yes, but then again, there's another side to me. I am a misanthropic humanist. It's a weird conflict when you are your own *bête noire*. Do like people? They're great *in theory*.'

A friend of Bill's and fellow graduate of the Houston comedy school was Sam Kinison, the controversial stand-up rant artist who died in a car smash earlier this year. Kinison was often accused of spreading hate, although Hicks himself employs far more gentle tactics.

'Thank you so much for seeing that. A lot of people compared Sam and Andrew Dice Clay and I thought that was completely untrue. Sam was a *satirist*. Dice Clay's a *moron*. Sam made some odd choices, and I guess as the venues get bigger you've got to get broader. You lose the subtlety, the click with the audience.'

Hicks spent two years in LA in his early 20s and hated it. Ever the pragmatist, he decided to return there when he recently turned 30. And he still hates it.

'I live in Los Angeles. I just moved there but I'm moving back to New York. I hate LA with all my heart, the sooner it falls into the ocean due to a major earthquake the better the world will be. I hate it so much, I hate people who like it. I'm going across the board on this one. I don't like Los Angeles.'

Stop being wishy washy and evasive, Bill, do you like LA or not?

'Oh, it's alright. Who am I to complain? Haha!'

Oh dear, Bill Hicks is not entirely happy being a comedian. For as long as he can remember, he has yearned to be – wait for it – a rock star. He is even signed to a UK-based record label, Invasion, and is currently touring British rock venues with support from wry, introspective folkies Balloon. How serious are these musical ambitions?

'Serious enough that I'm following up on it. I'm in a band, and when I get back from England I'm going into the studio to do an album of music with my comedy over the top of it. An experimental album, but I think its time has come, and I don't think anyone else could pull it off but me and my friends.'

Hmm. So when can we expect Bill to ditch comedy for good and go all-out rock on us?

'It's really hard to schedule this being-a-rock-star thing. There's no date on that, ha ha!'

Bill's manager calls him a 'rock 'n' roll comic'. What does that mean?

'Now it means nothing, because rock 'n' roll is dead and so is comedy. Ha ha ha ha ha!!!'

Not for the first time, Bill Hicks tosses back his huge insect head and erupts into fits of strange, cricket-like laughter. Now it all makes sense.

Recorded Live at Laff Stop, Austin, TX (December 1992)[51]

Haven't been here in a while, man. Living out in ah Los Angeles now. LA, or as I call it, Hell A, and ah, I just like getting outa there at any point, you know, just to go anywhere, you know, for the weather. They don't have fucking weather there, you know. Hot 'n' sunny every day. Today: hot 'n' sunny in LA. Yesterday: hot 'n' sunny. EVERY DAY: hot 'n' sunny. And they love it. 'Isn't it great? Every day: hot and sunny. Hot and sunny every day. Isn't that neat?' What are you, a fuckin' lizard? Only reptiles *feel* that way about this kind of weather . . . you know? I'm a mammal. I can afford scarves, coats, cappuccino and rosy-cheeked women, and all are available for sale . . . on the streets of New York. Now. Where I will soon be returning because LA is a nightmare city and the sooner it falls into the ocean due to a major earthquake and is flushed away like the *turd* city it is, into the Pacific Bowl, the better this world will be. Thank you, good evening. Yes, good evening. How are you tonight? Good. Thank you. The comedy of hate, join me. It's the newest thing. Join me. Hell, I'm spreading Christmas cheer. Welcome. Oh, won't we party hard when LA goes kersplash? Oh, grin from ear to fuckin' ear, won't we? LA fell in the ocean? Ha ha ha ha ha! (*singing*) 'There is a God. He loves us all so much.'

LA is a nightmare place, man. You always meet this one guy out in LA, you always– this real smarmy guy. He always says this: 'Yeah, I love calling back east January 1st. What are y'all doin'? Snowed in, huh? Bummer. Me? I'm out by the pool! Ha ha ha haaa!' What a *dick* this guy is. It's why I used to love to call LA when I lived in New York: What are y'all doin'? Talking to TV producers, huh?

Bummer. Me? I'm reading a book! Yeah, we're *thinkin'* back east. Yeah, we're *evolving*. Is that the big one I hear in the background? Bye you lizard scum! Bye! (*whoosh*) Ha ha ha ha! It's gone, it's gone, it's gone. Ah, it's gone. All the shitty shows are gone, all the idiots screamin' in the fuckin' wind are dead, I love it. Leaving nothing but a cool, beautiful serenity called . . . Arizona Bay. Ha ha ha! That's right. When LA falls in the fuckin' ocean and is flushed away, all it will leave is Arizona Bay.

So anyway. LA, man. LA, what a nightmare place. Home of the pedestrian right of way law. You ever heard of this law? It's true. Pedestrian right of way law. What this law is – believe this or not, it's absolutely true – if a pedestrian decides to cross a road in LA at any point, any time or anywhere on the road . . . that, they're just walking along, 'Oh, I wanna be over there now', step in road, every car by law has to stop – (*makes braking noise*) – and let this person cross the fuckin' road. Love to see those fuckers try that around here. Wouldn't that be fun? Some LA tourists here . . . stepping in the road, we just speed up, turn our wipers on, you know. Dum-ch, dum-ch, dum-ch. 'Bad call, brother. No great loss – he was from Los Angeles.' The stupidest fuckin' law.

How many of y'all wondered like I did during the LA riots when those people were being pulled out of their trucks and beaten half to death, how many of y'all wondered like I did . . . step on the fuck-ing gas, man! They're on *foot*, you're in a *truck* . . . I think I see a way out of this. It's that pedestrian right of way law. Gang of youths stepped in front of their trucks, Molotov cocktails, clubs in hand, every one of these California idiots: (*makes braking noise*). Freeze-frame! (*singing*) 'Da da da da da da da. Da da da!' That fuckin' Reginald Denny, that truck driver? Never gonna stop again, I guar-antee you. Could be an old woman with a baby carriage crossing the road, he's just (*makes repeated truck-horn sound*). 'Not today, lady. Not today. Tried stoppin' once, didn't work out too well for me. Some of y'all may have caught me getting my ass kicked on the news . . . go ahead and mail that 25-dollar ticket to me, brother. I'll take that over the 25 hundred stitches I had in my left fuckin' CHEEK!' That poor guy, Reginald Denny, Jesus. Everyone, all over the world, people watched this guy get his ass kicked repeatedly, and everyone in the fuckin' world in every country was thinking the same thing: step on the goddamn gas! What are you *doing*? Every country – French people: 'Why you no step on the petrol? The petrol . . . the truck, the [. . .] truck surely outrun the gang of people, I . . .' He could have avoided all this with just one little [. . .] like that. (*makes roaring noise*) You're through 'em at that point. Tap the fuckin' peddle. (*roaring noise*) Chinese — 'Why you not step on gas? Why you–' Man. I bet you anything that Reginald Denny is an exemplary employee at that trucking service he works at, man. His boss is thrilled to have him now.

'Wow, it's Reginald. Here again ahead of schedule. Ha ha! Unbelievable. He's ahead of schedule every run he makes now. It's as though . . . he ain't *stoppin'* out there. It's incredible. I'd love to give him a raise, but every time I run up to the cab he starts backing away.' (*truck horn*) 'Seems rather skittish.'

I was over in ah England. I went over to England the day the LA riots occurred. I left LA the day the LA riots occurred. *Unbelievable* timing. I left LA:

'Bye Bill, enjoy England.'
'I will, y'all have fun while I'm gone.'
'We will, Bill. Bye.'

I land at Heathrow Airport eleven hours later, pass a newspaper stand: 'LA Burns to Ground.' Holy shit. Did I leave a cigarette lit? How much are these? See if my picture's in here, man. It's literally the timing. And I'm over there in England, you know, trying to get news of the riots, you know, and all these Brit people are trying to sympathize with me:

'Oh Bill, crime is . . . horrible. Bill, if it's any consolation, crime is horrible here too.'
'Shut up. This is Hobbiton and I'm Bilbo Hicks, OK? This is the land of fairies and elves. You do not have crime like we have crime. I appreciate you tryin' to be, you know, diplomatic but . . .'

You gotta see English crime, if *only* we had crime like this, you know. It's hilarious. You don't know if you're reading the front page or the comic section over there. I swear to God. I read an article, front page of the paper one day in England: 'Yesterday some hooligans knocked over a dustbin in Shaftsbury.'

> 'Whoo-oo!'
> 'The hooligans are loose, the hooligans are loose. What if they become ruffians? I would hate to be a dustbin in Shaftsbury tonight. (*singing*) No one knows what it's like to be a dustbin . . . in Shaftsbury . . . with hooligans.'

What the hell are you *talking* about? Hooligans, ruffians – speak English! It's Crip, Blood. I mean, I'm sure it's a serious thing, hooligans, but it just sounds stupid, doesn't it? Picture a bunch of pale guys with penny loafers and no socks.

> (*singing*) 'We're the hooligans.' (*Pop!*)
> 'Hey, you fucker, come here.'
> 'Nope, got to catch us. You corner me, I might become a scallywag.'

You know, it's— yeah. It doesn't sound scary at all, does it? They have *proper* crime there. Yeah, I'd love to put the hooligans up against the Bloods in LA, that would be a . . . a short gang-battle.

> (*singing*) 'We're the hooligans.' (*Pop!*)
> (*three gunshots*) 'Huh? Hoola something, I didn't catch it all. Motherfucker danced up to me and patted me on the head. A *pale* motherfucker, *look* at that thing.'

It just wouldn't be a long gang-battle. I'm bettin' on the Bloods.

But ah . . . I was over there, I was over there when all the riots were occurring, man. It was really strange. An' I got to see while I was over there ah footage of the Rodney King trial, which I had never seen while I was here. I saw footage over there of the Rodney King trial. I *think* I figured out why the LA riots occurred. Did you guys see these cops testifyin', man? Did these guys have *balls*, or what, man? These guys carry their balls in a wheelbarrow, man.

"Scuse me, 'scuse me . . . Man with big balls is here to testify.'
'Place your right testicle on the Bible.'
(*whoosh, crash*)

This guy, Officer *Coon* . . . is life too fuckin' weird or what? Officer *Coon* looks in the camera and actually says, 'Oh, that Rodney King beating tape? It's all in how you look at it.' Courtroom murmurs, 'Jesus, what *balls*! I've never seen balls of this magnitude, this . . . he must have a specially fitted uniform . . . in which to place these large testicles. That's . . . that's incredible.'

'All in how you look at it, Officer . . . Coon?'
'That's right. It's how you look at the tape.'
'Well, would you care to tell the court (*incredulously*) how . . . you're lookin' at that?'
'Yeah OK, sure. It's how you look at it . . . the tape. For instance, well, if you play it backwards[52] you see us help King up and send him on his way.'
'Hmmmm. Not guilty!' (*bang*)
"Scuse me, 'scuse me . . . Man with big balls has just been acquitted.'

And I watch all the news reports, you know.

'Today Officer Coon, Officer Nigger Hater and Officer Keep Darkie Down . . . were acquitted on all racist charges. Here's Tom with the weather.'
'Hi Susie, it's 420 degrees Fahrenheit here in South Central LA right now. Probably a good time to get outa the fuckin' city, Susie. There's gusts of lead coming up Sunset.'

And then President Bush ah came out, and said, you know, not to worry, the justice system wasn't done with those cops yet. Yeah. Fact Bush called together a special committee made up of the surviving members of the Warren Commission to review all the evidence. Yeah. Yeah, well. They came up with the Magic Baton Theory. One baton blow just went outa hand.

'See it, it's bouncin' off his head – help! Would you believe I'm tryin' to stop it? Help me! Help me!'
'I'm gettin' my big balls away from that stick. Officer Keep Darkie Down, get Officer Nigger Hater to help ya.'
'Come on, Officer Coon!'

Boy, I love talkin' about the Kennedy Assassination, man. That's my favourite topic. You know why?

Audience: Why?

Bill: Because for me it's a great archetypal example of how the totalitarian government who rules this planet partitions out information in such a way that we, the masses, are forced to base our conclusions on erroneous— Oh, I'm sorry, wrong meeting. I thought this was the meeting ah . . . at the docks, no? Oh, shit. That's tomorrow night. All right. (*laughs*) Everyone *followed* that, that's the frightening fuckin' thing. Everyone here's going, 'Ah-huh.' Goddamn it! Are we that cynical? 'Yes we are, Bill. We will take any blow you give us. GO! We too will be at the meeting at the docks tomorrow, you fucker.' That was funny. Every one of ya, 'What was?' Wow. Cool.

But I, I love Kennedy, man. I was just down in ah, just up in where, I was just in Dallas, and ah . . . you know, you can go to the sixth floor of the School Book Depository. D'you know it's a museum called the Assassination Museum? D'you know that? True. I believe named that *after* the assassination, I . . . can't be sure of the chronology here, but . . . But it's really weird, you can actually ah, they have the windows set up to look exactly like it did on that day, and it's really accurate, you know, cos Oswald's not in it. (*laughs*) Yeah. So. I don't know who did their research, but I'm talkin' *painstaking* detail. It's true, man. It's called the Sniper's Nest and it's all glassed in with the boxes sittin' there; you can't actually get to the window. And the reason they did that of course, they didn't want thousands of American tourists getting to that window each year, you know, going, 'There's no fuckin' way! I can't even see the road! Oh my God, they're lyin'. It's a giant totalitarian government that rules the planet via the airwaves, partitioning off information in such a way—' Oh! There's no fuckin' way, man. Not unless Oswald was hanging by his toes . . . upside down from the ledge. Surely someone would have seen this. Either that or some pigeons grabbed on to him, and flew him over the motorcade. You know, there was rumors of anti-Castro pigeons seen drinking in bars the night before the assassination. Someone overheard them saying, 'Coup! Coup!' Aww . . . all right. Don't get on your we-hate-puns high horse. Fuck you! That is the best goddamn pun you will ever hear! Oh God. (*laughs*) Was kind of a rotten trick to make a pun out of that, wasn't it? 'You— ohhhh. Jackin' with us, man.' But you know, Oswald . . . I tell you seriously, man, talkin' about the Kennedy assassination, cos to me it really is this incredible example of something. I don't know what yet. It's pretty . . . engrossing to me. But ah, people's attitudes – it's just incredible to me, you know. People come up and, 'Bill, quit talkin' about Kennedy, man. Let it go. It's a long time ago, would you just forget about it?' I'm like, 'OK, then don't bring up Jesus to me . . . you know, as long as we're talking shelf life here.'

'Bill, you know Jesus died for you.'
'Yeah, it was a long time ago. Let it go. Forget about it.'

How 'bout this: get Pilate to release the fucking files. Quit washing your hands and release the files, Pilate. Who else was on that grassy Golgotha that day? Oh yeah, the three Roman peasants with the hundred-dollar sandals. Yeah, right!

So what else happened, man? I'm over in fuckin' England, and Bush fuckin' loses![53] Must have been a secret . . . it must have been a secret service plot to keep me out the country the night he lost . . . just to protect Bush, you know . . . his eardrums from shattering when I shrieked with fuckin' laughter. AAAH-HA HA HA HA! He's dead! It's dead! The Republican beast is fuckin' dead! Twelve years of that rampaging Republican fuckin' elephant-beast finally brought to its knees. (*trumpets like elephant, then makes crashing noise*) Yes! You're dead, you fucker! You fuck! You fuck, you're dead! Dead! Dead! Dead! We hate you! Hate you! Now do you know it? Now do you feel it? Feel the fuckin' hate. Feel it. Call off your dogs. Call your little Vietnamese pot-bellied Rush Limbaugh back to your fold, you demon fuck! Bring Pat Buchanan back![54] Call him back, you lost! Finally . . . the Republican beast-elephant brought to its fuckin' knees. Cos I feel like me and my friends and all the artists in the fuckin' country were like little pygmy tribes shootin' darts at that elephant for twelve years, and finally (*elephant trumpeting, then crashing noise*). Do our little pygmy dance: (*singing*) Na na na na na na na! Na na na na na na na! Na na na! Yes!

Boy, I tell you, politics does make for strange bedfellows. That's true, man. I read a quote in the paper two days after the election from Saddam Hussein, and ah he said – oh, they had to wait two days to get a quote from him, you know. They had to wait for him to quit *gut-laughing* . . . some bunker in Baghdad, you know: 'Aaah-ha ha ha ha ha ha ha! Haah! The elephant is dead.' Saddam Hussein says in this quote, 'We have nothing against America. We just want to see George Bush beheaded and his head kicked down the road like a soccer ball.' And I was thinking, that's so weird, cos . . . that's what *I* wanted to see. Wow, me and Hussein, we're like *this*. Who woulda thunk it?

'He's a Hitler.' You know, they find out, you know, Bush has been selling weapons to Iraq since whenever, and we knew that – I knew that, during the Persian Gulf War those intelligence reports would come in:

> 'Iraq – incredible weapons, incredible . . . weapons.'
> 'How do y'all know that?'
> 'Well . . . we looked at the receipt. But as soon as that cheque clears, we're goin' in. What time's the bank open? Eight? We're goin' in at nine . . . for God and country, and he's a Hitler, and hey, look, a foetus, so whatever you need, let's go! Whatever you, the apathetic, docile masses, need to get behind– here, here's a foetus. Come on!'
> 'Ah, it's a little foetus, look. It's a little foetus. I hate this man all of a sudden. He's a Hit— he's holdin' a little foetus.'

I tell you one thing: I'm glad fuckin' Bush lost to get rid of those pro-life fucks off my TV! That little foetus got more TV time than I did last year, goddamn it! I don't know who that little foetus' agent is, but *goddamn it*, that little foet– he was on more TV than me! He had some agent.

> 'You're gonna be big one day, kid. You're gonna be huge. I'm gonna have you swimmin' in pools of formaldehyde, kid. You're gonna be a big foetus, oh yeah. I'm gonna have you the wacky next-door-neighbour foetus, kid. You're gonna be *huge*. Move out to LA, kid. I'll introduce you to some of Drew Barrymore's children.'

Yes, come on. Let it out. Let it out! LET IT OUT!

But you know, I'm just so sick of this whole deal. We arm the world, we arm these little countries and then we send troops over to blow the shit out of 'em, you know? We're like the, we're like the bullies of the world right now, do you know that? We're like Jack Palance in the movie *Shane*, throwing the pistol at the sheep herder's feet.

> 'Pick it up.'
> 'I don't wanna pick it up, mister. You'll shoot me.'
> 'Pick up the gun.'
> 'Look, mister. I don't want no trouble. I just came to town to get some hard-rock candy for my kids and some gingham for my wife. I don't even know what gingham is, but . . . she goes through about four or five rolls a week of that stuff. I don't want no trouble, mister.'
> 'Pick up the gun. (*three gunshots*) You all saw him: he had a gun.'

Another great thing about ah . . . 'bout ah Bush being gone, it ends twelve years of fundamentalist Christians . . . in the fuckin' White House. Thank you, God. Finally my prayer got through. I was on hold with that prayer for about eight years, with fuckin' ringing: 'God, help us. God, are you there? Surely this is a really bad fuckin' joke, God. This B-actor idiot, fuckin' illiterate bozo-lookin' fuck can't be the President of the country, can he, God, not really? Reach your hands down from the clouds and pinch my butt, make sure

I'm not DREAMIN'!' Finally my prayer got through. Did ya'll know
– you wanna hear something absolutely – this is *fascinating* to me,
this is *ab*solutely fascinating: fundamentalist Christians believe the
world is 12,000 years old. Is that . . . let's just *think* about that.
Isn't that great? And I ask 'em, 'How do you think that? Why do
you think the world's 12,000 years old?' They go:

> 'Well, we added up all the people born from Adam and
> Eve, added up their ages: roughly 12,000 years.'
> 'Well, how scientific. I can't fuckin' argue with that kind
> of, you know, research. You think the world's 12,000
> years old?'
> 'That's right.'
> 'K. Can I ask you a question?'
> 'Sure.'
> 'It's a one-word question.'
> 'Fine.'
> 'Dinosaurs.'

I mean, if the world's 12,000 years old and the Bible covers it, why
didn't someone bring up fuckin' dinosaurs? You'd think someone
woulda brought that up . . . somewhere in the goddamn book:

> And Jesus and the disciples walked down the path
> towards Nazareth, but oh, the trail was blocked by a
> giant Brontosaurus . . . with a splinter in his paw. And
> the disciples did run a-screaming, 'What a big fuckin'
> lizard, Lord.'
> 'I'm sure gonna mention this in my book,' said Luke.
> 'Well, I'm sure gonna mention it in my book,' said
> Matthew.
> 'I'm not sure what I saw,' said Thomas.
> Timothy nudged him: 'It was a big fuckin' lizard, hey
> Thomas?'
> But Jesus was unafraid, and he took the splinter from
> the Brontosaurus' paw, and the Brontosaurus became
> his friend. And Jesus sent him to Scotland where he
> lived in a loch, O so many years, attracting the fat

American families with their fat fuckin' dollars to look
for the Loch Ness Monster. And O the Scotch did praise
the Lord: 'Thank you, Lord. Thank you, Lord.'

Twelve thousand years old. I asked this guy, said, 'Come on, man
– dinosaur fossils. What's the deal?' He goes:

'God put those here to test our faith.'
'I think God put you here to test *my faith*, dude. I think
I've figured this out.'

Does that— That's what this guy said. Does that bother anyone
here? The idea that *God* might be fuckin' with our heads? Anyone
have trouble sleepin' restfully with that thought in their heads?
God's runnin' around, burying fossils: 'Ho, ho ho! . . . We'll see who
believes in me now. Ho ho! I'm a prankster God. I am killing me.
Ho ho ho ho!' You know. You die, you go to St Peter:

'Did you believe in dinosaurs?'
'Well yeah, there was fossils everywhere. (*crash*) Aaargh!'
'What are you, an idiot? God was fucking with you!
Giant flying lizard, you moron! That's one of God's *easi-
est* jokes.'
'It seemed so plausible! Aaaaargh!'

Bound for the Lake of Fire.

You ever notice how people who believe in Creationism look really
unevolved? Eyes real close together, big furry hands and feet. 'I
believe God created me in one day.' Yeah, looks like he rushed it.

Now we have women priests. What do y'all think of that? Women
priests? Yeah. I think it's fine, women priests, you know. So what?
Now we got priests of both sexes I don't listen to. Fuck, I don't
care. Have one with three balls and eight titties, I don't fuckin'
care, you know. Have a hermaphrodite one, I don't, I don't care.
Have one with gills and a trunk – I might go to that service. (*makes
noise like elephant trumpeting*) I don't give a fuck, OK? While I
appreciate your quaint traditions, superstitions and, you know, I,
on the other hand, am an evolved being who deals solely with the

source of light which exists in all of us in our own minds. No middle man required. (*laughs sarcastically*) But anyway, I appreciate your little games and shit, you putting on the tie and going to church, a da da da da. But you know there's a LIVING GOD WHO WILL TALK DIRECTLY FUCKIN' TO YOU! Sorry, not through the pages of the Bible but FORGOT TO MENTION DINOSAURS!

By the way, if anyone here is in marketing or advertising . . . kill yourself. Thank you. Just planting seeds, planting seeds is all I'm doing. No joke here, really. Seriously, kill yourself, you have no rationalization for what you do, you are Satan's little helpers. Kill yourself, kill yourself, kill yourself now. Now, back to the show. Seriously, I know the marketing people: 'There's gonna be a joke comin' up.' There's no fuckin' joke. Suck a tail pipe, hang yourself . . . borrow a pistol from an NRA buddy, do something . . . rid the world of your evil fuckin' presence. OK, back to the show. Plantin' seeds. Will they bear fruit? I don't know. Feel better plantin'. You know what bugs me, though? Everyone here who's in marketing is now thinkin' the same thing: 'Oh, cool. Bill's going for that anti-marketing dollar. That's a huge market.' (*crying*) Quit it, quit it. Don't turn everything into a dollar sign, *please*! 'Oooh. The plea-for-sanity dollar – huge! *Huge* market! Look at our research.'

You know, isn't marketing the most evil concept ever? Like for instance, I saw this – you know what they do to movies now? This just drives me crazy. They show movies now to test audiences before the movie is released, and then change the movie depending on how these 200 *random* . . . *yahoos* – underline 'yahoo', point some fingers at it with a big exclamation fuckin' point – *ya-fuckin'-hoo* liked it or did not like it. As though we are all the same, as though we have the same taste, as though, as though, as though. For instance, saw a movie this year called *Basic* . . . *Instinct*. Now. Bill's quick capsule review: piece of shit. Thank you. That's all it was, by the way. Don't get caught up in the phoney hysteria surrounding this *piece of shit* film. 'Was it too sexist, and what about the leg, did you think that maybe—' Tha tha tha tha tha tha tha tha you're way off base. You've forgotten how to perceive correctly. Take a deep breath (*breathes*), watch it again: 'Hey, it's a piece of shit.' Exactly. That's all it ever was, was A PIECE OF SHIT. I just had to say that and clear it up. This *phoney hype* around this piece of shit film drove me crazy. Anyway, after I saw it about eight times . . . come to find out, after seeing this film, all of the lesbian sex sce– let me repeat this part of the show – all of the lesbian sex scenes were *cut* out of this film, because the test audience . . . was turned *off* by them. (*laughs*) Boy, is my thumb not on the pulse of America. I don't wanna seem like Randy Pan the Goatboy . . . but that was the only reason I went to that piece of shit film. Sorry. If I had been in that test audience, the only one out front protesting that film woulda been Michael Douglas demanding his part be put back in.

'I *swear* I was in that movie. I *swear* I was!'
'Well Gee, Mike, the movie started, Sharon Stone was eating another woman for an hour and a half . . . then the credits rolled. Ha ha ha! I don't remember seeing your scrawny ass. Ohh! Was that you in the corner when she flipped her over and started eating her butt? Was that . . . oh yeah, you were good. You were really good. I was a little, I was watchin' something else, but I saw you real briefly. She flipped her over, opened her ch— ahhhhh, started eating her ass, and I said, "Was that Michael Doug– oh, who gives a fuck. Look at that."'

See, what I'm saying is it'd be a different film if *I* was the test audience, that's all I'm trying to get at here. Don't try an' talk for me, please.

You know though, I don't get it, man. I tell you what, I have this new fear. Cos I know, I know that I'm in a case of arrested development emotionally. I know that now. Cos I realize, you know, like ah if you— anyone can go to the video store near my house and see what I've rented the past year. It's fairly frightening, you know? Unbelievable evidence of an emotionally, you know, ah . . . digression goin' on here. Porno movies and video games. What am I, *thirteen* emotionally? You know what I mean? I'm sitting there looking at this receipt I got from them, it's like *Clam Lappers* and Sonic Hedgehog. That was one *weekend*. That was *Easter* weekend. Something's going on with me, man. That's pretty scary way to celebrate the resurrection of Christ . . . with *Clam Lappers* and Sonic fucking Hedgehog. You know? I'm . . . my big fear now is I'm gonna go rent a porno film at this one store I go to a lot, I'm gonna go rent a porno film and take it to the front, you know, and give it to the guy, and he's gonna do that little 'doot!' and suddenly (*makes sound of alarm*): 'You've just rented your millionth porno tape!' (*alarm*) 'Get a picture of him with it! *Anal Entry*, volume 500 – he made it through every one of 'em!' (*alarm*) Give me the little trophy. Millionth porno tape, wow! Lucky fuckin' me. *And* along with Super Mario 2. I wish they'd combine video and porno. That would be great, man, you know? Video games and porno films? I'd have high score on *Clam Lappers* by now. I wish they did have interactive porno – you know they come out with this thing now, interactive movies? They're showing it in New York right now. Interactive movie – you watch the movie and then you determine which way you want the plot to go. This is fucked! This is technology solely for porno films . . . as far as I'm concerned. You know what I mean? I am so sick of being ripped off – if you've got enough courage to make porno films, go ahead and be *creative* about it. You're, you're already over the, you know, you've jumped the chasm here. 'We're gonna film people fuckin' and suckin'.' Cool! Now go crazy. You already made the jump. You are within the Dark Lord's terrain at this point. There's no reason to get *coy*. You're drugging up runaways down at fuckin' Sunset Boulevard right now. I don't think you need to have morality plays goin' on in the porno tape. Go ahead and satisfy my carnal base fuckin' needs. Interactive porno – that's the future, my friends. Then all dating will be history. Ah well. It's backed-up Wil— this is backed-up Willie talking. I always get my most depressed when I'm backed up, man.

No, but you know . . . it's hard to have a relationship in this business, man. You're always travelling, keeping weird hours, you know. It's gonna take a very special woman, you know . . . or a bunch of average ones. Which, I mean I'm saying that either way . . .

But anyway, I'm reading this article in the paper a few years ago about Ted Bundy.[55] Now, this is absolute— listen, there's still cheering for him: 'Whoo!' I think you're thinkin' of a different Ted Bundy here . . . not the shoe salesman on the TV show, this is . . . I don't know what the other connection. Well, this . . . the guy I'm talkin' about used a shoehorn once, but I won't tell you what for, because . . . But anyway, Ted Bundy the mass murderer's who I'm referring to. If you're gonna pick a hero, you know, do your research. Now . . . no, but anyway, this is absolutely true. If anyone can verify this it'll help, cos it's gonna sound absolutely far-fetched, *but* I read an article in the paper. Ted Bundy's on trial in Florida, on trial – twenty-four women the guy killed, I don't know. Twenty-four women – he's on trial. The paper says the courtroom is filled with women . . . trying to *meet him* . . . and give him LOVE LETTERS AND WEDDING FUCKIN' proposals. Does anyone remember reading this fuckin' article? (*cheers and claps*) That's enough to continue the bit. Now . . . if no one had applauded, I'd still be doin' it. How? We don't know. You have to rationalize on your feet. All I know is I got a script and I'm headin' towards the ending. I will not be stopped. Courtroom filled with women trying to meet Ted Bundy, give him love letters and wedding proposals – this is what the article says. And I'm sorry to say the first thing I thought when I read that was, 'And *I'm* not gettin' laid.' What am I doing wrong, you know? A natural question. So I read another article in the paper, ah . . . woman is suing the state of Wisconsin. Why would anyone sue the state of Wisconsin? Well, here's why. She married a fella . . . on Death Row. Why is he on Death Row? He killed eight women. She married him (*laughs*) there's more . . . he has Aids – let's up the ante of the story. You wanna? Who wants to still play with my story now? Cos I'm upping the ante – he is on Death Row for killing eight women, he has Aids, she married him, and is suing the state for the right . . . of conjugal visits! Now, I'm sorry to say the first thing that crossed my mind when I read that was . . . And *I'm* not gettin' laid.' Hey. What exactly are you ladies lookin' for here? These guys must've been *heavy* on the sense of humor thing you seem to love so much in your little ladies polls. 'Ted Bundy, that old whip. He's *hilarious*. Some of the things Ted would do, he *kills* me. Hoh, what a sense of *humor* he had. Ah. I overlooked the mass murder thing cos he kept me in *stitches*.' But you know, it's just depressing, you know what I mean? You know, Michael Bolton, Garth Brooks, Achy Breaky fuckin' dick this guy is, Ted Bundy getting wedding proposals, you know – we're fucked up here, man. I guarantee you Satan's gonna have no problems on this planet, cos all the women are gonna go:

'What a cute butt!'
'He's *Satan*.'
'You don't know him like I do.'
'He's the Prince of Darkness.'
'I can change him.'

And I bet that's true. I wouldn't put Satan– give Satan a snowball's chance in hell against a woman's ego, man. He'd rule the earth for a day, a week later we'd see Satan out cuttin' the lawn. (*makes lawn-mower noise*)

'Hey, aren't you Satan?'
'Shut up.'
'Whoa, Mr Prince of Darkness. You forgot to edge–'
'Shut up!' (*lawnmower noise*)

See him at the supermarket buying tampons:

'Tampons, aisle 3. Hey, aren't you Satan?'
'Shut up!'
'You're pussywhipped! You're not Prince of Darkness, you're Pussywhipped of Darkness!'
'Quit it, I'm Satan.'
'Ah, bullshit! You dropped your tampons, Satan.'

Thanks, you've been great. Hope you enjoyed it! Great to see y'all. You're the greatest crowd in the world. I hope you enjoyed it very much. Thank you. Good night.

Part 3:
Early to Mid 1993

Bill Hicks: Comedy for the Head
By Cree McCree *High Times* (April 1993)

'Come on into my twisted fuckin' soul.' Thus Bill Hicks begins a 'giggle tour' of mass murderers, whose highlights include a Jeffrey Dahmer Tupperware party. But what he really lays bare tonight, on the eve of an impending European tour, is the twisted fuckin' soul of Just-Say-No America.

'My biggest pet peeve,' the pallid, black-garbed Texan confides to a hipper-than-usual crowd at Caroline's comedy club in midtown Manhattan, 'is the war against drugs. Actually, it's a war against your civil rights.' Amidst a loud consensus of claps, Hicks continues: 'Marijuana's against the law. Marijuana, a drug that kills no one . . . Ever.'

That single word 'ever' elicits more laughter than many comedians milk from a fistful of one-liners.

A no-bullshit libertarian – he's enthusiastically pro-porn – with an acute sense of the sardonic, Hicks has made his own war against the War on Drugs a comedic *cause célèbre*. That he himself is now totally straight, following a collision course with booze and cocaine that landed him in recovery, has, if anything, strengthened his stance.

'My honest-to-God belief about drugs?' he asks onstage, not at all rhetorically. 'God let certain drugs grow naturally on this planet to help speed up our evolution. Do you think psilocybin mushrooms growing on top of cowshit was an accident? Where do you think the phrase "that's good shit" comes from?' Amidst hoots and whistles,

Hicks demonstrates 'god's little accelerator pad for our evolution': the discovery of 'shrooms by Planet of the Ape types, a grunt-and-gobble *tour de force* which climaxes with his incantation of 'The 2001 Theme.' 'Ommmmmmmm,' he chants in blissful elation. 'I think we can go to the moon now!' Pause for the organic laughtrack, then the tagline: 'That's exactly how the fuck it happened.'

More hipster monologist than stand-up comic, Hicks really believes that's exactly how the fuck it happened. After the show, he greets me warmly. Not once does he plug a career launched by David Letterman and nurtured by HBO. A sponge for quirky detail and useful data, he's as fascinated by my 'shroom experiences (not excerpted here) as his own. Bill Hicks is a dead serious and wickedly funny conversationalist who treats an interviewer just like his audience: as collaborator, not consumer.

Your management was reluctant for you to do a HIGH TIMES interview. Did they think it would spoil your image?
Well, 'Heroin Quarterly' had me first . . . no [laughs]. I have no idea what the problem was. I think all drugs should be legal – across the board, effective immediately. Law enforcement doesn't stop anyone from doing drugs. All it does is make criminals out of them.

Do you think there's any danger that, if drugs are legalized, corporate interests will take over?
Anything corporate is dangerous and harmful. [Drugs] should all be legal and free. Profit should be against the law. That'll stop those fuckers.

When you went through recovery to quit drinking and cocaine and clean up your whole act, did pot have to go along with everything else?
Oh, absolutely. That's part of the deal with the program. Everything goes. There's no middle ground.

Back in the days when you were still smoking pot, what's the most fun you ever had?
Well, to be honest with you, I was never a big pot fan. Which is very ironic, because I always espouse the virtues of marijuana. My thing was mushrooms.

I didn't know there was such a thing as a mushroom abuser.
There isn't. I went to AA, not MA. It wasn't abuse. It was right on
the money. To tell you the truth, the reason I quit doing mushrooms was because I had a UFO experience.
So that's a true story? That's not just a comic riff?
No, that's true. What's frustrating is that every time I tell the story,
the first thing people ask is were you tripping? And I go, yeah. And
they go, oh yeah, right. But it was really profound, and I want to
experience it again. Totally straight. So I can tell people I was straight.
**Have you read Terence McKenna's The Archaic Revival?[56]
Because your routine about apes discovering psilocybin is
part of his whole theory of evolution.**
I haven't, but I did read the *Esquire* article and it sounds incredible. But it's nothing that anyone who's ever experienced it doesn't
already know. And we go, yeah, cool, insects – I'm with you! The
insect consciousness.
**Tonight's audience really got off on your drug riffs, but I'm
sure you get some negative feedback too.**
Oh yeah. What really bugs me is that a lot of people don't even
have a tie-in with alcohol as a drug. I've never been attacked by a
pothead, but I've had drunks scare the shit out of me. Also, it does-
n't always register that people who smoke pot are under arrest in
a lot of places[57] and their belongings are taken from them by the
government. It's amazing how scared they've made everyone. They
can suspend the Bill of Rights and people think *it's a good thing*.
'Just Say No' is the extent of our drug education in this country.
All my friends said yes and I'll guarantee you we learned a lot more
about drugs. Just say yes, and you'll learn.
If you were elected President, what's the first thing you'd do?
I'd make Bush pay for his war against humanity crimes. Same for
Reagan.
What kind of punishment would you mete out?
I'd make [Reagan] watch his movies.
What about Bush?
I'd make him sleep with his wife. Because you know that is not
happening.
And Quayle?

He's the only guy I'd pardon. I want him. He's the jester of America, man. I'd put him on TV 24 hours a day . . .

His very own C-Span. Q-Span!

Exactly!

What's up for you in 1993?

I'm going to record a new album with my band, Marblehead – a comedy album but with music all the way through. Totally overboard with music and a spoken-word type poem. A rant. Maybe I'll call it 'Bill's Iliad.'

I feel a lot better knowing you're out there in the world. We need more people speaking out about real life.

Hey, I appreciate that. And I'm sorry about the delay on the HIGH TIMES interview. But those managers who made that little decision? They are no longer! HIGH TIMES will prevail.

Outside Broadcast, Branch Davidian Compound, Waco (8 March, 1993)[58]

Could be the end is nigh for Mr Koresh, aka Jesus, aka Vernon. Had he stuck with the name Vernon, the only people out here reporting right now would probably be the local farm report: 'Vernon's got some pigs locked up in a hole. We don't know what's happening, but Vernon's locking some pigs up there.' But the fact that he named himself David Koresh just goes to show a rose is just a rose by any other name, it's just a ah Yahweh. Anyway, we're outside Mount Carmel camp. The Davidian-Yahweh division, Latter-day Saints and Lutheran-Jehovah-Witness-Baptist-Methodist break-off group who believes in ah . . . that the literal interpretation of the Bible in Genesis is actually not exactly true. The literal story of creation in Genesis is true, and after that God created the sub-machine gun. Man named all the animals and then began shooting them one by one. Sort of a new breed of Christianity here in America, and one that ah, well, suffers no quarter. And there's forgiveness enough for everyone here, I'm sure. All I know is there's gonna be hell to pay when David Koresh aka Jesus aka Vernon Howell makes his final move for the Lord. We all come to this position at some point in our lives, that big chasm, that gap you have to jump into, and it's called faith. Unlike the rest of us though, David Koresh is armed to the gills, and when he makes the big leap it's gonna be hell to pay all around him. Anyway, we're out here, out at Mount Carmel, the Branch-Davidian-Latter-day-Saint-Adventist-Seven-Day-Church-Lutheran-Yahweh division breakaway group that believes of course in forgiveness, that Christ died and was resurrected, and then he's come back to kick some major ass. It's all out there. Looks like Grandma's house. In fact I think Grandma is being held hostage right now by the Branch Davidian-Adventist-Latter-Day-Saint-Yahweh division breakaway group, led by David Koresh, aka Jesus, aka Vernon. 'That's not Jesus, that's Vernon.' Anyway, it's day seven. It can't go on for ever. We'll be here till something happens.

> Pornography is good.
> All drugs should be legal.
> War is wrong.
> The rich get richer.
> The poor get poorer.
> Thank you I'll be here all week.

Ceremony Program, American Comedy Awards, March 1993

Recorded Live at Laff Stop, Austin, TX, and Cobbs, San Francisco, CA (Spring and Summer 1993)[59]

Well, folks, this is kind of a sentimental evening for me because . . . this is my final live performance I'll ever do, ever. No biggie, no, no, no, no, no hard feelings, no sour grapes whatsoever. I've been doing this sixteen years, enjoyed every second of it – every plane flight, every [. . .], every delay, every canceled flight, every lost luggage, living in hotel rooms, every broken relationship, playing the Comedy Pouch in Possum Ridge, Arkansas, every fucking year. It's been great, don't get me wrong.

But the fact of the matter is, the reason I'm gonna quit performing is I finally got my own TV show coming out next fall on CBS. So – thank you. I know. It is *not* a talk show. (*heavy breathing*) Dear God, thank you, thank Jesus, thank Buddha, thank Mohammad, thank Allah, thank Krishna, thank every fucking god in the book. (*heavy breathing*) Please rela— (*heavy breathing*) No, it's not a talk show: it's a half-hour weekly show that I will host, entitled 'Let's Hunt and Kill Billy Ray Cyrus'. So y'all be tuning in? Cool, cool. Cool, it's a fairly self-explanatory plot, ah . . . Each week we let the hounds of hell loose and we chase that jar-head, no-talent, cracker asshole all over the globe . . . till I finally catch that fruity little ponytail of his in the back, pull him to his knees, put a shotgun in his mouth like a big black cock of death (*shotgun boom*) and we'll be back in '95 with 'Let's Hunt and Kill Michael Bolton'. So.

Thank you very much. I'm just trying to rid the world of all these fevered egos that are tainting our collective unconscious and making us pay a higher psychic price than we imagine. In fact, that's how I pitched it to the networks exactly, I said ah . . . 'I'd like to do a show where I rid the world of all these fevered egos that are tainting our collective unconscious', and the guy at CBS said, 'Will there be titty?' And ah I said, 'Sure, I don't know, sure.' Boom! A cheque falls in my lap and ah . . . I'm a producer. I never knew it was that easy. All these years I been trying to write scripts and characters and plots and stories that had meaning. 'Will there be titty?' Sure. Boom! I'm a . . . I'm a producer now. 'Where've you been all our life, boy? We been lookin' for you in Hollywood. What are these titties gonna do? Jiggle? You're a fuckin' genius. Give him another cheque. I can't write enough cheques for you. You've answered our prayers in Hollywood. Jiggling titties, who would have thunk of it?'

I was over in Australia during Easter, which was interesting. Interesting to note they celebrate Easter the same way we do, commemorating the death and resurrection of Jesus . . . by telling our children a giant bunny-rabbit . . . left chocolate eggs in the night. Now . . . I wonder why we're fucked up as a race. Anybody? Anybody got any clues out there? Where do you get this shit from, you know? Why those two things, you know? Why not goldfish left Lincoln Logs in your sock drawer, you know? As long as we're making shit up, go hog-wild, you know? At least a goldfish with a Lincoln Log on its back, going across your floor to your sock drawer, has a miraculous connotation to it.

'Mummy, I woke up today and there was a Lincoln Log in me sock drawer.' 'That's the story of Jesus.'

Who comes up with this shit? I read the Bible, I can't find the word 'bunny' or 'chocolate' anywhere in that fucking book.

D'y'all have different books of the Bible than I do? Are y'all Gideons? Who *are* the fucking Gideons? Ever met one? No! Ever seen one? No! But they're all over the fucking world, putting Bibles in hotel rooms. Every hotel room: 'This Bible was placed here by a Gideon.' When? I've been here all day. I ain't seen shit. I saw the house-keeper come and go, I saw the minibar guy come and go, I've never laid eyes on a fucking Gideon. What are they – Ninjas? Where are they? Where're they from – Gidea? What the fuck are these people? I'm gonna capture a Gideon. I'm gonna make that my hobby. I am. I'm gonna call the front desk one day: 'Yeah, I don't seem to have a Bible in my room.'

People suck and that's my contention. I can prove it on scratch paper and a pen. Give me a fucking Etch-A-Sketch, I'll do it in three minutes to prove the fact, the factorum, I'll show my work, case closed. I'm tired of this backslapping, aren't humanity neat bullshit. We're a virus with shoes, OK? That's all we are.

What do you say we ah . . . lighten things up and talk about abortion. You know . . . I feel like I'm losing some of you here and I wanna win all of you back with this one. Let's talk about abortion. Let's talk about child-killing, and see if we can't get some chuckles rippling through the room here. Let's talk about mass murder of young, unborn children, see if we can't coalesce into one big healthy gut-laugh. Ha ha ha ha ha ha ha! Boy, I've never seen an issue so divisive. You ever seen – it's like a civil war, in'it? Even among my friends, who are all very intelligent, they are totally divided on abortion. It's unbelievable. Some of my friends, for instance, think these pro-life people are annoying idiots. Other of my friends think these pro-life people are evil fucks . . . How are we gonna come to a consensus? You oughta hear the arguments around my house. They're annoying, they're idiots, they're evil, they're FUCKS! Brothers, sisters, come together. Can't we once just join hands and think of them as evil, annoying idiot-fucks? I beseech you. But that's me, Libra rising: the Scales. And, strangely enough, Shiva the Destroyer. (*laughs*) Who would have thunk it? 'We're pro-life.' Ooh, you look it. Look like you're filled with life. All the little kids:

> 'Please don't adopt me, please don't adopt me.'
> 'We're your new Christian pro-life parents.'
> 'Oh, where's the tower, where's the gun, where's the tower, where's the gun? I was adopted by pro-life

Christians when I was a kid. (*gunshot sounds*) Does my
penis make me a bad boy? That's what they told me.'
(*gunshot sounds*)

Please, give me the Satan-worshipping family down the block. The
ones that have the good albums. Suddenly I'm adopted by the
Flanders, you know. 'Hi Bill, in'it a beautiful God-created morning?'
Heurf! 'We're pro-life'. What does that make me? You know what I
mean? You're so pro-life, you're so pro-life, do me a fucking favor.
Don't block med-clinics, OK? Lock arms . . . and block cemeteries.
Let's see how fucking committed you are to this premise.

'She can't come in.'
'She was ninety-six. She was hit by a bus.'
'There's options.'
'What, have we gotta have her stuffed? What are you
talkin' about? She's dead.'
'We're pro-life. Get her out of that casket, get her out!
She's not going. We're pro-life people. They'll be no
death on this planet.'

Pro-life. And I always think, you see my theory, here's my actual
theory beyond ah . . . the huge, hilarious jokes I have. Here's my
real theory, so: if you're so pro-life and you're so pro-child, then
adopt one that's already here that's very unwanted and very alone
and needs someone to take care of it, to get it out of a horrible
situation. OK? People say, 'Why don't you do that?' and I say, 'Cos
I hate fuckin' kids and could care less.' Couldn't give a fuck. Don't
care at all about abortion. It's your choice, case closed, the end,
bottom line. And by the way, that three-month-old kid in your belly
is not a fuckin' human being, OK? It's a bunch of little congregated
cells. You're not a human . . . till you're in my phone book. (*laughs*)
There. My hat is now in the political ring.

There is a new party being born: The People Who Hate People
Party. People who hate people: come together! 'No!' We're kinda
having trouble getting off the boards, but you know.

'Are you gonna be there?'

'Yeah.'
'Then I ain't fucking coming.'
'You're our strongest member.'
'Fuck you!'
'That's what I'm talking about, you asshole.'
'Fuck off!'

Damn, we almost had our meeting going. It's so hard to get my people together.

(*quietly*) Dont give a fuck about little fucking kids. 'I'm pro-life.' God, I wanna hang with you and play Twister. 'That's pornographic.' Damn! I hate playing with the pro-life people. And oddly enough, that face . . . is the exact same face . . . non-smokers have, too. 'I'm a non-smoker. I'm pro-life. I'm a pro-life non-smoker.' Let the party begin. Ow, (*singing*) do do do do do do.

I been getting that look a lot recently, cos I started smoking again. (*audience cheers*) See, I don't know how with a support group like you I fucking failed, you know? Damn it. How did I fail with y'know, everyone helping me out? 'Bill's gonna kill himself, whooooooo! Bill's gonna lose a lung, yeahhhhh!' [. . .] No, but I've been getting that look a lot lately, cos I started smoking again and . . . performing abortions, so. I mean everywhere I turn now, you know what I mean? I don't wanna get out of bed most days to be honest with you. Scraping a uterus here, it don't bother me. Is this bad for a dead foetus? Is this – oh, once the baby's dead this doesn't matter, does it? OK. Hate to hurt the little piece of flesh in there. Don't let the clothes fool ya, it's still fucking me!

But I've always found religion to be fascinating. Ideas such as how people act on their beliefs. Pro-lifers murdering doctors. Ha ha ha ha ha ha ha ha! Pro-lifers murdering people. Ha ha ha ha ha ha ha ha! I . . . ah, you know, it's irony on a base level but I like it. You know what I mean? It's real basic irony, but still you can get a *hoot*. It's a *hoot*. It's a *fucking hoot*. 'We're pro-life, and we'll kill your ass.' That's what fundamentalism breeds though, no irony, you see. They take the word literally, you know. Fundamentalists, yeah,

yeah. Well, once again I recommend a healthy dose of ah . . . psilo-cybin mushrooms ah. Three weeks ago two of my friends and I went to a ranch in Fredericksburg, Texas, and took what Terence McKenna calls 'a heroic dose'. Five dried grams. Let me tell you, our third eye was squeegeed quite cleanly. (*makes squeaking sound*) Wow! (*makes squeaking sound*) And I'm glad they're against the law. Cos you know what happened when I took 'em? I laid in a field of green grass for four hours, going, 'My God . . . I love everything.' The heavens parted, God looked down and rained gifts of forgive-ness . . . on to my being, healing me on every level, psychically, physically, emotionally. And I realized our true nature is spirit, not body, that we are eternal beings, and God's love is unconditional: 'n' there's nothing we can ever do to change that. It is only our *illu-sion* that we are separate from God, or that we are alone. In fact the reality is we are one with God and he loves us. Now, if that isn't a hazard to this country. Do you see my point? How are we gonna keep building nuclear weapons, you know what I mean? What's gonna happen to the arms industry when we realize we're all one. Ha ha ha ha ha! It's gonna fuck up the economy! The econ-omy that's fake anyway! Ha ha ha! Which would be a real bummer. You know. You can see why the government's *cracking down* . . . on the idea of experiencing unconditional love, ah. It's interesting, introducing the two drugs that are illegal – alcohol and cigarettes – two drugs that do absolutely . . . *nothing* for you whatsoever, and drugs that grow naturally upon this planet, drugs that open your eyes up, to make you realize how you're being *fucked* every day of your life. Those drugs are against the law. Wow! Coincidence? I don't know. I'm sure their motives are pure. But ah . . . isn't that great? Mushrooms grow on cow turds. I love that. I think that's why you giggle the first hour.

> 'Hee hee he ha ha ha ha! This grew on cow turds! Heaven is in a cow's butt! Ha ha ha ha ha ha ha! I know where heaven is!'
> 'Where?'
> 'In a cow's ass! Ha ha ha ha ha ha! Zchurrrrrrrrrrrrrrrrr. Oh my God! Lift me up out of this illusion, Lord. Heal

> my perception that I may know only reality and only
> you.'

Stuff like that.

'I took mushrooms and went to Astroworld and I had a really bad time.' You're a moron. They are sacred. Go to nature. Who wants to be on the Black Dragon, tripping. I would fucking be puking, man, about fifty yards, with each hurl of the Black Dragon. (*screeches*) Possessed Dragon. I just think it's interesting to see how people act on their beliefs, you know what I mean? Cos all your beliefs, they're just that. They're nothing, they're how you were taught and raised. That doesn't make 'em real. That's why I always recommend a psychedelic experience, cos it does make you realize everything you learned is in fact just learned and not necessarily true.

There's dick jokes on the way, please relax. (*laughs*) You're going, 'This guy better have some good dick jokes, I'll tell you that, honey. I mean, this guy better have a big, long, purple-vein dick joke to pull himself out of this comedy hole.' Throw down the big purple-vein dick and I crawl out of it and that's gonna be the joke at the end. Ha ha ha ha ha! Oh, hey, the clown got the laugh: cool.

OK folks . . . it's confession time. It's a confession in the way of a question. Is anyone here like me in that they are compelled, obsessed and drawn beyond their will . . . to watch the show *Cops*[60] every fucking night? I'm not alone? (*hysterically*) Oh, thank God! Thank God! I thought I was alone! Hi, I'm Bill and I'm a *Cops* watcher. 'Hi Bill.' I am OBSESSED by that fucking show. I can't . . . I can't not watch it. I'm like a guy with a sore tooth: I can't quit touching it, you know. Ow, ow. Oh, *Cops* is on. Ow . . . owwww. I've never *been* in so many trailer parks, *ever*. Ow. Each night I'm in a different – I could buy a trailer right now, I know that much about 'em from the show *Cops*. Ow – ooh, a double wide . . . oww. This is sick, man, I can't . . . you know. And I love it, cos every night it's the same show. A woman has been beaten by her husband, her head looks like a melon, the cops are called on a domestic call, cos . . . the trailer next door . . . couldn't hear the results of the *American Gladiators* contest or something, over her shrieking. I don't know why they called. I don't know how they had a phone, but anyway . . . The cops are called, right? And they come into the trailer, her fourteen little cracker spawn are peering around her gingham skirt. Their eyes are so close together, the left eye is in the right socket and the right eye is in the left socket – some genetic mutation due to inbreeding here, I don't get it. What does their family tree look like? A *stump*? And every time the woman stands up for the fucking guy. Head looks like a melon.

> 'He didn't mean to hit me, Officer. He didn't mean to
> hit me. He's a good man. Don't take him away. I fell
> asleep in the driveway and he run over my head with
> the truck. He's a good man. He don't mean no harm.
> He's passed out under the trailer right now with his dog,
> Skeeter.'

Fuck cops, send in the swat team. She doesn't need children. K? And that's a judgement call that I'm making but it also happens to be true, which gives it the force, that extra oomph. She needs no more children. K? OK. Can't support 'em! Can't feed 'em! Can't raise 'em! Don't even love 'em! Poink. Bring 'em out, why don't you just get the fucking *Cops* camera to shine it up your fucking pussy and film the little criminal COMING OUT! This is crime preven-tion. Here comes another illiterate, unwanted child. Cuff him, Banano. Wah! Wah! Wah! Can you calm down on your *rutting* just for a couple of seconds, until we figure out this FOOD/AIR DEAL? 'Well, who are you to judge? Who are you judging? What makes you think you know better than Jesus?' 'He didn't mean to hit me, Officer.' And she stands up for this guy! This fucking cracker's balls deep in that whore every night! I haven't been laid in three fuck-ing years! It's not right!

I got backed up semen that's about to make my head explode. Next time I come it's gonna be like a wax dart shooting outa my dick. Sh-dooom! Some one-eyed chick my girlfriend, you know.

'I'm not blowing you again. I wan– I'm gonna get through
this life.'
'Baby, I'll buy you a dog. Please blow me.'

I don't mean to let you all in on more than you care to know about
me, but . . . it blows my mind.

What is the psychology of women that put up with wife-beaters,
man? You know? What the fuck's the psychology to that? It really
makes you feel hopeless, man. You try and be a good guy, a nice
guy, an' an' an' you ladies, yeah, I know, and you know what? I know
y'all love Billy Ray Cyrus. Don't lie to me. He's a . . . I'm talking
to the *women* here. Yeah, bullshit! Fuck you. You do. Oh yeah, he
sold 5 million albums and now all the guys here bought 'em. Fuck
you! 'He's a hunk.' Fucking homunculus mongoloid. No wonder
this country's becoming like dog patch if that's who you wanna rut
with. Fuck, any woman here would fucking almost break her *pelvis*
opening her legs for that mongoloid fuck . . . to drop his filthy
cracker seed into your fucking womb. Liar! Liars! LIARS!

All right, man. Good evening everyone– oh, Jesus Christ. I've had
more people in *bed* before than this. Fuck, man. In fact they were
at the hotel. I left them to come here and do this. Don't I feel like
a fucking idiot? Y'all . . . don't – OK. This could be one of my last
performances, ladies and gentlemen. This week. I'm serious. I've
had it. Sixteen years I've pounded my head against the mentality
of America, which I, I, I ascribe to about . . . I'd say it's about an
eighth-grade emotional level that we're at, as a country. And ah . . .
you're doubting that? You don't think so? Really. OK. Well, anyway.
You know, go watch *Who's the Boss* and then we'll chat later, I ah
. . . please don't debate me, it's my one true talent, OK? I have
twenty-three hours a day to develop these little webs of fucking
conspiracy, so please. Relax and enjoy your hair.
     And your little cracker spawn are back at the hotel, choking
down the minibar contents, probably fucking each other and
producing more little crackers to come fuck with my life . . . you
inbred, redneck, hillbilly, fucking tourist, you. Good evening. How

are you tonight? Welcome. Welcome. Welcome to No Sympathy Night. Welcome to You're Wrong Night. Boy, I'm in a mood. You know . . . could be this haircut. Every time I look at my hair I go, 'Fuck it, someone needs to die.' Generally I think it's me, but ah, I don't have the balls to do it so . . . so I continue to walk around with my hair.

Ha ha ha! OK, shut up. Shut the FUCK up. FUCKING morons. You FUCKING morons!

And God wept, I believe is the next verse. As did the world. As more knobby-kneed white guys walk the planet with their black nylon fucking socks, their fat, fucking tick-like wives and their little, fat, fucking hateful children. Blocking the doorway, it's a doorway, MOVE IT! 'Huh, we're on vacation.' You're on a *mental* fucking vacation, that's what you're on, pal. Try waking up and enjoying the *life* you've chosen, OK? Instead of calling the travel agent and getting the big budget deal. It's a T-shirt nirvana.

I am your herder. Kneel in front of me.

Tonight, check politics on your fucking porch while your wife wiggles her fucking dong and fucks her own pussy with it, you fucking redneck, hillbilly piece of shit, you. Fuck America, if that's America, then fuck you too. Good evening, everyone. How y'all? Good? Everyone good? Welcome to my show. Hey . . . (*laughs*) 'Moo. Moo.' Coupla cows are getting arrogant out there. 'Moo. Moo.' Come on, Shep. Get that one cow who's leaving the pack. (*barks*) 'Moo.' Go back to the herd, moron. OK? I have this weirdest style, don't I? I . . . ha ha ha ha ha ha! 'Bill, you do a little kind of joke that's kind of funny, then you start telling us you hate us and you dig a fucking hole. Where's Bill going? He's going to comedy death. Boom! He pops out of it with another joke.' It's my particular style. Just— it's OK. It's all been done in ah . . . in hate. Now. I am like the angry sheep-herder. That's what I am. I'm ranting under the stars with my herd. 'Gee Bill, are you talkin' to us?' I'm talking metaphorically about America, all right? Not y'all. I give y'all more credit. I assume that you're ah enjoying this, or if not at least *emotionally* involved, which is important. Even if it's anger. Really. It's OK, man. That's what this is all about, man. It's supposed to be a fucking catharsis, man, you know? It's supposed to be release

from the fucking daily grind. I wish it worked for me. (*wheezy laugh*)
I'm killing me, join me.

I was over in Australia and I was asked, 'Are you proud to be an
American,' and I was like, 'I don't know. I didn't have a lot to do
with it, you know. My parents *fucked* there, that's about all. You
know, I was in the spirit realm at that time. "Fuck in Paris! Fuck
in Paris!" but they couldn't hear me, cos I didn't have a mouth. I
was a spirit without lungs or a mouth or vocal cords.' They fucked
here. OK, I'm proud. I hate patriotism. I can't stand it, man. Makes
me fucking sick. It's a round world last time I checked, OK? You
know what I mean? I hate patriotism. In fact, that's how we could
stop patriotism, I think. Instead of putting stars and stripes on our
flags, we should put pictures of our parents fucking. Gather people
round that flag and see your dad hunched over your mom's big
four-by-four butt. See if any boot rally mentality can circle round
that little fucking image. God . . . damn, I'm out of here! Fuck it!
Get your mom, shut up! Let's go garden.

You never see my attitude in the press, that's what bugs me. You
never see *my* point of view. For instance, gays in the military. Now,
I don't know how y'all feel about it. Gays who wanna be in the
military. Here's how I feel about it, all right? Anyone DUMB
ENOUGH to wanna be in the military should be allowed in. End
of fucking story. That should be the only requirement. I don't care
how many push-ups you can do. Put on a helmet, go wait in that
foxhole, we'll tell you when we need you to kill somebody. You
know what I mean? I'm so sick – I watched these fucking congres-
sional hearings and all these military guys and all the pundits,
'Seriously, aww the *esprit de corps* will be affected, and we are such
a moral'— excuse me! Aren't y'all fucking hired killers? SHUT UP!
You are *thugs* and when we need you to go blow the fuck out of
a nation of little brown people, we'll let you know. Until then . . .
when did the fucking military get all these morals— 'We are the
military. Is that a village of children and kids? Where's the napalm?
Sh-boom! I don't want any gay people hanging round me while
I'm killing kids. I just don't wanna see it.' And don't tell me it's

the military protects our freedom. Hey, ladies and gentlemen, there ain't no one out there who's a fucking threat to us, OK? They don't exist. Oh – I'm talking now only of countries we don't arm first. All right, if you wanna split hairs, you got a point. 'Bill, what about the nations we sell arms to and then go blow the fuck out of 'em?' OK, they might be scary for about a day. We give them the old weapons, we use the new ones on them, you know. Fucking Iraq found that out, huh? You have the Scud, we have the Patriot. The SCUD TIMES TWO, you fucks! Just keep selling 'em the shitty shit, you know. We'll be fightin' them next, they'll have muskets. Dhoosh!

> 'America won a war with this.'
> 'Yeah, a hundred years ago! They got new shit now.'
> 'Fuck!'
> (Sssssssss)
> 'What is that?'
> 'It's musket repellent.'
> 'I can kill you by looking at you.'

Oh, there's a threat to America, yeah, yeah, yeah. Back to that fucking *Cops* show, cos I'll tell you who the threat to freedom . . . no, no, not the threat to freedom. I'll tell you who the threat to the status quo is in this country – it's us. That's why they show you shows like fucking *Cops* so you know that state power will win and we'll bust your house down and we'll fucking bust you any time we want. That's the message. Why don't they just have a show called *Stormtrooper*? Or better yet, how about *IRS*? Argh! Every week the IRS has a special celebrity guest.

> 'This week it's Red Fox on *IRS Bust*.'
> (*singing*) 'Da da da da! Da da da! Da da da da!' (*Ding dong!*)
> 'Who dere? Who dere at my door? What y'all want?'
> 'The rings on your FUCKING FINGER!'
> (*singing*) 'Da da da da!'
> 'See you next week when we go down to Texas and meet Willie Nelson! On *IRS*!'

Cos that is the message they wanna leave you with. To keep you afraid and keep you fucking impotent. Keep these lying scumbags doing their fucking dirty work.

'What about Clinton? Is there any hope in Clinton?' There's no fucking hope in that guy. They're all the same. I'll show you politics in America. Here it is, right here.

> 'I think the puppet on the right shares my beliefs.'
> 'I think the puppet on the left is more to my liking.'
> 'Hey, wait a minute. There's one guy holding up both puppets!'
> 'Shut up! Go back to bed, America: your government is in control. Here's *Love Connection*. Watch this and get fat and stupid. By the way, keep drinking beer, you fucking morons.'

Ba ba ba na.

(*two gunshots*) Hicks was shot by a quiet loner. Though the shots had two different calibrations, we feel that one gun shot them both. He was a quiet loner who had a family and kids.

How are you a loner with a family? How does that work?

I'm kind of bummed because I'm missing right now, even as we speak, my favourite cultural train wreck: *The Tonight Show with Jay Leno*. I'm like a rubber-necker, man. Every night it's the crash of fucking metal when that show starts. Me and my friends have a little office pool wondering exactly which episode and which guest is gonna be on the night Jay finally puts a 9mm in his mouth and blows his Dorito-shilling head off his fucking body. I think it's gonna be Joey Lawrence from the show *Blossom*, ah . . . other of my friends beg to differ and think Patrick Duffy a more likely culprit.

> 'Oh, hi everyone. Welcome to the show. Tonight we have Joey Lawrence. Hi Joey, how are ya? It's good to see you again. Boy, it was always my comedic dream to be forty-four years old and interviewing a little Tony Danzer

wannabe every three months. Boy, I'm fulfilled as a
human spiritually. So . . . so, so, so anyway, Joey, you're
sixteen now? You're sixteen years old?'
'Yeah.'
'That's great, you're sixteen. You got a licence? You
drivin'? You drivin'?'
'Yeah.'
'That's great, you're sixteen, you got a licence. You got
a car? You got a car?'
'Yeah.'
'You got a girlfriend, hmmm? You dating somebody?
Anybody special?'
'Yeah. No. Well, she thinks so. I don't. Hee hee hee hee.'
'Good God, what have I done with my life?'

BOOM! His brain splew out, forming an NBC peacock on the wall
behind him. Cos he's a company man to the bitter fucking end. It all
started when he did the Doritos commercial. Here's the deal, folks.
You do a commercial, you're off the artistic roll call for ever. End of
story. OK? You're another corporate fucking shill, you're another whore
at the capitalist gang-bang. And if you do a commercial, there's a price
on your head, everything you say is suspect, and every word that
comes out of your mouth is now like a turd falling into my drink.
(*makes choking, then splashing sound*) Selling Doritos on fucking TV.
What a fucking whore. And not even when he needed the money,
either. You know, if you're a young actor, OK, I'll look the other way.
But the guy, you know, he makes 3 million a year, he decides to hawk
Doritos to make *more* money. You don't got enough money, you fucking whore? You gotta sell *snacks* to fucking *bovine America* now? 'Hi
everyone, I'm Jay Leno. Anyone remember when I was . . . when I
was funny? Here, eat Doritos. They're good—' (*makes choking sound*)
Satan fucking him in the ass on national TV. (*snorting and snarling*)

'They're good 'n' crispy. Here Satan, try the nacho-
flavoured ones.'
'Cool and flavourful.' (*snorting and snarling*)
'Tonight on the show, er, we have Joey Lawrence and
Patrick Duffy.'

Yes, tonight's the night! Fuck, if that was his line-up he'd use an Uzi in his mouth. (*makes machine pistol sound*) Rrrrrrrrrrrr! Just chewing fucking lead. Arrrrrrrrrrrrrr! Arrrrrrrrrrrrrr! 'What have I done with my fucking life?' Arrrrrrrrrrrrrrr! 'I used to be funny!' Arrrrrrrrrrrrrrr! Arrrrrrrrrr! Oh, quick, change his clip! Arrrrrrrrrrrr! Arrrrrrrrrrr! Arrrrrrrrrrr! He's a fucking blood-sprinkler! Pow! Pow! Pow! Arrrrrrrrrrrrr! Arrrrrrrrrrrrrrrrrrrrrrrrrrrrrrrr! The next night: (*singing*) 'ba da da da da. Ba ba ba da!'

> 'Ed, Ed ah, did you enjoy your vacation?'
> 'You are correct, sir.'
> 'Doc, that's a really nice red coat. Is that the colour of
> it or is that Jay's brains?'

Ha ha ha ha ha! 'He's just jealous cos he's never been on the show.' You're so right.

Do a commercial, you're off the artistic roll call, every word you say is suspect, you're a corporate whore and ah, end of story. And yes, I have been offered commercials, so I'm not jealous, and I turned them all down because I'm not a salesman. Aha, oop! And I don't need money that is built on blood. So.

Man in audience: Who offered to you?

Bill: Well, in England I did this really . . . this is classic England. I got offered a . . . this is the product. You ready? Orange drink. I'm going, 'What's the name of it?' 'Orange drink.' Classic England, right? Just such a socialist fucking nightmare over there, right? (*laughs*) That's the drink. 'It's orange drink.' I said, 'Yeah, you really got my act down good, guys. That'll be great. You know, when I'm ah done ranting about elite power that rules the planet under a totalitarian government that uses the media in order to keep people stupid, my throat gets parched. That's why I drink orange drink.' Yeah, right. See, don't you see how it'll all fit in. Don't you see how every word I said would be hollow and filled with nothing.

You do a commercial, you're off the artistic roll call for ever, and that goes for everyone . . . except Willie Nelson. Twenty-four-million-dollar tax bill, Willie was a little looser than the rest of us.

I just avert my eyes when he sings about tacos, you know what I mean? It's so fucking . . . (*singing*) 'I'm sitting here, selling tacos, oh waiting for the woman in the rose tattoo. My butt is so loose.' Oh, this is so sad. Is he done yet? No. (*singing*) I love picante and iced tea. Taco Bell hasn't called me. Oh, my butt hurts so bad.' Oh, this is so sad. Is he finished yet? No? (*singing*) 'I love nachos with chips 'n' dippin', love the things that I can get 'n, oh my butt is hurtin' me.' Oh, poor Willie. Poor fucking Willie. Oh God, let's pass the hat. Get him off the Taco Bell commercial! We gotta save Willie!

You know what I mean? You want a better world, ladies and gentlemen? Legalize pot right now. You wanna end the deficit? Legalize pot right now. I am so sick of hearing about the goddamn deficit, I could fucking *puke blood.* (*vomiting noise*) There ain't no fucking deficit, it's a FUCKING lie and it's a FUCKING illusion in the first place. But you wanna end it, you wanna end it, legalize pot: biggest cash crop in America. Deficit's gone. But I am so sick of hearing about, 'Well, your leaders misspent your hard-earned tax dollars, so you, the people, now have to tighten your belts and we got to start paying this back, because we, your leaders, misspent your money.' You know what'd make tightening my belt a little easier? If I could tighten it around Jesse Helms'[61] scrawny little chicken-neck. Ah, I feel better about the sacrifice right now! You fucking, tobacco-pushing, motherfucker! You are the worst fucking drug-dealer in the fucking world! You scrawny, rightwing, fear-mongering piece of sucker of Satan's COCK! YOU SUCK SATAN'S COCK! YOU FUCKING CHICKEN-NECKED LITTLE FUCKING CRACKER! I'd tighten my belt if that were the case. I'd eat bolony for a week, you know what I mean? I'd sacrifice. Boy, Jesse Helms. Isn't that a great one, i'n't he? Just another little fevered ego tainting our collective unconscious. Cos you know, anyone – like Swaggart[62] – anyone that far to the right is hiding a very deep and dark secret. You do know that, right? I'm an armchair fucking psychologist, but *anyone* that – you know when Jesse Helms finally dies, he's gonna commit suicide first of all in a washtub out back underneath a pecan tree. He's gonna slash his wrists and he's gonna write in blood, 'I been a bad boy.' But you know they're gonna find the skins of young children drying in his attic. Swarms of horse-flies going in and out of the eaves, and on CNN, over and over, his wife going, 'I always wondered about Jesse's collection of little shoes.' Anyone that far to the right is fucking hiding a deep, dark secret.

Speaking of Satan, ah . . . I was watching Rush Limbaugh the other day. Doesn't Rush Limbaugh remind you of one of those gay guys who likes to lay in a tub while other men pee on him? Am I the only one? Can't you see his fat body in a tub while Reagan, Quayle, and Bush just chhhhhhhhhhh! Just stand around pissing on him, and he can't– his little piggly-wiggly dick can't get hard.

'Aargh, aargh, I can't get hard. Reagan, pee in my mouth.'
'Well, how's that, Rush?'

Still can't get hard, so they call in Barbara Bush. She takes her pearls off, puts 'em up his ass, then squats over him, undoes her girdle, her wrinkled, flaccid labia unfolds halfway down to her knees, like some ball-less scrotum. 'Aargh, aargh, aargh.' She squeezes out a link into his mouth. Finally his dick gets half-hard. 'Ohhhh.' A little clear bubble forms on the end with a maggot inside. The maggot pops the bubble and runs off and joins a pro-life group somewhere. Am I the only one who sees that, or . . . or not? Thank God I'm not alone. Thank God I had the insight to notice Rush Limbaugh is a scat-muncher. He munches *scat*. *(laughs)* 'Jesus, Bill.' I'm so proud of that little dark poetry there. Started, I came out with the word 'scat-muncher' and it went from there, and I just . . . immediately thought of Rush.

Folks, it's time to evolve ideas. You know, evolution did not end with us growing thumbs. You do know that, right? Didn't end there. We're at the point now where we're going to have to evolve ideas. The reason the world's so fucked up is we're undergoing evolution. And the reason our institutions, our traditional religions are all crumbling is because they're no longer relevant. Ha ha ha ha ha ha! They're no longer *relevant*. So it's time for us to create a *new* philosophy and perhaps even a new religion, you see. And that's OK, cos that's our right, cos we are free children of God with minds who can imagine anything, and *that's kind of our role*. How do you evolve ideas? I'll give you an example right here. By the way, there are more dick jokes coming: please relax. I know I'm starting to lose them a little bit here with this shit, I'm like digging a fucking hole right now. And another thing . . . 'Where the hell did Bill go? He dug himself right through the planet.' I can hear people heckling in Chinese right now. 'Why . . . why you gonna do dick joke? Do dick joke. [. . .] No one want to hear your philosophy; they want to hear dick joke.' Oh, what a completely rational heckler, hmmmm. 'They pay to hear dick joke, not to hear you talk about the President Bush.' Here's how you evolve an idea; I'll give you an example. Why is the drug Tsar of this country – well, let's go back. Why do we *have* a drug Tsar in this country, a)? b) Why is he a cop? Why isn't he a guy in recovery, who's had an alcohol and/or drug addiction and overcome it? And why doesn't he help people with the same problem with compassion rather than condemnation? Why do we put people who are on drugs in jail? They're *sick*. They're not criminals. Sick people don't get healed in jail. See, it makes no sense. And if we *evolve* the idea, you see, the planet might be more *compassionate* and something like HEAVEN might dawn. I want everyone here to take the five dried grams I taped under y'all chairs right now. Under your chairs: check 'em out. Let's go, man. The fucking UFOs are waiting in the fifth dimension. Let's go! We'll do it later. We'll do it as a closer.

Shit, man. Mushrooms grow naturally on the planet. They're against the law. Marijuana grows naturally on the planet. It's against the law. Do you think making nature against the law seems a bit, I don't know . . . unnatural?

I was down in Australia when the Waco debacle ended, and I was very bummed because I thought that was the most fascinating story of the year, bar none. And everyone was so upset with that guy cos he called himself Jesus, right? And I said, 'Come on, you know. The guy's real name . . . is Vernon. Let him be Jesus for a couple of months, you know what I mean? What's it to you?' Who's gonna follow a messiah called Vernon, anyway. You gotta be Jesus, that's part of the Messiah deal. 'And Vernon spake.' Yeah, yeah, what are we doing?

> 'I'm followin' Vernon.'
> 'Where y'all going?'
> 'To the drive-in. Heyah! Joe-Bob Briggs said the movie
> was real good. Vernon's going. He's my Messiah. He said
> he'd get us some beef jerky. Whoo!'
> 'I follow Vernon.'

Isn't that weird, though. People always snap and think they're Jesus. How come no one ever snaps and thinks they're Buddha? Particularly in America, where more people resemble Buddha than Jesus.

> 'I'm Buddha.'
> 'You're Bubba.'
> 'I'm Buddha now. All I gotta do is change two letters on
> my belt. Bubba – Buddha. Come over here and read my
> Scripture. Vernon's a false prophet. Bubba-Buddha's the
> real man.'

I was in Australia, and the Australians had a big contingency at the Branch Davidian compound, and I'm from Texas so they were very curious. They were asking me all about it, you know. 'Oh, this guy's so weird, in't he? This guy Koresh is so weird.' And I was thinking, well, wait a minute. Frustrated rock musician with a messianic complex, armed to the teeth, and trying to fuck everything that moves. I don't know how to tell you this: sounds like every one of my friends in Austin. I don't know if this is gonna be an isolated incident. Waiting for Will Sexton to build a compound somewhere. I don't even know what that means. I don't even know what . . . that was an Austin name; I picked it out of a hat. Pick your own Austin guitarist. Have fun with the joke.

But I thought the whole thing was an absolute disaster and a debacle, and if any of y'all have been watching public access and seen the footage, which was not shown on any major news media source, of the tanks, Bradley tanks, shooting *fire* into the compound, which I think went against the party-line story, which was that they shot tear gas in order to help the mothers and the children to get out, to convince them – oh, they're destroying the compound, they're getting the moms and children out, you see . . . the soft sell is definitely the FBI's way. And anyway, so the major news said that the Branch Davidians started a fire. If I'm not mistak– correct me when I go off the story here – a-a-a-and that the Branch Davidians, and all they did was shoot in tear gas, and yet I've seen with my own eyes and my (*squeaking sound*) squeegeed third eye footage of a Bradley tank shooting *fire* into the *compound*, which . . . in't that odd that no major news source has picked up on that? Huh, you'd think that's newsworthy. Cos that basically means that the government, from the FBI, the ATF, up to Janet Reno and including Clinton, are ahm, *liars* and *murderers*. Ha ha ha ha! And – wait, there's more – and . . . I mean, the implications are vast. Ahm, you know. And if the ATF and FBI had any honor, if there was any honor left or dignity on this planet, they would commit hara-kiri while first admitting what they've done. They'd kill themselves, cos they are liars and murderers.

'Oh, we had to bust the compound down, cos we heard child molestation was going on.' Yeah, if that's true, how come we don't see Bradley tanks knocking down Catholic churches? I'm talking if child molestation is actually your concern. 'Well, there was a meth-amphetamine lab on it.' No there wasn't. And not one child came out of there saying they were molested. Not one child. They don't want the voice of reason spoken, folks, cos otherwise we'd be free. Otherwise we wouldn't believe their FUCKING horse-shit lies, nor the fucking propaganda machine, the mainstream media, and buy their horse-shit products that we don't fucking need, and become a Third World consumer fucking plantation, which is what we're becoming. Fuck them! They're liars and murderers. All governments are liars and murderers, and I am now Jesus. Now. And this is my compound.

I'm sorry if anyone here is Catholic, ah . . . I'm not sorry if you're offended, I'm actually sorry just the fact that you're Catholic. Got to be one of the most ludicrous fucking beliefs ever. Like these vampire priests sink their twin fangs of guilt and sin into you as a child and suck your joy of life out of you the rest of your fucking existence. And I love watching the Pope bounce around in his little Popemobile. That's the . . . that's got to be hoot number one on my fucking CNN list. Just, I want a whole show with the Pope just bouncing around in that all-terrain Popemobile, with the three feet of bulletproof Plexiglas around him. Boy, there's faith in action. You see, you know he's really the spokesman for God, because only God's spokesman would need Plexiglas bulletproof, don't you think? Don't y'all read that the same way?

I don't know. Christianity's the weird one though, you know. Christianity's such an odd religion, you know. I was raised that way, you know, and you can just suffer for it. You know, the whole image is that, you know, eternal suffering awaits anyone who questions God's infinite love. (*laughs*) That's the message, isn't it, that we're brought up with. Believe or die! 'Thank you, forgiving Lord, for all those options.'

I've been compared to Koresh before. People said I was like Koresh, except . . . without the guns or pussy. And ah . . . means I'm just a real annoying guy, basically.

> 'But you must understand the Seven Seals.'
> 'What, the seven— is this a circus? I'm with you. What?
> Seven seals. Right.'
> 'They hit the ball up their nose. Seven of them. I saw
> it when I was a kid. I don't understand it.'

And I knew Billy Clinton became one of the boys when he bombed Iraq.[63] Remember that? It was just a little news story for two days. Isn't that interesting? He launched twenty-two cruise missiles against Baghdad in retaliation for the *alleged* assassination attempt against George Bush, which failed. We killed six innocent people, launching twenty-two, I think 3-million-dollars-apiece missiles on Baghdad, killing six innocent people. Ahm, I think that's a little bit overdoing it, if you ask me. Ahm, you know what we should have done? We should have embarrassed the Iraqians, you know what

I mean? Here's how we could do it: *we* should have assassinated Bush, and said, 'That's how you do it, towel-head. Don't fuck with us.' And see, if *Bush* had been the one who had died, there would have been no loss of innocent life.

We should do a car-bomb derby with them, that's what we should do. Car-bomb derby. Put it on after *American Gladiators*. We'd just watch it, big ratings, 'It's good, I like *Car-Bomb Derby*. We beat the Iraqi team again. I love that.' And that way we'd all be on equal ground again. And I believe in equality. I believe there is a commonality to all humanity: we all suck. OK, thank you.

I have this feeling, man, cos you know there's a handful of people actually run everything. That's true. It's provable, it's not a fucking— I'm not a conspiracy nut. It's provable. A handful, a very small elite, run and own these corporations, which include the mainstream media. I have this feeling who's ever elected President, like Clinton was, no matter what your promises you promise on the campaign trail, 'blah, blah, blah', when you win, you go into this smoky room with the twelve industrialist capitalist scum-fucks who got you in there, and you're in this smoky room and this little film screen comes down, rrrrrrrrr, and a big guy and a cigar (*po po*) 'Roll the film.' (*po po po*) And it's a shot of the Kennedy assassination from an angle you've never seen before . . . that looks suspiciously off the grassy knoll. And then the film, the screen goes up, and the lights come up, and they go to the new President, 'Any questions?'

> 'Ah, just what my agenda is?'
> 'First we bomb Baghdad.'
> 'You got it.'

But we've got to come to some new, some new ideas about life, OK? I'm not being facetious about abortion. It might be a real issue; it might not. It doesn't really matter to me, cos what matters is, if you really believe in sanctity of life, then you believe it for people of all ages. That's what I hate about this fucking *child worship* syndrome going on around. 'Save the children. Think of the children. God, how many children were in the Waco? The children!' Hey, what does that mean? They reach a certain age, they're off your fucking love list? Fuck your children, if that's the way you feel, and fuck you with 'em. You either love people in general from all ages, or you shut the fuck up. 'Bill, what kind of philosophy is this, Bill?' I don't know yet. I'm chasing this philosophy like a hound. I don't know where it's heading. (*barks*) Trying to tree it, you know. 'Who are you to tell people when to have kids or not?' I'm me, it's true, shut the fuck up. Quit thinking you're gonna fucking make the world better by bringing more little *fucking* cabbages to the planet. Why don't you try loving the people that are already *fucking* here, OK? Instead of living for a future that never fucking comes. It doesn't exist. It ain't coming. There is no future. There's no such thing. It doesn't exist. 'You're our future! THE CHILDREN ARE OUR FUTURE!' There's no such thing, asshole! Take some mushrooms and squeegee your third fucking eye! (*makes squeaking sound*) 'Oh my God, there is only this moment!' (*makes squeaking sound*)

The argument doesn't work with me, flapjack. Go back to your fucking crackerjack lifestyle, and I'll meet you at the evolution bell-curve. I'll be sitting there awhile. It's kind of a tortoise-and-the-hare-story. (*makes sound of crickets chirruping*) That's Bill, waiting for people to catch up. (*crickets chirruping*). 'We think science is gonna save us, Bill!' Oh, FUCK! (*crickets chirruping*) Take mushrooms, folks, squeegee your third fucking eye. (*makes squeaking sound*) The TV has clouded it over, OK? TV is like taking black paint to your eye. Chhhhhhhhh! Take mushrooms. (*makes squeaking sound*) What do you think, mushrooms were here by accident? You think it's a *fucking accident* mushrooms grow on cow shit? Where do you think 'That's good shit' came from?

Childbirth . . . isn't natural. I'll let that sink in. Childbirth isn't natural. We're not supposed to give birth. We're not supposed to age or die. Did you know that? We're supposed to live for ever. We're supposed to be in a garden right now, leaning against a tree, naming animals, and the fact that you don't know the name of every animal in the world tells me something. You know what it tells me? We left the garden too soon.

> 'What's that?'
> 'I don't know.'
> 'It's a wombat.'
> 'Shut up and go back to the garden. No rutting till you name all the animals.'

We have to have a beautiful world where children can come to. OK? That would be knowing your world. (*laughs*) OK. *Men* don't want children. No man in this room wants children. Any man who thinks or says he wants children is no longer a man but a pussy-whipped freak of nature, who should be at home reading leather-bound copies of Donahue transcripts, renting Alan Alda films and buying Michael Bolton's CDs, cos you're no longer a man and you're out of the man club. You're out.

'I don't know with all the margaritas we buy we can afford a child, honey.' And I'll go you one *further*. And this is the one, folks, this is the idea that has made me virtually an anonymous figure in America for the last sixteen years. I have watched my crowds dwindle, I am going nowhere, and nowhere quick. If you have children here tonight, and I assume some of you do, I am sorry to tell you this: they are not special. Oh, wait, wait, wait, hold on. Let's not have any— wait, wait, wait, don't misunderstand me. I know a lot of y'all: 'What? Well, I don't . . .' Wait, wait, let's be clear on this. I know *you* think they're special. Ha ha ha ha ha ha ha! I'm aware of *that*. I'm just trying to tell you, they're *not*. Ha ha ha ha ha!

Do you know that every time a guy comes, he comes 200 million sperm. Did you know that? Two hundred *million* sperm. And you mean to tell me you think your child . . . is special? Because one out of 200 *million* sperm *that load* – we're talking *one load* – connected. Gee, what are the fucking odds? Two hundred – you know what that means? I have wiped entire civilizations off of my chest . . . with a grey gym-sock. *That* is special. Entire nations have flaked and crusted in the hair around my navel. Maybe even Gidea. *That* is special. And I want you to think about that, you too . . .

egg-carrying beings out there. With that holier-than-thou, we-have-the-gift-of-life *attitude*. I've tossed universes . . . in my underpants . . . while napping. Boom! A Milky Way shoots into my jockey shorts. Ohhhhhhhhh! What's for fucking breakfast?

Thank you very much!

Zchurrrrrrrrrrr. Oh my God. Lift me up out of this illusion, Lord. Heal my perception that I might know only reality and only you.

Wake Up America
(Summer 1993)

This show is designed to be a vehicle for politics and cultural satire. A topic-driven half-hour nightly program hosted by Bill Hicks, each episode will deal in depth with a single topic. Be it censorship in America today, political leaders, or the hypocrisy of the 'politically correct' movement, each show will attempt to lampoon the current conventional wisdom on said subject.

Bill's opening monologue will introduce and frame the topic of the day. In our desire to break from the tired monologue concept currently employed on most talk shows, this will be delivered sans audience. Instead of a series of corny one liners, Bill's monologue will be delivered in a conversational mode. The writers will put together an outline for him to work from, including pertinent information, jokes, etc. Then instead of a rigidly delivered night club style routine, we will have an extemporaneous stream of conscious delivery that promises to be much more interesting and exciting.

We feel we have come up with a unique way to do this. On any given topic, the writers, with Bill, will put together the outlines. We will then go onto the set and shoot any where from fifteen minutes to an hour of Bill's take on the subject. Off camera, will be the writers and others whom Bill feels comfortable talking to. Now instead of the conventional opening monologue, you have someone involved in an impassioned satirical conversation with his friends. Once this process is complete, we will edit the monologue to three to seven minutes for that evening show.

Using all the latest video technology available to us, we hope to do with television what ROLLING STONE did for journalism. A gonzo, guerrilla type show that infuses Bill's editorial best. Let's say the topic is censorship. Instead of the same pseudo celebrities and usual suspects droning on like so many talking heads, we will be sending crews out on the street to interview dozens of people from all walks of life. 'How do you feel about censorship? What should be censored? Why? Do you think nude dancing should be protected by the first amendment? Do you think it should be allowed in bars? Do you think it should be allowed in church? From these we can pull the most interesting, air them and then allow Bill to comment on each one. This same technique can and will be implemented using news footage of politicians, professional news makers, (Al Sharpton[64], Randall Terry[65]) etc.

Have you ever sat in front of your TV thinking, 'why didn't they ask that question or wouldn't it be funny if the host said that?' That is what we want to do here with Bill as our representative.

Many different 'set pieces' can be interspersed throughout. From staff editorials à la Pat Paulson on the old Smothers Brothers Show, to music videos. The set piece that we envision as part of our nightly show is entitled 'IF THEY HAD THEIR WAY'. In the case of a show covering censorship, it could be a filmed montage of empty libraries, a cop chasing and shooting at a newspaper blowing down a street past an empty newsstand, a Leave it to Beaver type family, sitting home watching TV and every channel has Pat Robertson and only Pat Robertson.[66]

Using the format described above has some definite advantages. A: no one else is doing it. B: it allows Bill to do what he does best, which is simply to show the fallacy and hypocrisy that often passes for reason in our world. C: from a practical point of view, the format allows to gather huge amounts of material in a short amount of time. By sending out many different interview crews asking a wide variety of questions, we can gather the material needed for several shows at once. It also gives us the flexibility we will need to do shows on late breaking, unexpected happenings, such as earthquakes, riots, assassinations, all that good stuff.

There is a definite need for a show that can cover our times in a unique and funny way. A show that doesn't hold back, but moves forward and has a point of view. Like him or not, a huge part of Rush Limbaugh's[67] success is the fact that he holds deep seated opinions and is not afraid to express them strongly. That's what this show will do from the opposite end of the spectrum. ONLY WE WILL BE FUNNIER, BETTER TO LOOK AT AND RIGHT.

The Wicked Christians (Thoughts on the ONE TRUE religion) (June 1993)

I spent Easter in Australia. It was interesting to note they celebrate Easter the same as Christians all over the world – commemorating the death and resurrection of Jesus by telling our children a Giant Bunny Rabbit left chocolate eggs in the night. (Gee, I wonder why we're fucked up as a race?) I've read through the whole Bible. I can't find the words 'Bunny' or 'Chocolate' in the whole damn book. Where do we get this stuff? And why those two things? Why not a goldfish left Lincoln Logs in your sock drawer? I mean, as long as we're just making this shit up . . .

Last night, after my show, a group of people from a Catholic church got up to complain to the management about my material. 'We're Catholics, and we're offended!' Look, here's the deal – if I did my show uninvited at your church, you'd have every right to be offended. But . . . you're at my church NOW, so shut the fuck up! (All I said was, 'If the FBI's motivating factor for busting down the Koresh compound was child abuse, how come we never see Bradley tanks smashing into Catholic churches?' Geez, it's like these people never read a newspaper or something . . .)

More news on anti-abortion activists, or pro-lifers, as they like to be called. If they're so pro-life, I wish they'd lock arms and block cemeteries rather than medical clinics, and shoot morticians rather than doctors. Then I'd *really* believe in their commitment.

God, it never seems to end. These meddlesome Christians with their insistence on pushing their dogma and agendas down my throat. Their smug self-assurance, theirs is the ONLY WAY. The legacy of fear and reprisal from their just GOD, whose vengeance rains upon his beloved children like fire and brimstone from the sky. Hallelujah, Brother and Sisters! There will be a mighty come-uppance for those who don't think like them. And for they who don't think like we. And for you who doesn't think like me. AMEN!

And look how well their belief works. Take Waco for instance – the god-fearing ATF storming the compound, guns blazing. The Branch DAVIDIANS returning fire . . . churchgoing Christians one and all. 'You can tell a tree by the fruit it bears.' This fruit lays shot and bleeding, burning, screaming. And both sides, still believing they and only they are right.

Look, I understand the philosophy. I was raised Southern Baptist in Texas! You don't think I got the message? P-shaw, my Brothers and Sisters! I got the ONE TRUE message. And I know, because this is how I was raised, that even you poor, misguided Christians from other denominations are wrong. So load your guns and prepare to do Holy Battle in the name of Jesus, the lamb of peace.

This is the message of Christianity:

> Eternal suffering awaits anyone who questions God's infinite love. (?!?)

Or, to paraphrase:

> I will make your life a living Hell if you don't think like me.

The first thing the indoctrinated Christian is taught is not to *ever* question his own faith. No matter how sound an argument is supporting another belief, or debunking existing beliefs, the strength of the argument is proof positive of its evil origins. In the Christian's mind's eye, it is Satan's foremost duty to make them question their own faith and thus make them susceptible to the Dark Lord's evil machinations. It's an almost foolproof built-in defense system, for no matter how reasonable, logical, sound, or sure an argument is, if it at all makes one question their belief, it *by definition must be evil* and *untrue*. In fact, the only unforgiveable sin in Christianity is to question one's own belief, or to hold it up to the light of reason. Conversely, the *denial* of even the most *obvious* facts that don't jibe with *The Belief* is proof positive of the steadfastness and purity of one's faith.

This is the reason Christians are so meddlesome. And annoying. And . . . well, unchristian. They don't believe in God, but they do believe in a Devil. They don't believe in Heaven, but they do believe in Hell. They don't believe in Salvation, but they do believe in Sin. They don't believe in Forgiveness, but they do believe in Condemnation.

It never occurs to Christians they might need God's word a little more than other people. Or, that they may be among the last on Earth to GET IT. They're like an annoying child from grade school, who, after learning basic math, goes up to a physicist and tries to convince him how much he's missing from his life from not realizing two plus two equals four. ('Thanks a lot for that knowledge, kid. Here's a bunny and a chocolate egg. I'll get back to you. . .')

So, that's what I think of the Wicked Christians. And if you don't believe me, just listen to Jesus himself in Luke, chapter 5, verse 32:

> 'I come not to call the righteous, but sinners to repentance.'

God, I pray the Christians get the message soon. . .

Letters of Response

8 June 1993

Dear Sir,[68]

After reading your letter expressing your concerns regarding my special 'Revelations', I felt duty-bound to respond to you myself in hopes of clarifying my position on the points you brought up, and perhaps enlighten you as to who I really am.

Where I come from – America – there exists this wacky concept called 'freedom of speech', which many people feel is one of the paramount achievements in mankind's mental development. I myself am a strong supporter of the 'Right of freedom of speech', as I'm sure most people would be if they truly understood the concept. 'Freedom of speech' means you support the right of people to say exactly those ideas which you do *not* agree with. (Otherwise, you don't believe in 'freedom of speech', but rather only those ideas which *you* believe to be acceptably stated.) Seeing as how there are so many different beliefs in the world, and as it would be virtually impossible for all of us to agree on any *one* belief, you may begin to realize just how important an idea like 'freedom of speech' really is. The idea basically states 'while I don't agree or care for what you are saying, I do support your right to say it, for herein lies true freedom.'

You say you found my material 'offensive' and 'blasphemous'. I find it interesting that you feel your beliefs are denigrated or threatened when I'd be willing to bet you've never received a *single letter* complaining about your beliefs, or asking why they are allowed to be. (If you have received such a letter, it definitely did not come from me.) Furthermore, I imagine a quick perusal of an average week of television programming would reveal many more shows of a religious nature, than one of *my* shows – which are called 'specials' by virtue of the fact that they are *very rarely on.*

All I'm doing in 'Revelations' is giving my point of view in my language based on my experiences – much the same way religious broadcasters might organize their programs. While I've found many of the religious shows I've viewed over the years not to be to my liking, or in line with my own beliefs, I've never considered it my place to exert any greater type of censorship than changing the channel, or better yet - turning off my TV completely.

Now, for the part of your letter I found most disturbing . . .

In support of your position of outrage, you posit the hypothetical scenario regarding the possibly 'angry' reaction of Muslims to material they might find similarly offensive. Here is my question to you: Are you tacitly condoning the violent terrorism of a handful of thugs to whom the idea of 'freedom of speech' and tolerance is perhaps as foreign as Christ's message itself? If you are somehow implying that their intolerance to contrary beliefs is justifiable, admirable, or perhaps even preferable to one of acceptance and forgiveness, then I wonder what your true beliefs really are.

If you had watched my entire show, you would have noticed in my summation of my beliefs the fervent plea to the governments of the world to spend less money on the machinery of war, and more on feeding, clothing, and educating the poor and needy of the world . . . A not-so-unchristian sentiment at that!

Ultimately, the message in my material is a call for understanding rather than ignorance, peace rather than war, forgiveness rather than condemnation, and love rather than fear. While this message may have understandably been lost on your ears (due to my presentation), I assure you the thousands of people I played to in my tours of the United Kingdom got it.

I hope I helped answer some of your questions. Also, I hope you consider this an invitation to keep open the lines of communication. Please feel free to contact me personally with comments, thoughts, or questions, if you so choose. If not, I invite you to enjoy my two upcoming specials entitled 'Mohammed the TWIT' and 'Buddha, you fat PIG'. (<u>JOKE</u>)

Sincerely,

Bill Hicks

June 1993

Dear Mr Christian,

I thank you again for your immense generosity in giving me another listen. I know you have zero obligation to justify your subjective response to an artist, yet I feel a need to point out a few things, and more importantly – a burning curiosity to know exactly what you meant.

No one holds comedy in higher regard than myself. *No one*. And I like to understand everyone's point of view about it, no matter how misinformed or arcane, in order to better understand for myself exactly what comedy is and how to do it best. Unlike many people, I do not think comedy is for 'escaping from the daily grind of reality to just kick back and *not* think for awhile. To just laugh at some . . . jokeblower like Carrot Top.' (To me, Carrot Top is the comedy equivalent of a streaker. Remember streakers? 'Hey, there's a nude guy running by! . . . wow . . . OK, anyway, what were we talking about?')

If comedy is an escape from anything, it is an escape from *illusions*. The comic, by using the Voice of Reason, *reminds* us of our True Reality, and in that moment of recognition, we laugh, and the 'reality of the daily grind is shown for what it really is – *unreal* . . . a *joke*. True comedy turns circles into spirals. What before seemed a tiresome, frightening, or frustrating wall, the comic deftly and fearlessly steps through, proving the absurdity of it all. The audience is relieved to know they're not alone in thinking, 'This bullshit we see and hear all day *makes no sense*. Surely I'm not the only one who thinks so. And surely there must be an answer . . .' Good comedy helps people know they're not alone. Great comedy provides an answer.

It is a most rarified air the great comics must breathe, who've transcended their own preconceived notions as well as the audiences at the *same time*. Here the comic is one with audience. He is a vessel, empty of himself, yet full of wonder and joy and creation – for these are the fruits the Voice of Reason bears. The Voice of

Reason is in us all, and it is the *same voice* that is in us all. And when it is voiced, it is heard by all and everyone can recognize it, because it *makes sense*, and *everyone* benefits from it . . . equally. There is no downside. There is no other shoe.

It is, and has been, and will forever be, this world of ours, a fucking *joke*. The real world lies beyond its veil, and the Artist, all Artists, have lifted that veil for themselves, and therefore for all, because we really are All One. (By the way, Larry, this is the very philosophy that has kept me virtually anonymous in America for fifteen years. Hmmm . . .) (Perhaps I should dye my hair blue and call myself Popsicle. Then I'd *really* be 'hot'!)

This is what confused me about, again, the idea of my not having a 'unifying theme'. Isn't Reason vs. Unreason, Sanity vs Insanity, Sense vs. Nonsense a *theme*? Isn't coaxing, cajoling, convincing the audience into fearlessly going on your inner journey *with* you a *theme*? (Particularly an inner journey such as my own, which to the provincial must seem, at first, quite profane?) What was Richard Pryor's 'unifying theme' other than his own idiosyncratic point of view? And who said it best and first? And no, it *wasn't* a comedian. Give up? It was Lenny Bruce. I *am* my own Unifying Theme, Mr Christian, and unfortunately there is no label, book, nor prop in which to name it. ('Social Critic' is not too far off the mark.)

You know, many reviewers have compared me to Lenny Bruce, and many have asked me how I feel about that comparison. My answer is always the same. First of all, since I didn't make the comparison, I don't have to justify it. But, to answer the question in earnest, I actually do feel we are similar. We are similar in that he was himself on stage, and I am *myself* on stage. Simlarly, Richard Pryor was himself, Charlie Chaplin was himself, Buster Keaton was himself, W. C. Field was himself, and the *only* pertinent question regarding these men's work – was it fucking funny? (Plus, I was doing a comedy show, not a term paper.)

You ended your piece on me with the single most baffling sentiment I have ever heard expressed regarding a comic. '. . . How are we to ever know if Mr Hicks is prophetic, or merely a crackpot?' *CRACKPOT!?* (Surely my show didn't remind you of Professor Irwin Corey's.)[69]

Since when in the *history* of comedy reviewing has *any* comic *ever* been held up to such remarkable standards? A prophet! A crackpot! Holy shit! (I'm still tossing and turning in bed over that.) Think about it, Larry. If you are willing to hold me up to such an unbelievable standard such as a *prophet*, or willing to dismiss me as some kind of *crackpot*, surely you understand my desire for you to reassess exactly what it is I do. And I think you are right when you said we might both learn something from each other with further dialogue. Apparently it is not clear to a *lot* of people what it is I do, so you know what? I'm just going to come out and tell you. No beating around the bush. Ok, here goes . . . I, like *all* artists in Western cultures, am a *shaman*. (That's somewhere between prophet and crackpot, by the way . . . though much closer to prophet.)

There, now you have it. I am a Shaman come in the guise of a comic, in order to heal perception by using stories and 'jokes', and always, always, *always* the Voice of Reason, that people may have Hope and Peace, by healing their misperceptions. I am a *shaman* and my goal is to . . . drum roll . . . be myself! And the effort that takes is . . . Another drum roll, please . . . *none*! And my message is . . . Drum roll, then cymbal crashes . . . *Be Yourself*. I am a *shaman*, a *healer* and truth is my medicine. Laughter makes the bitter swallowing of truth, for some, a little easier.

We live in a world of denial, Larry. And the shaman comes to remind us of our Truth. Shamans come in many shapes and forms. The form I've come in – me – is best expressed through the unfortunately limiting label of 'comic'. Yes, it must be confusing to some people. Gee, it took me *years* to realize what I was. (Years and years and years . . .) And always I've heard the same thing from the supposed 'powers that be' – 'We love you, Bill, but we just don't know what to do with you.' Really? Hmmm . . . That's very funny to me, because they obviously know what to do with the chumps, and the clowns, and the fakes, and the non-talents. Hmmm. . .

But, here's the good news – I finally realized who it is I am, and I no longer chase the carrot (tops), and I have no more hoops to jump through. I only have things to share with those who are willing or interested.

Let me tell you what a relief it is to finally know who you are!

The weight of the world has *literally* been lifted from my shoulders, and now I see *new hope* and *new happiness* being born everyday. And, strangely enough, *new opportunities* are coming at me all the time. ('Be yourself and all else will follow.') It's really that easy. And what effort does it take to be yourself?

A long time ago, a lawyer friend of mine told me something I found very enticing. He told me the word *Enthusiasm* cames from the latin words *En Theos*, which means – the God Within. 'In other words,' I thought to myself, 'do what excites you, for that excitement is God telling you – "we're on the right path, and we are together and isn't it *fun!*"' And it has been fun for me these last few years, and it's getting more fun everyday.

I'm writing to you now en route to W. Palm Beach, Florida, where I'll stay a few days before heading on to London. There we will take the first official step in realizing my vision for a show that came to me and my friend about three years ago. It is a show for visions and visionaries, for the Enlightened and those who wish to be Enlightened. It's called 'The Counts of the Netherworld', and its time has come. It's time to air the Voice of Reason. And, by the way, Larry, I am not a 'cult figure' in London, where I've been performing only for two years. I am a *star*. I *am* a cult figure in *America*, where I've been touring *ceaselessly* for over a decade. And, I might add, turning down every banal, stupid, trite, unfunny thing that was ever offered to me.

No, sir, I have a great respect for comedy. And it pains me to see it treated so . . . shamefully. There is no *context* for the bullshit we see on TV. There is no *center*. This country has swallowed the fucking lie hook, line, and sinker, and wallows in it like some fat swine – *proud* of its ignorance. As H. L Menken said – 'America's biggest failing is its inability to take comedy seriously.' And I couldn't agree more. Now, it seems, more than ever, our deranged country staggers aimlessly about, seeking, but it knows not what for. If only the mule would stop chasing the carrot, he would lay his tired weary carcass down and see the beautiful fields of grass on which to eat, that have been there all along. And, Larry, I think you are so right to point out the part the media has played in our national nightmare.

Whatever. The Truth will always be there, and it is only ourselves we are hurting. Shit, I *know* because I did it to myself for so long. And though I have taken the long route, what's the difference in the context of Eternity?

Anyway, I am *most* curious to hear your take on the Waco Documentary. Everyone, including myself, who's seen it, has the same response – what the hell am I seeing? Why haven't we seen this on the news? And can someone just please explain it? Your guess is as good as mine, although I think the footage speaks for itself. (Then again, I thought the Rodney King beating tape spoke for itself. Boy, was I wrong. I didn't know, as the cops helped me understand, that it was all in how you *looked* at the tape. Well what do you mean? 'Well, if you play the tape *backwards*, you see us help King up and send him on his way.' Oh . . .)

Also, I've included the videotape of my *final show ever* (?), which was shot at Igbies the day after you saw me. If you have the time and interest, I would greatly appreciate you giving another gander at what I do. The show at Igbies was so much warmer and I think a truer representative of what it is I actually do. Maybe now that you are, hopefully, over that bad cold, you can, at your leisure now, in the comfort of your own home, kick back and watch this tape and maybe even get a hoot out of it. (You were most definitely correct in assessing that [. . .] Improv – what a fucking morgue!)

Jeses, I've been writing now for over two hours. Even a crackpot can take a hint once in a while. I'll close by saying 'thanks' again for your openness in calling me back and hearing me out.

Sincerely,

Bill Hicks

P.S. Comic as shaman? Now *there's* a fucking unifying theme!

My Philosophy
(August 1993)

I love to smoke. To me, everything about smoking is cool. When I hear 'Kinda Blue' by Miles Davis, a cigarette magically appears in my hand, and I am THERE. Smoking is Miles Davis. Smoking is Tom Waites. Smoking is Bob Dylan. Smoking is Keith Richards.

Billy Ray Cyrus does not smoke. Michael Bolton doesn't smoke. Paula Abdul doesn't smoke. Is this clear? I'm not saying people who don't smoke aren't cool – although there does seem to be a pattern. I'm saying a lot of cool people smoke, and smoking is part of their coolness. I know I surprised a few people when I toured the UK last year. During the first tour, I was smoking and discussing my love of smoking onstage. By the time the second tour had begun, I had quit smoking, and all the people who liked what I did before seemed genuinely hurt and betrayed. People were yelling 'Judas!' and 'Traitor' and throwing cigarettes at me onstage. It was like Dylan going electric. While it was all done in good fun – except the lit ones – I explained my new lifestyle quite ingeniously. (There's nothing quite like a hail of burning embers raining down upon you to make you quick on your feet.) I told everyone the point of my old smoking routine was that I should have the right to smoke even if you think I SHOULDN'T. Now, I should have the right NOT to smoke even if you think I SHOULD. The point is – THE FREEDOM TO CHOOSE. After explaining this to the audience, they calmed down somewhat. While cigarettes were still thrown fewer and fewer lit ones were flicked at my head.

I don't want to toot my own horn here – you couldn't hear it from this distance anyway – but, I think I'm fairly open-minded when it comes to the idea of Freedom. I think I'm one of the only former drug abusers and alcoholics who doesn't decry the years I partied, or regret them. Instead, I look on those experiences as fun and exciting, and crucial to getting me where I am today. And I believe all drugs should be legal and available. In fact, I believe that as long as you don't harm another person, or get in the way of their freedom, ALL THINGS should be legal and available. As no amount of laws passed seem to prevent people's love of freedom, nor squelch their curiosity, nor their basic humanity, we would do better to look through the eyes of love and compassion, rather than condemnation and fear.

Drug abusers are not criminals in my mind's eye. At worst, they are just sick, and I know of no jail that has ever healed anyone.

I ascribe to a philosophy of Gentle Anarchy. I believe people are inherently GOOD, and left to their own devices – with the free exchange of ideas and information – a joyful lightness would spread across the face of our dour world.

I am aware there are many people who do not feel this way. This is why I figured out a way to make everyone happy, while also furthering the idea of Freedom. Here it is: for those people who think smoking, drugs, abortion, and prostitution should be legal and available – make them legal and available. And for those people who think smoking, drugs, abortion, and prostitution should NOT be legal and available – they're not, they never were, don't worry, we're cracking down. There. That way, the world would remain exactly as it is now, only without the onus of guilt, shame, and legality.

Does this mean I am suggesting people smoke, take drugs, get abortions, or go to prostitutes? No. I recommend you do what you want to do, which is what you're going to do anyway. I am merely suggesting we accept life on life's terms instead of drowning in a quagmire of niggling SHOULDS and SHOULDN'TS which have done NOTHING to free our spirits from the cloud of guilt and shame that shrouds this planet. Again – forgiveness rather than condemnation, compassion rather than judgement, and love rather than fear. And keep in mind, this radical philosophy is coming from me – an avowed misanthrope. If I can feel this way, surely there is hope for us all. Have we learned anything from all this? I have. The next time I tour the UK, I'm not going to tell the audience I quit smoking. I'm going to tell them I quit fucking, just to see what they throw at me then. I look forward to seeing you.

Part 4: Late 1993–94

Free Press or The Observer
Show Idea
(October 1993)

The story of William Harrison, son of the fabulously rich and unethical industrialist Dwight William Harrison, and also the inheritor of a two-hundred million dollar trust fund from a loving aunt. William Harrison has totally rejected the values and lifestyle of his parents and has started an alternative newspaper in the small college town from which he's from – say Austin, TX. The cast of characters who work at the *Free Press* – a weekly paper known as *'The Observer'* – all share the values of the counter culture.

There's Rainbow, a delightful free soul who believes and lives fully the ideals of the sixties. Rainbow channels the alien Sibius for an advice column in the newspaper called 'Sibius Responds'. She absolutely adores William, and loves people in general. She worships the ground William walks on for starting the paper and allowing 'the true nature of our reality to be printed and made available to the people'.

There's Dutch, a college student and jock whose football injury has sidelined him forever, relegating himself to sports writer for the *Free Press 'Observer'*, he's a goodhearted fellow, though totally confounded by Rainbow, new-age culture, and the start of the paper in general. He is happy to be able to keep his toe in sports in any way and writes florid, poetic accounts of the ongoing efforts of the college's sports teams. His dreams of being a serious writer are apparent, and William hired him for his innocence and genuine love of poetry. Dutch acts tough, but deep inside he's just as idiosyncratic as Rainbow, and treats his job at the *Free Press 'Observer'* as a salve for the regrets of failing at the one thing his parents willed for him – professional football.

There's also Tricia – a third-year journalist major whose gung-ho attitude at the paper is generally at odds with the easygoing spirit of the place. She's seeking major journalistic coups, uncovering corruption, injustice, human rights violations as though she were expecting a Pulitzer prize before even graduating. Many of her stories center on the brazen, corrupt Dwight Harrison, Industrialist/ Developer supreme of the small town. His acts range from pollution of streams and lakes, the building of golf courses over forest, and condos to block the views of the natural beauty of Texas Hill country. She too is frustrated and perplexed by the laidback attitude of the editor and chief of the *Free Press 'Observer'* She has no idea that William is Dwight Harrison's son, nor that William started *'The Observer'* as an act of complete rejection of his father's values. A situation he is slightly uncomfortable with as he watches Tricia single handedly going about trying to dismantle his father's empire. Tricia constantly reminds him she's destined for greater things than the flakey paper that hired her. She is a raven haired beauty, stiff and fiery, and little does she know how much she needs the laidback attitude of the editor and chief and the other members of the staff. William finds her quite attractive and her anger and frustration towards him speaks volumes of the other feelings she has not yet acknowledged that run deep inside her. As editor of the magazine, William writes his own philosophical ideas and opinions which sound like mumbo jumbo to Tricia. Still he gives her free rein on any story she chooses and backs her 100%.

Also on the staff is Lyle – music reviewer, concert-goer supreme. He believes music is the lifeblood of the paper and life in general and lives for music. His long hair and slacker speech annoy Dutch, who, although a poet at heart, was raised in a much more conservative atmosphere. Lyle thinks Dutch is a dumb jock. He is also always trying to hit on Rainbow. Rainbow, however, remains pure, just in case her hero – William – should ever need her or want her. William meanwhile fights his own personal demons – being the son of a corrupt, immoral industrialist who rules the town with an iron fist. And his own inner sense of justice and love of humanity. While

William and his father never see eye to eye, his mother understands her son's need to free himself from the oppressive atmosphere of the super-driven, super-rich, the super-immoral. She spends her time and money throwing charity events and other philanthropic activities. She loves her son dearly and is proud of the choices he has made. Dwight Harrison, on the other hand, feels betrayed by his only male offspring. The *Free Press 'Observer'* by its nature is a thorn in his side. He's torn between destroying the *Free Press* and whatever filial emotions he feels towards his only son. He lives in the constant hope his son will 'see the light' and come to work for him and eventually take over the empire. His feelings towards the gung-ho *Free Press* star reporter Tricia are rabid to say the least. She is constantly airing his dirty laundry in that small-time rag as though it were a personal vendetta. Tricia views him as the embodiment of evil itself, and in her uncovering his crimes and busting his empire, her ticket to greener pastures – the *Washington Post* or even the *New York Times*. She sees herself as a cultured woman of the world, and hates small town attitude of laidback slackers that make up the readership of the *Free Press 'Observer'*.

There's also Doyle, another reporter at the *Free Press* who is a loveable slob. Doyle is a forty-year-old burn-out who believes he's reached the pinnacle of success by working for the *Free Press*, and is content just slopping together stories of political corruption in the state's capital. Doyle is cynical and world weary and likes the image of the hard-nosed man on the street. Rainbow is always offering Doyle new-age remedies for his attitude which Doyle rejects in hand. 'The only problem with me, honey – is the whole fricken world.' Doyle, once a young idealist, has had his hopes shattered so often [in] his covering of state politics and politicians, it will take a miracle to piece them together again. Subconsciously, Doyle has come here for this miracle, which may perhaps lead his opinions to feelings for Rainbow in some unexpected ways. Tricia views Doyle as a bad luck burnout and steers clear of him unless absolutely necessary. Doyle views Tricia as an uptight twit looking for a big fall. Doyle would like to provide that fall if at all possible. He feels his seniority at the *Free Press* and in journalism entitles him to story choices. This constant battle is waged in front of William's desk, who always has the final say. Basically, Doyle wants to feel redeemed and gain back the ideals of his youth. Through the leadership of William, Doyle relearns how to live and that life is worth living. Even the arcane editorials William writes make sense to Doyle on a subconscious level, but as of yet, he's been unable to consciously grasp the true agenda of the *Free Press*. And just what is that agenda? To speak for the disenfranchised. All those lost souls who find no sustenance in mainstream news or media. All those seekers who found alternative lifestyles to replace the ancient crumbling institutions that have failed them, to voice the air of reason and open-mindedness in the ever increasing bland fascist consumer society, where the little guy is made smaller and more insignificant every-day. To try and recover our basic dignity and regain a sense of hope and even awe at the world around us. The *Free Press* is William's way of healing his past and offering an opportunity for all the idio-syncratic personalities who work there to heal their own special needs and find amongst this cast of social misfits and odd char-acters, a bond stronger than blood, a family of like minded broth-ers who can and will offer a different view of the world than the one that's grown so tired and familiar. They are obviously fighting an uphill battle, but what other battle is more worth fighting, and when little victories occur, what battles offer more rewards and rekindling of hopes than that of the loveable underdog who's finally overcome the odds? This is not just the story of the *FREE PRESS* but that of '*THE OBSERVER*' . . . The quiet, personable, animated observer who witnesses the tapestry of life with a loving eye, a whimsical smile, a sense of humor, and always, always hopefulness and rejoicing as each and every underdog finally defeats his own inner demons and the enemies that appear to be outside them, keeping them from peace.

In the end – all will be healed.

CapZeyeZ Live! with Dave Prewitt (24 October 1993)

Presenter: You're the first on the air tonight. What can we do for you?

Caller 1: Hallo. Mr Hicks, I got a coupla questions. First of all, I caught your act on HBO, the HBO special, and I was wondering, I know you're playing at the Laff Stop tomorrow, and I was just wondering, what kind of venue do you normally play? Do you play the Comedy Stops or do you do concert halls? Cos I know a lot of your stuff is borderline, I'm not sure if you're, for lack of a better term, like a social commentator or a comedian. OK. And I was just wondering what you had to say about that, and if you were thinking about getting any kind of more deeply into your subjects, rather than just, like I say [. . .] with a light brush, a light touch. Anyway, I'll get off the line.

Bill: Great questions, very astute questions. I will tell you this, that in England I play concert halls solely. And in America . . . ah, I'm on at the Laff Stop – does that explain anything to you? In England something happened between me and the audience, and I'll tell you what happened was they aired things like that HBO special the gentlemen just talked about and other specials that I've done, unedited on their four channels – they have only four channels. So they aired it, unedited, at prime-time TV, so consequently the audience that saw it – a huge audience in the UK – they had a good portion of people see it and like exactly what I really do. It wasn't edited, there was no . . . it wasn't like going on TV here. So there was huge crowds. It's been beautiful over in England.

Presenter: Course not here.

Bill: It hasn't happened here, and there's . . . you know, I could nitpick, but I will say things have picked up here. But as far as the material, much more am I getting into the subject matter, and if you come out to the show, there'll be nothing I did on the HBO show that you will see here. And the material is . . . I don't consider it really comedy. I don't even consider it the difference between comedy and drama, to be honest with you. I think as long as it's entertaining and interesting and hopefully funny, that it has merit as entertainment, and I appreciate the question. I would love to get out of comedy clubs and play theatres. I think social criticism is much needed in America, and unfortunately it's like Noam Chomsky said, 'The emperor wears no clothes, but he doesn't like to be told it.' Ha ha ha! Those emperors.

Caller 2: Hello, I was asking Bill that the difference between London humor and American humor is just ungodly, and . . .

Bill: So is the difference between English accents and yours. (*laughs*)

Caller 2: I just don't understand what . . . like the Bill Clinton and everything up here, I just don't get it. What is the thing that makes you sell your humor.

Bill: Makes me sell my humour? Tell my humour?

Presenter: What was that?

Caller 2: Tell your humor. Where do you get your ideas for jokes from?

Bill: OK, good question Mr Faux Englishman. (*laughs*) That accent's worse than the one I do, and mine's pretty bad. I do the only Englishman with a drawl, I think, in the world. Anyway, where I come up with material particularly is . . . it's very simple. Anything that defies my sense of reason. I don't look outside myself for answers. I kind of feel like everyone has a voice of reason inside 'em, and I believe that's been quelled to a large degree by our multimedia society that we live in, but anything that defies my voice of reason comes out, and you hold it up to the light of reason – that's the premise – and then you start nailing it, and those are the jokes, until what's left is a laughter, I think, of recognition of a truth. If that's not arcane and metaphysical enough for you, put on the special glasses.

Caller 3: Hey, I just want to say that I think that's bullshit about that David Letterman stuff, and as far as I'm concerned, I'm not gonna watch that show any more until Dave quits sucking that corporate cock. I'm behind you 100 per cent, man.

Bill: Well, I tell ya . . . I been watching the show since this incident happened with a different light in myself, and I have always . . . I've liked Dave and he's always been – well, I can't say he's been supportive, because in fact I feel like I've finally realized something: I've been for the last – however many times I've done it – in an abusive relationship that I keep going back for more. 'Bill, we love you, cos you're so edgy and hip. But when you come on our show could you not be that way?' And I made the mistake of doing it, thinking, 'Oh well, you know, I'll rewrite everything so it fits', and now I have no interest in doing that whatsoever. I would rather be on Dave's show here on Public Access than play to three million yahoos, who think they're watching something radical or rebellious.

Caller 4: I think that you've become one of the few really good visionary comics. I think like you and Dennis Miller and Will Durst are probably on that cutting edge, that Mort Sahl/Lenny Bruce type thing.

Bill: Oh, I appreciate that. There's a handful of others who you haven't heard of cos they're even more on the edge and you're never gonna hear 'em.

Caller 4: Why not?

Bill: Because there's no venue. Comedy clubs won't book 'em, and America does not take comedy seriously, social criticism seriously. If you look at even the careers of Mort Sahl and Lenny Bruce, you'll notice that one was basically run out of the business and the other one killed himself due to lack of work. This is how America supports social criticism . . .

HBO didn't censor me, and I got to give 'em credit for that. But Mort Sahl – there's a great documentary I saw on Mort Sahl on PBS, and he seems to be . . . he seems kind of at peace with himself, and in a way – I don't want to get too, again, esoteric – but I'm kind of at peace with myself as well. I don't really care any more. There are venues and there are avenues, but they are not going to be mainstream. But that's why I love Public Access, that's why England has opened up for me, and HBO was nice enough not to edit anything except due to time constraints. I think there's a change coming up, man. You can't put out puerile crap twenty-five hours, cos eventually there's gonna be chaos in the streets, which there already is, because people are frustrated not having their voice of reason confirmed. And everyone has that voice of reason that goes, 'This is bull, man. What I'm watching is bull.' And yet the media does not confirm it, so after a while people get . . . they begin to think they're insane. And that's the bummer about it, but that's why I love non-mainstream stuff, because you actually hear honest emotions, and that's what you won't hear on mainstream TV ever, is honest emotions.

Caller 4: Before I . . . I'll hang up now, but before you get out of there, give me your take on two things. Give me your take on the Palestinian Peace Accord, and what the hell are we doing in Somali and Haiti? What the hell is that all about? Now they're talking about . . . did you hear the news today about the bomb in Northern Ireland?

Bill: No.

Caller 4: Oh yeah, somebody threw a bomb into a shopping complex, a downstairs shopping complex where nobody can escape, killed nine, injured about fifty, and we're supposed to send some sort of peace envoy over there to try and work this all out between the Catholics and Protestants, like that's gonna happen. Why don't we have the Crusades all over again.

Bill: Right. Well, my take on any of the foreign affairs of the US Government is at best cynical and completely doubtful that their motives are our motives or anything other than the elite maintaining the status quo. As far as the Palestinians specifically, they were there, they need their land, and Israel is a satellite of this country. We sell them nuclear weapons, and you can just imagine what kind of deal the Palestinians are gonna get. And as far as the Somalia/Haiti, what we're doing is spreading democracy at gunpoint. In other words . . .

Caller 4: Well, they'll have health care at least.

Bill: Well, they're gonna need it, cos McDonald's going in first . . . I can't answer those questions, and I tell you who I love to read is Noam Chomsky, and if y'all can get into Noam Chomsky at all, he will definitely take a squeegee to your third eye, and that's what we need to have happen. But thanks for calling. I appreciate it.

Presenter: Are you planning on going back to Dave? I know he had expressed wanting to have you back.

Bill: Yeah, after this *New Yorker* article comes out on Monday, I don't know if they're gonna express that same feeling.

Presenter: Well, you know, we each have our thing to do, and I don't know if being on Dave would have been that other step, you know?

Bill: I don't really care any more, cos you know what? I've never been me on Dave. You know, out of all the other eleven appearances I've done on the show, I've never had anyone come up to me and go, 'I saw you on Letterman last night. You were great.' And the reason that is, I've never been me on that show. And I don't really know if it's enough respect for myself to go on and play a game that's not me, so I don't really care any more, to be honest with you. And that's it. I don't really care. There's other venues and there's other outlets, and let them play their game. And I tell you what: it is, as another caller mentioned, everyone's getting screwed now, and it's becoming so transparent they're fucking lying that it's laughable, and that's all I want to say on that.

Unresolvable Problems – Resolved! (November 1993)

Bosnia-Herzegovina, Bosnia-Herzegovina, Bosnia-Herzegovina . . . That's all you hear in the news these days. The general consensus amongst the press is one of perplexity and puzzlement, as the pundits keep asking themselves (aloud) how it is 'Americans can sit back and let this carnage in Bosnia-Herzegovina continue? How can the American people sit back so apathetically and watch this terrible carnage and "ethnic cleansing" take place? The images of horror we pump into American homes around the clock have had no discernible effect. Why is that?' (Etc. Etc. Adnauseam.)

I'd like to venture a guess here. Could it be because you, The Media – acting as the mouthpiece for the elite state power you serve, have lied about EVERY SINGLE STORY you've ever reported on? From the 'inhuman savagery' of Native Americans, to the unchallenged 'he's a Hitler' statement regarding Saddam Hussein, perhaps we're just a little tired of having our emotional chain yanked by you agenda-setting wastrels. Perhaps we're tired of being played like a cheap violin. Maybe, just maybe, you've cried 'Wolf!' one too many times.

Bosnia-Herzegovina conveniently took center stage in your nightly newscast just as the Iraq war petered out and George Bush slinked away defeated. It's most impressive how this thousand-year-old conflict only recently became headline news, and TOP STORY significance. What a scoop! You eager Truth Seekers definitely can't be accused of dragging your feet. I guess you had to wait for the discovery of America and then the invention of television in order for the images you pass on [to] be extremely graphic and appalling, and therefore, hopefully, insuring a speedy end to this now Vital conflict. (Now that is thinking ahead!)

Do you really care about Bosnia-Herzegovina? Or is Bosnia-Herzegovina just another in a long series of UNRESOLVABLE PROBLEMS you shrilly go on about in order to keep the general populace anxious, confused, helpless, ultimately – controllable? Well?

I'm not suggesting what is happening there is not tragic. It is. And just to show you I'm not totally insensitive to the plight of the . . . Serbs? Bosnians? Muslims? Croatians? Women? Children?, or whomever you're going to feature in tonight's newscast in order to push our buttons . . . I will solve this Unresolvable Problem right now – free of charge. And just to show you I'm not some pie-in-the-sky, peacenick, spoilsport – I guarantee we'll still get to use the full extent of our military strength. (Whew!) Here's how we do it: We find out where the Bosnians, Serbs, Muslims, whomever, are getting their weapons and then we blow up those suppliers with extreme [. . .] I'd be willing to bet enthusiasm for 'ethnic cleansing' will wane if only sticks and rocks are available for the warring parties. (Hey, something just occured to me. If civilization had a No Tolerance attitude towards the makers of weapons, maybe there'd be less war . . . sorry.)

I know, I know . . . you're thinking 'Blow up the arms dealers!? How could that possibly help?' Well, just think how much we Americans will save on petrol. Our planes can just drop their bombs on take-off! A secondary target could be those propaganda outlets that stoke the fires of our hatreds and keep us at each other's throats while the powers that be continue to enact their agendas with impunity. Imagine how entertaining that would be – sitting at home watching the finest war machine the world has ever seen, bombing their own bases and munitions factories, then heading towards Atlanta and the CNN bunker where they will perform their final kamikaze mission for peace. One by one, our TVs suddenly go blank. We turn them off and breathe a collective sigh of relief. Our shared nightmare has ended. Mordor has fallen. We could then turn to our friends, our neighbors, our gardens, our books, and even to our own thoughts, listening as songbirds provide the soundtrack for our reborn earth, and the dream of forgiveness dawns gently on our healing minds.

And what about the press? what part could you now play? Well, in light of the spineless servility you've shown to state power, and the function you've played as propagandist for the ruling elite, for your blatant obfuscations of facts, your agenda-pushing histrionics, your trivialization of all things good and important, your focusing on the trivial in order to deny serious thought and therefore keep Unresolvable Problems Unresolved, thereby assuring your continued employment, there seems to be only one HONORABLE thing left for you to do. But don't worry, it will be remembered in your obituaries that ultimately you made the correct editorial choice. i.e. – editing yourself from the Truth Seeking, journalistic process.

Dear Scallywag,[70]

Please feel free to call me anytime at 310-***-**** with questions, suggestions, or just to chat. I realize we've never even met. I'm sure it would be a delight.

Sincerely,

Bill Hicks

Introducing . . . Bill Hicks
Scallywag No. 14
(Autumn 1993)

Bill Hicks, the fastest up and coming alternative comedian in the States is arriving to these shores this Spring to star in his own Channel Four TV series. He has developed a cult following after a nationwide tour. He is joining *Scallywag* to write regularly from America.

SYMPATHY FOR THE DEVIL
Anyone needing additional proof just how serious this global recession has become needn't look any further than a certain mid-Manhattan courtroom last Friday when Lucifer (yes, the Devil himself!) filed for Chapter 11. Whew! I knew Old Scratch was bankrupt spiritually, but financially as well! How could this happen?

Apparently, the Prince of Lies made some particularly bad deals in the eighties that were now coming back to haunt him . . . (Fade Out).

(Fade In – Penthouse Suite – Four Seasons Hotel – N.Y.N.Y)

Michael Bolton lays on a couch reviewing last night's concert receipts. A cold breeze ruffles the pages he is holding. Bolton looks up and sees the Devil sitting across the table from him.

Devil: Hello, Michael. Are you enjoying your worldly success?

Michael Bolton indicates the room around him as if to say 'What's not to like?'

Devil: Good! You would agree then that I have lived up to my end of The Bargain?

Michael Bolton nods slowly.

Devil: Excellent! Then you know why I've come. It's time for you to live up to your end of our little deal, Michael. I've come for your soul.

Michael Bolton stares at the Devil, then slowly shakes his head. The Devil smiles patiently.

Devil: You don't seem to understand, Michael. We have a . . . DEAL.

Michael Bolton sits up and leans into the Devil's face.

Michael Bolton: You don't seem to understand. Devil-Man . . . I have no soul to give you. Sorry! Ha! Ha! Ha!

The Devil gasps and recoils in horror as Michael Bolton throws back his head and laughs maniacaly – his paltry locks whirling about his misshapen balding pate like fistfulls of tiny snakes, and his sharp little teeth clicking together like bones rattling in the night.

Devil (weakly):   But . . . we . . . had . . . a . . . deal . . .

Michael
Bolton: Ha! Ha! Ha! Sorry! You should have done your research! Even the phone company does a credit check! Ha! Ha!

Suddenly, he stops laughing and snaps his fingers. Out of the shadowy corners of the room step two burly bodyguards, who grab the Devil by the arms and pull him roughly towards the door.

Devil: But . . . But . . .

The bodyguards hurl the Devil into the hallway, where he stands sway-
ing and confused.

Michael
Bolton: Maybe you'll have better luck with your other clients.
           So long! And again . . . Sorry! Ha! Ha! Ha!

With that, the door slammed in the Devil's face, and a sick feeling began to grow inside him, and things went from bad to worse.
He had no luck with his other eighties clients. Between Michael
Bolton, MC Hammer, Vanilla Ice, Marky Mark, Mariah Carey, Paula
Abdul, and a host of other daft twits he had turned into inexpli-
cable stars, all reneged on their end of The Deal, having no souls
to turn over in the first place. Now, the Devil is out of a job, and
a new Evil rules this sorry Earth . . . an Evil unbounded by any
standards of quality, code of ethics, pride, or integrity. And a cold
wind blows in the hearts of Man. And a maniacal shriek of laughter echoes in the night . . . with a bullet.

On Smoking
(undated)

I need to quit smoking cigarettes – not because it's unhealthy. I only need enough breath each morning to cough up the requisite amount of phlegm. And not because it's a filthy habit, because the nicotine stains is the closest thing I've ever come to a tan. No. The reason I need to quit is because by smoking, I contribute to the tobacco industry, which in turn supports Senator Jesse Helms of North Carolina. Jesse Helms comes up for election every six years. In that time I figure I spend over $11,000 on cigarettes, a portion of that then finds its way into his campaign war chest, which he uses to get re-elected to the United States senate. The Surgeon General's warning ought to read: 'Smoking has been determined to cause cancer, heart disease and Rednecks with seniority'.

Now since I really don't want to quit smoking, I'll strike a deal with the tobacco people . . . I'll continue to make them rich by killing myself and others around me, if they will allow me to earmark how my money is to be spent during Senator Helms next election. I would like them to take the money I could be spending on hookers and give me five seconds on one of Jesse's television ads. Any specific message? The Bill of Rights – void where prohibited. Otherwise, I'm investing in a year's supply of chewing gum and massages that roam, not far, but wisely.

On the Fall of Communism (undated)

In the midst of all the elation over the fall of communism in the Soviet Union, one important fact has been overlooked – the United States has lost its 'Bogeyman'. Without the Soviet Union, who will fuel our latest paranoia? Who will the CIA spy on? Ok – its own citizens like it always has, but now how will they justify it? Saddam Hussein of Iraq? I think not. Sure, he has the look of a first class villain. But if looks were all it took, every other month we could just kick the tar out of Jack Palance. No, we need a country that not only has its own nuclear weapons, but also represents a threat to democracy. In other words, we need The United States of America. That's right – our next Cold War ought to be with ourselves. We're the logical choice. After all, who possesses the biggest danger to the American environment – we do. Who's responsible for our venal and corrupt government – we are. Besides, we could save money if we were our own worst enemy – for instance, the Hotline would become a local call. And if you thought McCarthyism in the 50's was irrational, think of the fun we could have asking Americans if they are now, or have ever been An American. Done right, we could blacklist seventy-five per cent of the people working in television and film. Just think, that's all but one of The Golden Girls. So turn those missiles around 180 degrees and remember – Better Dead Than Us.

Two Myths Explored, Debunked, and Other Rantings (undated)

I was reading the 'Letters to the Editor' section of *Rolling Stone* Magazine the other day. In it were letters in reponse to an article that appeared in the magazine the week before about gun control. Judging from the points of view expressed in the letters, the article had presented the usual two sides you hear regarding this issue, insuring that nothing would be resolved and the argument would rage on and on ad infinitum until we all wished someone would just shoot us so we wouldn't have to hear it anymore.

The two points of view that are allowable in the narrow spectrum of debate in America regarding gun control are these: first, those people who believe it is our constitutional right to bear arms (these are the 'you'll get my gun when you pry it from my cold dead fingers' bunch – the National Rifle Association, and basically every yahoo goober you'll ever meet in America), then there are those who believe it is our constitutional right to bear arms, *but only* after a one week waiting period before being able to purchase a gun, and/or psychiatric and criminal records check. In other words, they feel some type of gun control measure should be enacted so it's just a little harder to purchase a gun, while not infringing on our 'Guaranteed Consitutional Right to Bear Arms.' (There is a third point of view on the gun control issue, those who I refer to as THE VICTIMS, but they remain strangely silent and unorganized.)

Well, here I was again reading these letters, these pathetic attempts at logic from tiny-brained, right-wing fearmongers (i.e. 'if you outlaw guns, only outlaws will have guns', and 'Guns don't kill people, people kill people') and letters from the timid, cowering 'left' having the gall to suggest that 'while it is people who kill people, they do it much more readily and handily with guns than without them', and 'while outlawing guns would leave only outlaws with guns' doesn't take into account the fact that many of the victims of guns are children shot by other children – outlaws neither one. And, of course, there was no acceptance of the statistical correlation between the number of deaths caused by handguns (over ten thousand just this year alone) in America, where guns are readily available, compared to the paltry number of deaths caused by handguns in England (22!) where guns are *not* so readily available. The simple fact that where there are lots of guns – there are lots of people dying from guns, and where there aren't a lot of guns – not many people die from guns, is an equation the bloodthirsty, hate mongering horde of gun freaks that maintain it is their 'consitutional right to bear arms' don't understand is more than a little frightening. Shouldn't you be able to comprehend simple leaps of logic before being able to purchase a gun? 'No!' they cry. 'It is our right!' And so they believe.

Well, I took it upon myself to peruse a copy of the Bill of Rights to find out exactly what this article in the constitution states. What I discovered shocked me quite profoundly, for two reasons. First because I realized what level of ignorance I was dealing with here – pre-school at best, and second, because what I found so easily in Article Two of the Bill of Rights has *never* been mentioned before (as far as I know) in this neverending debate.

I'll quote Article Two[71] of the Bill of Rights first, then present my simple realization and perhaps, God willing, this ludicrous issue can be resolved once and for all. (Yeah, right . . .) Here goes: 'A well-regulated militia being necessary to the security of a free state, the right of the people to keep and bear arms shall not be infringed.' (!) As far as I can tell, that's *one sentence*. This issue doesn't need to be debated by constitutional lawyers. This whole debate could be cleared up by my first grade English teacher, Mrs Farmer. Article Two says, essentially, that: 'In order to maintain a free state a *well-regulated* militia (the National Guard) is necessary, and to that end *only* (at least according to the grammatic content of the sentence) people (the National Guard) have the 'right to bear arms'. If you reverse the two parts of the sentence it becomes even more crystal clear: 'The right of the people to keep and bear arms shall not be infringed, in order to maintain a well-regulated militia.'

This sentence, this *one* idea, this complete thought in and of itself does *not* say every Floyd, Clem, or Burl has the right to bear arms. It does *not* say every psychopathic yahoo in the country should be able to own a gun. It doesn't say that *at all*, and anyone with an education higher than the first grade *should* be able to comprehend this. Again, I believe people should be able to glean the true meaning of a simple sentence before we even *begin* to discuss their owning automatic weapons for 'hunting purposes.'

I can't help but wonder why the simple and obvious meaning of this sentence has never been mentioned before. Perhaps this is old news to the gun control debaters, but that still doesn't change the meaning of the sentence. Are gun rights advocates arguing that roving gangs of young people shooting innocent bystanders constitutes a 'well-regulated militia'? Or that Clem shooting Burl because he mistook him in the dark for a 'nigra' constitutes a 'secure and free state'? What, exactly, is their argument based on? Because it is *not* based on *any* 'guaranteed right' in the constitution. A child could explain this to you if he or she wasn't busy ducking for cover, or being strip-searched on the way into their grade school.

Here is the problem as I see it – a lot of very fearful and confused people in this world are heading towards realizing their own self-fulfilling prophecy. They're advocating a right that *does not* exist (at least constitutionally, as we've seen) to arm themselves to the teeth and 'protect' themselves from unnamed predators who, they believe, want nothing more than to break into their homes, rape their fat wives, and then steal all their bowling trophies.

They want to 'defend' themselves against some giant social war that appears to them to be breaking out everywhere, threatening their very existence itself. And just who are these poor and twisted souls that flap helplessly in the winds of change like a klansman's sheet rustling against his legs as he chases a 'nigra child' in the night? They are . . . you guessed it! . . . *Christians!*

Fundamentalist Christians to be exact. Uh-oh! Dial 911 and call the logic police – this *is* an emergency! Turn your phazer to your own head and press 'stun'. Slip into some bib-overalls, put a corn stalk between your teeth and pull up a stump, because you are about to experience philosophical thinking at its *best*! These are some *deep*, *deep* thinkers here. They've left more than one man stuttering in amazement, silenced by their swift grasp of 'THE TRUTH'! which is stated so clearly in the Holy Bible, which is the 'literal word of God'. Watch as every sane and logical argument falls helplessly against their wall of faith. Their beady little pig eyes flare red with fear and hate when the 'Good Book' is held up to the Light of Reason. Watch out! Those Christians might bite! After all, they've got God on their side, and there's no question in their little cracker minds about that. I guess they assume they're forgiven for every form of grevious persecution they've committed against 'non-believers' over the centuries. Be careful! There's nothing more dangerous than an angry Christian. With that lethal combination of ignorance combined with self-righteousness! Keep your hands in the car at all times, and *no petting*. It's Christian Country safari, or as it's more popularly known in this, the latter part of the twentieth century as – Amerikkka.

Now don't get me wrong. Some Christians are fun. Take the Pope for instance – why, he's a downright hoot! I could watch him for *hours* bouncing around in his little POPE MOBILE, surrounded by three feet of bazooka-proof plexiglass that I guess we're supposed to believe was forged in Heaven by the angel Gabriel to protect the Pope from Satan's Assassins. Now, *there's FAITH IN ACTION*!

No, I'm speaking more specifically about right-wing, fundamentalist Christians – those who believe the Bible is the 'literal word of God'. *These* are the folks that frighten me, being as they are, in the equivalent of spiritual kindergarten, while *also* holding positions in the *highest* levels of the US Government. (Ronald Reagan, George Bush, Jimmy Carter, and Bill Clinton come to mind, just off the top of my head.)

How can the Bible be the 'exact and literal word of God', when in the first four chapters *alone* God is already stumbling about and placing his claim of omniscience in a very suspicious light? In chapter two of Genesis, we read that 'God formed man out of dust from the ground' and this man's name was Adam. Also in chapter two, we're told that 'God caused a deep sleep to fall upon the man then took one of his ribs and fashioned a woman from the rib', and this woman's name was Eve. (Now remember, I'm not questioning the miraculous power of God, only the claim by fundamentalists that the Bible is 'the exact and literal word of God.') In chapter three, we learn of Adam and Eve's fall of grace from EDEN. Now, in chapter four, Adam and Eve have 'relations' and Eve gives birth to a son – Cain. Next she gives birth to Cain's brother Abel. Cain kills his brother Abel and Cain then 'went out from the presence of the Lord, and settled in the Land of Nod, east of Eden.' *Then*, in the next verse we're told 'and Cain had relations with his wife . . .' Whoa! Hold on here. His wife? Where the hell did she come from? How does this work? You see, the Bible may be the 'literal word of God', but apparently it's not the 'complete works of God'. (That'll be out this Christmas along with the Led Zeppelin 16-disc box set.)

When posed with these obvious questions of veracity, fundamentalists will then start backpedaling and offering up their pseudo-intellectual philosophies to 'fill in the gaps' so to speak of God's 'exact and literal word'. (You won't find people more presumptuous than Christians.) They'll say that Adam and Eve had other children besides Cain and Abel, daughters, who aren't mentioned in the Bible. Already we're open to interpretation, and assumption, and, I might add, if it's true – INCEST! You would think the 'exact and literal word of God' would be clearer and more understandable and not so open to anyone and everyone's assumptions and interpretations which have kept even fellow Christians at each other's throats, not to mention the vast chain of guilt, shame, condemnation, and religious persecution they've imposed upon others since the Prince of Peace was first born.

As for me, I believe that God is Love, and that he created us, and that we are his beloved children. I believe his love is *unconditional*, and that there's nothing we could do to ever change that. I believe it is our own misperceptions of who we really are that leads to *every* self-created hell you'll find in this world. I also believe forgiveness is the key to healing our perceptions and allowing us to remember God and his everlasting love for us.

Whatever other dogma or rhetoric you want to add to that simple belief is your business I guess. Or however you wish to interpret it. Like gun control and fundamentalism – these are the nature of the problems that arise in a country of people who are seventy per cent functionally illiterate. I just pray you'll let my own form of practice be my business and keep your little fearful hands off the weapons for a while. I for one am going to take what Terence McKenna refers to as an 'heroic dose' of psylocybin 'MAGIC' mushrooms with my friends and head for the woods, where the word of God can be heard quite effortlessly and quite clear and without the 'thee's and thou's.' Hopefully, just before we leave, we'll catch a shot of the Pope bouncing around in his little Pope Mobile on the news. That'll give us something to giggle about for the first forty minutes before God starts speaking and we hush in silent reverie, and bask in his neverending, holy love.

Igby's Comedy Club, California (September 17 1993)

I got a really shitty stereo. I brought my Dylan tapes down here. You know he sings? I mean, this opened up a whole new fucking world. All these years I'm buying his albums, G chord, C chord, G chord, C chord. What kind of genius is this? There's lyrics – some quite profound. I think he has potential.

Glad you brought a book in case this show bores you. Very nice. Hope you all brought reading material with you tonight. If not, we can pass *Juliette* around the room. Anyone at any point feels like you want to read *Juliette*?

Audience member: He's big in Montreal.

Bill: He's big in Montreal? Oh, I love Montreal. Is that where you're from? Let's get back to my show. I ah . . . end of audience participation. Now. I'm not that quick on my feet, you know. It's an illusion.

Anyway, folks, I appreciate you coming out. It's a very sentimental evening for me and a very exciting one, but this is my final live performance I am ever going to do stand-up comedy-wise. True. No, no, no, don't get my wrong. It's not sour grapes. I've loved every, you know, moment of the sixteen years I been doing it in total anonymity in the country I love, and every delayed flight, every Econolodge, I've loved it all. Playing the Comedy Pouch in Possum Ridge, Arkansas, every three months. It was *my* treat. Every broken relationship was a hoot, but . . . No, the reason I'm quitting is actually good news. I finally got – I found out today – I got my own TV show on CBS coming out in '94. (*audience whoops and claps*) Yeah. It's not a talk show. (*makes sound of crowd cheering*) Thank God, thank Krishna, thank Buddha, thank Mohammed, thank Allah. (*makes sound of crowd cheering*) Calm down. It's not a talk show.

It is a half-hour weekly show that I will host entitled 'Let's Hunt and Kill Billy Ray Cyrus.' (*audience claps*) Thanks. So y'all'll tune in? Cool. Cool. It's fairly self-explanatory. Each week we let the hounds of hell loose and we chase that jarhead, no-talent, cracker asshole all over the globe till I finally catch that fruity little pony-tail of his, pull him to his knees, put a gun in his mouth (*makes sound of gun*) and we'll be back in '95 with 'Let's Hunt and Kill Michael Bolton.' Thanks a lot. Thank you. You see the run is fairly limitless with this idea. We're not gonna run out of storylines any time too fucking soon here. And we're kicking it all off with our Marky Mark/Vanilla Ice/MC Hammer Christmas spectacular, and I don't want to give away any secrets, but the first one we hunt and kill on the Christmas special is Marky Mark, because his pants kept falling around his ankles and he couldn't run away. It's hilar– he's hopping along, I crossbow him right in the abs. And there's something really neat to see him laying face-down in snow and his blood seeping out and the snow melting and he just sinks from view. I'm telling you, it has the weirdest . . . you just kinda aaaaah, he's gone, oh, you stretch, your bowels loosen, aaaaah. My first solid shit in a year, yeah! I had no idea the psychic price I was paying that he existed simultaneously with me on the planet! I didn't know the burden that I carry every day, every fucking bill-board, 'Oh, there he is again.' When he goes down, I'm telling you, the clouds lift, birds are chirping (*mimics birds chirping*), sunlight, 'Hey brother', everyone's walking with a step, it's . . . All I'm trying to do, folks, is rid the world of all these fevered egos that are taint-ing our collective unconscious and making us pay a higher psychic price than we can fucking imagine. That in fact is how I exactly pitched it to the network. Seriously. I went in and I said, 'I wanna do a show where we rid the world of all these fevered egos that are tainting our collective unconscious', and the CBS guy goes, 'Will there be titty?' And I said, 'Yeah, all right, sure. Sure.' Boom! A cheque falls in my lap, I'm a producer. We've had creative meet-ings.

'What are these titties gonna do?'
'Ah, jiggle?'

'Son, you're a genius. Where have you been all our lives?'
'Oh, at the Comedy Pouch in Possum Ridge, Arkansas, you
fuck. I had no idea if I said the word "titty" I'd get my own
show, but er . . .'

Damn it! Damn me for not thinking of that. What does everyone
love? Titties, yes. I do hope Marky Mark's abs count as titties, but
I don't know. Don't be disappointed. I'm sure there's enough egregious women on this list that I'll find somewhere down the line.
None yet, but . . .

I don't know what the deal is, folks. I'm like a 31-year-old
curmudgeon, man, you know? Went to a dance club the other night,
give you an example. Obviously I wasn't driving and ah . . . so we
wound up at a dance club. Now, I go to dance clubs about once
a year, just to justify the other 364 days of the year I spend in my
apartment going, 'God, what fucking idiots!' and ah . . . yeah, takes
one day. I'm like a camel. I go to a dance club, I fill my hump with
hate (*makes sucking sound*), and I can go about a year and the hump
starts to go down, and I go back to the dance club (*makes sucking
sound*). I'm the hate camel, you see. And it just takes a brief interlude with humanity to fill my hump and I'm good for about a year.
I read *Juliette* by Yves Beauchemin, big in Montreal, and suddenly
I get itchy. I think, 'Maybe people are OK. Maybe I should get out.'
I go out, (*makes sucking sound*) and the hump . . . I'll see ya in a
fucking year, you know. Anyway, this girl asked me to dance, which
I thought was hilarious. 'Would you like to dance?' And I was like,
'Ah, you read my mind', you know. 'That's why I'm leaning in the
darkest corner closest to the exit, you know . . . I'm about to boogie.
I'm about to cut a rug.' But it's so weird. Women – some women
– have this weird myth: you can tell the way a guy is in bed by
how he is on a dancefloor. I think that's so ridiculous. I mean, first
of all what does it matter? You know what I mean? If a guy's on a
dancefloor really getting into it and enjoying himself and expressing himself, what does it matter how he is in bed? He's gay. So
. . . real men don't dance. They sit, sweat and curse. Oh, fuck.

OK, speaking of homosexuality, something has come to my attention that I feel I must comment on, and let me preface this by

saying first of all I am a very open-minded person. I mean, I really am. Being a fella such as myself, who over the course of his life has several times taken his bodyweight in psilocybin magic mushrooms, I've had my mind fairly opened. My third eye has been squeegeed. (*makes squeaking noise*) UFOs? Seen 'em! OK, you know what I mean? I'm out on a limb with Shirley MacLaine, she's clinging to the trunk, I'm hanging by a twig at the end of the limb. 'Come on, Shirley! Let's go! Take another cap, the UFOs are honking! Let's go!' 'Bill, you're really out there, dude!' I'm pretty open-minded . . . *but* something has come to my attention. Now, have you heard about this? These new grade-school books for children to help explain to them the gay lifestyle? You know what I'm talking about? One of 'em is called *Heather's Two Mommies*. The other one, *Daddy's New Room-mate*. Folks, I'm gonna have to draw the line here and say I find this really fucking disgusting. You know, it's abhorrent and I think it's fucking evil, all right? And I'm talking of course about *Daddy's New Room-mate*. *Heather's Two Mommies*, on the other hand . . . wow! Quite a fetching read. I ah . . . Oooh, they're hugging on page seven. Ooh, go mommies, go! Heather's such a lucky girl. I wish I had two mommies. Ooh, they kiss in chapter 11. Ooh! So that is cool, but the other one . . . You know, there's actually people in the world who consider that a double standard. (*laughs*) People! What are we gonna do with 'em! Which kills me about being back in LA, the home of fucking phoney false cult religions such as the inner child, this bullshit. God. You know, I'm real tired of this backslapping humanity fucking movement going on. 'Aw, humans, aren't we neat! Come on, we're keen!' Folks, we're a virus with fucking shoes, man. That's all we are. And this 'Get in touch with your inner child' – do me a favour: get in touch with your outer fucking adult, all right? Get off my couch, get a fucking apartment and quit hugging me. You know what'd make your inner child real happy? Get a fucking job. 'The inner child.' I think our country's fairly childish enough. I think we're in touch with that. Let's move on to our outer adult – ready? OK. It's time to evolve. Ready? Go! OK, I'll go first.

But . . . no, I'm really down on humanity and it all comes from watching TV, cos when I meet people everyone's sane and reasonable, right? Then you go home, turn on the TV and you're like,

'What the fuck world is that?' You ever do that? Just watch CNN, just watch the top of the hour. 'This half hour: war, death, famine, Aids, homeless, recession, depression, deficit, drought, flood, earthquake, fire!' Then you open your curtain and you look out . . . (*makes sound of crickets chirruping*) Where's all this shit happening? I think Ted Turner's making this shit up! I think Jane won't fuck him some nights, he goes, 'Fuck you, I'll ruin the whole world. Here, read that on the air. By 1994 we will all have Aids – read that on the air. I don't get laid, no one gets laid.' I'm writing letters: 'Jane, blow him, fuck him, jack him off – something! Calm Ted down.' How about a story about hot-air balloons or something. You know, and I'm drawn to it, you know, you can't not. It's like watching a homeless woman give birth in a dumpster to an armless, flippered child – you gotta peek. She's breastfeeding him Sterno, you gotta . . . he's flippered and walking around, already nudging garbage cans off with his nose, the lids. You gotta peek. I mean, Jesus! It's human fucking nature. But do we have to dwell on it? Some little flippered thing, you know. Do we have to keep talking about it? I don't know.

But you know who's really pissing me off, truthfully, is pro-life people. Pro-lifers. Here's the deal, pro-lifers, if any of y'all are here tonight. Ready? You lose, shut up, go home. It's real simple: you lose. You lose. Bye-bye. Go home. See you later. You know . . . pro-life. You ever look at their faces? 'We're pro-life.' Don't they look . . . don't they just exude joie de vivre, you know? You just feel like playing Pictionary with them all night long, don't you?

> 'Er . . . is that a cross?'
> 'That's right.'
> 'Er, is that another cross?'
> 'That's right. You're very good.'
> 'Well, you're kinda easy to predict . . . being a fundamentalist and all. I'm way ahead of you. I've already read the fucking book, boh!'

Fundamentalist Christians – they're something to deal with, folks. My dad's one, it's fucking frightening. My dad: 'I believe the Bible's the literal word of God.' I go, 'No, it's not, Dad. It's just not.' 'Yeah, well, I believe it is.' 'Well, you know, some people believe they're Napoleon, that's fine, beliefs are neat, cherish 'em, but don't share 'em like they're the truth. You see, I have taken my bodyweight in mushrooms (*makes squeaking sound*). My third eye has been squeegeed. If it was the exact word of God . . . you ready? It'd be real clear and easy to understand! (*laughs hysterically*) God's got a way with words, being the creator of language and all.' (*laughs hysterically*) OK. You have fifty different sects of Christianity. You know, you can't even agree on it amongst themselves. But my dad's just, 'I believe it's the literal word of God.' And I go, 'It's not. I can prove it to you. Give me your Bible.' He goes and gets his Bible. 'OK.' I go, 'What's it say on the front?'

> 'Holy Bible.'
> 'What else does it say?'
> 'King James's Version.'
> (*laughs*) 'There you go. That's King James's Version. Let's
> listen to King Willy's version here.'

Do you ever notice how people who believe in creationism look really unevolved, you ever notice? They always have big furry eyebrow ridges, long fingers and hairy hands. 'I believe God created me in one day.' Looks like he rushed it, but ah . . . me? Billions of years to get the fucking hardened cynic you see before you. God tinkered with me. Kept adding spice. 'I'm going to make a William. This will take longer than a day. First I must break his fucking heart for sixteen years. I must have women tell him they love him, then leave him. Ha ha ha ha ha! I am creating a William!'

It's not as simple as 'poof', there you are, you know? But pro-life, you know. What does that make us? You know what I mean? You're anti-choice is what you are. But let me tell you something, if you're so pro-life, do me a favor, OK? Cos I might agree with you. Let's just say if you're so pro-life, don't lock arms and block medical clinics, OK? Lock arms and block cemeteries. Let's see how committed you fucking are to this premise.

> 'She can't come in.'
> 'She was ninety-eight, she was hit by a bus.'

'There's options.'
'What, are we gonna have her stuffed and mounted?
She's starting to stink. Let's go!'

I wanna see pro-lifers at funerals with crowbars opening caskets,
going, 'Get out! We're pro-life. Just look at my face. Don't I exude
love of life?' Boy, I wanna hang with you. You know what I mean?
And I tell you something, watching their actions on the news
has really helped me decide how I feel about abortion, and it is
a difficult issue. That age-old question: at what point does the
foetus become a human being? And I tell you, watching those
pro-lifers in action, I realize there's a lot of adults who haven't
become human beings yet, so start scraping wombs, who could
give a . . . you know. I maintain, look, why don't you adopt a kid
that's already here. Jesus, there's millions of unwanted kids, man.
If you're so fucking pro-life, adopt a kid who's in a fucking orphan-
age and give him a loving home, you know, there's millions of
them. 'Oh, why don't *you* do that? Why don't *you* do that?' I hate
kids and couldn't give a fuck, ah . . . I was recommending to
you something. I couldn't care a fucking less. I ah . . . sorry, I'm
throwing my hat in the ring. A new party's just been created: the
People Who Hate People Party. It's so hard to organize 'em,
though.

'People who hate people, come together!'
'Will there be people there?'
'Yeah!'
'I can't make it then.'

I know they're out there. I just can't get 'em to fucking organize.
People who hate people – join hands! You know, it's just . . . it's
not working out so far, and I know it's a majority of people. 'I'm
pro-life.' Strangely enough, that's the same face non-smokers use.
'I'm a non-smoker. I'm a pro-life non-smoker.' Let the party begin.
I been getting that look a lot lately, because . . . I started smoking
again. (*audience claps*) Thank you. With support like that, I wonder
why I ever quit. 'Hey, whoo! Bill's smoking, yay!' What, do you live
in Raleigh, North Carolina, what's your . . . what? Suddenly the

economy gets a boost? Fuck! No, I been getting that look a lot lately cos I started smoking again *and* performing abortions, so, you know, I mean . . . everywhere I turn these . . . Sometimes I can hardly get out of bed. But I just love smoking, folks. I'm sorry. I went nine months without 'em, and I mean what can I tell you? The hook is fucking deep, man, I'm telling you. They just dropped the bait back in the water, ploop, plop! (*makes sound of line being drawn in*) They weighed me, you know, hung me up. 'Caught a big one.'

But I have this theory – actually it's a hope – that if that scenario is at all true when you die and you go to heaven and St Peter meets you at the gate, if that's at all true, I believe the first thing he's gonna ask you is: 'You got a light?'

> 'You mean y'all smoke here?'
> 'Yeah, that's why it's heaven. These aren't clouds, this is cigarette smoke, buddy. Hell is non-smoking. You wanna look down at them for a minute?'
> 'All right.'
> 'I can't believe what they do to their bodies. It smells like an ashtray. I'm trying to eat my food. Why would they wanna do that to themselves? Do they know how stupid that is?'
> 'God, how hellish.'
> 'No shit. Light up and come on in. Hendrix is on harp tonight.'
> (*singing*) 'Let me stand next to your fire, yeaaahh.'

Man, no one beats Hendrix, man. Fuck Eddie Van Halen, fuck Steve Vai, no one beats fuckin' . . . Hendrix was an alien, OK? His ship landed, they said, 'Jimi, show 'em how it's done and we'll pick you up in 28 years.' And you know what Jimi said? 'All riiight.' He plays his cock, did y'all know that? They just strung his cock. He played it with his teeth. Does that make him gay? (*imitates Hendrix playing 'Star Spangled Banner'*) I love people who are dead, for some reason. All my heroes are dead. Keith Richards, for instance. What do you say we do some comedy? I always like to put some comedy in my shows. Here's an impression of Keith

Richards. (*puts his cigarette in the microphone stand*) Some people start talking to him, it's so real. 'Keith!' Boy, Keith went over the edge years ago. He went over the fucking edge, right, and everyone thought that's it, Keith's gone. And then they looked over the edge and there was a fucking ledge, and he had hit and landed on it. There's a *ledge* beyond the edge! Keith was like, 'I hit a fucking ledge. I'm all right. Throw down me guitar, I got a song.' (*imitates opening of 'Jumping Jack Flash'*) (*in English accent*) 'There's a ledge beyond the edge. Keith landed on it, the lucky bloke. A lot of people missed the ledge.' I love dead people.

Been travelling a lot as usual. Was over in Australia – very interesting place. Anyone ever been to Australia? Fascinating place. Dig this. Dig this, man. Picture this. Put it in your head and get ready. Clear out your head of everything else: as big as the US is geographically, with as few people living there as are in this room right now. Lot of leg room down under. Literally. 'No worries, mate.' Apartments: dollar a month. Two-thousand-acre den. How do you furnish that? 'With beer caps, mate. A carpet of beer caps.' But it's interesting. I found this out. I think it's so weird that the Australians were originally the criminal class of Great Britain, and the Brits, in order to punish them, sent them to Australia, their own prehistoric, Eden-like island continent. Bummer. (*laughs*) Boy, you don't wanna get on the wrong side of them Brits. They'll fuck you good. What the fuck? What do you wanna bet the crime rate really soared in Great Britain when people figured out where they were gonna be sent to.

> 'Let me get this straight. You keep the shitty food and
> the shitty weather, and [. . .] we get the Great Barrier
> Reef and lobsters the size of canoes. I'm Jack the
> Ripper.'
> 'No, I'm Jack the Ripper.'
> 'I'm Jack the Ripper.'
> 'We're all Jack the Ripper. Where's the fucking boat?'
> (*makes sound of boat horn*)

That's me going over the horizon. (*boat horn*) It is down under. That's true too.

But I was over in Australia during Easter, which was real interesting to note they celebrate Easter the exact same way we do –
commemorating the death and resurrection of Jesus by telling our
children a giant bunny rabbit left chocolate eggs in the night. Now,
I wonder why we're fucked up as a race. Anybody got any . . . ?
You know, I've read the Bible. I can't find the word 'bunny' or 'chocolate' anywhere in the fucking book. Where do you come up with
this shit? Why not goldfish left Lincoln Logs in your sock drawer,
you know? As long as you're making shit up, go hog wild. At least
a goldfish with a Lincoln Log on its back going across your carpet
has some miraculous connotations.

> 'Mummy, today I woke up and found a Lincoln Log in
> me sock drawer.'
> 'That's the story of Jesus.'

Who comes up with this shit? The Gideons? By the way, who the
fuck are the Gideons? Ever met one? No. Ever seen one? No. But
apparently they're everywhere, running around, putting Bibles in
hotel rooms. Every hotel room: 'This Bible was placed here by a
Gideon.' When? I been here all day, I ain't seen shit. Saw the house-
keeper come and go, saw the minibar come and go, saw the minibar guy come and go again . . . those were the old days. I've never
laid eyes on a fucking Gideon. What are they, Ninjas? Where are
they from? Gidea? What the fuck are these people? I'm gonna
capture a Gideon. That's my new hobby. I am. I'm gonna capture
one, man. I'm gonna call the front desk one day and go, 'Yeah, I
don't seem to have a Bible in my room.' Probably come through
the window on a grappling hook, some Gideon helicopter on the
roof, ready to whisk him back to the island of Gidea, where non-
stop Bible printing is going on. 'God, I did see one. He was masked
and had a fucking samurai sword. They are out there.'

I think it's interesting the way people act on their beliefs, you
know? I'm always interested in that. That's my new little hobby of
study. Why . . . how do you act on your belief, you know what I
mean? For instance, a lot of Christians wear crosses around their
necks. Nice sentiment, *but* do you think when Jesus comes back
he's gonna want to see a fucking cross? Ow. Kind of like going up

to Jackie Onassis with a rifle pendant on, you know? 'Just thinking of John, Jackie. We love him. Trying to keep that memory alive, sweetie.' Back and to the left, back and to the left, back and to the left . . . which, by the way, that action you see on the Zapruder film, was caused by a bullet coming from . . . up there, yeah! I gotta go back and take physics again, cos apparently I missed that day. Maybe that's why Jesus hasn't shown up yet. He's up in heaven, going:

> 'Dad, they're still wearing crosses. I'm not going. Fuck
> it. No, they totally missed the point. No. Fuck it. No
> way, man. No! . . . OK, I'll go back as a   bunny, but
> I'm not . . .'
> 'Hey, aren't you Jesus?'
> 'No, I'm a fucking rabbit. Shut up. Here's a chocolate
> egg – that's about all you can handle spiritually right
> now. Could y'all evolve by next Easter? This
> suit is real fucking itchy. OK! I'm Jesus the bunny.'

(*sips drink*) Nothing better than water. They haven't made it and it ain't coming. God, I love water. Folks – and by folks I mean y'all – it's time for a confession. This is not easy, but it's my last show ever. I'm serious. But I'm gonna make a confession in the form of a question, all right? Is anyone here like me, in that they are compelled . . . beyond their will . . . to watch the show *Cops* every fucking night that it's on? Someone? I'm not alone? Ohh. Thank God. Hi, I'm Bill, I'm a *Cops* watcher. 'Welcome Bill. You're in the right place.' Oh, thank God I'm not alone. I'm like a guy with a sore tooth – I can't quit touching it. I swear . . . Ow, owwww. Oh, *Cops* is on. Oww. Owww. I have never been in so many fucking trailer parks, man. I swear to God. I could *buy* a trailer right now, that's how much I've learned about 'em from fucking *Cops*. Owww. Oh, that's a Double-Wide. Owww. And what's so compelling about it is every night it's the same fucking show: a woman has been beaten by her husband, her head looks like a fucking melon, you know, someone makes a domestic call, right? The trailer next door, apparently, over her screaming couldn't hear the results of the *American Gladiator* contest or something. I . . . I was surprised they had a phone, but . . . anyway, the cops show up, and every fucking time the woman stands up for the guy. 'He didn't mean to hurt me, Officer. He didn't mean to hit me.' Her fourteen little cracker spawn are peering around her gingham skirt. Their eyes are so close together the left eye is in the right socket and the right eye is in the left socket. It's kind of genetic mutation due to inbreeding. What does their family tree look like? A stump? 'He didn't mean to hit me, Occifer. I fell asleep in the driveway and he run over my head wi' de truck. He's a good man. He's passed out under the trailer with his dog, Skeeter.' What is the mentality of standing up for a wife-beater? I don't get that, ladies. I know it's a self-esteem thing, but fuck, it makes me feel bad. Cos I'm kind of like a nice guy, and I haven't seen pussy in like three years, and meanwhile Burl in Plot 14 is balls deep in this hillbilly whore every fucking night, and you know, I'm just a little bitter about it, you know? I'm showing up with flowers, and meanwhile Burl's hitting her with a crowbar and she's sticking by her man, you know? And I know this is backed-up semen talking, I'm not lying to you, folks. I'm not gonna try and kid you either. I mean, next time I come it's gonna be like a wax dart shooting out of my cock. 'Woman killed by semen dart. News at eleven.' 'Sorry, baby, it's been a while.' I mean, I'm a little upset by it. I even went to one of those rebirthing . . . you ever do that? You go to rebirth class to re-experience your birth, just to remind myself what a pussy was like. And I even got a woody, which is pretty scary. Freud's doing backflips, meanwhile I'm in my mom's pussy, going, 'Oh, that's what it's like. All right. Just had to remind myself. It's been so fucking long.' 'Oh, he's a good man. He don't mean to hit me wi' de crowbar.' Burl gets pussy every night, sure. Maybe I should have a dozen crowbars next time I go on a date. No, but it just makes me feel a little . . . It's just weird. I know it's a self-esteem and we live in a very sick society, but . . . and standing up for wife-beaters when there's good guys out there, and also, ladies, I'm not fooled. I know you like Billy Ray. Don't lie to me. The guys here didn't buy his fucking albums. I know you think he's a hunk. Bullshit. Don't fucking lie. And you would break a *pelvis* trying to open your legs wide enough to get his cracker fucking member into your body to pump his homunculus seed into your womb. Don't fucking lie to me. You would chainsaw your legs off to give him better access, to have that phoney, talent-less fucking hump shoot his tainted, probably whisky-brown fuck-ing semen into your body, Tennessee whisky-brown semen, cos you think he's a hunk. And same with that fucking ratlike Michael Bolton. This little rodent-appearing human. Now, I looked in the mirror, I don't look like a rodent, and yet you like that guy, and don't fucking lie to me. I'm a little upset by it, man.

And you know what? Also the ramifications are frightening too. It occurred to me that we're just fucked. You know, I'm sorry. I'm not a bitter . . . but we're fucked. Satan is gonna have no prob-lems ruling this planet. None! You know why? All the women in the world are gonna go, 'What a cute butt!'

> 'He's Satan!'
> 'You don't know him like I do.'
> 'He's the Prince of Darkness!'
> 'I can change him.'

I bet you can, too. I really do. I don't give Satan a snowball's chance in hell against a woman's ego. No fucking way. He'll rule the planet for about a day, a week later we'll see him out cutting the lawn, you know? (*makes lawnmower sound*)

> 'Hey, aren't you Satan?'
> 'Shut up.' (*lawnmower sound*)
> 'You forgot to edge out back, Mr Prince.'
> 'Shut up.' (*lawnmower sound*)

He'll be at the supermarket.

> 'Tampons. Price check. Tampons. Satan's here buying
> Tampons for his girlfriend.'
> 'Shut up. I'm the Prince of Darkness.'
> 'Yeah, you dropped your Cotex, Mr Prince.'
> 'Shut up.'
> 'I'll rule this planet . . . next weekend when she's outta
> town. Grrr.'

Get outta here. A pussy-whipped Satan – that's what's in store for us. And hopelessness reigns. Until you see our *Full House* – 'Let's

Hunt and Kill the cast of *Full House* Easter Special.' Then I think hope will be reborn on the planet.

Speaking of Satan, I was watching Rush Limbaugh the other day. Very scary world we're living in, folks. Doesn't Rush Limbaugh remind you of one of those gay guys that likes to lay in a tub while other guys pee on him? Don't you see . . . do you see that? You know what I mean? Can't you picture his flabby little corpulent body in a tub, and Reagan, Bush and Quayle around the edge? His little piggly-wiggly dick can't get hard. 'Uh-uhh, I can't get hard. Piss in my mouth, Ronnie.' He still can't get hard, so they call in Barbara Bush. She sticks her pearls up his ass, squats over his face, undoes her girdle, her wrinkled, distended labia unfolds halfway to her knees, like some ball-less scrotum. 'Uh-uh-uh.' She squeezes out a link into his mouth, finally his dick gets half-hard, 'Urghhhhh', a little clear bubble forms on the end with a maggot inside, pops the bubble, rushes off to a pro-life meeting or something. Am I the only one that sees that? Sorry if any of y'all ordered the nachos a minute ago. He's a scat-muncher and we all know it. He munches scat – deal with it.

My dad is into him, of course. My dad . . . it's unbelievable. I go through the den the other day, my dad goes, 'Bill, Rush is on.' I go, 'Yeah, the rush *is* on, Dad, bye-bye.' And he goes, 'Why don't you just listen to the man?' I said, 'Dad, you know, I've listened to this before. It was in 1972 and it was a show called *All in the Family* and the character was Archie Bunker. This is . . . I've heard it. Unfortunately there's no meathead playing counterpart with this fucking idiot.' But anyway, I'm listening to talk radio shows, and everyone: 'You know what Rush said about NAFTA? You know Rush is talking about NAFTA. I heard Rush the other day say about NAFTA . . .' What y'all looking for, a new dad? Grow the fuck up. Take responsibility for your fucking lives. What do *you* think about NAFTA, man? I'll tell you what I think: the cock-sucking elite who own and run everything in this fucking country are selling it out from under us, tomorrow. There ain't no battle over fucking NAFTA, that's a fucking charade, like our elections are a fucking charade, and tomorrow, ladies and gentlemen, they're selling your fucking life out from under you. Don't you ever fucking forget it either.

There's dick jokes coming up, please relax. Folks, here's the deal: I editorialize for forty-five minutes, the last fifteen I pull my 'chute, we all pull our 'chutes, and float down to Dick-joke Island together. We will rest our weary heads against the big, purple-veined trunks of dick jokes while bouncing on our spongy scrotum bean-bag chairs and giggle away the night like good American comedy audiences are supposed to, goddammit! With pee-pee jokes. 'You know what Rush said about pee-pee jokes. "Dad, I've heard it." It's called Archie Bunker, who was another fat, white, fear-mongering, conservative, stupid white male ego talking. Hah, I've heard it! Rush has nothing to offer me. See Dad, there's this little weird thing that grows on a cow turd. It's really weird. Let's go listen to it talk.'

Folks, it's time to evolve, man. That's why we're troubled. Cos you know why our institutions are failing us? The Church, the state, everything's failing? It's cos they're no longer relevant. (*laughs*) They're not relevant any more. It's . . . we're supposed to keep evolving. You know, evolution didn't end with us growing opposable thumbs, did you know that? There's another ninety per cent of our brains that we have to illuminate. Illuminate. That brings me back to that little thing that grows on a cow turd. 'Come on, Dad, I wanna . . .' Actually, I tried to get my dad to trip with me, which is . . . very dangerous, you know. That could be very heavy duty for the man, he's seventy-five, and I don't know if he'd get what I get out of it, you know what I mean? He might get into a . . . I'd hate to have my dad weeping next to me:

> 'I just love Rush.'
> 'Dad, Dad, this is not the outcome we're supposed to get from this. It's supposed to be where your ego dissolves and you realize the true nature of our reality, which is mind, and that we literally all are one and there's no such thing as death and our bodies are an illusion, and God's eternal love is unconditional and never have we left it, other than the dream of the Fall from grace, which is just an illusionary dream, and never has God been unloving to us, and we can wake up and remember God's eternal, unconditional love.'

'I just wanna watch Rush.'
'Oh shit, Dad's not getting off on these like I am.'

I guess I have to do the only thing I can do: acceptance and forgiveness. It's the only tools that you've got left. And evolution, if you're interested in it.

I was down in Australia when the Waco debacle ended, the fiery inferno, which we all saw. And I was really bummed I was not here for it, because I thought it was the most fascinating news story of the year, bar none. And everyone was so pissed off about that guy cos he called himself Jesus, and I was saying, 'Come on. The guy's real name is Vernon. Let him be Jesus for a couple of months. What's it to ya?' Who's gonna follow a messiah named Vernon anyway, you know? You gotta call yourself Jesus, it's sort of part of the messiah deal. 'And Vernon spoke and he spaketh and he sayeth . . .' You know, what? 'Let's go get some beer, whoo!' You know, Vernon just doesn't have the necessary spiritual weight that I'm looking for.

But anyway, isn't that weird too how everyone snaps in our country and thinks they're Jesus? How come no one ever snaps and thinks their Buddha? Particularly in America, where more people resemble Buddha than Jesus.

'I'm Buddha.'
'You're Bubba.'
'I'm Buddha now. All I gotta do is change two letters on
my belt. Bubba.'
'Buddha. Vernon's a false prophet.'

Isn't that weird, though? And it's funny, it's real funny, cos these Australians had a big contingency in the compound that burned down, and they were of course curious, and I'm from Texas, and I actually went to the compound the seventh day of the siege, cos it was right outside Austin, and I went to it, but these people in Australia were like, 'Oh, Bill, isn't he . . . he's such an oddball, isn't he? He's so odd. He's such a strange character.' And I'm thinking, 'Well, let's think about this. Frustrated rock guitarist with a messianic complex, armed to the teeth, trying to fuck everything in skirts. I don't know how to tell y'all this, but sounds like every one of my friends.' I'm waiting for the Eric Johnson compound to come out, you know. I don't know. I don't think Eric's frustrated, but . . . but anyway. And they said, you know, they had to break down the compound because child abuse was stepping up. Well, if that's true, how come we don't see Bradley tanks knocking down Catholic churches, you know? If in fact child abuse is your concern. Actually, folks, I don't know if any of y'all have seen this, it's a tape, kind of bootleg going around, showing film of the Bradley tanks not knocking, as the official story was, small holes to insert tear gas, but crashing the building off of its fucking foundation and fire shooting out of the tanks. The FBI and the ATF are liars and murderers, and Janet Reno and President Clinton either a) knowingly passed on a lie, or b) are so out of touch with their own fucking arms of their government that they're incompetent and Clinton should be impeached immediately. Case fucking closed. And y'all haven't probably seen the footage, but it's sort of different than the official story, isn't it? Small holes, tear gas/giant holes, flame-throwers. Ha ha ha! They burned these people in their homes. OK. That's our government. OK. I've seen the tape and it's fucking real, and whatever. Make your own conclusions. You haven't seen it, so it's . . . you know, whatever. But all Clinton . . . you know, I have no illusions about these cock-suckers. I know there's twelve guys who run the fucking world, and they own every company, and it's a fact. You can look it up. I'm not a conspiracy nut. This is all on paper. There really are twenty-two families who run and own fifty per cent of the mainstream media, which is where we get our news. And it's true. It's a fact. You can look it up. I don't, you know . . . I can't be this big of an asshole without having the truth to back me up; otherwise I'd be a fucking nut doing this. But see, if you have the truth with you, you can do this. Gee, I'm starting to sound like Koresh, aren't I? Fuck. People have often said I remind them of Koresh. I'm like Koresh only without the guns or pussy. So basically I'm just an annoying fellow, but ah . . . and a frustrated rock guitarist, too.

But I knew Clinton was in with the big boys when he bombed Iraq. Do you remember that? Two-day news story: Clinton launches twenty-two cruise missiles on Baghdad in retaliation for the *alleged failed* assassination attempt against George Bush. We launched twenty-two, three-million-dollars-apiece cruise missiles to Baghdad, killing six innocent people. I think that was a little overdone, you know? You know what we should have done? We should have embarrassed the Iraqians. *We* should have assassinated Bush and said, 'That's how you do it, towel-head. Don't fuck with us.' And see, if Bush had been the one who had died, there would have been no loss of innocent life. Yeah, so you see. I mean, that would have saved us, ah, hundred million dollars. And I love that too, how the media called it . . . everyone in the government and the media called it a cowardly act on the Iraqians' part, because some Iraqian guy was gonna drive a Toyota car bomb and blow himself up in the process of trying to kill the president of the United States, because that's all they can really do since we're the imperialist rulers of the New World Order, and we call that a cowardly act. Meanwhile, we're launching cruise missiles 200 miles away from floating iron islands. Who are the cowards again? OK. This is the material, by the way, that's kept me virtually anonymous in America. You know, no one fucking knows me, no one gives a fuck. Meanwhile, they're draining the Pacific and putting up bench-seats for Carrottop's next show-time special. Carrottop: for people who didn't get Gallagher, you know?

> 'That Gallagher was a little heady. I ah couldn't folla half of his stuff.'
> 'Carrottop's more my speed. You see, first of all he's got red hair, an' that just cracks me up all the time. I don't even need material, ask my wife, I'm on the floor. Red-haired man! Red-haired man on TV! Whoo-oo! Don't even need material or ideas. Red-haired man. So he's got that goin' for him.'
> 'What do you like about him?'
> 'He's got red hair.'

You know, Gallagher. Only America could produce a comic named Gallagher, who ends his show by destroying good food with a sledge-hammer. Gee, I wonder why we're hated the world over? All these fat Americans on the front row: 'Haw, haw, haw, haw! Now *this* is comedy. Haw haw haw! That Bill Hicks is jus' bitter. I get tired listening to him. Why can't he hit fruit with a hammer? He's just jealous he didn't think of it.' Folks, I did think of that. I was *two* at the time, and I said, 'This is real stupid.' Fucking idiot. I could have been the young Gallagher in diapers, walking around being a millionaire, franchising myself, but no. I had to have this weird thing about trying to illuminate the collective unconscious and help humanity. Fucking *moron*! Gallagher destroying good food – I guarantee you there's gonna be no Gallagher world tour any time soon, and if there are there will be no dates in Somalia, OK? I don't know if those little bags of skin and bones would be able to appreciate Gallagher's particular wit.

> 'He destroys good food with a hammer. We must go and get front-row tickets and hopefully catch a watermelon rind and live another day. We are here to see Gallagher. We must live another day. Put us on the front row, so my child Hibiscus can eat one more day.'
> 'Will that be in the horsefly or non-horsefly section?'
> (*makes sound of fly*)
> 'We are here to see Gallagher and see his ending show.'

Gallagher. Meanwhile, this is my last show ever. I'm tired, folks. Tired of spreading the news. Folks, it's time to evolve ideas. That's all we're left with. There's gonna be no more thumbs coming down the pipe, it ain't happening. Sure, they'll be aberrations in evolution – people who take steroids, those fucking guys who pump up, people who do punctures and, you know, tattoo . . . there's gonna be different aberrations. But the true evolution is to evolve ideas. What do I mean? 'What do you mean?' What do I mean? Well . . . well, for instance, how about this? Why is the drugs tsar of this country – first of all, why is there a drugs tsar? Forget that – why is the drugs tsar of this country a cop? Why isn't he instead someone who's been through recovery, who has had an alcohol and/or drug addiction and overcome it, and offer instead hope and compassion, rather than condemnation and jail sentences to drug abusers? See, that would be evolving an idea. See, drugs abusers, folks, are not criminals, they're sick, and putting sick people in jail . . . does that make sense? (*singing*) 'Na da da na da da.' It really doesn't. And the fact they wonder why kids do drugs, well, you know, the reason is a) they feel good, but b) the hypocrisy of watching beer pushed down our fucking throats every commercial with women basically almost the bottles in their twat at this point. 'Beer. Pop that beer, honey. Boy, it tastes good, makes you look good and feel good, too.' The fact that alcoholism is totally a fucking scourge in this country and responsible for every fucking broken home, every fucking beaten child, every fucking beaten wife . . . we overlook that, wink, wink, nudge, nudge. Cigarettes: death – you know, nothing. Pot, meanwhile, a drug that kills . . . no one – and let's put it in a time frame – ever . . . pot is against the law. Now does that make sense? Do you think your child is supposed to accept that, or is he supposed to look at you and go, 'You hypocritical mother-fucker, I'm shooting heroin in the vein under my cock, cos I hate your fucking lying society and your lie that you fucking live.' That's why your kids do drugs. OK? Because they see that we're not growing up and taking responsibility and we're fucking liars, you see, and kids sense that immediately. They have that instinct. Anyway, if you want a better world, legalize pot. That's my point. You wanna end the deficit, legalize pot. Pot is a better drug than alcohol, and I'll prove it to ya. You're at a ball game, you're at a concert, someone's really violent, aggressive and obnoxious. Are they drunk, or are they smoking pot? (*audience*) 'Drunk!' Wow, we all know the truth. I've never seen people on pot get in a fight, because it's fucking impossible.

> 'Hey, buddy!'
> 'Hey what?'

End of argument. Say you get in a car accident and you've been smoking pot. You're only going four miles an hour. (*makes sound of car crash*)

> 'Oh shit, we hit something.'
> 'Forgot to open the garage door, dude.'
> 'It's OK, I forgot we were going in reverse.'

At least no one was hurt. The garage door has to be replaced – boom! A job has been created. I got new stuff, Mr Kreskin. I'm just building a case. See how confident you are in a minute. We ain't even pulled our 'chutes yet.

They lie about marijuana. Marijuana makes you unmotivated: lie. When you're high you can do everything you normally do just as well, you just realize it's not worth the fucking effort. There's a difference. 'Sure, I could get up at dawn, get in traffic, go to a job I hate that does not inspire me creatively whatsoever for the rest of my life, sure I could *do* that. (*inhales, as if from spliff*) Or . . . I could sleep till noon, get up and learn how to play the sitar. (*exhales*) (*in monotone, repeatedly*) 'Now ning now ning ning ning now ning now ning ning ning now ning now ning ning ning now ning now' – what is it, one string? How fucking hard is that? 'now ning now ning ning ning now ning now' (*makes sound of crickets chirruping*) In harmony with the crickets! 'Now ning now' (*crickets*) Here comes the mother ship! We shall rock on! The universe is our playground. That's how you evolve ideas, OK?

I'll give you another example. Confucius used to say, 'What is the sound of one hand clapping?' And he said it as an enigmatic way to say there would be no sound, but you know what I say to that? (*claps with one hand*) Fuck Confucius, let's move on. It's time for a new philosophy, folks. One based on, yes, the principles of Jesus, which were love your brother as yourself, because you know what? He is yourself. Literally. Ha ha ha ha ha ha! We are literally all one. OK. The body is an illusion, you see, cos God doesn't create things that can be destroyed . . . cos he's God, dig it? *We* have miscreated this world. It's a dream. What's that old song – 'Row, row, row your boat, gently down the stream, merrily, merrily, merrily, merrily, life is but a dream'? See, we knew it as children. We forgot it since. Maybe it was just me. Maybe y'all are going, 'Bill, we knew that the whole time. Bill, do you know that you're at a comedy club and . . . this is not your compound? And, you know, you're kind of funny at times, but we got babysitters and ah, you know, it's a cute show, you dance around, you make faces, you know, it's fine, but you're not telling us anything we don't already know, Bill. Come out with the good stuff.'

OK, here's another idea that needs to be punctured, then evolve. a) The idea that childbirth is a miracle. *Now*, I don't know who started this little hur-rumour, but it is not a miracle. Sorry. It's not a miracle, no more a miracle than eating food and having a turd fall out of your butt, all right? It is a chemical reaction and a biological reaction, the end. OK? You wanna hear a miracle? A miracle's raising a kid who doesn't talk at a fucking movie theatre. There . . . miracle. A miracle's raising a kid that doesn't run into my crotch at the supermarket cos they have no peripheral vision.

> 'Where's that little miracle, come here!'
> 'Mommy!'
> 'Come 'ere!'
> 'Mommy, where's my two mommies?'

I might have to forgive this human and go meet his two mommies. I've never met two mommies. You must be a lucky little boy. Two mommies . . . do they hug and kiss on the couch? God, I love that. Nothing more beautiful than a woman making love to a woman. Sorry to be so crass, but that's a fact. Now, must move on to my show. I'm just . . . my final show, I might add.

I'll go you one further: childbirth is not only not a miracle, childbirth isn't natural. 'What do you mean, Bill? It's the most natural thing in the world.' Wrong. First of all, no guy in this room wants children. No guy wants children. No. They don't. Any guy who thinks or says he wants children is no longer a guy but a pussy-whipped freak of nature, who should be at home reading Donahue transcripts, renting Alan Alda films and buying Michael Bolton albums, cos you're no longer a guy and you're out of the guy club. You're out. Guys don't want children, because guys *are* children and we don't want the competition. That simple. 'You mean there's gonna be something in the house cuter than me? This must be stopped. I'm already sulking. They're not even born yet and all you do is talk about the little baby. It's women! Women!' This is my new character. It's all I do with it, but I think there's potential. 'It's women! Women!' I don't know, I think the character's gonna grow, and along with my bitterness until boom, a tower and a gun. And you'll . . . finally I'll have my own special. (*laughs*) Women have this *unholy void* inside of them.

> 'I need something to love.'
> 'Love me, you bitch, I'm right here!'
> 'You're acting childish.'
> 'Perfect! I will be your child-man. Honey, if I promise
> never to mature . . . I think I can pull this off.'

And I'll go you one further, and this is the routine that has virtually ended my career in America. And I'm gonna end on this, but ah . . . you've been a great crowd. If you have children here tonight, and I assume some of you do, I'm sorry to tell you this: they are not special. I'll let that sink in. La da da da da. I know a lot of parents who are getting their backs a little stiff right now. 'Hey, wait a minute. My child's special.' Don't get me wrong, folks. I know you *think* they're special. *You* think that. I'm telling you they're not. See, I know . . . they're not. Do you know every time a guy comes, he comes 200 million sperm, did you know that? 200 million sperm, and you mean to tell me you think your child is special, because one out of 200 million sperm connected that load? Gee, what are the fucking odds? (*laughs*) 200 million – do you know what that means? I have wiped entire civilizations . . . off of my chest . . . with a grey gym-sock. *That* is special. Entire nations have flaked and crusted in the hair around my navel! *That* is special. And I want you to think about that, you two-egg-carrying beings out there, with that holier-than-thou, we-have-the-gift-of-life attitude. I have tossed *universes* in my *underpants* while *napping*. You've been great. I hope you enjoyed it. Thanks a lot. Thanks for coming to my final show.

(*Plays out to 'Killing in the Name of' by Rage Against the Machine. Hicks places a watermelon on a stool, lifts mike stand like a sledgehammer, looks at audience and throws stand down. Mimes 'motherfucker' in time with music while giving audience the finger with both hands. Walks away.*)

Letter to John Lahr
(January 1994)

Dear John,

Here is the material (verbatim) that CBS's Standards and Practices Found 'unsuitable' for the viewing public in 1993, Year of Our Lord. THESE are the 'Hot Spots' I believe were most mentioned. I'm going to include audience response as well, for it does play a part in my thoughts on the incident which will follow the Jokes. Jokes, John, this is what America now fears – one man with a point of view, speaking out unafraid of our vaunted institutions, or the loathsome superstitions the CBS hierarchy feels the masses (the herd) use as their religion. Oops! I'm getting ahead of myself with my thoughts. Let's go now to the afternoon of October 1st, 1993. The place: The Ed Sullivan Theatre, where The Late Show With David Letterman now reigns supreme amongst the many Late-night talk shows that have sprung up like poisonous mushrooms since Johnny's retirement. The time – 6.40 p.m. 'Time for the final guest of the night, a 'very entertaining comedian – Bill Hicks. Bill, come on out here!' The audience applauds as I stroll out in my new bright fall colors – an outfit bought just for the show, very unlike my usual all black ensemble and reflective of my bright and cheerful mood. I'm feeling good. The set I've prepared has been approved and reapproved by Mary Connelly, the segment producer of the show. It is the same exact set that was approved for the previous Friday, the Night where I was 'bumped' due to lack of time. It is the Material that I'm excited about performing for it best reflects – out of all the other eleven appearances I've made on the show – myself. Let us begin . . .

Bill: Good evening! I'm very excited to be here tonight, and I'm very excited because I got some great news today. I finally got my own TV Show coming out as a replacement show this fall!

The audience applauds.

Bill: Don't worry, it's not a talk show.

The audience laughs.

Bill: Thank God!

Bill (cont.): It's a half hour weekly show that I will host, entitled 'Let's Hunt and Kill Billy Ray Cyrus'.

Audience bursts into laughter and applause.

Bill: I think it's fairly self-explanatory – each week we let the Hounds of Hell loose and chase that jar-head, no talent, cracker-idiot all over the globe till I finally catch that fruity little pony-tail of his, pull him to his Chippendales knees, put a shotgun in his mouth, 'Pow!'

Audience is applauding and laughing through-out this run.

Bill (cont.): Then we'll be back in '94 with 'Let's Hunt and Kill Michael Bolton'.

Audience laughs and applauds.

Bill: Yeah, so you can see with guests like this, our run will be fairly limitless.

Audience laughs.

Bill: And we're kicking the whole series off with our M.C. Hammer, Vanilla Ice, Marky Mark Christmas Special . . .

Audience laughs and applauds.

Bill: And I don't want to give any surprises away, but the first one we hunt and kill on that show is Markie Mark, because his pants keep falling around his ankles and he can't run away . . .

Bill Mimes a hobbling Markie Mark. The audience laughs.

Bill: Yeah, I get to cross-bow him right in the abs. It's a beautiful thing. Bring the family. TAPE IT. It's definitely a show for the nineties . . .

Audience applauds.

At this point I did a line about men dancing. Since it was never mentioned as a reason for excising me from the show, let's skip ahead to the next 'Hot Point' that *was* mentioned. (By the way, the Joke on men dancing got a huge laugh.) But let's move forward to the following Joke.

Bill: You know, I consider myself a fairly open-minded person, but speaking of Homosexuality, something has come to my attention that has shocked even me. Have you heard about these new grade school books for children they're trying to add to the curriculum, to help children understand the gay, lifestyle? One's called 'Heather's Two Mommies', the other one is called 'Daddy's . . . New Room-mate'.

Here I make a shocked, disgusted face.

Bill: Folks, I gotta draw the line here and say this is absolutely disgusting. It is grotesque, and it is pure evil.

Pause.

Bill: I'm talking, of course, about 'Daddy's New Room-mate'.

Audience laughs.

Bill: 'Heather's Two Mommies' is quite Fetching . . . you know they're hugging on page seven!

Audience laughs.

Bill (lasciviously):   Oooh! Go, Mommies, Go! Oooh! They kiss in chapter four!

Audience laughs.

Bill: Me and my nephew wrestle over that book every night . . .

Bill mimes his little Nephew jumping up and down.

Bill (as Nephew):   'Uncle Bill, I've gotta do my homework!'

Audience laughs.

Bill: Shut up and go do your Math! I'm proofreading this for you . . .

Audience laughs. We move directly into the next 'Hot Point'.

Bill: You know who's really bugging me these days? These pro-lifers . . .

Smattering of applause.

Bill: You ever look at their faces . . . 'I'm pro-life!'

Here Bill makes a pinched face of hate and fear, his lips are pursed as though he's just sucked on a lemon.

Bill: 'I'm pro-life!' Boy, they look it, don't they? They just exude Joie de vivre. You just want to hang with them and play Trivial Pursuit all night long.

Audience chuckles.

Bill: You know what bugs me about them – if you're so pro-life, do me a favor – don't lock arms and block medical clinics. If you're so pro-life, lock arms and block cemeteries.

Audience laughs.

Bill (cont.): Let's see how committed you are to this idea.

Here Bill mimed the pursed lipped pro-lifers locking arms.

Bill (as pro-lifer): 'She can't come in!'

Audience laughs

Bill (as confused member of funeral procession): 'She was ninety-eight. She was hit by a bus!'

Audience laughs

Bill (as pro-lifer): 'There's options!'

Audience laughs.

Bill (again as confused funeral procession member): 'What else can we do – have her stuffed?'

Audience laughs.

Bill: I want to see pro-lifers with crowbars at funerals open-
             ing caskets – 'Get out!' Then I'd really be impressed by
             their mission.

Audience laughs and applauds.
  At this point I did a routine on smoking that was never brought
up as a 'Hot Point', so let's move ahead to the end of my routine,
and another series of jokes that *was* mentioned as 'unsuitable'.

Bill: I've been traveling a lot lately, I was over in Australia
             during Easter. It was interesting to note they celebrate
             Easter the same way we do – commemorating the death
             and Resurrection of Jesus by telling our children a giant
             Bunny Rabbit . . . left chocolate eggs in the night . . .

Audience laughs.

Bill (cont.): Gee, I wonder why we're so messed up as a race? You
             know, I've read the Bible – can't find the words 'bunny'
             or 'chocolate' in the whole book.

Audience laughs.

Bill (cont.): WHERE do we get this stuff from? And why those
             two things? Why not 'Goldfish left Lincoln Logs in
             our sock drawers?' I mean, as long as we're Making
             stuff up, let's go hog wild.

Audience laughs and applauds.

Bill: I think it's interesting how people act on their beliefs.
             A lot of Christians, for instance, wear crosses around
             their necks. Nice sentiment, but do you think when
             Jesus comes back, he's really going to want to look at
             a cross?'

Audience laughs. Bill makes a face of pain and horror.

Bill: Ow! Maybe that's why he hasn't shown up yet . . .

Audience laughs.

Bill (as Jesus looking down from Heaven):   'I'm not going, Dad. No,
    they're still wearing crosses – they totally missed the point.
    When they start wearing fishes, I might go back again . . . No,
    I'm not going . . . OK, I'll tell you what – I'll go back as a
    bunny . . .'

Audience bursts into applause and laughter the band kicks into
'Revolution' by the Beatles.

Bill: Thank you very much! Good night!

Bill crosses over to the seat next to Letterman's desk.

*David
Letterman*:   Good set, Bill! Always nice to have you drop by with
    an uplifting message!

Audience and Bill laugh, we cut to a commercial.

During the commercial break Dave asks me how things are going.
I say fine, I'm working on a couple of albums these days. He asks
me if I've lost some weight. I tell him yes, I've been drinking about
a quart of grapefruit juice a day. Then Mary Connelly comes over
to the seat followed by Robert Morton, the producer of the show.
They're both smiling and saying, 'Good set!'. I ask them again how
they thought it went. They say, 'Great! Didn't you hear the audience response?' I'm relieved they feel this way. They leave the desk
area. Dave then leans over and asks if I've quit drinking. I find this
a rather odd question seeing as how I haven't touched a drop of
liquor in over five years and Dave and I have had this conversation before since then. I then tell Dave I've started smoking cigars,
and I ask him what kind he smokes. He names a brand which I
didn't catch, then hands me one of his very own. I say 'Thanks!'

And now we're back from commercials. There's about fifteen seconds left. Dave turns to me and says something to the effect of, 'Bill, good to see you again. Good job.' Then closes the show with . . .

Dave: I want to thank our guests tonight – Andie McDowell, Graham Parker, and Bill Hicks . . . Bill, enjoy answering your mail the next few weeks. Goodnight everybody.

The audience and Bill cracks up at Dave's closing line, and we're off the air. Again Mary Connelly comes up to me and says the show went great. When I enter the green room, everyone's sitting there watching the taping of the show applauds and says, 'Great set'. Graham Parker (who I'm a huge fan of) comes up to me with a big smile on his face and shakes my hand, saying, 'Great! Loved it, mate!' I finally start to relax a bit. It's over, and as far as I can tell, everyone enjoyed it. Bill Sheft, a comic and one of the writers on the show comes up to me saying, 'Hicks, that was great!' I ask him if he thinks Letterman liked it. Bill Sheft, whose other duties include warming up the audience and getting them to applaud when the show goes in and out of commercials – a job that he performs just to the left of Letterman's desk – says, 'Are you kidding? Letterman was cracking up throughout the whole set.' Now I feel even more relieved. Since I am a fan of Dave's and the show, it means a lot to me that he would enjoy my work. Finally I begin to relax in general. While it feels good to do a set on the number one talk show in America, and again, a show that I'm a huge fan of – it is extremely nerve racking. The stakes are much higher obviously, playing to eight million people than the typical three-hundred-seat club crowd comics are used to playing every night. The fact that it was over and by *all* accounts went fine was a huge relief.

At this time, I'd like to tell you the circumstances that led up to me being called at the last minute to do the show . . .

I was scheduled to appear on 'The Late Show with David Letterman' on Friday, September 24 – one week previous to the actual day when I went on – the show I just recounted. As I said earlier, the material I was to do was approved and reapproved by

Mary Connelly, the segment producer of the Letterman show. I flew up to New York, went directly to the studio, and Mary and I went over the set again then she graciously showed me around the beautiful, revamped Ed Sullivan Theatre. We both agreed every base had been covered, and I went back to my hotel to run through the set again and again – my typical procedure. That afternoon I went to the show. The other guests that night were Glenn Close and James Taylor. The show began, I got made up, and sat waiting in my dressing room for my spot. About half-way through the show, Mary Connelly called my manager Colleen McGarr and me into a hall way and told me she had some bad news – the show was running late, and there wouldn't be time to get me on. This is known as being 'Bumped' in talk show parlance, and isn't as bad as it sounds.

You still get paid, free hotel room, and your flight back to wherever you're going. The only downside really is that you're all pumped up with adrenalin and ready to go on, then – nothing. It's kind of like a cowboy might feel if he were sitting on the bull, wrapping his hands in the rope, psyching himself up, then the gate never opens. Of course I was a little bummed, because I wanted to get this over with and return to my more familiar world of three-hundred-seat comedy clubs and doing material the nature of which is unexpurgated, and only has to be approved by me.

Mary expressed her apologies, then went on to say I'd be rescheduled as soon as possible, perhaps in a couple of weeks. Colleen, my Manager, and I then went to The Palms restaurant and consoled ourselves with lobsters the size of canoes. We both felt fine about everything, and the next day I flew home.

The following week, I was back up in New York working Caroline's Comedy Club. On Friday, October 1st, I called up a Florida paper to do an interview for my next engagement at the Comedy Corner in West Palm Beach, Florida. Toward the end of the interview, the reporter said, 'Oh, by the way, congratulations,' I said, 'thanks, what for?' He said, 'Well, you're doing Letterman tonight.' Hmmm . . . I said, 'That's news to me, maybe I should get off the horn here and find out what's going on.' He said, 'Yeah, you better, they've been looking for you all day.' We hung up and

I called my Manager's office. Since Colleen, my Manager, was with me in New York, and was out shopping with her Mom, I assumed she'd heard nothing of this as well, I got a hold of Colleen's assistant, who went berserk when she got on the line, 'where have you been all day!? The Letterman people have been trying to reach you all day! They want you on the show tonight! Some other guest has fallen out.'

I was a little embarrassed by this inability to be found, for it was my fault entirely. You see, I had checked into the hotel room under the name Otis Blackwell,[72] in honor of the true author of some of Elvis Presley's biggest hits, including 'All Shook up' and 'Don't be Cruel'. Another reason I checked in under that name was kind of a private joke between myself and me regarding another comic who will remain nameless – hopefully forever, who had gained some popularity doing routines, mannerisms, and attitudes remarkably similar to my own. And *another* reason I checked in under an assumed name, and the most obvious in the world, I wanted to assure my privacy and avoid any over zealous creditors who might be lurking about trying to ruin my day and the beautiful weather we were experiencing that fall week in New York. Again, it was all my fault, though I make no apologies.

I hung up the phone and immediately called Mary Connelly at the Letterman show. She too berated me for being so mysterious about my whereabouts, then asked me if I could go on the show that night. I said 'of course'. It was now 3.30 p.m. Mary told me a car would be by to pick me up at 4.15. I got dressed, the adrenalin started pumping, and I went through the approved set again and again until the car arrived. My Manager, Colleen, and her mom and I excitedly jumped in the car and we headed for the studio. Colleen's Mom, a Canadian and another devout fan of the Letterman show, had already attended a taping that week. She was doubly excited for the opportunity to see the show twice in one week, and in this instance to experience the backstage goings on as opposed to watching the show as an audience member.

We got to the studio in plenty of time to hear about the guest who had been cancelled from the show – the former cook of the Gambino Crime Family, currently in the Witness Protection Program, had written a cookbook and wanted to go on television to promote his book. (These fellows aren't known for their brightness.) The stipulation if he chose to go on, from the government, was a) he would lose his protection entirely, and b) he would forfeit his four-thousand-dollar-a-month stipend he receives from the US Government for turning stool pigeon against the Mob. The cook still wanted to go ahead with the show. He must have some unbelievably good recipes in that book. Anyway, apparently throughout the day, the Letterman show received several calls from Italian-accented men who wanted to know if the stool pigeon cook was really going on the show, then, when told he was, they asked, 'What time does the show tape?' Understandably, the Letterman people begin to feel nervous about booking the former Mob cook. The Letterman people then decided to cancel his appearance. Unfortunately, the cook, living in a hideout in New Jersey two hours away from New York (perhaps under the name Otis Blackwell), was already en route to the studio. There was no way to contact him until he reached the studio with pots and paws and cookbook in hand.

Now, who exactly was going to tell him he wouldn't be going on the show after all? Twenty-four-year-old staff member Daniel Kellison drew the short stick and when the Mob cook showed up, Daniel broke the news to him as delicately and gracefully, I'm sure, as he could muster. By all accounts, the cook went berserk. He stormed off, pots and pans rattling, Daniel breathed a great sigh of relief and resumed his much safer duties on the show.

All of this was occuring during, and up to the time they were looking for me, to when I got to the show and heard the story. We all had a good chuckle, acknowledged the strangeness of life, then I went up to be made-up. What I didn't learn until after the show was that half-way through the taping, young Daniel received a call from the fuming Mob cook, who proceeded to call Daniel every name in the book, then threatened to kill him if it was the last thing he ever did. I was oblivious to this turn of events as I headed down to do my spot in the show. I wasn't even aware of the extra tension in the green room, the additional security, nor the ashen-faced Daniel standing sadly in the corner, focused as I was on the set I was about to do.

I stood in the wings, taking a final drag from my cigarette, then David Letterman introduced me, and I walked out to center stage and performed the set I recounted in the beginning of this ever-growing saga.

After the show, I returned to my hotel and took a long hot bath. It felt really good. All the tension of the day steamed away. I'd done the show. It had gone well. The pressure was off. I could finally relax. As I was getting out of the tub, the phone rang. It was now 7.30 p.m. Robert Morton, the producer of the Letterman show, was on the line. He said 'Bill; I've got some bad news . . .' My first thought was that Daniel had perhaps been chopped up and sautéed by the Mob cook. Robert Morton went on . . . 'Bill, we have to edit your set from tonight's show.' I sat down on the bed, stunned, wearing nothing but a towel. 'I don't understand, Robert. What's the problem? I thought the show went great.' Morton replied, 'It did, Bill. You killed out there. It's just that the CBS Standards and Practices felt some of the material was unsuitable for broadcast.' I rubbed my head, confused, 'Ah, which material exactly did they find . . . unsuitable?' 'Well,' Morty replied, 'almost all of it, if I had to edit everything they object to, there'll be nothing left of the set. So we just think it's best to cut you entirely from the show. Bill, we fought tooth and nail to keep the set as is, but Standards and Practices won't back down. David is furious. We're all upset here, Bill, this has nothing to do with how we feel about you. We loved the set and we take full responsibility for this. We love you and know how hard you worked on this set. What can I say? It's outa my hands now. We've never experienced this before with Standards and Practices . . . and they're just not gonna back down, I'm really sorry.' I was trying my best to digest all this. The tension creeping back into my body and my mind. 'But, Bob . . . they're so obviously jokes . . .' 'Bill, I know, I know, Standards and Practices just doesn't find them suitable.' 'But which ones? I mean, I saw this set by my sixty-three-year-old Mom on her porch in Little Rock, Arkansas. You're not going to find *anyone* more mainstream, nor any place more Middle America than my Mom in Little Rock, Arkansas, and she had no problem with the material.' 'Bill, what can I say? It's out of our hands . . .

Bill, we'll just try and schedule a different set in a couple of weeks and have you back on.'

I wanted at that time to say 'I don't think I can learn to juggle in that short of a time', but I just was too stunned. Then Morton said, 'Bill, we take full responsibility for this. It's our fault. We should have spent more time before hand working on the set, so Mary or I could have edited out those "hot points" and we wouldn't be having to do this now.' Finally, I came to my senses. I said, 'Bob, they're just jokes. I don't want them to be edited by you or anyone else. Why are people so afraid of jokes?' To which Morty replied, 'Bill, you have to understand our audiences.' This is a line I'd heard before and it always pisses me off. 'Your audiences!' I retorted. 'What do you grow them on farms? Your audience is comprised of "people", right? Well, I understand "people", being a person myself. People are who I play to every night, Bob, and we get along just fine . . .' 'Bill, look, it has to do with the subject matter you touched on, and our new time slot, we're on an hour earlier you know.' 'So, what? We taped the show at 5.30 in the afternoon, and your audience had no problem with the material then. What . . . does the audience become overly sensitive between the hours of 11.30 p.m. and 12.30 a.m.? And by the way, Bob, when I'm not performing on your show, *I'm* a member of the audience for your show. Are you saying my material is not suitable for me? This doesn't make sense, why do you underestimate the intelligence of the audience? I think that shows a great deal of contempt on your part . . .'

Morty bursts in with, 'Bill, it's not our decision. We have to answer to the networks, and this is the way they want to handle it. Again, I'm sorry. You're not at fault here. Now let me get to work editing you from the show and we'll set another date as soon as possible with some different material, OK?' 'What kind of material? How bad airline food is? Boy, 7–11s sure are expensive? Golly, Ross Perot has big ears? Bob, you keep saying you want me on the show, then you don't let me be me. Now, you're cutting me out completely. I feel like a beaten wife who keeps coming back for more. I try and write the best material I can for you guys. You're the only show I do because I'm a big fan, and I think you're the best talk show on. And this is how you treat me?' 'Bill, that's just the way it is sometimes, I'm sorry, OK?' 'Well, I'm sorry too, Bob. Now I've gotta call my folks back and tell them not to wait up . . . I gotta call my friends . . .' 'Bill, I know. This is tough on all of us . . .' 'Well, you gotta do what you gotta do . . . OK'. Then we hung up.

So there you have it – not since Elvis was censored from the waist down has a performer, a comic, performing on the very same stage, been so censored – now from the neck up, in 1993. In America. For telling Jokes.

I began getting dressed for my shows that night at Caroline's. It began to dawn on me there were greater implications than just me being censored. When I went up to my manager, Colleen's room, Colleen and her mom were getting ready to go with me to Caroline's. I told them the news. They didn't believe me at first, but my emotional state and the fact that I kept repeating 'they're just Jokes. They're just Jokes, they're just Jokes . . .' finally convinced them it was true. Colleen immediately went into the bedroom to call the Letterman people. I sat with her Mom and ranted for awhile. There were tears in her eyes. I think there were tears in mine as well. 'What are they so afraid of?' I yelled, and 'goddammit I'm a fan of the show. *I'm* an audience member. I do my best shit for them . . . they're just Jokes . . .'

My feelings for the show and my relationship with them were undergoing a metamorphosis, as were Colleen's Mom, I believe. It was like finding out there is no Santa Claus, only the implications of this realization were much more sinister. Here's this show I loved, that touted itself as this hip late night talk show, trying to silence one man's voice . . . a comic no less. A show that pretends to be so irreverent, yet buckles at the first hint of anything resembling, in their frightened eyes, edginess. Colleen came back into the room after talking to Mary Connelly of the Letterman show. Mary told Colleen exactly what Robert Morton told me. Colleen asked her if we could get a copy of the tape of my performance. Mary told her, 'No problem. We'll get it off to you on Monday.' Shellshocked, Colleen, Colleen's mom, and I headed off to Caroline's Comedy Club where I was to do two shows that night.

On Monday Colleen and I flew to W. Palm Beach, Florida, where

I was to perform a five-day run at the W. Palm Beach Comedy Corner. Colleen called the Letterman show and was again told getting a copy of my performance on Friday's show would be no problem. Colleen then gave her address and Fed Ex number, and she was told the tape would arrive the following day.

Meanwhile, we had walked into Maelstrom. The phones were ringing off the hook, and for the next three days I was continuously busy. You see, over the course of my sixteen years performing comedy all over America, I had made many friends and fans in the media-print, radio, and television. All of them were notified by 'my people' of my Letterman appearance that Friday. When my appearance on the night they were watching never occured – ironically replaced by a canned comedy performance by Bill Sheft – they were curious as to what the story was. As I told them, I heard word processors clicking in the background. Apparently, many of my Media Friends, fans, and supporters are also Letterman fans. They felt this was a story that was Newsworthy and expressed to me their own sympathy and outrage over what had occurred. The ball was rolling without any help on my part. While it's been tiring these last few days of *continuous* interviews, it's really easy on my part, for all I have to do is tell the TRUTH . . . over and over and over again. At least it's easy to remember.

Tuesday came and went without the arrival of the tape from the Letterman show. Throughout Monday and Tuesday, the interview requests kept pouring in. My managers Colleen McGarr and Duncan Strauss were pondering how to handle this situation. We all agreed that it wouldn't be fair to voice our thoughts until we received the tape of the show and saw for ourselves the set, my performance, and the reaction of the audience. We also thought it only fair to tell the Letterman people about all the calls we were receiving, and find out what their response might be. Thinking the tape still might be on its way – even though it was now two days since they assured us they had overnighted it – Duncan Strauss called up Letterman's producer Robert Morton, to tell him of all the articles and interviews that were pending.

Essentially, Robert Morton didn't like the idea of any press about what happened. He took a particularly 'dim view' of the upcoming

New Yorker profile, if it were to include any mention of this incident of me being censored. Mr Morton then reiterated how much they loved me at the show, and how well I'd done Friday. Duncan told him he looked forward to seeing the set on the tape and then they hung up. Now we all had heard 1st hand that a) The Letterman people loved my set. b) CBS Standards and Practices were responsible for the censoring. c) The tape was on its way. And d) They wanted to rebook me for another spot in the upcoming weeks.

When Thursday came and went and still no tape arrived, I took it upon myself to call Robert Morton personally. I asked him why the tape hadn't arrived yet. He said, 'Um . . . I don't know if we're legally allowed to send out a tape of an unaired segment of a show . . .' Hmm . . . I thought that was pretty off the top of his head. I said, 'Robert, I just want it for my archives, and my parents would love to see it.' Morty said, 'OK . . . I'll try. I'll see what I can do. I'll get you the tape. Are we OK, Bill?' 'Yeah,' I said, 'I'm fine. I'm just looking forward to seeing my act.' To which Morty replied, 'I understand, I'll get you the tape. And let's work on another set for a few weeks from now.' I said, 'Great!' And we hung up. To this day, no tape has ever arrived. What I've recounted here is the exact material I used, and the exact responses I received from the people responsible for producing the show, and the responses of the audience to the best of my memory. Since no tape of the set seems to be forthcoming, this puts me in the awkward position of having to recall these events and commit them to paper – basically to stand up for myself and tell the truth with all the possible information that's at hand at this moment. Since there was so much interest from the media, and no support from the Letterman people, we decided to go ahead and do these interviews, telling the exact truth as we knew it to be with as much information that was at our disposal. Reporter after reporter followed radio talk show after radio talk show for *five* solid days. Almost to a man, each and every one were fans of mine and of Letterman's show. And almost across the board the same outrage was expressed when I told them the material CBS Standard and Practices deemed 'unsuitable' for the viewing public. One such radio talk show – The Alex Bennet Show in San Francisco – had a live studio audience the morning I called in to be interviewed. The studio audience laughed at the Jokes as I told them, and applauded the points I made about television after hearing the Jokes. Someone who heard that broadcast took it upon himself to write a stinging letter to CBS, chastising them for their cowardice for not airing my set. They quickly received a letter in reply which was then faxed to my office. Its contents were most interesting and added a humorous twist to this already black comedy that was unfolding. I have CBS reply before me, and I quote '. . . It is true that Bill Hicks was taped that evening and that his performance did not air, what is inaccurate is that the deletion of his routine was required by CBS (!) In fact, although a CBS Program Practices editor works on that show, the decision was solely that of the producers of the program with that of another comedian. Therefore, your criticism that CBS censored the program is totally without foundation. Creative Judgements must be made in the course of producing any program, and while we regret that you disagreed with this one, the producers felt it necessary and that is not a decision we would override. (!) (By the way, the underlining of pertinent sentences was done by me.) Whoa! Here was a unique twist. This response from CBS was at total variance with everything I'd been told repeatedly by Robert Morton, the producer of the Letterman show, and Mary Connelly, the segment producer of the show and my set in particular. This response doesn't gibe at all with Morton's claim that 'Bill, the set was great! You killed! It's CBS Standards and Practices who want this particular material edited . . . we fought tooth and nail to keep the set as is . . .' etc., etc., etc. Then the darker implications of all this came into even clearer focus. I realized this is the only time weaselly capitalists ever pass the buck – when they're held accountable for their actions. Next, the scoundrels will be wrapping themselves in the flag, and the farce will be complete – just another minor footnote in the history of the ongoing saga of Freedom of Expression in the Land of the Free, and the Home of the Brave.

It's been exactly one week now since this odd story began. And believe me, none of this was planned, expected, nor sought after. I did what I've always done – performed material in a comedic way which I thought was funny. The artist always plays to himself, and

I believe the audience seeing that one person can be free to express his thoughts, however strange they may seem, inspires the audience to feel that perhaps they too can freely express their innermost thoughts with impunity, joy, and release, and perhaps discover our common bond – unique yet so similar – with each other. This philosophy may appear at first to some as selfish – 'I play to me and do material that interests and cracks me up.' But you see, I don't feel I'm different than anyone else. The audience is me. I believe we all have the Voice of Reason inside us, and that voice is the same in everyone. And if I may open up even more, I believe that voice (you may call it conscience) is the voice of the Holy Spirit that God has instilled in us all to gently lead us out of our own self-created hells – those feelings and thoughts of hopelessness, fear, sin, and guilt which have never and could never exist in Reality, for what God did not create, does not exist. And I pose a question you can Meditate on and find a great deal of peace from: 'What could oppose God's will?'

This is what I think either CBS, or the producers of the Letterman show and Networks and governments fear the most – that one man free, expressing his own thoughts and point of view, might somehow inspire others to think for themselves and listen to that Voice of Reason inside them, and then perhaps one by one we will awaken from this dream of lies and illusions that the world, the Governments, and their propaganda arm – the mainstream media – feeds us continuously over fifty-two channels, twenty-four hours a day. What I realized was – they don't want the people to be awake. The elite ruling class wants us asleep so we'll remain a docile, apathetic herd of passive consumers, and non-participants in the true agendas of our governments, which is to keep us separate and present an image of a world filled with unresolvable problems that they, and only they, might one day, somewhere in the never-arriving future, may be able to solve. Just stay asleep America, keep watching TV, keep paying attention to the infinite witnesses of illusion we provide you over Lucifer's Dream Box – television. I find it laughable and pathetic.

When I was a young boy, watching comics on television, I used to think, 'Boy, if they like this guy, they're going to love me.' And I began working quite young, writing, growing, maturing, always striving to top myself – to make people laugh hard at things they know and believe deep in their hearts to be true. It has been a long road, let me tell you; but after sixteen years of constant performing up until this little incident on October 1st, 1993, the cold realization finally struck me. A sobering answer to the wish of that young boy I once was back in Houston, Texas, all excited with the idea that 'if they like these guys, then they're going to love me.' The realization was – they don't want me, nor my kind.

Just look at ninety per cent of television programming. Banal, puerile, trite scat. And this *is* what they want, for they hold the masses – the herd – in such contempt. I've lost count of how many times I've been in a 'creative' meeting in Los Angeles, and after pitching an idea for a show heard the following statement: 'That's very Funny, but do you think it will play in the Mid-West?' As though the Mid-West were this vast wasteland filled with bib-overall wearing bumpkins whose intellectual level and comprehension could only be satisfied with 'American Gladiators', or 'Love Connection', or 'full house', or . . . etc, etc, etc. The list fills the one inch TV guide each week – the Bible of the herd. Like a menu for bad drugs that deaden the mind and drive a wedge between our conscious and unconscious minds, and between ourselves and each other, and between us and them, and between us and the experience of Life itself. Well, I've got some surprising news for you – I've played the Mid-West – all over the Mid-West, in fact, and you know what I've found? The people there are quite intelligent, well read, thoughtful and reasonable folks, just like most people I meet every day, everywhere, all over the world. But no wonder there's an evergrowing sense of disenfranchisement, apathy, and cynicism in our country. When we're all tuned in to the real drug of this country – television – brought to us by an elite class of 'unique' and 'special' people who find the dirty herd beneath contempt, and only there really to buy the useless products created to fill the imaginary 'wants' television really hawks between hours of puerile programming. Every few years, they cart out the old argument regarding television's role in our society. As usual, they pose to keep us divided and keep the problem unresolved, then it's back to 'business as usual'. The herd has been pacified by our charade of concern as we pose the two most idiotic questions imaginable – 'Is TV becoming too violent?' and 'Is TV becoming too promiscuous?' The answer, my friends, is this – TV is too <u>stupid</u>. It treats us like Morons. <u>Case Closed</u>. Truly, the only stupid people I've ever met, the most absolutely <u>clueless</u> are the very people that produce television. Unfortunately, self-awareness is not one of their long suits, regardless of how many hair weaves, breasts augmentations, Valiums, shrinks, or phony religions of the 'inner child' they've partaken of. Don't you find it ironic at all, that television pushes beer (alcohol, the number two killer drug in the world) down our throats twenty-four hours a day, with beautiful half-naked women and the promise of 'freedom and infinite sex appeal', while also maintaining a division of their corporate empire called 'Standards and Practices'? Exactly what <u>Standards</u> are you practising. I've even seen these commercials during 'in depth' reports on the war against drugs. At least drug dealers have enough shame to lurk on street corners and in alleyways, and not come over the tube into our homes with all the slick, glossy production values the beer hawkers muster as though they were offering manna from Heaven in a six pack.

But as I said before, their lack of self-awareness is only matched by their blatant hypocrisy. I remember one time I did the Letterman show, and the night before Robert Morton and I made the rounds of the comedy clubs in New York to hone the set. During the course of the night, Mr Morton had decided I should drop a few of the bits from my set because they weren't 'right for our audience'. The next morning I did a radio show, and the interviewer asked me if it was difficult to translate my club act to television. I responded by telling her of the previous night's activities. That afternoon, when I showed up at the Letterman studio, Robert Morton ran up to me and said, 'Hey, Hicks, why were you dissing us on the air today?' I asked what he meant. He said, 'you were saying we edit your stuff for TV, we've never done that!' Uh . . . Hmmm. How do you respond to the insane? I was speechless. Yes, lack of self-awareness and hypocrisy reign supreme in the world of television. Shoot, TV would still be hawking cigarettes if the government hadn't stepped in. Why the government stepped in in the first place is anybody's guess. Perhaps it's because we've opened so many new overseas markets to push the number one killer drug[73] in the world, that the future of tobacco products is still safe from encroachment. By the way, that's another issue never raised by our OBJECTIVE News media – the fact that we are pushing the number one killer drug in the world to unsuspecting Third World Nations with the same glossy, enticing advertising that was used in the US in the fifties. We should all kick back, pop open a beer, and breath a sigh of relief that the few are still making a profit, while the many are tightening their belts in this 'ever changing' global economy – the New World Order. As Don Corleone said in *The Godfather*, 'Follow the money'.

This leads me, hopefully, to my summation on my own personal involvement with Letterman and CBS, and television's involvement with society in general. Why was I censored from the Letterman show? Because some of my Jokes hit 'Hot Points' and were deemed unsuitable for the American viewing public. The fact of the matter is, this vast empire of network television called CBS are a bunch of shameless cowards who kowtow to very organized, although minority, special interest groups in America. They fear losing their corporate sponsorship, and that is the threat these special interest groups promise. What the networks don't realize, due to their total lack of contact with anything resembling Reality, is that the majority of people in America are in general, thoughtful, reasonable people. But it is the minority of fundamentalist morons pushing their fear mongering agendas that get all the attention. The squeaky wheel gets the oil.

You see, Reasonable people don't usually, write letters of complaint or praise to networks because a) Reasonable people have lives. b) Reasonable people know they're just jokes. c) If the Reasonable people don't find the jokes funny, they know it's just TV. d) Reasonable people know if something's on now which they don't like, there may just as well be something they do like coming up soon. e) Reasonable people know they can turn the TV channel, and f) Reasonable people know they can just turn the TV off and go about their day.

It's that insane <u>minority</u> the networks cower to, and play to in their imagined perception of the 'Mid-West', i.e. any state between Los Angeles and New York. That horribly unsophisticated herd that makes up the majority of Americans. Instead, one letter from some fundamentalist anything, written in crayon saying, 'I saw a guy talk about Jesus on your show. I'm offended, signed X', sends the network cowards scurrying to make amends and rid the show of the 'unsuitable' material. Well, I've got news for the Bureaucratic Capitalist Whore Cowards that run television. I'm offended too! I'm offended by the constant barrage of banal, trite, puerile scat you offer without any sense of shame or human dignity. And I've got something else to say to those people who say, 'I'm offended', like some five-year-old child throwing a tantrum. Ready? There are a lot of things in life that are offensive, life itself can be offensive, I myself have a large list of things that offend me . . . So what!? Grow the fuck up! We now live in the 'Age of being offended.' Get over it. Perhaps a little open-mindedness, tolerance, and acceptance may be the antidote to what ails you. Try it and see if your load isn't lifted just a bit. See if your pinched face of fear doesn't relax a tad. Why don't you exercise a little of the faith you say you believe in so much, and trust in God and his infinite, unconditional love. Why don't you fucking Christians start <u>acting</u> like Christians?

And now, the final irony. One of the 'Hot Points' that was brought up as being 'unsuitable for our audience' was my joke about pro-lifers. My brilliant friend Andy posited the theory that this was really what bothered and scared the network the most, seeing as how the 'pro-life' movement has become essentially a terrorist group acting with impunity and God on their side, in a country where the reasonable majority overwhelmingly supports freedom of choice regarding abortion. I felt there was something to this theory, but still I was suprised to be watching the Letterman show (I'm still a fan) the Monday night following my censored Friday night performance, and lo and behold, they cut to a . . . are you ready for this? . . . A pro-life commercial! This farce is now completed. 'Follow the money'.

In summation, I'd like to point out that I am not some curmudgeon with a chip on his shoulder regarding television. There are several shows on TV I absolutely love and never miss. 'Northern Exposure', 'The Simpsons', 'Seinfeld', 'The Larry Sanders Show' I find absolutely brilliant, hilarious, and inspiring. It's these exceptions to the rule that are truly entertaining, and treat the audience with love and respect as they deserve. And, I'd like to take my hat off to Roseanne Arnold for having balls the size of Montana, and overcoming much more serious odds than I've ever faced, to realize her artistic vision, keeping it pure, and silencing the white male elite ruling class by putting on, again, one of my favorite shows on television.

Folks, there are no bitter grapes on my part. I love what I do, and I will do it forever – creating and sharing and trying to shed some light and hope to my lovely lost Brothers who need to laugh and be free just like me. Whether I'll ever be asked to return as a guest on the Letterman show is of no consequence to me. I still think Dave does the best talk show on TV. (Along with Bob Costas and Charlie Rose.) I do not fear CBS, Letterman, or anyone or anything anymore. I'm at peace with myself and the world and my God. I only pray <u>everyone</u> will find that same peace within themselves, as I know in my heart they will. The Voice of Reason told me that, and if you think about it, it really is the only thing that makes sense. The answer to the philosophical question I posed earlier, 'What could oppose God's will?' is 'Nothing'. And God's will for his beloved children is perfect happiness and remembrance of Him and his eternal love for us. We are undergoing evolution, and will continue to do so until all of us awaken to this Truth. Our awakening can be as gentle or harsh as we want to make it. Personally, I prefer the gentle awakening I've experienced in my own life. But, as always, you are free to choose your own route to Heaven. In the end, it really doesn't matter. We'll all make it there in the end. I'm reminded of a quote by the brilliant Noam Chomsky, a personal inspiration to me: 'The responsibility of the intellectual is to tell the TRUTH, and expose lies.' While I do not consider myself an intellectual by any stretch of the imagination, his quote, coincidentally, is the same way my parents taught me how to live. So in honor of them, I'll continue doing what I've been doing, the best way I can. Then, I'll see you all in Heaven, where we can really share a <u>great laugh together</u> . . . forever and ever . . . and ever. With love,

Bill Hicks

Final thoughts . . . You know. This postulating on the power the pro-life movement wields against the cowards (co-conspirators?) of network television and mainstream media in general has finally led me to a conclusion I've been trying to draw on my own thoughts and Feeling about abortion. Here it is: the answer to that confounding question of when, exactly, does the foetus become a human being? Well, after my dealings with television producers and the bureaucratic twits that run the networks has led me to a rather novel answer to that question: I know now of some <u>adults</u> who have yet to develop into real human beings. This realization helps me rest easy with my own pro-choice stance regarding abortion. The pro-lifers themselves remind me less of human beings than a frothing pack of mad dogs impervious to logic, reason, or facts that seem to be the defining characteristics of human beings, and the difference between the 'lower' order of animals.

I'm reminded yet of another quote, one by Thomas Jefferson that I believe sums up my whole problem with mainstream television. He said, 'I know of no safe depositary of the ultimate powers of society other than the people themselves; and if we deem them too unenlightened to exercise their power with a wholesome discretion, the answer is not to take it from them, but to inform (them).'

If television considers itself in any way the moral arbiter of our society, I think it goes a long way towards explaining the awful situation our culture is in. For television has not 'informed' the people but instead deformed them by deforming reality and presenting it 24 hours a day on 52 channels . . . no wonder we feel so confused, afraid, and out of control when this is the reflection presented to us as 'life'. There can be only one answer – turn it off, open your window and listen to the breeze and the crickets and the silence that has nothing to sell to us, but gives freely – this is Reality.

Dave,

I just wanted to drop you a line wishing you a Merry Christmas and Happy New Year!

David, Apparently some misunderstanding has occurred between us all, leaving me in the dark with just my version of how things were, and many unanswered questions.

As we have been "in my mind's eye, at least" "friends in the business" I thought maybe You could help me understand one a little better.

Starting in January, I became a regular contributor for the prestigious (read: no money) newspaper – "The Nation." (For some reason, egg heads treat me as their own. Hmm... Oh well, they're nice enough folk!)

Anyways, I've enclosed a copy of my first contribution, to be used by "The Nation" as a running series entitled "Bill Hicks on television... sometimes." The events and aftershocks of that last "situation" on your show have inspired all these introspective ideas regarding television. If you have time, I'd love for you to read this, and perhaps add your version to my tiny understanding. I've yet to send the article to "The Nation", and I'd love to rewrite it so it has a happier ending. Again, at your leisure. But just so ever – they're going to request this soon.

Also, I've included a Macanudo Cigar, to return the wonderful favor of what you gave me that Cuban Beauty during the commercial break. I know Mac's don't hold a candle to what you smoke. Then again — my cases is not at the well-deserved lofty height of yours own.

Your "tv. pal",

Bill Hicks

P.S. I'm writing you on the eve of my 33rd Birthday. Christmas is just around the corner. You know what I want, leave us clearing the air? A copy of my last set on your show! My folks think I fouled up! Help?

A copy of the original letter from Bill Hicks to David Letterman.
A transcript of the letter is printed opposite.

LETTER TO DAVE LETTERMAN

Dave,

I just wanted to drop you a line wishing you a Merry Christmas and Happy New Year!

David, apparently some misunderstanding has occurred between us all, leaving me in the dark with just *my* version of how things were, and *many* unanswered questions. As we have been, in my mind's eye, at least 'friends in the business' I thought maybe *you* could help me understand just a little better.

Starting in January, I became a regular contributor for the prestigious (read: no money) newspaper – 'The Nation'. (For some reason, egg heads treat me as their own. Hmmm . . . well, they're nice enough folk!) Anyway, I've enclosed a copy of my first contribution, to be used by 'The Nation' as a running series entitled 'Bill Hicks on Television . . . Sometimes.' The events and aftershocks of that last 'situation' on your show have inspired *all* these introspective ideas regarding television. If you have time, I'd love for you to read this, and perhaps add your version to my tiny understanding. I've yet to send the article to 'The Nation', and I'd love to rewrite it so it has a happier ending. Again, at your leisure. But just remember – they're going to request this *soon*.

Also I've included a Macanudo cigar, to return the wonderful favor when you gave me that Cuban beauty during the commercial break. I know Macs don't hold a candle to what you smoke. Then again – my career is not at the well-deserved lofty height of your own.

Your 'TV pal',[74]

Bill Hicks

P.S. I'm writing you on the eve of my 32nd birthday. Christmas is just around the corner. You know what I want, besides us clearing the air? A copy of my last set on your show! My folks think I fucked up! Help!

JAY,

Just wanted to drop you a line, wishing you and MAVIS a very Merry Christmas and _Happy_ _New_ _Year_!

Look, my friend, I know I've perhaps seemed a bit... impassive (?)...in responding to your extremely cordial and personal invitation to be on your show.

The Reason is, as I said to you before (or tried to) was that I've finally got my own vehicle green-lighted for the prestigious (read: Artsy) Channel 4 in the U.K.

Literally, all of my time is being spent preparing for the show. (A situation I'm sure you're familiar with.) After I get this "bug" out of my system, if you are still interested, I'm all ears for your ideas. (JAY, I've been asked repeatedly to go back on Dave's show and have demurred for this exact reason... Well, there's a couple of other reasons as well, I'm sure you can imagine.)

Look, I can take a hint. For some unknown Reason, I've been allowed to "do my thing" in the U.K. where I'm totally accepted for who I am, and for all the Right Reasons. So I've had to go pull a Hendrix thing... So, what? Not a bad set of Artistic footprints to follow in, eh?

And one other thing: what I've ever said regarding your show, is being said by a lot of people other than myself. Alexander Woolcott of New Yorker fame to name just one. These things are not said in "hate", nor found by "enemies". It's more or less like how we all will "run down" our own best friend, (or even ourselves at times). "You know what Mavis needs to do is..." etc. etc.

These statements are done from a concerned and interested party. Not an "enemy". It is in fact a sign of how much an ... influence you've played in my life, that interest and intriguing kind of questions. I hope you don't take it personally, or seriously. Your friend,
Bill Hicks

A copy of the original letter from Bill Hicks to Jay Leno. A transcript of the letter is printed opposite.

Jay,

Just wanted to drop you a line, wishing you and Mavis a very Merry Christmas and *Happy New* Year!

Look, my friend, I know I've perhaps seemed a bit . . . impassive (?) . . . in responding to your extremely cordial and personal invitation to be on your show.

The reason is, as I said to you before (or tried to) was that I've finally got my own series green-lighted for the prestigious (read: artsy) Channel 4 in the UK. Literally, *all* of my time is being spent preparing for the show. (A situation I'm sure you're familiar with!) After I get this 'bug' out of my system, if you are still interested, I'm all ears for your ideas. (Jay, I've been asked repeatedly to go back on Dave's show and have demurred for this exact reason . . . Well, there's a couple of other reasons as well, I'm sure you can imagine.)

Look, I can take a hint. For some unknown reason, I've been allowed to 'do my thing' in the UK, where I am totally accepted for who I am, and for all the right reasons. So I've had to go pull a Hendrix thing . . . so what? Not a bad set of artistic footprints to follow in, eh?

And one other thing: what I've *ever* said regarding your show, is being said by a *lot* of people other than myself. Alexander Woolcott of *New Yorker* fame to name just one. These things are not said in 'hate', nor said by 'enemies'. It's more or less like how we all will 'run down' our own best friend (or even ourselves at times). 'You know what Mark needs to do is . . .' etc., etc. These statements are done from a concerned and interested party. Not an 'enemy'. It is in fact a sign of how much an influence you've played in my life, this interest and intriguing kind of questions. I hope you don't take it personally, or seriously.

Your friend,

Bill Hicks

The Vision
(18 December 1993)

I had a vision last night while getting my first massage in over five months. The masseuse's name was Lola and she brought out the best in me. As you know I've been trying to learn to '*transcend*' my whole life. Last night, while she massaged me to the music of Yanni (of all people), I transcended at least once, maybe twice. I'm absolutely positive I transcended once because I saw into the future and had a vision. The vision details how I, my lovely wife Colleen and my two children (also in the future) will leave this world, and this planet, and it was most fine. Let me tell you about this vision I had . . .

First of all, obviously Colleen and I were mates and had two children. The children were around four and five years old. I'm not sure if they were a boy and girl, or two boys, or two girls, but I can guarantee you one thing – they were one or the other. In fact, the more I think of it, I saw a boy around five, and a little pigtailed girl, around four, both with golden hair, wearing jeans and dungarees, just like their Pa. Pa was also wearing a cool hat and jacket like Jed Clampett of Beverly Hillbillies fame, or Paul Newman in Butch Cassidy and the Sundance Kid. Pa seemed to be around forty-six years old. By the time this occurred, Pa and Ma had built and lived in their house for several years. In fact, long enough for Pa's dog Lustre to mature and act as general to two Danes who were now three or four. We were all totally at peace, living Heaven on Earth, or so we thought at first, although there was still more to come – we were already living much of our dreams, had realized them, or were basically just rich in abundance beyond our wildest imaginings. We were free in all aspects of the word. We just kept giving love freely to make room for new love and new happiness. God was guiding and teaching us, and we were happy to follow, just basking in his peace and his never-ending love. On this particular day, we had been playing in the yard, swinging on swings, wrestling with our two Dane pups named Crotus and Chiron, cuddling with The General – Lustre, a handsome Border Collie who sometimes takes his duties far too seriously. Lustre was my best friend, my first dog. He's sharp as a whip and can keep Crotus and Chiron in line with one commanding yap. Crotus and Chiron 'look up' to Lustre. He is their leader, The General, and he's all dog in the best possible sense of the word.

Suddenly, the Danes and Lustre pricked up their ears, looked at each other, then me. They seemed excited and a little nervous. They began running in a circle around me, then suddenly took off, towards the rolling hills that surrounded our beautiful house. I called for them to come back, but they were really hot on the trail of something. A rabbit? No, they're better trained than that. Something 'big' had captured their entire attention, and off they went. Colleen and the children were laughing excitedly, then they went running after the dogs, laughing all the while. I was a little miffed, because I called out to them as well and their response was much like the dogs. Totally ignoring me. 'It's probably just a rabbit!' I yelled. But they didn't even hear me, intent as they were on 'getting in on the hunt', as it were. I sighed, then took off after them all. By this time, the dogs were out of sight, over a hill, and all I heard was their occasional manic barking. 'Wow,' I thought, 'maybe there's an intruder on the property.' With that thought in mind, I picked up the pace a little bit. As I closed the gap between me and my family, we were going up a rather large rolling hill. The dogs were just over the hill and they were barking furiously, though excitedly. As Colleen and the young 'uns reached the top of the hill they stared in wonder and pointed excitedly down into a little valley where the dogs were. Colleen then turned towards me, wide-eyed, and said 'Come here! You're not going to believe this!' Now I was most curious. I then noticed a sun in the sky. Not *the* sun, because *the* sun was setting behind and to the left of us. Another sun shone brightly in the sky, and in fact seemed to be floating right above the little rolling valley where all this interest was being focused. My jaw dropped a little, and I paused in my efforts to take a deep breath and ponder about what this could mean. Colleen yelled 'Come on! You don't want to miss this!' Finally I revived my pace and then was standing with my family in my arms looking at the new 'sun' and then down into the valley. 'Oh,' I thought, 'it must be time to go . . .' There in the valley, pretty as you please, sat a huge round disc. The sun overhead started circling rapidly around us and the disc. My hands were being tugged by the two children, and Colleen was pushing me from behind. 'Come on!' she said, laughing. 'This is what you've been waiting for your whole life!' We started down the hills towards the disc. The only dog visible was Crotus. He was standing on a ramp that led to a door into the ship. He was barking furiously at me to hurry up and come. We started running now towards Crotus, all of us laughing, crying, and trying to take everything in at once. We ran up the ramp to Crotus, who leapt up on his back paws and gave me a big sloppy kiss. Colleen pulled on my hand, and we stumbled on through the door onto the ship. There was this great whooshing sound. I stopped on the ramp and looked back one last time at our planet. So gentle and sweet our life had finally become, the beautiful golden rolling hills, I could see our footsteps in the grass and wondered what all this would look like after we left. Our front door was left standing wide open, our footsteps running through the grass, up the hill then down into this valley where they would disappear in a great impression left by the disc. 'What would people think?' I wondered. Then I began smiling, and then laughing, then roaring with pure joy and laughter. They'd think, 'Isn't this just like Hicks?' At this thought, I stepped into the craft, the door shut and we shot up fast into the space surrounding our planet. On we travelled till the earth was just a dot, then the dot disappeared and we were on our way to our *new* life and *new happiness*.

Amen

Bill Hicks Interview Taken From
Campus Activities Today
(January 1994)

After being censored by CBS **on his 12th appearance on** the Letterman Show, he might be considered America's most rebellious comedian. But is he? *The New Yorker* says this Texas comic might have gotten a raw deal. In this interview, you can decide!

On October 1, 1993, Bill Hicks, after making his 12th appearance on the David Letterman Show, became the first comedy act to be censored at CBS's Ed Sullivan Theatre. It was the Ed Sullivan Theatre where Elvis Presley was censored in 1956. According to New Yorker Magazine 'Presley was not allowed to be shown from the waist down. Hicks was not allowed to be shown at all. It's not what's in Hicks' pants but what's in his head that scared the CBS panjandrums. Hicks, a tall thirty-one-year old Texan with a pudgy face aged beyond its years from hard living on the road, is no motormouth vulgarian but an exhilarating comic thinker in a renegade class of his own.' (November 1, 1993 by John Lahr)

Bill Hicks is a thinker. A bit of a philosopher . . . perhaps a bit of a rebel. He believes that comedy should carry a message and it should be a learning experience. In a review for the San Francisco Chronicle, Gerald Nachman wrote, 'Bill Hicks is as American as Apple Pie à la cyanide. Love him or leave him, but listen to him. This rapidly emerging comic voice, cutting through the bland comedy-club air like a persistent, ear-shattering smoke alarm, is a different sound in contemporary stand-up humor . . .'

Rick Vanderknyff of the Los Angeles Times says 'When stand-up comedy experienced its renaissance in the late 70's, it was heralded as the new rock 'n' roll, a clearinghouse for cutting-edge ideas. It was going to be dangerous. It was going to be subversive. Anyone who follows comedy knows what has happened since. The scene flourished, but in all the wrong ways, becoming little more than a proving ground for faceless hacks hoping to land a sitcom or a movie or a TV commercial. Truly funny, original comedians are hard to find: funny comics with ideas should be put on the endangered species list. Bill Hicks is one such comic . . . When Hicks looks out at America, he worries, and when he worries, two things happen: He gets angry, and he gets very, very funny.'

We will admit to you readers. Bill Hicks is different. In this interview, you will have the opportunity to learn more about him . . .

CAT: Tell us a little bit about your style because it is probably a little different from what most schools are used to seeing.

BILL: Well, what I believe, and it is very archaic, by the way, I hold comedy in very high regard. I believe my style is kind of a letting everyone know – I believe that everyone has a voice of reason inside – I believe that it is quelled by the shrieking idiocy of mainstream media that we hear and it has added to our hopelessness on the planet because mainstream doesn't offer answers, they only continue the problems. And I believe the voice of reason inside of us has the answers if we'd only calm down and listen to it. But what I do on stage is let that voice speak through logic and reason. And of course, I make it funny. The medicine goes down a little easier. I don't know if that is different from other guys, but . . .

CAT: One thing you do is try to make a point. Some comedians are out there to frolic and carry on and to get somebody's attention but not really to deliver anything serious. I have noticed with your stuff that there is a message to be heard.
BILL: The message is generally reason versus unreason. What

makes sense and not what doesn't make sense. In other words, besides our preconceived notions about the world, the way that we are raised with certain religions and upbringings and the way we're told 'should' and 'shouldn't', let's see what really works. Everyone can benefit from logic and reason. That's kind of the way I take it.

CAT: When I talked to some of the agencies about interviewing Bill Hicks, they say 'You are not going to want to interview Bill Hicks because he is so blue . . . he is a club comedian.' Some of the things you say are certainly considered controversial.

BILL: Blue is another connotation. Blue is like I am some guy up there spewing filth out of my mouth and that is not the case. That is really annoying and I haven't heard that in a long time.

I think we transcended that. I think the profile in the *New Yorker*, brought out who I truly am by a very learned reviewer. Blue connotes such meaningless filth to me. It's like the old Red Foxx albums doing nothing but obscene jokes.

CAT: When you think of 'Blue,' you think of someone doing just filthy jokes . . .

BILL: And that is not what I do. Yeah, I use some discretionary language because that is the way I kind of talk, but at the same time the language is just part of the character. We all have to grow up. This is the 1990's. If you are shocked by a couple of slang words, it is your problem, not mine. Quite honestly being referred to as 'blue' by anyone not only bothers me but it really shocks me.

Yeah, I have some very dark poetry that I do in my show. We talk about things very openly. But, again, like you said, there is a point to it. It all comes clear if you actually listen and not just 'he's so bad . . . he's blue'. What can we do . . . change the world?

CAT: The bit you did for HBO, how well was it received?

BILL: That was a year ago, and it is better now. On a scale of 1–10 for me, I felt it was a 4. That went over a 23-date run and we filmed only one show, I was a bit tired. The meaning and the message were there but I am very critical of myself. It could have been much better.

CAT: Tell me a little bit about how you got started in this business.

BILL: I started in Houston at about thirteen. I started actually performing on stage at the Comedy Workshop in Houston when I was fifteen. That was about 1978. It was long before this comedy boom happened. It was very unique. When I first started, the guy came up to me and asked could I do 45-minutes. I said sure . . . but it was interesting. All the guys did that. People back then would come up to me and want to know how I had the courage to talk in front of people. Well, I think our nation has overcome that fear.

CAT: So you started in the comedy club in Texas. Where did it go from there?

BILL: I stayed there until I finished high school. I kept working at the club. When I graduated, I told my parents what I did. My brother and my sister went to college . . . it's what you do. I said, well, I'm going out to LA to be a comedian. They said 'Don't you have to be funny?' I said 'Dad, as a matter of fact, I've been working as a professional comedian for about three years.' It was really a shock to them. I left to go to LA with a guitar, $300 and a corduroy suit with a vest.

I landed there. I went up the Comedy Store and I got in there as a regular and I worked there for two years. I was very very miserable. I loved the comedy and I liked being creative, but I was in the wrong element. I moved back to Houston and right then the comedy revolution began. When I went back to Houston, I was so miserable that I said to myself that I was going to college . . . even if I had to be a frickin' accountant . . . anything but getting on stage again. Something was really weird about it.

But, I was in college about six weeks when the club called and said they had a guy fall out and would I come down and do a couple of sets. I went down and it felt right all of a sudden. Gigs kept poppin' and I kept going. Suddenly I am making a good living doing this.

CAT: There was a network there.

BILL: There was a network, there was a tour. I am now making great money as a twenty year-old kid. I'm thinking, 'Wow, let's not be foolish.'

It's like a mistress. It beats the hell out of me sometimes but it's actually saved my life too. I've never been more happy or at peace about it. It's been a long enough road, but what is length in the context of eternity.

CAT: What inspires you to do the kind of comedy that you do?

BILL: The first inspiration was when I was twelve actually. Suddenly I had become a night owl and they had the Late Show on, and what came on that night was a Woody Allen film called *Casino Royale*. I was a little kid and I was watching it and something struck me about it. Then the next week they had another film that he made, *What's Up Tiger Lily*. I don't know why, it just made me laugh. The next week they had *What's New Pussycat*. I kept saying, 'Wow, it's that guy again'. There was this guy who makes people laugh and that's what he does. I didn't even know that this could be a career or anything. That summer, I was walking through a book store and there was this book that had just come out '*Without Feathers*' by Woody Allen. I said to myself, 'There's that dude who makes me laugh.' And I picked it up and started reading it in the store. I was walking up to strangers crying

I was laughing so hard . . . . saying 'read this, read this!' Woody Allen was the first influence. I even wrote kind of like him then.

I saw Richard Pryor's first 'in concert' film and I went 'Oh, my God!' The guy totally used the stage and became characters. He was a one-man movie. That really loosened me up on stage. That is when I started using my personal life. All I knew then were my folks and the kids from high school.

The final influence was Sam Kinison. He started working at the club. What I learned from Sam was this. He was the first guy I ever saw go on stage and not in any way ask the audience to like him. That gave me extra confidence because then I knew you could just be yourself. Since then that has been my philosophy. Oddly enough your most oddball thoughts . . . the kind that most people say 'I couldn't tell that to somebody' when you tell them on stage, people laugh the hardest. The most personal stuff is what people respond to as being so funny.

CAT: What makes you so different from other comedians out there in the market these days?

BILL: I think it is the way I live and think. A lot of people look outside themselves for what will make the audience laugh . . . what will they like. I always think . . . 'What makes me laugh?' I think that is where there is kind of a myth. Most comics, you don't know who they are when they leave. We often tend to be like some 'joke blower'. I don't think that I am any different from the audience. So what will make me laugh, will make them laugh.

CAT: Do you think that your audience is more sophisticated than most other audiences? Obviously you have done a lot of research on the material that you use.

BILL: You have a really good sense of irony, and a great sense that you are watching a show. I have never gone around saying that I wish this audience was smarter or this town sucks. I have never thought that. I just always went out and did things that made me crack up and it was contagious. Most of what you see is in those gross terms about humanity. I think everyone is inherently good and I give everyone the benefit of the doubt. I think that I am real open and that opens people up. I have had just as bad or good a crowd in New York City as in Lafeyette, LA. Your crowd is the luck of the draw on some nights.

CAT: I noticed that some of your political type of satire . . . for instance your Kennedy stuff, if they are not up on the details, the whole thing might just go over their heads. After all, that was thirty years ago.

BILL: Good Point. I obviously have not found a mainstream venue for me in America. I can only hope that people want to have some knowledge of history and what is going on around them.

Just as you called I am finishing the touches on a show that I wrote that we are doing next year in London. If you want that mainstream bullshit, most of the audience can do the jokes with you. It is like a sing-along. Do you really want that?

CAT: You seem to be a pretty high profile star.

BILL: Well, I get a lot of critical acclaim. I have a cult following, but it is funny. That next level is elusive.

CAT: Why do you think the market is different in England?

BILL: For one thing, they only have four channels on TV. It would be like the old days here. When there is a special on, it is really special. They aired my Montreal special, unedited on prime time and over one quarter of the English market saw the show and then they re-ran it. In America there are 5200 comics that have 'specials'. So what the hell is special about it? In England it has happened in one year what in fifteen years has not yet happened in America.

CAT: What specifically, from your viewpoint, was the deal with the Letterman Show?

BILL: I believe that American television is afraid to have someone who makes sense on TV because that will inspire other people to think for themselves. . . . Not be a passive herd of consumers. And one by one people will go 'This is crap'. Instead of sitting there with a beer in their hands and watching these horrible, horrible images of America that I just don't believe in. I am eternally hopeful. The America that I know is one where people are generally reasonable. I meet a lot of people and everyone is genuinely perplexed by the state of affairs but they just can't believe that this box will produce so many lies on the news. They just won't believe it. Even my dad and I go round and round about this. I've told him that they just want you to feel hopeless so that you will buy their crappy products.

If it weren't true, Why would I be censored from Letterman. The jokes are harmless . . . They are just jokes. The censors say 'I'm offended'. Well good, I am offended by a lot of stuff. Where do I send my list? Life can be offensive. Why can't you just be an adult and move on.

I tell you something. That was my twelfth appearance on his show and I have never been more comfortable or happy with the material . . . ever. I felt it was like really me. It wasn't edited or pre-edited and I killed that night. And what a shock it was to get back to my hotel room thirty minutes later and find out the whole thing was not going to be shown.

LA is made up with a bunch of hopefuls just like me. You see all this junk on TV and you say to yourself 'if they like this guy, they are going to love me!' But they want what already works.

I have been to all these creative meetings out there (now there is a term for you 'creative meetings') and they say that this idea is really creative and really funny, but will it play in the midwest? If the people in the midwest knew the contempt that television holds for them. They think that they are Bibb-overall wearing crackers and they lower the standards to this imaginary stupid herd. That is what they do and I have heard it a million times. Thank God a couple of shows slip in. There has got to be hope. *The Simpsons*, one of the funniest shows ever, slipped in. *Northern Exposure*, another show I love, when they aired it six times and it didn't do that well, the studio canceled it. Then they needed a replacement for the summer and ran it again and Boom . . . everyone caught it. Give stuff a chance, man!

Everything is run by accountants and demographics and marketing. They need to look outside themselves. The people that write *The Simpsons* – you know they have fun writing that. They sit there and they say to themselves – THAT'S HILARIOUS.

That's the thing . . . back to Letterman, they have this preconceived notion. I wrote him a thank you note because it opened my eyes up to something that I have been missing. I love the Letterman Show and I am a fan of the Letterman Show. When they came to me and told me 'Bill, we love you and we want you on anytime.' Well I was kind of touched. I have turned down other shows to do them and I was really comfortable doing it. And yet, they would take me out to do material at the clubs before the show, they would cut out something. What I do is tell lengthy things that are all connected and when part of it is cut, it fragments the message and part of it can be lost. Therefore, what it appeared like was that I was just another joke blower. There was no continuity.

They come to me and say 'Bill, it is very funny but you have to understand our audience'. I asked 'What, do you grow them on farms or something? Is your audience comprised of people? Well I know them! I play to them live every single night all over the country. They have no problem with this material.'

I was like the wife who stayed with the abusing husband, but I finally had to say this is it. I have taken my final wack with the crow bar. I still love the show. I think Dave does the best talk show. But, I am bored by being limited. In England they say 'Can you come out with your vision and we'll produce it.'

You have people that want to hear comedy where they don't have to think about anything. To me they are missing the point. They say 'I just want to escape from reality'. No you don't. You want to escape from illusions.

God has this weird little hobby. He creates perfection. This world is not perfect. We have to learn to separate illusions from reality. The best comedy is where people wake up to that. They actually leave feeling lighter, they feel hope. It's like Dice Clay . . . 'I'm just giving people what they want.' Well you're creating a lynch mob.

CAT: What you're doing is dividing them.

BILL: Exactly! Exactly! Instead of being yourself and letting them be their true selves. Then, that to me is entertainment. Take the guys who write *The Simpsons*. It's funny to them. Well, guess what? It's funny to us too. We are all the same.

That is what I try to do with my show. Let the voice of reason speak. Make sense and be funny and just see what happens. My audience learns from me and I learn from them. Obviously, I'm a dreamer.

CAT: How long do you think it is going to take for the American audience to be as open as the English are?

BILL: You have got to keep in mind that there are so many levels in America. I am doing well here and they are open to it. But on a mass level, not yet. Why? Because they haven't been exposed to it.

I think we are going through our 'terrible twos' as a country. 'Get in touch with your inner child.' How about this: 'Get in touch with your outer adult.' Take responsibility and move on.

You have all this hype and all these shows about the terrible drug wars that are going on in America and in-between you have all these alcohol commercials. Come on, you can't tell me that you don't see the irony there. Cigarettes kill more people than all illegal drugs combined times 100. This is a fact and there is no way we can weasel around it.

You wonder why kids do drugs? Well they do drugs because they see their lying hypocritical parents drinking liquor, they see liquor being sold, they know the effects of liquor . . . every kid has gotten drunk and they go 'You're lying to me! And you're probably lying about drugs too!' You are never going to stop the drugs by saying 'Just Say No' or showing some guy who had a cocaine heart attack. That is not drug education.

Why is the drug czar of this country a cop? Why is it not a guy who has been through recovery and recovered from drug and alcohol abuse who can offer real answers and real hope for people who are sick . . . and that is what drug abusers and alcoholics are. They are sick! The voice of reason is that what we are doing isn't working and it is never going to work. How many lives must be lost? Why are we putting these sick people in our overcrowded jails? Have you ever heard of anybody getting healed in prison? What are the chances? It gets worse.

I was raised Southern Baptist. What is one of the first things that you learn? The Kingdom of Heaven is within you. I am saying that it really is in you . . . seriously. These aren't just hollow words that we repeat from generation to generation. The voice of reason tells you that it is within you.

CAT: One of things that scares people is that you are so convincing and probably not mainstream by the way they have been taught and it scares them to think that maybe you might be right.

BILL: That is an interesting point. I try to be a lot more funny and warmer now. I want them to get the message by acting as an example. I am not preaching at them anymore as much as I am living it. It keeps them from getting afraid. But why are we afraid of information, knowledge or someone's point of view?

That's what happened on Letterman. They were afraid of my point of view. Jesus, I listen to Geraldo and I want to barf. He's holding up people's dirty laundry and crowing about it. Isn't that ironic?

I have got to look at my own life. I have had people tell me things that made sense and I rejected them for a long time. Maybe it's just human nature. I'm getting better at it though because I'm living it rather than just saying it.

CAT: What are your long term goals? What do you hope to achieve?

BILL: I have no long term goals, whatsoever. My only real goal is to be myself. Here's a great one.

The word is 'enthusiasm'. It is from 'Enthios' which means the god within. You know what that means. You do what excites you . . . what really brings you joy. It God's way of saying you are on the right path. We are on it together and isn't it fun. Do what brings you joy and all else will follow.

CAT: Do you think some of things you tell people or bring out in your show might scare people because it is anti-establishment?

BILL: Sure. Sometimes my dad even gets on this kick . . . you hate this country, you hate the government and you hate religion. I have to tell him to step back. 'Dad, I really don't think you're watching me. I just hate being lied to.'

You hear so much about old family values. What about just *values*? Everybody should have values.

Last week was Kennedy week and Dan Rather was doing this special once again supporting the lone gunman theory. He was questioning why nine out of ten Americans think there was a conspiracy. Well since the Kennedy assassination all we've seen is corruption in government. From Vietnam to Iran Contra to Watergate to the phony oil crisis, you have no credibility . . . they are obviously liars. Why are we supposed to believe them?

CAT: Why do we keep electing them?

BILL: Many people don't think there is an option.

CAT: Excuse me, but I don't believe that. I hope this is not too liberal, but I think that if we gave everybody in the US Congress their walking papers today and elected a whole new group without any experience whatsoever, I don't think we could be in much worse shape than we are now.

BILL: I agree, but I don't think we should fire them. I think we should kill them on the air live. That would bring people hope. (Just kidding about the killing part.)

But you are absolutely correct. It is an old boys club that is about as corrupt as it possibly could get. They are getting kickbacks and pay-offs from major corporations and the last thing they are doing is representing humanity.

CAT: Innocent people are getting hurt in the meantime. People who have put their faith in an establishment that is full of corruption.

BILL: Let me tell you a story. This is a classic example of irony. My dad is a fairly well-to-do white man. He considers himself super patriotic and fought in WWII. Now, I love America but he doesn't understand why I love it. We are arguing about our policy in another country. I'm asking him why we have to be the watchdogs of the world. Why aren't we offering people education and food? There would be no animosity. My dad actually said this 'I don't think the peasants should be allowed to vote.' I said 'Dad. I think my version of Democracy – and maybe Thomas Jefferson said it best – 'I know of no safe depository of the powers of the nation other than the people themselves. And if we deem them too unenlightened to wield their power with healthy discretion, the remedy is not to take it from them, but to inform them.' How is that for a frickin' sentiment!

CAT: You seem very knowledgeable and educated in all these areas. How have you become so knowledgeable?

BILL: I tell you who opened my eyes up a whole bunch is a guy named Noam Chomsky. I will recommend a book, *Manufacturing Consent*. Noam is a linguistics professor at MIT. He is a critic of American policy in the name of patriotism. He dispels the rumor that you have to be liberal or conservative, Democrat or Republican. We are all these things at times. What we are, are people and let's move on from there. Noam Chomsky pours information into your head. It is interesting, fascinating and documented. He is the eighth most quoted man in history . . . we're talking Socrates, Shakespeare and this guy packs a wallop.

CAT: Bill, have you ever considered being a lecturer?

BILL: I have. I don't know what shape my life is going to take, but I would love to go around to colleges and offer something with the comedy in the context of something other than a comedy club.

CAT: People expect lecturers to be controversial and I think you might have less resistance in getting your message across. You could use the comedy in the lecture.

BILL: I'd love to be able to do that. Because we are watching another generation that are (A) going to be indoctrinated into the system and (B) a lot of people are seeking still and I'd love to get to them at that age.

I would love to be able to debate some of these issues. Thinking is its own reward.

I just had a new little miracle that happened in my life. Dell Publishing wants me to publish a book about anything that I want to write about. Obviously, I think what I would first write about is this discussion on reasonable thinking . . . sense versus nonsense. That's a good title right there. Let me write this down. I think that might be what it takes to introduce me as someone credible enough to do lectures. There are too many people already out there speaking on things that are just crap or they don't know crap about. I would want to be credible.

CAT: I have to tell you that when we got the pre-release of the HBO tape as we were considering interviewing you, there was some concern . . . not so much because of the language, but because of the interpretation of the material. 40% of the schools we reach are church supported schools. I was concerned as to how they might interpret your message. Yet as we are interviewing you, I am getting a completely different perspective. Yes, you probably can be considered a rebel and maybe some of the things you say could be considered radical to staunch conservatives, but as a magazine we need to give our audience a chance to decide for themselves. I have to tell you though, I don't think the tape accurately gives audiences a look at the real Bill Hicks.

BILL: Thank you for being honest with me and I agree about the tape you saw. To those staunch conservatives 'If you are secure in your position, then why are you afraid of my ideas? You can just reject it or listen to it on the level of the joke.'

You know what really bugs me about these Presidential debates? If there is never a third member there as a judge, then there is no one to say 'Wait, you didn't answer that question. You aren't moving on until you ANSWER the question.' The people want answers . . . boom, you lose a point! You've lost credibility.

The thing is, that most of the people in congress want us to think that every problem is so unsolvable. They just gloss over them and make us think that sometime in the 'near' distant future they will be resolved. So the people just think to themselves, 'Who knows better than this guy, I guess?'

CAT: Why are people scared of controversial comedians but not controversial speakers? You could go on Oprah, Donahue, Geraldo and a host of other shows and express your views without too much effort, if you were a speaker. But the fact that you are a comedian seems to put it in a different light.

BILL: One of the things that I have heard is that America's biggest failing is its inability to take comedy seriously. What you are saying and what I believe is that they take it too seriously. A real comic does offer solutions. Some people are afraid of that . . . they are afraid of someone who can truly express an idea and do it with all the convictions because this is the only idea that makes sense. It is irrefutable . . . until I hear more information, and I am willing to hear you out.

CAT: Was there ever a clear response as to why you were censored from Letterman?

BILL: Never! The first call was this: The show had to be censored. Why? Because CBS Standards and Practices found your material unsuitable. I said 'Well, did it not go over well with the audience.' The response was 'Yeah, it did.' 'Then what's the problem.' . . . again there was no debate judge there. The punchline was that I did a pro-life joke . . . a very clean joke about pro-life. The basic thing that I said was 'Don't lock arms and block medical clinics. Lock arms and block cemeteries.' Let's see how committed you are. We live in the USA, United States of Advertising and there is freedom of speech to this highest bidder. The next week there was a pro-life commercial during the Letterman Show.

New Happiness
(7 February, 1994)

I was born William Melvin Hicks on December 16, 1961 in Valdosta, Georgia. Ugh. Melvin Hicks from Georgia. Yee Har! I already had gotten off to life on the wrong foot. I was always 'awake', I guess you'd say. Some part of me clamoring for *new* insights and *new* ways to make the world a better place.

All of this came out years down the line, in my multitude of creative interests that are the tools I now bring to the Party. Writing, acting, music, comedy. A deep love of literature and books. Thank God for all the artists who've helped me. I [. . .] these words and off I went – dreaming my own imaginative dreams. Exercising them at will, eventually to form bands, comedy, more bands, movies, *anything creative*. This is the coin of the realm I use in my words – *Vision*.

On June 16, 1993 I was diagnosed with having 'liver cancer that had spread from the pancreas'. One of life's weirdest and worst jokes imaginable. I'd been making such progress recently in my attitude, my career and realizing my dreams, that it just stood me on my head for a while. 'Why me!?', I would cry out, and 'Why now!?'

Well, I know now there may never be any answers to those particular questions, but maybe in telling a little about myself, we can find some other answers to other questions. That might help our way down our own particular paths, towards realizing my dream of *New* Hope and *New* Happiness.

Amen

I left in love, in laughter, and in truth and wherever truth, love and laughter abide, I am there in spirit.

February, 1994

Appendix: Recorded Live in Denver, San Ramon, West Palm Beach and San Francisco (1990–93)

How are you doing tonight? Interpreter? I'm doin' pretty good ah . . . been on the road doin' comedy now for ten years, so bear with me while I plaster on a fake smile and plough through this shit one more time. Teasin'. It's magic every show.

Now, a lot of you non-smokers are drinkers. I'm a non-drinker and a smoker. To me we're trading off vices. That seems fair to me. Not to you, does it? 'Uh-uh, uh-uh, uh-uh, uh-uh, uh-uh. 'We don't care whether you drink.' 'Why should our lives be threatened by your nasty habit?' Yeah, but you know what? I can't kill anybody in a car cos I'm smoking a cigarette, OK? And I've tried. Turn off all the lights, rush 'em, they always see the glow. Huh huh. 'Man, there's a big firefly heading this way. Shit, it's knocking over shrubs! Goddamn, it just hit a mailbox!' Now you're going, 'Bill, who're you tryin' to kill in your car?' That's another story entirely.

I was a pathetic drunk, man. I'd get pulled over by the cops, I'd be so drunk I'd be out dancin' to their lights, thinking I'd made it to another club. Does not look good on the arrest report. You ask a state trooper to do-si-do, they tend to remember you. As opposed to ten years ago – you remember ten years ago, the attitude? You got pulled over, you were drinking, cop comes up to your car:

> 'Son, you been drinkin'?'
> 'Ohhh, yeah.'

'Oop, sorry to bother ya. Hope I didn't bring your buzz down any, ah . . . didn't know y'all were partyin', didn't mean to startle ya. All righty . . . Sure, I'll dance.'

A little more easygoing, right? Ten years ago? Yeah, it was. *Now* if you get pulled over and you been drinking, that's the end of the fuckin' chase. There could be bank robberies going on around you, kidnappings, terrorist activities, fuck it. Every cop car in the county pulls up . . . to watch *you* audition for your freedom. Oh yeah, that's their favourite show at night. They all get out with their coffee, they put you in the headlights of their car . . . and you're on: 'Thank you. It's great to be here at the overpass. Boy, it looks like we got quite a turnout here tonight. Lieutenant, how are you? Good to see you again. Apparently a season ticket-holder to our little weekend show.'

They put you through that field sobriety test, which is very deceiving. I don't know if you've ever been through this. It's very deceiving, field sobriety test, cos it's very easy at first. First thing they told me is walk a straight line. Pfftt . . .

'Son, you wanna come back?' (*three gunshots*)
'Come on Lieutenant, we do that joke every weekend. Goddamn it, that almost hit me. I'm comin' back, I'm comin' back. I'm comin'!'
'Touch yer nose.'

Easiest test I've ever taken! I'll touch my nose *and* walk a straight line. Get some extra credit on this motherfucker. Yeah, then comes the kicker: 'Say the alphabet . . . backwards.' . . . You got me. (*laughs*) I'm not even drunk. I'm obviously too stupid to be driving, goddamn it. Where the fuck did that one come from? We just changed gears on that test. 'Touch yer cheek. Touch yer hair. Do calculus.' I was doin' so FUCKIN' GOOD! Say the alphabet back– what does that have to do with sobriety? You know what I mean? I couldn't say it, you know, I couldn't *read* it backwards, I'm so . . . so used to that song. It's like you've been practising your whole life to fail the drunk test. Z Y, Z Y, ZY fuck it! (*singing*) 'A B C D E F G, I'm a moron get me off the road.' What does saying the alphabet backwards have to do with sobriety, man? I think they're making this shit up as they go. You're drunk, they're bored . . . they can say anything, you know?

> 'Touch yer nose. Walk a straight line. Hell, son, do a flip. (*whoosh, crash*) Pretty good, pretty good. Come 'ere, stick your dick in our exhaust pipe.'
> 'I've never heard of this one. Ah shit, they are police-men. They know what they're doin'. Goddamn, that's hot.'
> 'Shut up, we're gettin' out of that alphabet deal.'
> 'Oh fuck it. I'm sober now. We shoulda done this back at the bar. Damn! Now how long they been chasing us?'

They're makin' this shit up! And they pop you anyway . . . no matter what you do in that test, if they feel like it. So I say, forget it. Touch your nose, walk a straight line – aah, screw it, I'm drunk. I might puke if I start movin' around a lot. How 'bout this, Officer? How about you carry me to the back of your car? Think I'll start my eighteen-hour nap right now, buddy. You ever seen vomit go through that mesh screen between the front and back seats? Ah yeah, you're gonna rue the day you pulled *me* in, pal. I been eatin' bar olives for three days now.

> 'Yes sir, you got me. I'm drunk (*makes vomiting noise*). Whoo! Man, you got me outa my car and into yours just in time, Officer. I'm gonna be out of jail tomorrow, you're gonna be smelling this shit for weeks, buddy. Boy, hope I was worth it. (*laughs, then vomits*) Euch, sorry. Z Y . . . fuck it, you got me, dude. (*vomits*) Z Y Xxxx– (*vomits*). Boy, you'd better get me off the road before I fill this fucker up and we drown, buddy.' (*vomits*)

I don't recommend doing this. But it is a semi-true story. Well, there are such things as cops . . . that much is true.

Live in New York City. I moved up here after I got . . . after I quit drinking, and ah . . . New York City. I moved there from Texas, by the way. Get this, man: I left in Houston, Texas, my apartment – 1,400 square feet, balcony, thirty floors up, air conditioner, centralized, dishwasher, washer/dryer, free parking . . . drum roll: brrrrrrrrrrrrrrrr 400 dollars a month. Ha ha ha ha ha! What a fuckin' idiot, huh? I feel like a real moron. I moved to an apartment, I could touch one wall with that hand, the other wall with that foot . . . 1,000 dollars a month. It's Supermoron! (*sings excerpt from Wagner's 'Ride of the Valkyries'*) I can answer the door, answer the phone, take a leak, be in the shower, all at once . . . for I am Superfuckin'moron. It's unbelievable. All my friends call me up all the time: 'Hey, you living in New York. You been mugged yet?' I go, 'Yeah, as a matter of fact. The first of every month.' Ha ha. They got it systemized. Apparently it's legal. Little wizened guy: 'Give me all your money.' 'Yes sir, hu-huh.' It's not an apartment, it's a *com*partment. I shoulda read the fuckin' ad better. This thing has a Murphy tub. You know, the sad thing is, I tell people who live in New York about my apartment, they all, to a man, they go:

> 'You got a great deal.'
> 'Where the fuck do *you* live?'
> 'I live in your Murphy tub. 1,200 dollars a month.'
> 'I thought that was a roach.'
> 'No, it's me. Quit spraying me.'
> 'Geez, I'm sorry.'

That's not very good, you know, apartment relations. Spraying Raid on your neighbour.

Anyway, who am I? Ah, well, I'll give you an idea. Last few months I been doing a one-man show, like a lot of comics these days are doing one-man shows, and I'm no exception. Ah, I been doing a one-man show at the Improv in Stokey, West Virginia, for the last four months. Off off off off off Melrose. And ah . . . the theme of the one-man show is about my life . . . growing up as I did in a happy, healthy and loving family. And it's called 'Let's Spend Half a Minute With Bill'. And ah . . . well, hell, it's such a short show I could do it right now for ya. OK, here we go. It's about my life as I did growing up in a happy, healthy, loving family: 'Good evening everybody. Momma never beat me and Daddy never fucked me. Good night!' (*in deep voice*) 'T-shirts are on sale in the lobby.'

I don't know if this show will be able to relate to dysfunctional America, but that's the way I was raised. Sorry! Ha ha ha ha ha! No bone to pick. Supported me in everything I did – whoops! It's fun doing the show, though. In Stokey, West Virginia, people come up, real excited: 'That was a great show. Liked it a lot. Little long . . . but ah . . . my attention span wavered towards the end. One thing though: that part about your dad never fucking you – that's a joke, right?' Course it is. Is that a bus? I'm outa here.

Everything they tell you about pot is a lie. They tell you pot smoking makes you unmotivated: *lie*. When you're high you can do everything you normally do just as well, you just realize . . . it's not worth the fuckin' effort. Sure, I could get up at dawn, get in traffic, go to a job I hate which does not inspire me creatively whatsoever for the rest of my life. I could *do* that, sure . . . or . . . I could sleep till noon, get up and learn how to play the sitar. (*in monotone*) 'Dow ning now ning ning ning now ning now ning ning ning now ning now ning ning ning now ning now.' What is it – one string? How fucking hard is this instrument? 'Now ning now ning ning ning now ning now ning ning ning now ning now ning ning ning now ning.' It'd be a better world. If it were all these sitar players calling up fucking aliens from the fifth dimension to join us. See, I don't fit anywhere. No one else shares my fucking beliefs, man, you know what I mean? I don't get it. It's true. 'Bill, Bill, your, your beliefs are ludicrous.' 'Oh. OK, mom.'

It's like, you know, drugs, man. It's like I can't believe we have this war on drugs. You people actually think honestly that the government's true about this, right? You actually believe they're making adverts – don't make me giggle and fall off the stool. 'Oh no, Bill. We know they're lying cocksuckers. We're not fooled, that's why . . . we stole their drugs! Ha ha ha!' But you know what I mean. How can you have a war against drugs? All day long you see those commercials: 'Here's your brain', 'Just say no', 'Why do you think they call it dope?', and the next commercial: 'This Bud's for you',

'Hey, it's Miller time!' I got some other shocking information. Tell you this? I know you don't *know* this, so I feel it's my duty to tell you, thus to pass on knowledge: alcohol brrrrrrrrrrrrrr is a FUCKIN' DRUG! . . . a). b) – and here comes the big one – brrrrrrrrrrrr alcohol kills more people than crack, coke and heroin COMBINED EACH YEAR! Da na na, na na na. 'This Bud's for you, this *drug* is for you, *this* drug is for you. It's OK to *drink* your drug. Ha ho, yeah! We meant those *other* drugs. Those *untaxed* drugs. Those are the *bad* ones.' Aww, you knew that, right? Come on, yeah, you did. And thank God they're taxing alcohol, man. It means we have those great roads we can get fucked up and drive on. Thank God they're taxing this shit, huh? We'd be doing doughnuts in a wheatfield right now. Thank God we're on a highway. Whoooo! (*crash*) My point is, I wasn't a *criminal* when I did drugs. No more than you're a *criminal* cos you drink a beer. People who do drugs are not *crim*inals. They might be sick . . . but I don't think jail's gonna heal anybody. 'Yeah, thank God they caught me. Oh, what was I doing, ruining my life with that marijuana? I wanna thank Bubba, my new rehabilitator back there.' I would not come out of jail wanting to do less drugs. I would wanna come out mainlining heroin into my fucking eyeballs . . . think it would only escalate. Which, by the way, I think all evidence points to that. Ha ha! OK. I deal only in facts. That's why I'm a cocky fucking bastard. Ha ha ha! My life is infinitely better now that I've quit taking drugs. But my life would be infinitely worse had I ever been arrested for taking drugs. That's my fucking point.

I'll tell you, I'll tell you a story now. This is, I'm kinda . . . hanging here by nothing. I'm kinda tired. I flew in ah, yesterday. Four-hour flight, now . . . dig this. They don't allow smoking on airplanes, right? *But* . . . they allow children, OK? Now . . . a little *fairness* is all I'm asking for. Some woman on the plane: 'Well, smoking bothers me.' Well, guess what? Ha ha ha! Come here and let's chat about Junior for a little while. I think I could fill your fucking ear with some irritants, baby. Anyway, I luck out on this flight, right? Every seat next to me is empty. Cool, I'm going to sleep. No shame, every armrest goes up, pillows, blankets on the head, fuck it: I'm outa here, man. Which I love doin' cos it really bugs the business guys sittin' around. I actually had a guy say to me: 'Hey, is that allowed?' 'No, I bought every seat. Shut up. I love taking 6,000-dollar naps, you idiot. Go back to your Macintosh, monkey boy. Just cos you're in the sky don't mean you can't work for the man. Hey, I think I hear your jacket wrinkling in the overhead compartment.' So I'm asleep on this flight, blessedly, finally asleep, right? And I feel this tapping on my head, this non-stop, relentless . . . tapping on my head. And I look out of my little . . . cave of pillows, and there's this little kid . . . *loose*. Someone set it loose. And out of *all* the things on an airplane that might attract the attention of a little toddler, the top of my head beat out all the fucking competition. Fuck Barney the dinosaur! Put the top of my head on TV and your little spawn'll sit saucer-eyed for hours, tapping the fuckin' screen. I don't know what it is about the top of my fuckin' head, little kids go fuckin' nuts over it. And I look across the aisle at the mom. She's course grinning like an idiot, you know. Guy next to the mom: 'They're so cute when they're that small. Ha ha ha ha.' Isn't that amazing, though? Letting your kid run loose like that on an airplane? And then . . . the kid ran over to the emergency exit and started flippin' the handle to the door. And the guy next to the mom started to get up, and I went: 'Wait a minute. We're about to learn an important lesson. (*crash, sound of explosive decompression*) Boy, you're right: the smaller he gets, the cuter he is. Ah, God. Stewardess, since we got a breeze in here, can we smoke now?' True story. Semi-true story, ah . . . altered times for formal use, poetic licence, in order to ah avoid day work. (*laughs*)

How long you been smoking, sir? Fifty *years*? Did you start when you were one? Did you have like a cigarette mobile over your crib? (*makes noise of baby laughing, then crying*) 'Time to go change the baby's ashtray.' You look great. You feel OK?

50-year smoker: Die tomorrow.

Bill: Die tomorrow? Well, you got about thirty minutes. Thanks for spending it with me. You ever try an' quit? Right, see, that's every, I love that. Every smoker: 'You ever try an' quit?' 'Mm-hmm. I'm trying right now, believe it or not. You may find it hard this hard to believe, but.' Have you tried cold turkey? That's the hardest. Yeah. You gotta quit gradually. That's what I'm gonna do. Quit gradually. What I'm gonna do is I'm gonna lose one lung . . . little while later I'm gonna lose the other one. And that's it. I got a *plan*. Dude, can I bum a cigarette from you, man? I'm trying to quit buying. Thank you, sir! Fifty years of smoking – you're giving me fuckin' hope! I was gonna quit till I saw you. Fuck it.

But I have this hope. This hope . . . it's a hope, really. It's a theory, it's a dream, it's a wish, it's a prayer, it's a hope. That if that scenario is at all true when you die and you go to heaven – if St Peter is actually at the gate and he meets you – I hope and believe the first thing he's gonna ask is:

> 'Got a light?'
> 'You mean y'all smoke here?'
> 'Yeah, it's why it's heaven . . . These aren't clouds, this is cigarette smoke, buddy. Hell is non-smoking. You wanna look down at them for a minute?'
> 'Sure.'
> 'I can't believe what they do to their bodies. It smells like an ashtray. I don't wanna smell their secondary smoke while I'm trying to eat. Why would anyone do that to their bodies?'
> 'God, how hellish.'
> 'No shit. Light up. Come on in . . . Hendrix is on harp tonight.'
> 'My man, Jimi! . . .'
> (*imitates Jimi Hendrix playing American national anthem*)
> 'Yeah!'

Man, he's a fucking alien, no doubt about it, man. UFO dropped him off, said, 'Jimi, show us how it's done. We'll pick you up in twenty-eight years, all right?' He went, 'All right.' Fuck, that guy played his cock. They strung his cock with . . . guitar strings and that's what he played. Played it with his teeth. Does that make him gay? You know . . . 'Hey heeyyy, all righ'.' Hendrix language. I don't even . . . encompasses everything. 'Heeyeaahh.' Tripping his FUCKING ASS off. Playing the guitar like no one has ever played it since. Fuck Eddie Van Halen, fuck Steve Vai, fuck these phoney soulless piece of shits. Jimi Hendrix played his *cock*. 'All right, baby. Yeah. Playin' my cock.' . . . I don't think that makes him gay. Let's do some comedy. I always like to add some comedy to my show. Those who've seen me before might know that. There's another guy I love: Keith, man. Keith went over the edge years ago. You know, I thought, 'Ah, he's fucked, man.' Keith went over the edge, and then everyone looked down over the edge, and there's a fucking ledge and he'd landed on it! 'Ay, it's a ledge beyond the edge. What a lucky fucking guy I am. Throw down me guitar, got a riff.' Da dow da da da. There's a ledge beyond the edge. Who knew? Keith found it. What an *explorer*. What a fuckin' *bold* man. 'I'm over the fucking edge. Good night everybody.' Ew! Thonk. Goddamn it, there's a ledge over there. That lucky son of a bitch. 'All right. Yeaah. All right, baby.' What fucking language was Hendrix speaking anyway? Just the all-encompassing positive: 'Yeaah.' 'Bill, you're talking about musicians who died over twenty years ago. You ever thought about updating your fucking show?' Beethoven was wacky. Now I . . .

Now that I've been travelling a lot, and where have I been? Interesting places. Ah, I was in Australia. That was interesting. Anyone here ever been to Australia? (*audience member whistles*) One . . . one squeaking human over here. Some marsupial of some kind. (*makes mewing noise*) Australia's really interesting, ah . . . I didn't know anything about it, but dig this: first of all, it's as big as the United States is geographically. Seriously. As big as the US: picture that. With as few people living there . . . as are in this room right now. Lotta leg room down under. Apartments: dollar a month. Two-thousand-acre den: picture that. Would hate to vacuum, but fuck, think of the parties. But anyway, the Australians, I found out – this is interesting – were the ah criminal, criminal class of Great Britain, and the Brits, in order to punish them, sent them to Australia. Their own prehistoric, Edenlike island continent . . . bummer! Well, you don't want to get on the wrong side of the Brits – they'll fuck you good, Jack. How do you wanna bet the crime rate really soared in Great Britain when people figured out where they were going to be sent to, you know?

> 'Let me get this straight. You keep the shitty weather and the shitty food, and we get the Great Barrier Reef and lobsters the size of canoes . . . *I'm* Jack the Ripper.'
> 'No, *I'm* Jack the Ripper.'
> 'I'm Jack the Ripper.'
> 'I'm Jack the Ripper.'
> 'We're all Jack the fuckin' Ripper.'
> 'Where's the boat?'
> (*makes noise of boat horn*)

That's me going over the horizon. (*boat horn*) It is down under, but ah . . . you just see two Australians surfing the Great Barrier Reef:

> 'What were you, mate?'
> 'I was a murderer.'
> 'I was a thief.'
> 'All right. Hope we're not parolled.'

There are dick jokes on the way, ladies and gentlemen. Please relax. Feeling a little tension in the room here. 'He hasn't told any dick jokes. Doesn't he know he's in America? Doesn't he know about our puritanical self-hatred of our own body and its desires, the only way we can find relief is through the medium of penis material?' Yeah, I'm totally aware of where I am, don't worry. The dick jokes are on their way. Here's the deal, ladies and gentlemen: I editorialize for forty minutes. The last ten minutes we pull our 'chutes and float down to dick-joke island together. K? And we will rest our weary heads against the big, thick-vein trunks of dick jokes, while we sit in our big, cushiony, beanbag scrotum chairs and giggle away the dawn like any good, American comedy-club audience.

I went to a dance club the other night, very much against my will. I wasn't driving – there you are, stuck an' ah . . . I go to dance clubs, you know, about once a year, just to justify the other 364 days of the year I spend in my apartment going, 'God, what idiots!' And ah, takes about one day. I have to fill my hump – I'm like a camel. I go to the dance club, fill my hump with hate. I can go about a year then the hump starts to go down, I go back to the dance club (*makes sucking noise*) fill my hump of hate, and I'm off again. I'm the hate camel, don't you see how that . . . An' what am I doing here, you know? Anyway this girl asked me to dance, which really cracked me up. 'Would you like to dance?' And I was like, 'Ah, you read my fuckin' mind, you know. That's why I'm leaning in the darkest corner closest to the exit, you know, I ah . . . I'm about to boogie. I'm about to cut a rug.' But it's so weird, women have this weird myth you can tell the way a guy is in bed by how he is on a dance floor. I think that's ludicrous, man. And what does it matter, anyway? You know what I mean? If a guy's on a dance floor, really getting into it and enjoying himself and expressing himself, what does it matter how he is in bed? He's gay! Real men don't dance. They sit, sweat and curse.

Speaking of homosexuality . . . something has come to my attention . . . that has shocked even me. Now, I consider myself a very open-minded person, I'll be honest with ya. I think I'm very open-minded. Being a fella such as I am, who over the course of his lifetime several times has taken his body weight in psilocybin magic mushrooms, I've had my mind fairly opened, OK? UFOs? Seen 'em! (*laughs*) OK. Been *on* a couple. (*laughs*) Good gas mileage. OK. I'm out on a fucking limb with Shirley MacLaine at this point, all right? She's clinging to the trunk, I'm hanging by a twig. 'Come on, Shirley. Take another cap! Come on, the UFOs are honking. We gotta go!' I'm pretty open-minded – mother goddess, earth goddess, I'm there, I'm with you, believe me, in all ways. Now! And yet . . . something has come to my attention that absolutely shocked me. Have you heard about these – and I know you have – these grade-school books they're trying to put into the curriculum for children to help them understand the gay lifestyle? You know what I'm talkin' about? One of 'em is called *Heather's Two Mommies*. The other one – ready? – *Daddy's New Room-Mate*. Folks, I'm gonna have to draw the line here, and say that this is absolutely disgusting. I think it is grotesque, and I think it is evil. I'm talking of course about *Daddy's New Room-Mate*. *Heather's Two Mommies*, on the other hand . . . quite a fetching read. I ah . . . ooh, they're hugging on page seven. Go Mommy, go. That is such a lucky girl. Ooh, they kiss in Chapter five, oooh. I wish I were Heather. Me and my nephew wrestle over that book every night.

> 'Uncle Bill, I gotta do my homework.'
> 'Shut up! Do math. I'm proofreading again. Ooh, they're
> hugging. Oooh, what's six plus nine?' (*laughs*)

I just don't fit in with anywhere, man. I'm watching TV, you know. I'm down in Florida, man, and I was down there a couple of years ago when Bob Martinez was Governor of Florida, you know? And I'm watching him. They say, 'Here's Bob Martinez, Governor of Florida.' Yeah, I agree. 'Here's Bob Martinez, Governor of Florida.' He comes on. He goes, 'It's obscene. It's pornographic. It's filthy.' And I'm thinking, 'Cool, what is it?' Anyway, he's talking about thong bathing suits. Do you know what these are? Thong bathing suits? Well, I didn't know what they were, and I'm watching the fucking TV, and . . . here's some women on the beach of Florida in thong bathing suits, and over this Bob Martinez's voice: 'It's obscene. It's pornographic. It's filthy.' Let me tell you something real quick: any man that doesn't want women wearing thong bathing suits is a fuckin' freak. D'you hear that clearly? Good. Even the Pope was going, 'What are you, nuts? You can see their *asses*, Bob. Bob, I'm the Pope and I'm looking at her ass. Shut the fuck up! Do you want me to take this tall hat off, start banging you with it, you fucker? God created that ass, Bob. Worship. BOW to that ass, Bob.' 'Poe-naw-graphic.' That's what Jesse Helms calls it: 'Poe-naw-grah-fee. Poe-naw-grah-fee.' I don't think you should be against something . . . till you can pronounce it. Is that harsh of me? I think that's a good rule of thumb.

Let me ask y'all a question real quick. It's crude, I warn you up front, but there is a reason I'm asking. It's not done gratuitously, all right? I'll do that stuff in a minute. Are there actually women in the world who do not like to give blowjobs? That's the nicest way I can say that. Did you hear the question? See a lot of guys on dates got their fingers crossed here tonight. 'Well, it better not be true.' Reason I ask, I'll do this one more time. She goes down there for like three seconds and starts coming back *up*. And I'm going, 'Uh-uh . . . Uh-uh . . . Unless you're getting up to put ice in your mouth.' Anyway, without getting graphic . . . she actually said to me, 'I think you've had enough.' Really? Well, *I* think you're gonna *know* when I've had enough. Yeah, pretty definite ending to this. Fairly cut and dry. Anyway, it blew my mind and it's all it blew, so I been inquiring from audiences why you ladies don't like to do that to your guys. I cannot conceive of one reason why you don't make that your avocation while here on this planet. Why don't you wanna do that all the time to your guy? I don't understand. I actually had a woman last show go, 'Yeah, you ever try it?' I said, 'Yeah. Almost broke my back.' It's that one vertebrae, I swear to God, it's that close. I think that vertebrae is gonna be the thing to go in our next evolutionary step. Just a theory of mine . . . and a fervent prayer. It's great, all the guys are going, 'Honey, I have no idea what he's talking about right now. I think he's a devil child.' Yeah, that may be true but guys . . . *you* know what the fuck I'm talking about. Guys, if you could blow yourselves, ladies you'd be in this room alone right now . . . watching an empty stage. I hope I don't seem shallow.

But anyway, I asked the woman who said that, 'You ever try it?' I said, 'Well, let me ask you something. Why don't you like doing that to your guy?' She goes, 'Because it's disgusting.' Well, that's a tad harsh. And also, I might add, a double standard. Cos you know what? I have *never* heard you ladies say it's disgusting . . . when we're down between *your* legs, *gnawing* away. 'Oh, this is so gross. I'm gonna throw up. Oh, don't put your finger in my a– oh, that's ruude.' I've never heard that before. Guys, you ever heard that? Ever? Yeah, weird. Me neither, huh. Then again, maybe I can't hear it cos your thighs are clamped . . . Boy, my folks are proud of me.

> 'Bill honey, you still doing that pussy-eating sketch in your act?'
> 'You betcha, momma.'
> 'I wish your grandmother was still alive to see you do that pussy-eating skit, honey. That is so funny. Your

glasses going whicha way. Your grandma and grandpa woulda *loved* that piece. That comedy ah' journey under the moniker "cunnilingus skit".'

'Thanks, mom.'

'No biggy, honey.'

Someone actually asked me once: 'Who's your favourite New Kid?' The first one that dies! That's the poster that's going up in Willie's room. And I hope it's Donnie, that scruffy little rebel. Hope Donnie gets that one chin-hair he's been working on for three fuckin' years caught in the front wheel of his scooter, and it pulls his head off like a champagne cork comin' out. Pop! Pop! Pop! He's in the middle of the freeway like a plasma sprinkler. (*makes squirting noises*) That would crack me up for days. And his parents are there, and they see it too. Oh yeah, yeah. There's mom, his mom watches the whole fuckin' thing with her eyes open like Malcolm in *Clockwork Orange*. 'I can't fucking blink. I'm watching my son torn asunder.' Yeah, who's that in the corner of your eye? It's Bill, laughing his fucking head off. Shooting blood thirty feet into the sky like a fucking geyser. That, my friends, would tell me God is loving.

My old girl? Thanks for bringing her up, dude. My girlfriend left me, man. It's hard to believe. You know what's weird? She said she loved me, but when she left she took the TV, the bed and the VCR. Guess when ah . . . we were at home and she was saying, 'I love you, I love you, I love you', I was standing in front of either the TV, the bed or the VCR, and like an idiot, I thought . . . 'I love you, you big nineteen-incher.' Thanks, honey. (*laughs*) So she can't add. I'd come home, the Toshiba's gone.

S'OK that she left, dude. I don't care. What am I gonna do, get bitter? You know what? You can't get bitter, man. Just because someone tells you they love you, then they leave. You gotta, you gotta think that it's a reason that it happened, and you gotta look on the bright side, and you gotta move on, right? Right?

Audience member: 'Wrong.'

Audience member: 'Yep . . . sure.'

Bill: Yeah, sure. Yeah, right. Yeah, Bill, whatever, get to the fuckin' point. No. I'm not gonna get to the point. I'm gonna sit here and ramble into this fuckin' wall. On the bright side I'm glad she left, cos you know what? It helped my career. Cos I'm driven now. I'm driven by a fantasy that one day this girl who I loved more than anything in the world, and she said she loved me then left, one day she's gonna be living some day in a trailer park somewhere in Alabama . . . living with this ex-welder, 600 pounds, fur all over his back, drinks warm beer, farts, belches, beats the kids, watches *The Dukes of Hazard* every fucking night, and has to have it explained to him. She's gonna have nine, naked little kids with rickets that bring home dead animals from the side of the road for them to eat at night, burrs in their hair, mud on their face, rats laying babies in their ears at night. One night that welder's gonna be making love to her, and he's gonna be on top and suddenly his heart's gonna explode, and she's gonna be trapped under 600 pounds of flaccid, fish-belly cellulite, shifting like the tides of the ocean as blood, phlegm and bile pours out of his mouth and nose . . . into her face, and just before she drowns in that tepid puddle of afterbirth . . . she's gonna turn to *The Tonight Show* and I'm gonna be on it. So you see, I'm not bitter.

Well, folks, I did longer than I was supposed to do. The reason is I always do long shows when I'm in Denver, cos I know for a fact there's nothing else going on here. So, thank you very much. Good night. Hope you enjoyed it. Thank you very much.

Notes

Part 1: 1980-1991
Interview by Allan Johnson (14 September 1989)

1. Dick Clark (b. 1929) presented *American Bandstand* on the ABC network between 1957 and 1987. He was long known as 'America's Oldest Teenager'. To this day he retains his boyish good looks.

2. A former Pentecostal Preacher, Sam Kinison (1953-92) featured on numerous cable comedy specials and guested regularly on Saturday Night Live. In the late eighties he performed with Mötley Crüe and Ozzy Osbourne. His comedy was marked by a relentless and sometimes disturbing honesty about sex, politics and religion. He died in a car accident in 1992.

    Hicks was 17 years old when he started to work with Kinison and the other Texas Outlaws, Riley Barber and Carl LaBove.

    'Some people may think Sam Kinison's in one place, but I know where he is: He's upstairs; he's next to God.' Ozzy Osbourne.

3. Andrew 'Dice' Clay (b. 1958) started his career as an actor and became a highly successful and controversial stand-up comedian in the late 80s. He starred in the family sitcom *Bless This House* in 1995.

Recorded Live at the Village Gate, NYC, and Caroline's Seaport, NYC (1990)

4. Released in 1990 as *Dangerous*; re-released in 1997 by Rykodisc.

5. Homelessness rose sharply throughout the 1980s in New York City. In 1979 shelters housed just under 2,000 homeless single

adults each night. By 1990 they were registering around 9,600. In the winter the figure sometimes exceeded 11,000 (Source: Coalition for the Homeless).

6. Ronald Reagan won the 1980 Presidential election in a campaign that drew on the thoughtless verities of Hollywood patriotism. In his two terms he worked hard to support corporate interests while attacking a supposedly elitist and out of touch liberal intelligentsia.

7. Debbie Gibson's (b. 1970) career highlights include 'Only In My Dreams', 'Shake Your Love' and 'Lost in Your Eyes'.

8. Tiffany (b. 1971) had number 1 hits in the US with 'I Think We're Alone Now' and 'Could've Been'. Her career was launched by a series of promotional appearances at shopping malls. Discussing the mall appearances, her producer Brad Schmidt commented 'It started out as a marketing tool and as a way to get her in front of people and it turned into a phenomenon.'

9. Rick Astley was one of producer Pete Waterman's most successful pop acts, enjoying success on both sides of the Atlantic with 'Never Gonna Give You Up', 'Together Forever' and some other songs.

10. Founded in 1978 by Bob Guccione of *Penthouse* fame, *Omni* published both science fiction and non-fiction about controversial, 'cutting edge', scientific topics, including psychedelia and UFOs. The magazine finally folded in 1996 after a brief incarnation as an online-only publication.

11. After war service in the navy and a stint working in the oil business, George H. W. Bush (b. 1924) served in the US Congress from 1966. He was US Ambassador to the United Nations between 1971-73 and Head of the CIA between 1974-75. He served two terms as Vice President under Ronald Reagan where he took a particular interest in deregulation and 'anti-drug programs'. In 1988 he was elected the 41st President of the United States. During his time as President, Bush successfully invaded Panama and removed Saddam Hussein from Kuwait. He was unsuccessful in his attempts to defeat drugs. His son has now declared a War on Terror as well.

George Senior's own stand on terrorism was unambiguous;

'On the surface, selling arms to a country that sponsors terrorism, of course, clearly, you'd have to argue it's wrong, but it's
the exception sometimes that proves the rule.'

12. The Partnership for a Drug-Free America first aired the 'This
is your brain on drugs' commercial in 1987. The Partnership
describes itself as having 'deep roots in the advertising industry' and was founded in 1986 with funds from the American
Association of Advertising Agencies. It has tended to focus on
illegal and untaxed drugs (whose producers and distributors
are not heavy spenders on advertising) in its campaigns. It
stopped accepting money from tobacco and alcohol companies
in 1997 but continues to receive support from the pharma-
ceutical industry (source Fairness and Accuracy in Reporting
Website: www.fair.org).

13. Jim Fixx (1932-1984) wrote *The Complete Book of Running*
(1977) and *Jim Fixx's Second Book of Running* (1980).

14. At a demonstration in Dallas in 1984 Gregory Johnson doused
a US flag in kerosene and set it on fire outside the City Hall.
John was found guilty of 'desecrating a sacred object' under
the Texas Penal Code and sentenced to one year in prison. His
case went to the Supreme Court of the United States, which
ruled in June 1989 that Johnson's actions were a form of
symbolic speech and protected under the terms of the First
Amendment to the Constitution. In the course of delivering
the court's verdict, Justice Brennan remarked; 'If there is a
bedrock principle underlying the First Amendment, it is that
the Government may not prohibit the expression of an idea
simply because society finds the idea itself offensive or disagree-
able.'

Recorded Live at the Vic Theatre, Chicago (November 1990)

15. Released as *One Night Stand* in 1991, Laughing Stock
Productions Ltd.

16. A certain amount of repetition is inevitable in a collection of
stand-up routines. The editors have decided to include all the
main routines, so that the reader can see how the treatment
of the same themes changes between 1990 and 1993.

17. James Vance and Ray Belknap entered into a suicide pact in 1985. Belknap died at the scene while Vance died three years later. Their parents sued the heavy metal band Judas Priest, claiming that the subliminal message 'do it' in their song 'Better By You, Better Than Me' caused them to act as they did. In 1990 the judge in the case ruled in favor of the band. Incidentally he also stated that subliminal messages did not qualify as constitutionally protected speech.

18. The US courts have spent many years trying to provide an adequate definition of obscenity, including Potter Stuart's famous 1964 attempt, 'I know it when I see it'. In the 1973 case, Miller v. California, the US Supreme Court ruled that a work would be considered obscene in law if it satisfied the following three conditions:

    i.) '"the average person, applying contemporary community standards" would find that the work, taken as a whole, appeals to the prurient interest ...'

    ii.) 'the work depicts or describes, in a patently offensive way, sexual conduct specifically defined by the applicable state law . . .'

    iii.) 'the work, taken as a whole, lacks serious literary, artistic, political, or scientific value.'

Live at the Funny Bone, Pittsburgh, PA (20 June 1991)

19. Recorded Live at the Funny Bone, Pittsburgh, PA (20 June 1991). Released in 2002 as *Flying Saucer Tour, Vol. 1* by Rykodisc.

20. Emmanuel Lewis was a popular 1980s child actor best known for the character Webster in a popular TV show. Phyllis Diller is a veteran US comedienne.

21. Jack Lalanne (b. 1914) is an important figure in the creation of the health and fitness movement. He is credited with the remark 'Death would ruin my image.'

22. A 'stogie' is slang for a cigar or cigarette.

23. Iraq invaded Kuwait on 2 August, 1990. A US-led coalition backed by a UN mandate began a series of air strikes against Iraqi positions on 16 January. On 24 February coalition forces

entered Southern Iraq. On 27 February President Bush declared Kuwait liberated. In around one hundred hours the US military inflicted devastating casualties on the Iraqi military.

24. Arsenio Hall is a popular US talk-show host and comedian.

25. See especially Alfred McCoy, *The Politics of Heroin: CIA Complicity in the Global Drugs Trade* (Chicago: Chicago Review Press, 2003). First published in 1972, Lawrence Hill and Co. published a new edition in January 1991, six months before the Pittsburgh gig. Also notable in this context are Gary Webb, *Dark Alliance: CIA, The Contras and the Crack Cocaine Explosion* (New York: Seven Stories, 1998), Alexander Cockburn and Jeffrey St Clair, *Whiteout: The CIA, Drugs and the Press* (London: Verso, 1998), and most recently Douglas Valentine, *The Strength of the Wolf* (London: Verso, 2004).

26. Lynette 'Squeaky' Fromme (b. 1948) was an associate of Charles Manson. In September 1975 she attempted to murder the US President, Gerald Ford.

27. Neil Bush, son of George Bush Senior, who was accused of real estate fraud in the early 1990s.

28. Stuckeys is a chain of southern US roadside candy stores.

29. US card game; British version is called 'Find the Lady'.

Recorded at Laff Stop, Austin, Tx (14-17 December 1991)

30. Released as *Relentless* in 1992; re-released in 1997, Rykodisc. An edited version broadcast on 2 January, 1992 on Channel Four.

31. Clarence Thomas (b. 1948) is a Justice of the Supreme Court. In 1991, during his Senate confirmation hearings in October of that year, a former colleague of Thomas, Anita Hill, alleged that, 'After a brief discussion of work he would turn the conversation to a discussion of sexual matters. His conversations were very vivid.'

32. Paul Reubens (b. 1952) found huge success through his comic alter ego, Pee-Wee Herman. In July 1991 Reubens was arrested for indecent exposure in an adult cinema in Sarasota, Florida.

Reubens continues to work as an actor, but Pee-Wee Herman has retired from show business.

33. Senator Edward Moore Kennedy (b. 1932) is usually known as Ted or Teddy. Hicks is perhaps referring to him, for some reason.

34. The 19 October 1987 edition of *Newsweek* ran a long, generally sympathetic article about then Vice-President Bush's Presidential ambitions. The headline read 'George Bush – Fighting the "Wimp" Factor'.

   Bush never quite got over the word, and in 1991 he commented, 'You're talking to the "wimp". You're talking to the guy that had a cover of a national magazine, that I'll never forgive, put that label on me.'

35. A large number of UFO sightings were recorded in Fyffe in 1989 and 1990. The area is also notorious for unexplained cattle mutilations.

36. The Joad family are the central characters in John Steinbeck's novel of the Depression, *The Grapes of Wrath*.

37. Arrested in July 1991, Jeffrey Dahmer was found guilty of murdering seventeen young men and boys in February 1992. Dahmer died in November 1994, killed by another inmate in a Wisconsin prison.

38. Sharper Image is an outlet for innovative consumer goods.

39. Released in 1991, *Dollman* told the story of Brick Bardo, a cop from the planet Arturus. Hicks might have watched it, who knows?

40. In Christian terms heretical, Hicks' identification of God, love, and the Universe recurs in mystical traditions of worship throughout the world. Interestingly it irritates fundamentalists and atheists in pretty much equal measure.

Part 2: 1992
Recorded Live at the Dominion Theatre, London (November 1992).

41. Broadcast as *Revelations* early in 1993 on Channel Four Television.

42. On 29 April 1992, three of the four officers caught on tape beating Rodney King were cleared on all charges, prompting three days of rioting.
43. This joke re-emerged in the controversy surrounding the 2003 invasion of Iraq, most noticeably in David Hare's 2004 play, *Stuff Happens*.
44. Hicks might be referring to the now notorious reports that Iraqi soldiers removed premature Kuwaiti babies from incubators and allowed them to die. In October 1990, the main source for the story, a 15-year-old girl Kuwaiti girl identified only as Nayirah, claimed that she had seen 'hundreds' of babies being killed in this way. In fact there were only a handful of incubators in the entire country. Nayirah herself was the daughter of Kuwait's ambassador to the United States. After the war an Amnesty International investigation found 'no reliable evidence' for the story. For more on the propaganda build-up to the 1991 and 2003 wars against Iraq, see Sheldon Rampton and John Stauber, *Weapons of Mass Deception* (London: Constable and Robinson, 2003).

    President Bush likened Iraq's takeover of Kuwait with the Nazi *blitzkrieg* in Europe in the 1930s. The Western media enthusiastically took up the theme, likening Saddam Hussein with Hitler. By equating resistance to the war with appeasement of Hitler this approach helped secure and sustain public support.
45. The British government was rocked by a scandal involving the illegal sale of arms in the years preceding the 1990 invasion of Kuwait. An official inquiry began in November 1992. In 1996 it concluded that parts of the UK state were indeed breaking their own arms embargo.

Recorded live at the Oxford Playhouse on 11 November 1992
46. Released as *Shock and Awe* in 2003 by Invasion.
47. For more on this, see G. Grandin's *The Last Colonial Massacre: Latin America in the Cold War* (Chicago: University of Chicago Press, 2004).
48. The 'Crips' and the 'Bloods' are Los Angeles street gangs famous for a series of inter-gang conflicts in the late 1980s.
49. Hicks is referring to the April 1992 general election. As in

the US election of the same year, tax played an important part in the campaign strategy of the right-wing incumbent. It is not clear whether Labour lost because of fear of a 'tax bombshell' or more general doubts about their managerial competence.

50. Earl Weaver is a baseball player and manager, who Bill may be confusing with Dennis Weaver – best known for long-running television series *Gunsmoke and McCloud* and, more recently, as the host of the Western Channel. He appeared dressed in a hat and cape and riding a horse.

Recorded Live at Laff Stop, Austin, TX (December 1992)

51. Recorded between the 14-17 December 1991, released in 1992 as *Relentless*; re-released in 1997, Rykodisc.

52. Martin Amis' 1991 novel, *Time's Arrow*, explores a similar idea at much greater length.

53. George H.W. Bush lost the Presidential campaign to Bill Clinton in November 1992.

54. Pat Buchanan (b. 1938) is a conservative politician and writer and former aide to President Richard Nixon. He served as White House Communications Director in the Reagan administration between 1985 and 1987. In December 1991, Buchanan challenged George H.W. Bush for the Republican Presidential nomination, receiving 3 million Republican votes on a protectionist ticket.

55. Theodore 'Ted' Bundy (1946-1989) was a prolific serial killer and rapist. He married Carol Ann Boone during his trial and received hundreds of letters from women claiming to be in love with him. In his last interview before execution, Bundy blamed pornography for his own and others' violent hatred of women.

Al Bundy, played by Ed O'Neill, was the central character in the long-running TV sitcom, *Married with Children*.

Part 3: Early to Mid 1993
Bill Hicks: Comedy for the Head by Cree McCree (*High Times* April 1993)

56. *LA Weekly* called Terence McKenna 'the culture's foremost spokesman for the psychedelic experience'. The book referred to here is a collection of essays and interviews published in the same year as the *High Times* interview — *The Archaic Revival: Speculations on Psychedelic Mushrooms, the Amazon, Virtual Reality, UFOs, Evolution, Shamanism, the Rebirth of the Goddess and the End of History* (San Francisco: HarperSanFrancisco, 1993). His most famous book is *Food of the Gods: The Search for the Original Tree of Knowledge* (Rider: London, 1992). Hicks cites McKenna on more than one occasion in his later routines.

57. See especially Eric Schlosser's *Reefer Madness* (London: Penguin, 2003) for details on America's war on pot smokers.

Outside Broadcast, Branch Davidian Compound, Waco (8 March, 1993)

58. On 28 February 1993, ATF officers launched a raid on the compound of Branch Davidian leader, David Koresh. Four agents and an unknown number of Branch Davidians died in the subsequent gunfight. On 19 April the FBI attempt to storm the building. Koresh and 76 of his followers died in fires.

   Hicks visited the scene of the siege on 8 March 1993 and later expressed doubts about the official account of how the fires started. In 1999 the BBC reported an official FBI statement that 'the FBI may have used a very limited number of military-type CS gas canisters on the morning of April 19 in an attempt to penetrate the roof of an underground bunker 30 to 40 yards away from the main Branch Davidian compound . . . the military canisters may have contained a substance that is designed to disperse the gas using a pyrotechnic mixture . . .' (source: http://news.bbc.co.uk/1/hi/world/americas/ 431348.stm)

Recorded Live at Laff Stop, Austin, TX, and Cobbs, San Francisco, CA (Spring and Summer 1993)

59. Released in 1997 as *Rant in E Minor* by Rykodisc.

60. Sometimes called the original reality TV program, *Cops* first aired in 1989. It is still broadcast on US television.

61. Jesse Helms (b. 1921) was the Republican Senator for North Carolina from 1973 until his retirement at the end of 2002. When confronted with evidence that the President of El Salvador's Constituent Assembly was directing death squads he replied, 'All I know is that D'Aubuisson is a free enterprise man and deeply religious' (Source, Eric Bates, *Mother Jones*, May/June, 1995).

62. The most popular televangelist of the 80s, Jimmy Swaggart (b. 1935) had a regular audience of 2 million families for *The Jimmy Swaggart Telecast*. His businesses had an annual turnover in excess of $100 million. In February 1988, accusations that Swaggart had engaged in improprieties with a New Orleans prostitute resulted in a sex scandal that severely dented his credibility. Swaggart's difficulties also damaged Pat Roberts' bid for the Republican nomination in the same year.

63. During George H. W. Bush's visit to Kuwait in April 1993 to commemorate the coalition's victory over Iraq in operation Desert Storm, Kuwaiti authorities arrested sixteen people alleged to have been planning a car bomb attack on the former President. A Kuwaiti court later convicted all but one of the defendants. On 26 June, President Clinton ordered the firing of 23 cruise missiles at Iraqi Intelligence Service headquarters in Baghdad in retaliation for the assassination attempt. Seven of these missiles went astray and landed in civilian areas. Clinton said he was acting on 'compelling evidence' of Iraqi involvement in the assassination plot.

In the run-up to the Iraq invasion of 2003 President W. Bush called Saddam Hussein 'the guy who tried to kill my dad.' No evidence of Iraqi involvement has emerged since the American occupation.

Wake Up America (Summer 1993)
64. Al Sharpton (b. 1955) is a civil rights campaigner and politician. He ran as a Democratic candidate for the Senate in 1992 and 1994, and campaigned to become the Democratic Party's Presidential nominee in 2004.
65. Randall Terry (b. 1959) is an anti-abortion campaigner and the founder of Operation Rescue.
66. Pat Robertson (b. 1930) is a Christian evangelist. He is the founder and Chairman of the Christian Broadcasting Network. Greg Palast investigates Robertson in his 2003 book, *The Best Democracy Money Can Buy* (London: Constable and Robinson, 2003).
67. Rush Limbaugh is a highly controversial broadcaster and one of the foremost propagators of the myth of the 'liberal media' in the USA. He is acknowledged as a popular mouthpiece for the Republican right across America, and is accused by his critics of making millions by distorting facts while targeting liberal policy.

Letters of Response
68. Two priests wrote to Channel 4 to complain about 'Revelations'. These two letters form part of Bill's correspondence with them.
69. Irwin Corey is a surrealistic comic under the soubriquet 'The World's Foremost Authority.'

Part 4: Late 1993–94
Unresolvable Problems — Resolved! (November 1993)
70. *Scallywag* was an underground newspaper/scandal sheet, critical of establishment ideas. http://www.scallywag.org/

Two Myths Explored, Debunked and Other Rantings (Undated)
71. The first ten amendments to the US constitution are known as the Bill of Rights. Most versions of the second amendment read: 'A well regulated Militia, being necessary to the security of a free State, the right of the people to keep and bear Arms, shall not be infringed.' The extra comma after 'Militia' does not materially affect Hicks' argument.

Letter to John Lahr

72. In April 1993 Hicks was quoted in Austin Comedy news speaking about Denis Leary, 'I have a scoop for you. I stole his act. I camouflaged it with punch-lines, and to really throw people off, I did it before he did.'

73. For more about the international tobacco business see Noam Chomsky, *Deterring Democracy* (London: Vintage, 1992).

Letter to Dave

74. Speaking in the documentary, *It's Just a Ride*, David Letterman (b. 1947) said, 'Well, our relationship with Bill Hicks came to kind of a peculiar ending, made all the more peculiar by the man's death. And I have personal regrets about how our relationship developed prior to his death. So it makes me doubly sad that he is now not around so that we can, I think, correct mistakes that were made on his behalf. So I feel a personal sense of regret regarding that.'